W9-AXJ-106

The Supreme Court
and Constitutional Theory,
1953–1993

The Supreme Court and Constitutional Theory, 1953–1993

Ronald Kahn

University Press of Kansas

© 1994 by the University Press of Kansas
All rights reserved

Published by the University Press of Kansas (Lawrence, Kansas 66049), which
was organized by the Kansas Board of Regents and is operated and funded by
Emporia State University, Fort Hays State University, Kansas State University,
Pittsburg State University, the University of Kansas, and Wichita State
University

Library of Congress Cataloging-in-Publication Data

Kahn, Ronald C.
The Supreme Court and constitutional theory, 1953–1993 / Ronald
Kahn.
p. cm.
Includes bibliographical references and index.
ISBN 0-7006-0666-1 (cloth)   ISBN 0-7006-0711-0 (pbk.)
1. United States. Supreme Court. 2. Judicial process—United
States. 3. United States—Constitutional history. I. Title.
KF8748.K38 1994
347.73'26—dc20

[347.30735]   93-39805

British Library Cataloguing in Publication data is available.

Printed in the United States of America
10 9 8 7 6 5 4 3 2

The paper used in this publication meets the minimum requirements of the
American National Standard for Permanence of Paper for Printed Library
Materials Z39.48-1984.

In memory of my father
Robert S. Kahn
and
Professor J. David Greenstone

Contents

Acknowledgments

Professor J. David Greenstone, my mentor and friend, demonstrated that one can aspire to the most rigorous standards of scholarship and also be personally caring and empathetic. David taught me the process of critical thinking. He read proposals and papers that formed the intellectual core of the book. Most of all, David taught me to "keep the faith." I also want to thank Grant McConnell, and Theodore Lowi, Duncan MacRae, and Leonard Binder, who, along with David, taught and inspired me during my years at the University of Chicago.

I wish to thank my colleagues in the Department of Government, now called Politics, at Oberlin College, especially Marc Blecher and Harlan Wilson, for many years of stimulating intellectual companionship. I am also grateful to colleagues in the wider Oberlin community, especially Professors Norman Care, Jack Glazier, Associate Provost David Love, and our recently appointed colleagues in the Department of Politics, for sustaining an atmosphere in which creative scholarship and scholarly teaching are the norm.

The following scholars read drafts of chapters, papers, and articles, associated with this project: John Brigham, Jonathan Entin, Leslie Goldstein, Joel Grossman, Sandy Levinson, Michael McCann, and Karen Orren. I am grateful for their comments. I also want to thank Michael Briggs, my editor at the University Press of Kansas.

I am most grateful to the talented Oberlin students who have contributed to this project as research assistants: Jeffrey Auerbach, Anita Cicero, Stuart Christie, David Glenn, William Hirshorn, Jennifer Mezey, William Wimsatt, and Adam Zemans. The Dana Foundation's gifts to Oberlin College made it possible to employ these students as research assistants. I especially want to thank Mark Neath and Ben Gibson, two superb graduates of Oberlin College, whose critical comments on the final drafts were crucial to its completion.

While I was working on this project I received generous support from Oberlin College's Committee of Research and Development. My thanks go to Harvard University Law School, which provided a most stimulating atmosphere in which to germinate my ideas about the relationship of law, theory, and politics when I was a Liberal Arts Fellow in Law and Government in 1979–1980. I am also grateful to the National Endowment for the Humanities for supporting my attendance at an inspiring summer seminar taught by Professor Alpheous Thomas Mason at Princeton University in 1979 and an-

x other at Stanford University in 1984. I especially want to thank Oberlin College for providing a Research Status Appointment in 1988–1989, during which I worked on this book.

Last, but really first, I want to offer my thanks to my mother, Beatrice Kahn, who nurtured my early intellectual growth, and to my wife, Diana Grossman Kahn, and daughter, Rachel Melanie Kahn, whose continuous support and liveliness, both intellectually and socially, bring joy to my life.

Part One
Historical Antecedents of the Burger Court

Chapter One

*Introduction: Supreme Court Decisionmaking
and Doctrinal Change*

The Burger Court era (1969–1986) has been viewed in several unique ways. It has been perceived as having neither a definable vision of moral values nor a clear vision of American political institutions and individual rights behind its jurisprudence. It has been viewed as uniquely pragmatic, nonideological, and lacking in coherence. Finally, the primary identifying characteristic of its jurisprudence has been that it was not different from the previous Court era—that it did not produce a "counterrevolution" to the doctrinal innovations of the Warren Court (1953–1969).[1] I believe these views are wrong.

My principal objectives in this book are to define and explore the nature of our misperception of the Burger Court, to offer a revisionist view of the Court, and, most importantly, to explain why it came to be (mis)perceived in these terms. Special emphasis will be placed on analyzing Warren Court decisionmaking and doctrinal change and on how, and why, that Court was perceived by scholars and the nation both at the time and later. Because the Warren Court became the standard of evaluation for its successor, misperceptions of the decisionmaking process and process of doctrinal change on the Warren Court offer insights as to why the Burger Court continues to be misperceived.

Misperceptions of both Courts are based on disagreements among scholars as to whether the Supreme Court should be viewed primarily as a political or as a legal institution in analyzing its internal decisionmaking process and the degree of autonomy of the Supreme Court and law from politics. Political models of Supreme Court decisionmaking, which emphasize that justices act like policymakers and are influenced by changes in the wider political system, have dominated the intellectual landscape, especially among political scientists. Legal approaches emphasize the importance of following precedent, the independent effects of internal Court decisionmaking, and, most important, the effect of the application of long-term polity and rights principles on the development of constitutional law. The legal approach continues to be the primary view held by many legal, law school–based scholars and a significant number of political scientists who specialize in American constitutional law.

I call the political approach to Supreme Court decisionmaking and doctrinal change the instrumental approach, primarily because it emphasizes that justices use polity and rights principles, and all constitutional theory, instrumentally, as means to achieve their policy objectives. I refer to the legalist approach as constitutive because it emphasizes the place of developing polity and rights principles, precedent, and constitutional theory as significant to the Court's "constituting" constitutional law and principles. A constitutive approach also assumes that there is a far greater autonomy of law, and the Supreme Court, from politics than the instrumental approach argues.

The constitutive approach does not claim that changes in the wider political, social, and economic systems have no impact on Supreme Court decision-making; rather the constitutive approach emphasizes the importance of precedent, polity and rights principles, constitutional theory, and the Court decisionmaking process as key mediating forces in the development of the law. The constitutive approach emphasizes that justices, at crucial times, make decisions that are in conflict with their personal policy wants or those of the presidents who selected them. They do so in part because they view the Court as a countermajoritarian legal institution and share a concern for the legitimacy of the Supreme Court and the rule of law.

I argue that the instrumental approach has greatly—and wrongly—influenced our perception of both the Warren and Burger courts. By viewing Supreme Court decisionmaking as constitutive we can better understand the decisionmaking process in each Court era and the relationship of the internal Court process to outside forces. In Part One, which focuses on the Warren Court era, I argue for a constitutive interpretation of doctrinal change and Supreme Court decisionmaking, one that does not view justices as policymakers, but rather as jurists who seek to work out polity and rights principles in a dialogue with what Owen Fiss has called "the interpretive community."[2] A study of the predominant constitutional theories and interpretations of American politics in the different Court eras can be used to understand how standards of evaluation of the Supreme Court change and to place Court decisionmaking in the wider ideational concerns of legal scholars and political scientists and theorists.

In Part Two I contend that the Burger Court also engaged in constitutive decisionmaking and that the predominant "no counterrevolution" interpretation of the Burger Court, which emphasizes that the major contribution of the Burger Court was that it did not engage in a counterrevolution to Warren Court jurisprudence, is wanting. It is the primary cause of our misperception of the Burger court, the process of Supreme Court decisionmaking, and the external factors that influence the development of constitutional law.

I ask how well the constitutional theory of the Warren and Burger Court eras functions as a guide to Supreme Court decisionmaking and find them wanting in important respects. In Part Three, I explore whether the Rehnquist Court also engages in constitutive decisionmaking and consider whether we can expect contemporary civic republican constitutional theory to provide a better guide to Rehnquist Court decisionmaking than occurred in previous Court eras.

Because instrumental rather than constitutive interpretations of Supreme Court decisionmaking and doctrinal change inform our vision of the Warren Court, we have misperceived that Court. Two instrumental interpretations of the Warren Court have been most influential: the *election returns* approach[3] and the *policymaking* approach.[4] Both of these approaches assume that principles, including long-standing legal principles about American political institutions, polity principles, and individual rights principles, are used instrumentally by justices who, like elected officials, seek to achieve specific policy outcomes.[5] These two are the most sophisticated of the instrumental approaches because they include both an analysis of *internal* decisionmaking and a description of factors *external* to the Court that are said to explain doctrinal change.

Another instrumental approach, the *safety-valve* approach, is in fact an important variant of the policymaking approach. In this view of Supreme Court decisionmaking, the primary objective of the Supreme Court is to ensure that the pluralist political system functions well. The Court's primary role, then, is to make up for the inability of the executive and legislative branches to accommodate incremental change and fair access to government by all groups of citizens and to provide the political system with the means to counter malfunctions or to enact reform.[6]

The interpretation of the Warren Court by G. Edward White, biographer of Chief Justice Warren, and perhaps the foremost legal historian of the Warren Court, differs from all these. Although Warren Court decisionmaking was viewed by White as constitutive until 1962, when Justice Frankfurter retired, his *biographical* approach is based primarily on instrumental assumptions about Warren Court decisionmaking that likewise lead us to misperceive the Warren Court.[7] Furthermore, instrumental visions of the Warren Court as dominated by a concern for equality and pure moral principles and as uninterested in polity principles grossly misinterpret Warren Court decisionmaking patterns and the resulting equal protection doctrine.[8] In Warren Court opinions involving rights of access to courts, voting rights, and the crucial fundamental rights and interests areas of the right to travel, education, and receipt of government benefits, I find that polity principles—justices' views of American political institutions—were as important to Warren Court justices as were visions of equality. In the Warren Court, as in prior eras of the Supreme Court and the Founding Period, a combination of polity and rights principles, and not merely visions of equality, informed judicial choices.

"Chief Justice Eras" as Units of Analysis

This book is based on the premise that in order to explain why we misperceive the Burger and Warren Courts and the limitations of instrumental interpreta-

6   tions of Supreme Court decisionmaking and doctrinal change, we must talk about "Court eras." Treating Court eras as units of analysis does not result in an oversimplification of the analysis of the decisionmaking process on the Supreme Court or blur ideological differences among individual members of the Court. As G. Edward White argues, comparing Court eras identified by their chief justices can offer much in understanding Supreme Court decisionmaking and the process of doctrinal change.[9]

The approach here is not to analyze the ideological premises of each Warren and Burger Court justice in all cases within a doctrinal area or in all, or most, major doctrinal areas. Rather, polity and rights "moments" are identified in landmark cases when justices pinpoint polity or rights values that inform the approach they will take in subsequent cases across or within doctrinal areas. The recent joint opinion by Justices O'Connor, Souter, and Kennedy in *Planned Parenthood of Southeastern Pennsylvania v. Casey* (1992) is a superb example of a polity and rights "moment" of significance.[10]

Nor can we study the place of polity and rights principles in all important doctrinal areas in one book. I have chosen to focus here on equal protection in the Warren and Burger Court eras (Chapters 2 and 5) and on church and state cases in the Burger Court era (Chapter 4), because scholars who employ instrumental interpretations consider that these areas best epitomize the validity of instrumental assumptions about Supreme Court decisionmaking and doctrinal change. If constitutive rather than instrumental assumptions about Supreme Court decisionmaking and doctrinal change are borne out through a study of these doctrinal areas, there are additional reasons to question instrumental interpretations.

I do not argue, as some scholars have, that the intellectual and political skills of the chief justice so dominate each Court era as to explain the differences between the Warren and Burger Court eras. The intellectual and leadership skills of Chief Justices Warren and Burger, and those of other justices such as Brennan and Powell, are noted, but in the end I reject explanations of doctrinal change that emphasize "internal" Court process over external factors, as I do instrumental analyses of doctrinal change that do not respect both the autonomy of law and politics—of the Supreme Court from elected bodies—and the impact of the dialogue between the Supreme Court and interpretive community on doctrinal change. Thus I explore the complexity of Supreme Court decisionmaking in order to puncture the conventional holistic visions that many scholars and the lay public have of these two Court eras, the Supreme Court decisionmaking process, and the process of doctrinal change.

At times I refer to the Warren and Burger "Courts" as a shorthand way to discuss and criticize conventional and overly simplistic interpretations offered by scholars who are too willing to define the Warren Court as primarily concerned about equality and the Burger Court as primarily outcome-oriented and pragmatic or dominated by centrist justices. I view the terms "Burger Court" and "Warren Court," and, more importantly, the traditional conceptualizations of the two court eras as oversimplifications by the academy and the wider legal and lay public. I discuss why this oversimplification is ironic, given the evidence that both polity and rights principles inform the jurisprudence of individual justices.

When this is done we shall see that our simplistic ideas about the Warren and Burger Court eras obscure more than they illuminate the doctrines and decisionmaking processes in each Court era. We will see that polity principles were important to liberals on the Warren Court, just as principles of individual rights were important to conservatives on the Burger Court. We also will see that polity and rights *principles*, not mere pragmatism, were important to left, right, and centrist justices on the Burger Court. Finally, the fact that blocs exist and coherence in polity and rights principles and doctrine pervade each era supports an analysis that emphasizes the coherence of polity and rights values rather than random case decisions.

Instrumental Approaches to Supreme Court Decisionmaking
The Election Returns Approach

In the 1950s, political scientist Robert Dahl presented the first and most influential formulation of an instrumental interpretation of Supreme Court decisionmaking and doctrinal change, the election returns approach.[11] Richard Funston in the 1970s and Gerald Rosenberg in 1991 also offered studies of Supreme Court decisionmaking and doctrinal change that are based on assumptions similar to Dahl's.[12] The election returns approach views the Supreme Court decisionmaking process as not significantly different from that of elected and appointed officials in legislative and executive policymaking institutions. It argues that the Supreme Court must be analyzed in similar "political" terms because it is concerned largely with making "policy" choices. Dahl asks about the Supreme Court what he would ask of any political institution: "Who gets what and why?" and "What groups are benefited or handicapped by the Court?" Dahl contends that the Supreme Court is built on a "fiction that it is not a political institution but exclusively a legal one" that must go outside legal criteria found in precedent, statute, and the fundamental values of the Constitution. This is especially so in landmark cases because there is controversy, both in society and among legal scholars, about how to read the facts, the law, and the possible outcomes in a case and about which values to choose.[13]

Dahl demonstrates his legal-realist roots when he denies that principles of natural rights and fundamental rights are significant bases of Court action and limits on society.[14] He argues that natural law and fundamental rights were more acceptable as bases for judicial choices in an earlier day, when it was be-

8   lieved that certain rights were natural and self-evident, at least to all reasonable creatures.[15] His approach also denies the importance of separation of powers polity principles, including the special role of the Supreme Court and judicial review as a limit on electoral politics and as an explanation of doctrinal change.

Dahl argues that national politics in the United States, as in other stable democracies, is dominated by relatively cohesive alliances that endure a long time, followed by a period of intense struggle and change. Except for transitional periods, "the Supreme Court is inevitably a part of the dominant national alliance. As an element in the political leadership of the dominant alliance, the Court of course supports the major policies of the alliance." Dahl views the Court by itself as almost powerless to affect the course of national policy. The glue that binds the Supreme Court to the majority coalition is the recruitment of justices by presidents with the political preferences of the dominant coalition in mind. Doctrinal change results when the president selects nominees to the Supreme Court who reflect his and his majority coalition's political philosophy, public policies, and polity and rights principles.

Thus, Dahl argues that while the Supreme Court is not an agent of the governing coalition, neither is it independent of it. He notes that legislatures tend to be overruled by the Supreme Court only when their lawmaking majority is weak, and Congress reverses the Court's policy in a majority of cases, often within four years of Supreme Court action. When there is no agreement within the dominant alliance on a national policy, any attempt by the Court to make policy leads to disaster, as in the *Dred Scott* case and the early New Deal period.

As in most instrumental approaches, Dahl asks whether the Supreme Court violates what he considers to be the primary value in our democratic political system—majority rule. Having assumed that majority rule is at the core of the polity principles in the Constitution, and fearing that a Supreme Court of nine justices appointed for life might undermine this majority principle, Dahl sees the central question as whether the Supreme Court as a policy-making institution has been countermajoritarian. For him, the Court's most important role is to confer legitimacy on the majority coalition's interpretation of the Constitution. "The policy views dominant on the Court are never for long out of line with the policy views dominant among the lawmaking majorities of the United States." Because the Court's legitimacy is jeopardized when it flagrantly opposes the major policies of the dominant alliance, it will not normally counter the constitutional interpretations and laws of that alliance. The Court is most effective when it sets limits on public officials in state government, bureaucracies, and regions of the nation to force them to stay within the policy objectives of the governing coalition. Dahl views the Supreme Court's discretion to make national policy as similar to that of a committee chair in Congress who is powerless to nullify the policies of the rest of the dominant party leadership.

Not only can the dominant coalition be trusted to support polity and rights values in the Constitution when it makes public policy, Dahl argues, but at crucial times in our history, when the Court has invoked rights and justice as a norm along with its role as the protector of fundamental rights, it has more often than not worked *against* the interests of the weak. In some very significant cases the Supreme Court's delay in implementation of congressional policy, sometimes up to twenty-five years, has denied fundamental rights to the weak. The Supreme Court has used the Fifth, Thirteenth, Fourteenth, and Fifteenth amendments to preserve the rights and liberties of relatively privileged groups at the expense of submerged groups: slaveholders at the expense of slaves, whites at the expense of blacks, and property holders at the expense of wage earners and other groups.[16]

The finding that the Supreme Court does not protect minorities any better than the majority coalition is not alarming to Dahl because of his faith in the pluralist political system: "Thus to affirm that the Court supports minority preferences against majorities is to deny that popular sovereignty and political equality, at least in the traditional sense, exist in the United States; and to affirm that the Court *ought* to act in this way is to deny that popular sovereignty and political equality *ought* to prevail in this country. . . . If the Court did in fact uphold minorities against national majorities . . . it would be an extremely anomalous institution from a democratic point of view."[17]

Thus, for Dahl the standard of evaluation of the Supreme Court as an institution is not whether it protects individual rights or whether it honors the polity principles in the Constitution. Dahl has chosen to reinterpret the place of judicial review in our constitutional scheme based on principles that view the majority coalition, rather than the Supreme Court, as a protector of individual rights. These views are in violation of separation of powers principles, views about judicial review held by the Founders, and basic constitutional principles that restrict the powers of elected officials because of fears that they will undermine individual rights and the rights of minorities.

Also, Dahl argues that there is no need for strong law and courts to limit politics. Our faith in political institutions is at least as well placed as our faith in the Supreme Court and perhaps more so, he maintains, since their actions, unlike those of the Supreme Court, do not violate Madisonian democratic principles as he views them.

Dahl's instrumental assumptions also affect his view of the interpretive community and doctrinal change. He argues that changes in precedent and past legal formulations as well as the ideas held by political theorists, legal scholars, jurists, journalists, and others in the interpretive community are peripheral to doctrinal change, as are the changing ways that constitutional the-

10   ory organizes polity and rights values into a coherent statement of their relationship to each other.

Dahl assumes that the Court uses principles instrumentally to justify the policy positions of justices, which are not very different from those of the presidents who appointed them. It assumes that justices think in terms of policy rather than neutral polity and rights principles whose substance and relationship are informed by evaluative norms in changing constitutional theory. The Supreme Court, as Dahl sees it, is not autonomous of the wider political system in which it operates. Nor is it a legal institution in which stare decisis and legal, as opposed to policy, choices are made. To Dahl, it is simply an instrument of politics.

The Policymaking Approach

Like Dahl, Martin Shapiro, the most cogent proponent of the policymaking approach, argues that the Supreme Court should be viewed in instrumental terms as a major policymaking rather than a legal institution.[18] Justices muddle through and fashion arguments to support their policy positions, because, as in politics, there are no clear solutions to problems. Like public officials, justices decide what policies they desire and use polity and rights arguments to support those policies. They are also careless and arbitrary in their choices, they let issues stew so that all can be heard, they experiment with different approaches, and they are responsive to public sentiment and the general political climate. Like politicians, justices calculate and ponder the major policy issues confronting the Court and make choices based upon immediate facts and broader notions of the good life and the good state.

Shapiro argues that collaborating, debating of principles, and bargaining among the justices rarely occur:

> The Supreme Court is not a place where nine scholarly men think, study, discuss and carefully ponder their decisions and then write reasoned elaborations of the careful path of legal analysis that they have pursued before coming to a conclusion. . . . There is little purpose in his rethinking the basic questions, seeking to convince or bargain with his fellow justices, or spending time carefully honing an elaborate opinion. . . . In short, like most other government policy makers, the justices are usually confronted with choices that they can treat as incremental variations on choices that have been made in the past.

Deliberation among justices is not crucial to doctrinal change, Shapiro argues, since clerks, not the justices, read briefs and do much of the work, including the writing of opinions. Justices in the majority as well as those dissenting often fail to read each other's opinions.[19] Shapiro views oral argument as weak and seldom influential in decisionmaking and emphasizes that judges do not consider the constitutional theory behind different visions of basic polity and rights principles as they make their constitutional choices. Precedent is used merely as fodder for arguments on behalf of policies that a justice wants.

The Warren Court, according to Shapiro, wrapped its policy wants in theoretical language. For example, because a justice of the Warren Court followed the "preferred position" analysis articulated in the *Carolene Products* case does not mean that this theory was the basis for judicial decisionmaking. Rather it was a justification for imposing policies to pay off the New Deal coalition. After the famous *Carolene Products* footnote the Supreme Court used civil liberties language to make judicial policies that favored economic redistribution, the poor, blacks, intellectuals, government employees, and other elements of the New Deal coalition created by Roosevelt. Thus the Warren Court switched from supporting the needs of Republican businessmen to those of the Democratic lower class: "Rarely has a Supreme Court doctrinal pronouncement been more transparently political."[20] Thus, for Shapiro, judicial self-restraint and preferred position advocates were "stablemates" rather than seriously contending wings of the Court. Shapiro calls the preferred position analysis which identifies rights within the Bill of Rights and situations of malfunction by political institutions for special scrutiny, a New Deal "myth" that becomes "ideology," because it is a selective version of reality that guides and shapes the interpretation of all subsequent reality.[21]

Shapiro argues that the Warren Court, like the *Lochner* Court, deviated from the past norms to impose its policy wants. Post-1937 Courts, especially the Warren Court, merely changed their clients and social theory. Both *Lochner*-era and post-1937 Courts created rights and said that government cannot overcome them except for compelling reasons; the scrutiny in both Courts of national and state legislation, for Shapiro, was a wide-ranging social, economic, and political investigation. However, in the Warren court, "the premise is now: that government is best which governs equally."[22]

Shapiro's policymaking approach accords a central role to the interpretive community in doctrinal change in the Warren Court era. He argues that although the Court follows the policy wants of the interpretive community, rather than those of the majority coalition, current constitutional theory about polity and rights principles and their relationship does not affect Court choices independent of commentators' policy wants.

On the Warren Court the judicial self-restraint bloc, led by Frankfurter, and the preferred position bloc, led by Warren and Brennan, represent the two wings of a New Deal coalition whose ideology "totally dominated" the Court and the major law schools. "That ideology held that the Supreme Court must either abdicate to the president and *his* Congress, or, if it had any authority to act at all, it was only [to act] on behalf of personal and civil

12   rights—that is, on behalf of those interests that carried the New Deal certificate." Therefore, Shapiro's argument is that both Frankfurter and Harlan supported New Deal outcomes, needed reasons to overcome judicial self-restraint
and let Congress and the president make policy, and employed ideas in the interpretive community to justify those policies. Using the preferred position
approach, the Court began more aggressively to promote the agenda of the
New Deal and, under the guise of civil rights, to force states to demonstrate
why they had failed to produce economic equality. By the end, the Warren
Court was moving toward the creation of constitutional guarantees of national
basic minimums in education, housing, subsistence, legal services, political influence, birth control devices, and other facets of the modern welfare state for
all persons regardless of race—that is, securing specific policy outcomes.

Shapiro's emphasis on the economic policy preferences of justices and his
rejection of the notion that constitutional theory and polity and rights principles had an independent effect on Warren Court decisionmaking is clear in his
analysis of *Shapiro v. Thompson* (1969). In that case the Supreme Court voided
one-year state residency requirements for welfare recipients—not, he argues,
because they infringed upon a right to travel, as the majority opinion claims,
but rather to meet the policy needs of members of the New Deal coalition, as
part of a trend to develop a right to economic equality and survival through
welfare payments. "What right could be more purely and fundamentally economic than the basic subsistence provided by welfare benefits? Yet the Court's
first entry into this area, *Shapiro v. Thompson* (1969), comes wrapped in, of all
things, an alleged civil liberty, the right to travel." Shapiro argues that it
sought a redistribution of economic resources to pay off a constituency—pure
and simple—because it supported the classical New Deal policy goals. The
right to travel and the polity principles the Court purported to uphold are
merely window dressing; the Court sought to establish in constitutional law
the policy wants of the justices and the New Deal coalition.

The emphasis on policy wants is also at the core of the Warren Court's definition of the right to privacy as protecting a married couple's use of contraceptives:

> Its ground-breaking *Griswold* decision, which struck down state bans on
> birth control and led the way to later abortion decisions, supposedly rested
> on a whole range of constitutional grounds—of which the equal protection
> clause was not one. Yet, it was obvious that the Court's judgment really
> rested on the conclusion that birth control services were in fact widely
> available to the middle classes and the basic effect of the state statutes was
> to deprive only the poor of such services. It is indicative of the egalitarian
> thrust of the Court that its most confused and indecisive record was in the

area of freedom of speech, which seemed to it to raise liberty rather than equality issues.

Thus, for Shapiro as for Dahl, the game is not about polity and rights; it is about desired outcomes:

> Once the doctrine is understood in this light, it can be seen that what appeared to be a bitter battle between two schools of commentators and two wings of the Court—the judicial activists and the judicial self-restrainers— was in reality a New Deal consensus on the validity of the New Deal myth and the virtue of the New Deal clientele. At worst there was only a difference of opinion on whether the Supreme Court should leave the President alone or actively assist him in the care and feeding of the New Deal coalition.

Shapiro specifically rejects Dahl's thesis about doctrinal changes on the Supreme Court. Although he views the Supreme Court as a policymaking institution, he does not see it as part of the majority coalition. "All of the major and many of the minor interventions occurred quite independently, without the cooperation or encouragement of other parts of government or of either of the political parties. . . . The Supreme Court has shown a capacity for independent action that has been surprising in light of the total subservience—indeed, the near demise—of judicial authority that New Deal commentators and justices often announced" as a reaction to the Supreme Court's overturning liberal legislation before 1937. Except for school desegregation, which was spurred by the NAACP, "the major policies and many of the minor ones were judicially initiated without the support of substantial organized constituencies, interest groups, or identifiable blocs of voters."

Shapiro argues that the parallelism between the general drift of American life and thought and what the Court has done means that "it is difficult to depict the Court as a pure example of a political elite doing whatever it pleases. In the light of its massive policy initiatives, it is also impossible to depict it as a mere ritualistic legitimizer of what those political actors more closely linked to particular political forces choose to do." In contrast to Dahl, Shapiro sees the Supreme Court acting independently or in advance of the trend by the central government to nationalize efforts to meet the problems facing its citizens, not automatically as an agent of it. The degree to which the Supreme Court invalidates national legislation is not a valid indicator that it is fulfilling the wants of the majority coalition.

How does Shapiro explain the Supreme Court's policymaking in light of the lack of strong support by organized interest groups and the active opposition of many people to its decisions? First, he argues that the distinguishing

14   feature of the Supreme Court's intervention into policymaking is not its utility in building a support coalition of politically powerful, focused constituencies. Rather, "it has been their consonance with some widely held but inchoate values of the American people and with ideas whose 'time has come.'"
The argument here is that the Court had stated basic democratic values (for
example, one person, one vote) that could not be attacked by politicians. Defendants' rights, Shapiro tells us, were politically viable because "most Americans cannot help believing that everyone accused of a crime is entitled to a fair
trial. . . . Few white Americans outside the South could openly defend official government discrimination against Negroes. . . . By the 1960s and 70s
American sexual mores had so changed, that the Court's recognition in its obscenity, birth control, and abortion decisions of both the prevalence and
problems of sexual expression was little more than a legal confirmation of the
felt necessities of the times."

The Supreme Court's authority, according to Shapiro, lies in its ability to
tap into the public's highly diffuse but strong support for principles in the
Constitution, such as freedom of speech or a fair democratic process, that
rarely generate sufficiently focused or organized support to produce direct
action in legislatures and administrative bodies. The Court can also add to
these principles, as in the area of desegregation, where it can key into inchoate
values. For Shapiro, these inchoate values are instrumentally important. They
resonate with the policy choices of the Supreme Court and act as a post hoc
basis for legitimating the desire of the Supreme Court to provide for those in
the New Deal coalition. The Court is autonomous from direct influence by
the governing coalition but not from those who have benefited from the New
Deal and who support New Deal policies. Therefore, Shapiro views the Warren Court as promoting the policy interests of blacks, the poor, defendants,
and liberal scholars—what he calls the New Deal Coalition—who seek equality
and redistribution of wealth and political power.

Shapiro and Dahl both view the Court as meeting the policy needs of external entities: the majority coalition for Dahl and the members of the New
Deal coalition for Shapiro. However, Shapiro does not support Dahl's direct
line of causation: from elections and interest groups, to governing coalition,
to Court nominees, to doctrinal change. Shapiro believes that the Court rarely
makes policy choices based on the support of interest groups. The Court
makes many decisions that organized interests oppose, such as its decisions on
school prayer. However, implementation takes a long time in such cases. For
Shapiro the Court may be more countermajoritarian than for Dahl: "If, as we
are so often told, the Supreme Court follows the elections returns, it nevertheless does not act in a directly election-oriented way." However, the election returns and policymaking approaches are very similar in this important re-

spect: they do not consider that polity and rights principles, stare decisis, and legal theory have an independent effect on Supreme Court decisionmaking.

The Safety Valve Approach

The major exponents of the safety valve approach, Anthony Lewis and Archibald Cox, like Dahl and Shapiro, view Supreme Court decisionmaking in terms of a direct instrumental objective. Lewis presents the Supreme Court's primary objective as that of ensuring that the pluralist political system functions well. Under this approach (also called institutional functionalism), the Supreme Court's primary role in the American system of government is to make up for the inability of other branches of government to accommodate the incremental change and to provide access to the political system for all groups of citizens. Both of these elements are necessary for a vital political and legal system.

Like the election returns and policymaking approaches, this approach accepts the idea of equilibrium in the pluralist political system—a notion consonant with the pluralist interpretations of the American political system in favor in the 1950s. However, unlike Dahl, Lewis argues that such equilibrium requires a skeptical, critical Court rather than an acquiescent Court. The Supreme Court must act to ensure this equilibrium by countering the institutional malfunctions of Congress, states, and bureaucracies.

Like Dahl, Lewis demonstrates a faith in the ability of the overall political system to meet demands for policy change and change in its political structure. However, this faith is justified only if we can trust the legal system to play a major role in reform, which in turn depends on the maintenance of the autonomy of law from politics and of legal institutions from political institutions.

Like Shapiro, who views the Supreme Court as responding to inchoate values held by the American people, Lewis sees the Court as responding to changing moral values: "If the Court has changed, it is because we have changed."[23] Thus the Warren Court responded to changes in national moral values. Lewis argues that the national consciousness had no way to express itself except through the Supreme Court, and the Warren Court acted when the political system was stymied.

Although the safety valve approach does perceive the Supreme Court as having a role autonomous of the dominant majority coalition and the specific policy wants of the justices, it, like the other instrumental approaches, also sees the Supreme Court as using polity and rights principles in instrumental ways—that is, to secure specific policy outcomes. In this case, the instrumental value is the smooth functioning of the pluralist political system.

The Biographical Approach

The most complex and filigreed of the instrumental approaches to Supreme Court decisionmaking and doctrinal change is that offered by G. Edward

16   White, the preeminent biographer of Earl Warren. In contrast to the instrumental interpretations just discussed, White centers his analysis of the Warren
Court, at least up to 1962 when Frankfurter retired, on the centrality of polity
and rights principles in the Court's constitutional choices. For White, judicial
philosophies, and the different polity and rights principles held by individual
justices, are independent bases for doctrinal choices, not ideas used instrumentally to secure policy wants. The different groups of justices are not "stablemates," as Shapiro would have us believe; nor do the justices use ideas
merely instrumentally. Internal debate on the Court is not epiphenomenal to
outcomes. Rather the justices are informed by their own polity and rights
principles, and the differences that arise can be explained by biographical
events.

Until 1962, White argues, the Warren Court split into two major groups
that defined its controversies. He explains the differences between the two
groups of Warren Court justices in biographical terms. The first group, Black,
Douglas, and Warren, were children of poverty. They did not like the effects
of privilege and viewed a strong Court as supportive of equality in political,
economic, and social institutions. Warren was, for example, a California Progressive who abhorred interest group politics and mistrusted politics as a
means for meeting the needs of the underprivileged. The second group,
Harlan and Frankfurter, were children of the elite who had received their training at major business and legal institutions. They tended to support political
institutions and a limited role for courts as agents of political change. They
also favored slow, incremental change through the law and well-crafted decisions as guides to the legal community. The debate centered on differences
over the judicial role and the nature of the American polity. White defined
one view as "process jurisprudence" or "process liberalism," the other as
"substantive liberalism." Process jurisprudence accepts law-making by judges
but confines it to limited areas of intervention; emphasizes the antidemocratic
character of the judiciary and the inability of judges to achieve detailed technical expertise; and supports government agency action as long as the agency
stays within its expertise and views courts as "disinterested," legislatures as
"representative" of popular opinion and able to canvass a wide spectrum of
views, the executive as "efficient," and administrative agencies as "flexible"
and "expert."[24]

Substantive liberalism holds that some values supersede, rather than com-
pete with, others. These values are embedded in the Constitution and in society and include the egalitarianism and libertarianism that compelled the eradi-
cation of economic inequality. White summarizes the substantive liberalism of
the Warren Court: The Constitution is the supreme law of the land and its
mandates displace all competing laws, legislative or judge-made. The judiciary
alone is the ultimate interpreter of the Constitution, and it must use the literal

words of the Constitution and the works of the Founders and of the framers of later amendments. That way the justices could say they were not substituting their own values for those of the Framers but doing only what the Constitution compelled them to do. Questions of the reach of judicial power, the appropriate balance between values, and the substantive content of the equal protection and due process clauses were thus avoided. Process liberalism, then, put a brake on court action in areas where legislatures, agencies, and the executive were taking no action, such as reapportionment. Substantive liberalism required no such brakes. It did not merely stop intentional discrimination but was more affirmatively egalitarian in advocating that the Court intervene where no legally defined wrong existed.

White argues that when Chief Justice Warren joined the Supreme Court he did not have a well-developed "philosophy of judging," but that the *Brown v. Board of Education* (1954) decision shaped Warren's approach to his office. "His [Warren's] longstanding beliefs that government should be responsive to the people at large, not to special interests, [were] transposed into an image of an energetic court protecting the rights of all Americans, especially the downtrodden and disadvantaged. His moral indignation over corruption and dishonesty metamorphosed into an undeviating interest in the abstractions of fairness and justice, and a conception of law as inexorably linked to ethics."

Up to 1962, White observes, the unity of the Warren Court did not suppress its diversity but was merely superimposed upon it—the Court was not a melting pot but a mosaic. No individual emerged as its intellectual leader during the sixteen years of Warren's tenure. Its dominant justices retained their distinctive points of view, harmonizing with one another only sporadically and superficially. Several powerful justices, such as Black, Frankfurter, Harlan, Douglas, and Warren, stood in "trenchant opposition or an uneasy coexistence." No theory of constitutional interpretation of judicial performance captured the Court, and much of its energy came from a clash of competing prudential attitudes. Differences over polity, rights, and the role of the Court, not over policy wants or equality principles, informed the choices of the Warren Court, at least until Frankfurter (and Whittaker) retired in 1962.

Like the instrumental scholars, White contends that a humanitarian impulse gained momentum in the Warren Court after Frankfurter's retirement:

> The original debate metamorphosed into something resembling an ideological confrontation. At stake in the debate was more than the delineation of proper techniques of opinion-writing or even the designation of social values deserving of judicial implementation; at stake was the viability of the process theory of appellate judging. . . . [Warren] expanded his horizons, encouraging judicial reform of legislative apportionment, criminal

18 procedure, Church-State relations, anti-trust laws, labor relations, and the boundaries between the federal government and the states.

The Court competed with Congress to produce change in the area of civil rights. The Warren Court saw American institutions and society as complex and industrialized and American citizens as victims of that complexity. Thus the Court had a concern for the effectiveness of government. The major conflict among the justices before 1962 was over the proper role of Court intervention in modern society; polity values had a central place in Court controversies. However, once the Court had dealt with the polity issues of judicial self-restraint and political questions, it moved to activism in its rights jurisprudence. After Frankfurter's retirement, the Court was far less concerned about polity principles as limits on Court action. It minimized "analytic barriers" to its actions and, White argues, "revealed itself as having a distinctly ideological character."

Thus, White argues that the Warren Court shared a general commitment to social ends such as efficiency, humanitarianism, equality of economic opportunity, and equal treatment before the law—the basic tenets of modern liberalism. The justices disagreed over methods of attaining these ends and, most importantly, over the proper role of the Court in doing so, before but not after the Frankfurter retirement. Therefore, while White sees polity and rights principles as important to the Warren Court, his theory, like the other instrumental approaches, views the Warren and Burger Courts as moving toward substantive liberal jurisprudence, toward concern about outcomes, toward a dying debate about polity principles.[25]

Constitutive Interpretations of the Supreme Court

The constitutive approach tends to focus on the Supreme Court as primarily a legal, not a policymaking, institution in which the rule of law—the Constitution, precedents, and fundamental rights and legal principles—influences judicial decisionmaking. This approach considers that the polity and rights principles held by the justices are central to Supreme Court decisionmaking. The constitutive approach presented here is informed by the important scholarship of Robert McCloskey, a leading political scientist and commentator on the Supreme Court in the 1950s and 1960s, and of political scientist Walter Murphy.[26]

McCloskey discusses "the deep and ineradicable tension in the American political tradition between the value of electorally accountable policy-making and certain other values or ideals."[27] These other fundamental rights values or principles, which limit raw electoral politics, include due process of law, liberty, equality, and the principle that individuals are responsible only for what they do, not for ascriptive categories others apply to them.

McCloskey believes that doctrines of popular sovereignty and fundamental law ought to be distinct, held side by side, not fused in the Constitution. "This propensity to hold contradictory ideas simultaneously is one of the most significant qualities of the American political mind at all stages of national history, and it helps substantially in explaining the rise to power of the United States Supreme Court." The courts are guardians of fundamental law and legislatures are guardians of the will of the people. Having both types of guardians, McCloskey argues, in language reminiscent of the relativist political theory of the 1950s, "insured public support for the institution that represented each of them."[28]

McCloskey does not pinpoint the effect of polity and rights values on Court choices, but views the Court as part of the pluralist "genius of American politics" interpretation put forward by his generation of scholars. Its genius was to be not too far ahead of or behind public opinion or autonomous of politics: "The Court seldom strayed very far from the mainstream of American life and seldom overestimated its own power resources. To put [it] in a different way, the Court learned to be a political institution and to behave accordingly; and this fact above all accounts for its unique position among the judicial tribunals of the world." McCloskey sees electoral accountability as a fundamental value and as an important reason for the Court to be cautious: "Public concurrence sets an outer boundary for judicial policy-making; . . . judicial ideas of the good society can never be too far removed from the popular ideas." McCloskey believes that the Supreme Court is in a reciprocal relationship with public opinion, emphasizing that the Court engages in judicial self-restraint—that constitutional law is the science of the possible.

McCloskey's is a 1950s outlook, in which the equilibrium among institutions of the American political system is prized uncritically. However, unlike Robert Dahl and other leading scholars of the day, McCloskey introduces into his analysis the centrality of polity and rights principles. These principles are not case-specific or merely employed instrumentally in the name of securing a public policy or meeting the needs of "history."

The dualism between popular sovereignty (polity principles) and fundamental rights is found in the legal, political, and social philosophy of every era; we have never resolved the conflict between popular sovereignty and fundamental law. McCloskey does not accept the legal realist view that a court is merely a political institution that makes policy choices as a legislature does; polity choice, fundamental law, and the myth of an impartial, judicious tribunal are necessary to keep legitimate the Court's claim on the American mind. Although they do make policy, justices cannot shed the duty to follow fundamental law. McCloskey argues that the Constitution is not an immutable code because it leaves too many questions open, with popular will and higher law principles fighting it out in the crucible of judicial politics.[29] Nor does Mc-

20   Closkey view polity principles and fundamental rights values as part of a dialogue among the Court, the interpretive community, and the wider society; it is as if the Court is merely responding to "history."

The work of Walter Murphy has also informed the constitutive approach. In *Elements of Judicial Strategy* (1964), Murphy viewed Supreme Court justices as policymakers in a political system. However, his view was far more subtle, and based on less instrumental assumptions about justices' motivations, than the theories of Robert Dahl and Martin Shapiro. Murphy argued that Supreme Court decisionmaking is shaped by both bargaining within the Court and pressures from outside the Court system. However, he argued that legal precedent, individual rights, and polity principles shaped justices' constitutional choices more than they do those of elected policymakers. Also, in contrast to Dahl and Shapiro, by the late 1970s Murphy had eschewed instrumental assumptions about Supreme Court decisionmaking and argued that justices decide cases primarily on their determination of the proper relationship between polity and rights principles.[30]

Polity Principles

In the constitutive approach, polity and rights principles are the basic filters through which doctrines of popular sovereignty and fundamental rights confront each other. One can compare polity and rights principles and identify significant moments when a group of justices makes a clear statement of principles that set boundaries for future decisionmaking. For example in *Planned Parenthood of Southeastern Pennsylvania v. Casey* (1992), the case that upheld the right of abortion choice first stated in *Roe v. Wade* (1973), the joint opinion by Justices Souter, Kennedy, and O'Connor on the importance of precedent and a concept of Court role and legitimacy is a significant polity moment on the Rehnquist Court.

By polity principles I mean justices' deeply held ideas about where decisionmaking power should be located when deciding questions of constitutional significance. Polity principles involve beliefs about whether courts or electorally accountable political institutions are the more appropriate forum for constitutional decisionmaking. They also include beliefs about whether state, local, or national levels of government are proper forums for making such decisions.

Central to a justice's polity values is his or her attitude—critical or trusting—toward legislative and interest group politics. Different Court eras will exhibit different mixes of trust in and criticism of states as venues for making constitutional choices, for example, and for whether the national government and federal courts can be trusted to oversee states and state courts. Therefore, a belief in the polity value "states' rights" is a point on a continuum of polity principles. With regard to separation of powers, another major polity principle, justices will differ as to whether they believe the political system or the courts should intervene to mediate conflicts between the branches.

Polity principles also involve questions of how complexly or simply justices view structural inequality as a basis for the Court's increasing its power of judicial review. These questions are at work in all areas of public law, including such individual rights areas as equal protection, procedural due process, First Amendment freedoms, and questions of substantive due process, such as the right to privacy. The term "polity principles" also refers to less formal views about the American political system held by jurists, such as their views about how well the pluralist political system is operating. For example, in cases involving equal protection and the fairness of school funding schemes, justices' views about whether local school systems, states, or federal courts are the most appropriate forum for decisionmaking were central to Court choices; justices did not simply ask whether supporting an individual's First Amendment freedoms requires that there be a fundamental right to education. Polity principles about the intrusion of government into individual behavior and the formation of discrete and insular groups also informed Court choices. For example, on the question of whether to allow cross–school district busing to end segregation, the Court's support of local control of schools was central to its ban on such busing for districts that were found not to be in violation of the equal protection clause. In public aid to religion cases, justices' polity values about whether local and state politics can be trusted to settle conflicts between groups and religions were central to Burger Court decisionmaking.

Finally, polity principles inform the debate in constitutional law, practice, and theory about whether federal courts or electorally accountable institutions should make choices and about the *degree* of institutional autonomy that should be granted to electorally accountable institutions and to courts. Courts must decide how much weight polity principles should be given when balanced against individual rights, which are usually of a less defined and potentially more substantive, open-ended nature. At their most persuasive, judicial decisions based on polity values are grounded *structurally* in powers enumerated in the Constitution, polity principles that are informed by these powers, and the overall principles of governance embodied in the Constitution. For some justices these values imply judicial self-restraint, reliance on existing political power structures, and a firm faith in participational and access norms to ensure a normally functioning democratic system. The polity principles of other justices lead them to favor judicial activism and support for expanded individual rights as a counter to "malfunctions" in the political system.[31]

Rights Principles

Rights principles are defined as beliefs (held by justices, as well as judicial advocates and constitutional scholars) about legally enforceable claims for individual powers, privileges, or immunities guaranteed under the Constitution, statutes, and law. Thus, many rights relate to "cocoons" that shield citizens from government intrusion, such as the fundamental rights and interests embodied in the Bill of Rights. Rights principles do not usually include issues of power among branches of the majoritarian political process as much as they involve decisions about entitlements for individual citizens from agencies or other parts of the political system.

Rights may be prohibitions against government interference with the liberty of individuals or groups; these include the basic freedoms in the Bill of Rights. They also may be composed of federal courts' determinations of affirmative responsibilities on the part of government, as in modern equal protection law.[32] Rights may include the assurance that goods and services that are allocated by legislatures and declared essential to life and liberty are distributed under a set of rules and processes that is neither capricious nor arbitrary.

Rights principles force one to think about the individual or group and about individual liberties like freedom of speech and the right to privacy. Polity values, on the other hand, force one to think about the nature of governmental powers, the political process, and the judicial process. Thus, while polity and rights principles may be viewed as analytically distinct, for heuristic purposes they work together to form the bases of an individual justice's approach to constitutional questions and to changing doctrine in different Court eras. Justices and Courts differ in the way they view and balance polity and rights principles and whether they see them as complex, rigid, or permeable; through these differences we can explain the growth of constitutional law and see how the wider society and interpretive community are in a dialogue with the Supreme Court. However, we must first establish that the relationship of polity and rights principles is central to the development of constitutional law and constitutional theory.

The Founding Period

The juxtaposition of polity and rights visions has informed the development of constitutional law, with the balance between the two changing over time. In this country the clash between them extends back to the Founding Period, when the Article VII structural credo necessary for ratification of the Constitution was countered or, for some, buttressed by the first ten amendments.[33] A central issue was the distribution of power among state and local political institutions, on the one hand, and national institutions on the other. The Founders perceived this issue as a question of whether individual rights could be better protected through polity principles establishing limits on national or state power or through a Bill of Rights or commitment to natural law.

Of central concern to both Federalists and Anti-Federalists was whether governing bodies of small or large constituencies offer better protection for individual rights. The Anti-Federalists wanted to protect state sovereignty because they felt that states, being smaller and more homogeneous, would be better forums for the teaching of civic virtue. They supported small-constituency government, state and local government power, because they believed that the very rich and the very poor, who were prone to forming factions, would be less likely to dominate small governments than a government of strong national political institutions. The possibility of instability and conflict would be reduced if small-constituency government prevailed, because it fostered more direct contacts between citizens and elected officials and thus would have better success at gaining the confidence of citizens. Finally, Anti-Federalists believed that citizen trust in government would decline with the growth in national political institutions and structural complexity. They questioned the Federalist assumption that national political institutions and the separation of powers under a theory of national supremacy of law would protect citizen rights, add to citizens' confidence in the Constitution and the new governing institutions, and protect against the problem of majority and minority factions, a key concern of the Federalists.[34]

The Federalists were concerned primarily about stability. They believed that continued state sovereignty would cause a decline in property rights, retard economic development, and lead to a poor national defense—outcomes they thought would decrease public confidence. The Federalists believed that the larger constituencies and more heterogeneous bases of the House and Senate, in contrast to those of state legislatures and towns, would reduce the possibilities of oppression by minority factions and control by a majority faction with narrow interests. The representative scheme of large constituency bodies would result in better-educated, more-skilled leaders coming to the fore and a greater likelihood of the cross-checking of interests. Thus, structural complexity, national government–large constituency power, the power of judicial review, and good administration would limit the misuse of power by political leaders and protect citizen rights and interests under the new Constitution.

The Federalist theory of government won out over Anti-Federalist arguments, in part because some of the Anti-Federalists themselves feared that the effects of minority factions in the states would retard the economic development and military security of the nation. Yet the Anti-Federalists, having lost most of the battles over polity principles, secured the listing of individual rights against intrusion by the national government in the Bill of Rights and the main body of the Constitution. Both Federalists and Anti-Federalists saw the power of judicial review and judges' lifetime tenure as a means to limit the effects of faction.

Thus, the relationship between the structure of polity and the protection of individual rights was of central concern to both the Anti-Federalists and the Federalists.[35] The Federalists also linked their polity concepts—beliefs in na-

24   tional political institutions, federal courts, and national supremacy of the law—to the protection of rights.[36]

The Supreme Court before the Warren Court

While scholars have differed over the degree to which concepts of rights and polity dominated the thinking of the Supreme Court during the Marshall and Taney eras, all agree that both polity and rights principles informed Court choices. Gerald Garvey argues that in the Marshall Court the protection of what he calls "buyer-seller" relationships (rights principles) predominated, while in the Taney Court concerns about the power of state legislatures to make policy were prominent.[37] Edward S. Corwin contends that the power of the states and national government was not fixed in the Marshall Court but was left unclear to be reinterpreted in each era so law could reflect changes in political power and the new problems facing the nation.[38]

The Civil War amendments, especially the Fourteenth Amendment with the open-ended language of its equal protection, due process, and privileges and immunities clauses, allowed the Supreme Court and Congress to protect a wider range of individual rights against encroachment by the states. As typified by the Supreme Court's narrow interpretation of the Fourteenth Amendment in the *Slaughterhouse* cases (1883), before the *Lochner* era (1905–1937) the Court chose not to interpret that amendment in an open-ended, rights-protective way. The Court did not permit significant limits on state action, except with regard to invalidating the most extravagant limits on the rights of blacks to participate as a matter of law in civil processes, such as on juries.

Garvey argues that in the *Lochner* era the Supreme Court reintroduced in a more stringent form the need to protect "buyer-seller" transactions between citizens and corporations in their contractual relationships.[39] The *Lochner* Court also accepted the Taney Court's notion that principles of federalism allow expanded state, not national, police powers. Corwin argues that a "no-man's land" resulted, one in which neither state nor national legislatures could make economic laws to protect the health and welfare of factory workers.[40] The *Lochner* Court defined manufacturing as a local activity subject only to state regulation, in contrast to commerce, the actual movement of goods, which was subject to national legislation. The Court declared unconstitutional many laws designed to protect the health and welfare of factory employees. It viewed these laws as interference in the rights of contract between individuals and corporations found in the substantive definition of liberty in the due process clause of the Fourteenth Amendment as applied to states and in the Fifth Amendment as applied to the national government. These definitions of commerce and manufacturing and conceptions of legal rights of contract were derived logically; the Court did not view economic relationships as a matter of unequal economic and political power subject to state regulation in the public interest.

However, like many scholars, Garvey oversimplifies the nature of constitutional decisionmaking in the *Lochner* Court by emphasizing the place of rights principles.[41] A more precise analysis of the *Lochner* era indicates a dovetailing of novel rights and polity concepts. It was the strong ideological parallelism of these concepts that created Corwin's ''no-man's land,'' which arose from the reintroduction of the sanctity of contract as a matter of right *and* the introduction of novel, clearly delineated (''bright-line'') distinctions between state and national police powers.

The *Lochner* era cannot be fully understood in pure rights or pure polity terms. To view that era primarily in Garvey's terms of rights, ''buyer-seller'' relationships protected by the Supreme Court, overstates the role of rights conceptions and disregards the innovation in polity principles. It also obscures the reason the *Lochner* Court declared so much national legislation unconstitutional and fails to explain why the Court permitted state legislation affecting conditions of some factory workers, for example, women. Thus, Garvey's failure to present an integrated theory of polity and rights leads to his failure to explain the *Lochner* era and why the *Lochner* Court was so out of touch with views about economic and social change that were emerging in the wider political system. To characterize each era as either one of rights protection or polity clarification is merely to describe an outcome. It does not show the relationship between rights and polity concepts in the development of the law. Concepts of polity and rights should be viewed as intimately related to each other, yet analytically distinct; for no constitutional question involves only rights or polity principles. There is no pure rights or polity syntax, even though some constitutional scholars have attempted to create one.[42]

Jurisprudence since World War II has been concerned with the political power of insular minorities, groups that historically have received prejudicial treatment from majoritarian political institutions. Garvey argues that the post-*Lochner* Court has developed a new syntax, which he calls a ''ruler-subject'' syntax, in which the Court centers its analysis on power relationships in society, usually political power relationships.[43] Since 1937 the Court has placed its faith in political institutions to regulate economic relationships, while the Court's role has become ensuring equal formal access for all citizens to political institutions. The Court sees society as a network of interdependencies rather than as separate, clearly defined spheres of action and relationships. The self-policing economic transactions of the *Lochner* era have given way to choices by the Supreme Court that allow government regulation by political institutions, and protection of ''buyer-seller'' relationships has been limited, at least through the Warren Court period, to questions of First Amendment rights and other individual liberties protected by the Bill of Rights.

26   In an age when the bright-line distinctions of the *Lochner* era are no longer
possible, concepts of polity and rights continue to structure Supreme Court
choices. Justices have what J. David Greenstone and Paul E. Peterson have
called in another context ideological interests in a certain type of regime or political structure.[44] They refine these interests during their tenure on the Supreme Court.

The Twentieth Century: Lessons from Supreme Court Voting Studies
Quantitative studies of Supreme Court voting confirm that polity as well as
rights values are enduring predictors of constitutional choices by justices.
They also suggest that polity principles differ among justices and are more significant to Court choices in some areas of constitutional doctrine than others.

A study by John Sprague demonstrates that justices' views about the role
of state and national political institutions have influenced judicial choice and
have been the basis for bloc voting on the Supreme Court since the 1890s.[45] In
federalism cases there is an intensification of voting structures, that is, a tendency for greater rates of agreement and disagreement, as measured by ranges
of association scales for each justice.

In the classic study of voting on the Roosevelt Court, C. Herman Pritchett demonstrates that different groups of justices supported state and local
autonomy as a polity value at different rates. For example, Justices Frankfurter
and Jackson had higher standards for evaluating denial of the rights of criminal
defendants in federal as compared to state cases than did Justices Black and
Douglas. Black and Douglas used higher standards and allowed less deference
to alleged rights violations at the state and local levels than to violations by the
national government. "Obviously, the desirability of states retaining control
of their own standards of criminal prosecution is a value which Frankfurter
rates considerably higher than do Black and Douglas."[46] Sprague and Pritchett
also suggest that polity principles are central not only to justices such as Frankfurter or Jackson, who believed in judicial self-restraint, but to liberal justices
as well.

Doris Provine finds that in federalism cases between 1947 and 1957 polity
concepts about the role of the Supreme Court as allocator of power offer the
best explanation of case selection politics. "The most plausible explanation
for the tendency of the Court to decide these cases on the merits . . . is that
the justices feel that the Court, as a forum of last resort, must play a crucial
role in preserving amicable and efficient relations among quasi-sovereign governmental units."[47] However, in cases specifically relating to federalism, both
Pritchett and Provine report that this tendency is weaker.[48] Their data suggest
that polity concepts have an independent effect on judicial choice, separate
from justices' views of individual rights.

An important question is whether all justices, or only the more conservative ones, use polity principles to inform their choices. Pritchett reports that those he calls "libertarian-activists" on the Court were more review-prone than justices who were less oriented toward civil liberties.[49] Libertarian justices wanted to help the underdog, that is, obtain more individual rights, but this goal was less important in federalism cases.[50] Thus polity and rights principles may interact in different ways depending on the area of constitutional law. Clearly the relationship of rights and polity principles is complex and cannot be adequately explored by reliance on quantitative data.

Of most significance is Provine's finding that justices' policy wants and efforts to secure power and influence within the Court decisionmaking process are not central to their decisions about whether to vote for Supreme Court review of cases. Provine finds that "most justices who tend to vote frequently for review do so in a wide variety of cases", "while less review-prone justices are restrictive with their votes across the board." A comparison of votes to review with votes on the merits in the same cases suggests that members of the Supreme Court do not simply vote their policy preferences in case selection, "nor do justices appear routinely to calculate probable outcomes on the merits in deciding whether or not to vote for review. . . . Judicial views of the proper role of the judge and judicial conceptions of the appropriate work of the Court on the merits are important in case selection," rather than simply sympathy for litigants.[51] Thus, polity principles have consistently played a role in federalism cases since 1889—as principles, not post hoc rationalizations for justices' policy wants.

Harold Spaeth and Stuart Teger try to prove that justices on the Supreme Court merely vote their policy preferences rather than deciding issues on the basis of polity principles.[52] They argue that justices defer to states and national regulatory agencies when they agree with the substance of policy and favor judicial activism when they do not. Of the forty justice cells they identify in their study, ten indicate voting influenced by activism and restraint. But policy wants alone do not inform judicial choices; Spaeth and Teger find that judicial self-restraint as a value is present in Supreme Court review of federal regulatory decisions and cases involving federalism, civil rights and liberties, and access to federal courts. Concepts of judicial activism or restraint, rather than mere policy choice, informed the decisionmaking, in at least one of these doctrinal areas, of the following Burger Court justices: Douglas, Brennan, Stewart, White, Marshall, Powell, Rehnquist, and Stevens (justices had to defer to states in over 50 percent of the cases to be seen as holders of judicial self-restraint ideas, a tall task in this day of court activism). As expected, judicial self-restraint is a more important basis of choice in federalism cases than in the area of civil liberties and, especially, First Amendment law.

Most significantly, in the area of access to federal courts we see a confirmation of Provine's findings on the role of polity principles. Spaeth and Teger ar-

28   gue that Burger Court justices between 1969 and 1976 responded to a mixture of motivations. "For some the dominant influence was administrative/legal concerns; that is, judicial self-restraint. Rehnquist and Stewart fit this pattern. Other justices responded to a political attitude toward access; concern with the policy of the cases. The third group of justices, the bulk of the Court, were motivated by a combination of the two attitudes." Spaeth and Rathjen's data allegedly show that polity principles, not pure policy wants, motivate votes on access. When they compared justices' votes on access with their place on a liberal-conservative continuum, they found the proportion of votes cast to open court access to be identical to the ordering of justices on the continuum—evidence, in their view, that substantive policy wants control justices' voting behavior.

This conclusion is unwarranted—a mere correlation does not tell us about the thought processes of justices. It is quite possible that polity principles and substantive policy concerns, such as trusting courts over legislatures and seeking access to the courts for the poor, correlate with a belief in equality as a rights principle. Such correlations do not demonstrate that polity principles do not inform choices; they show only that the direction of polity and rights values may be similar in some cases. The fact that justices make choices in support of or opposition to expanding rights, or make choices using different doctrinal bases, suggests that much more is at work than justices seeking their policy wants.

A number of conclusions can be drawn from the studies discussed here. Both polity and rights principles are active in Supreme Court decisionmaking, but polity principles are more active in some areas of constitutional law than in others. State and local autonomy and judicial self-restraint have consistently been polity values since the 1890s. The Burger Court, the Warren Court, and earlier Courts differ in the degree of reliance that justices placed on polity and rights principles. Justices do not make decisions on the basis of desired policy outcomes alone; they have continuing ideas about the role of states and the place of courts in our political system. But polity and rights principles are more dominant in the jurisprudence of some justices than others—clearly so in the cases of Justice Frankfurter[53] and of Justice Rehnquist today.

Justices at the center are not the only justices who take both process *and* rights values seriously; justices of the left and right do not base their judicial decisionmaking on either pure rights or pure polity concepts. Implicit in the thinking of justices such as Brennan and Marshall, who have been called rights-oriented justices, are concepts of polity that are important to them. Implicit in the opinions of justices such as Rehnquist, Burger, Frankfurter, and Harlan, who have been labeled polity-oriented justices, are concepts of rights that are important to them. It is curious that even though the Founders, Supreme Court justices, and most scholars have understood that process and rights values exist in the Constitution, the analysis of their role by constitutional theorists and scholars of American courts and political institutions has been faulty.

The way polity and rights principles dovetail, or fail to dovetail, in each Court era defines the Court. Also, within Court eras the nature of the meshing of polity and rights principles can change with a change in personnel, as on the Warren Court after Frankfurter retired, and on the Burger Court in the late 1970s. Natural groupings of justices result, which are different among and sometimes within Court eras. I use the word "natural" because identifying a bloc and measuring the degree of fit across many issues are less important for understanding the place of complex polity and rights principles in judicial decisionmaking than the identification of instances in which specific justices identify the choices and at times balances among polity and rights principles.

Justices seek coherence in polity and rights principles to increase their influence over the development of constitutional principles within the Court and wider society and thus make a place for themselves in history. They ask themselves what fundamental rights may be viewed as "in" the Constitution and how these principles are to be applied in a particular case, in view of their polity and rights principles, precedent, and the facts in a case. Justices create personal constitutional visions in which their views of polity and rights principles, their underlying moral values, and their attitudes toward the history of the Court and nation are central. These personal theories, which inform judicial choices, evolve over the course of a justice's years on the Court as the justice seeks to develop a coherent approach to constitutional questions. To achieve coherence, a justice cannot think only of the case outcomes, or the individual case, but must consider the implications of each choice for later applications of polity and rights principles.

Chapter Two
Equal Protection on the Warren Court

I argued in Chapter 1 that the relationship of polity and rights principles, both in Court practice and in constitutional theory, holds the key to understanding the development of constitutional law and to why we misperceive the Burger Court. In this chapter, the analysis centers on the Supreme Court under the stewardship of Chief Justice Earl Warren from 1953–1969. I examine commentators' views about the place of polity and rights principles in its consitutional choices, their criticisms of the Warren Court, and the causal role they ascribe to principles such as polity and rights values in doctrinal change.

Most commentators argue that the Warren Court is unique in the history of the Supreme Court for its concern with ethical or rights values, particularly the value of equality, rather than polity principles. On the other hand, many criticize the Warren Court for a lack of craftsmanship, improperly exercising legislative and executive power, and furthering a decline in the rule of law and legitimacy for the Supreme Court. However, analysis of Warren Court *decisionmaking*, primarily in the areas of equal protection of the law and the fundamental rights and interests strand of equal protection, reveals that the traditional view of the Court overstates the level and quality of its innovation and underplays the importance of polity principles to Warren Court justices.

Before we can understand why we misperceive the Burger Court, we must analyze the Warren Court, because the instrumental assumptions about the Warren Court's decisionmaking process and process of doctrinal change continue into the Burger Court. Because the Warren Court became the benchmark for evaluating its successor, our faulty perception of the former has led to a faulty view of the latter.

Instrumental Views of the Warren Court
The Primacy of Ethical Values and Pure Forms

When scholars describe the Warren Court, they emphasize its sense of moral responsibility, its desire for justice, and particularly its view of equality rather than its views about the place of political institutions and courts in our system of governance. This interpretation predominates whether the scholar subscribes to the election returns, policymaking, safety valve, or biographical explanations of doctrinal change on the Supreme Court. For example, Richard Funston, who along with Robert Dahl is the major proponent of the election returns approach, asserts that "the Warren Court's commitment to equality was unique in the history of American judicial politics."[1] Martin Shapiro, the most articulate advocate of the policymaking approach, emphasizes that the Warren Court consistently used equality as the standard in an astounding array of doctrinal areas. Shapiro views the Warren Court as involved "in a consistent and comprehensive constitutionalization of the New Deal's fundamental vision of social justice, while violating its fundamental political theory of the strong presidency." In the Warren Court, he argues, there was a consensus on the New Deal "which the Warren Court pursued and in terms of which its achievements can be defended and rationalized." The activism of the Warren Court served the poor, racial minorities, and government workers—not big labor or business. Black, Frankfurter, and Douglas took possession of the Court's inner bastions, and preferred position doctrine on speech, voting, and criminal process won out over judicial modesty.[2]

Vincent Blasi, another advocate of the policymaking approach and the major proponent of the no counterrevolution theory of the Burger Court views the Warren Court as "fired by a vision of the equal dignity of man" and as having a "moral vision and an agenda." "Doctrinal compromises took place against a background in which the direction of constitutional development was both clear and, to many, inspiring."[3]

Anthony Lewis, the chief proponent of the safety valve approach, argues that the one constant in three dramatic examples of Warren Court change: criminal justice, Negro rights, and reapportionment was "the ethical element"—a response to national moral demands.[4]

Even G. Edward White, the proponent of the biographical approach and the Warren Court scholar who concedes most fully the place of polity and rights principles in Supreme Court decisionmaking, argues that matters of institutional powers became nearly irrelevant in the Warren Court era. "If a branch of government had engaged in or tolerated a practice that Warren found inconsistent with his conception of American citizenship under the Constitution, the power of that branch was thereby undermined. Warren's perception of constitutional values overwhelmed institutional values in his decision making calculus." White emphasizes that "ethical imperatives" were the key element in Chief Justice Warren's and Warren Court jurisprudence. "Principles of fairness, decency, individuality, and dignity were, for Warren, constitutional imperatives that the Court was under an obligation to consider in its decision-making." Warren espoused a "twentieth-century version of 'natural law'—his ideas of imperatives emanating from the ethical structure of the Constitution."[5] These imperatives and his duty as judge to implement them were so apparent to Warren that doctrinal interpretation was simple.

Other scholars of the Warren Court also subscribe to the importance of ethical values and the value of equality on the Warren Court. Philip Kurland

32   argues that equality principles pervade Warren Court jurisprudence.[6] Archibald Cox views the demand for racial justice as the most powerful factor shaping Warren Court jurisprudence, with "egalitarianism" as the second most powerful factor.[7] To Leonard Levy the most significant aspect of the Warren Court was that it espoused liberal values.[8]

Scholars such as Vincent Blasi also emphasize that unlike those of political institutions or the Burger Court, Warren Court decisions consisted of "pure forms" rather than compromises among justices. The Warren Court was viewed as highly principled and less accommodating than the Burger Court to law enforcement officials in criminal defendant rights cases and less solicitous of state legislatures in reapportionment decisions. According to Blasi, on important issues Warren Court justices made fundamental choices. The decisions of the Warren Court (but not the Burger Court) had a "generative quality or a moral force"; they were less prone than the Burger Court to "ad hoc accommodations," which Blasi argues can "reshape political conflicts for a time."[9] Like all other commentators on the Warren Court, Blasi argues that the activism of the Warren Court was rooted in fundamental equality concepts.

Warren Court Polity Principles

Less prominent in the contemporary vision of the Warren Court is the place of polity principles concerning the roles of courts and American political institutions. When scholars do discuss the polity principles in the Warren Court, they tend to emphasize the Court's mistrust of pluralist politics, legislatures, and interest group politics. Richard Funston writes:

> What seems to have been a thread running throughout the Warren Court's decisions was a profound contempt for legislative agencies of government. Indeed, perhaps the most important characteristic of the Warren Court's decisions as a whole was a general disparagement not of liberal, democratic results but of the democratic process, especially as represented by the legislative process. The Court apparently had little or no confidence that legislatures and the legislative process would produce "right" results.[10]

According to G. Edward White, Warren had very clear views on the differences between legislatures and courts. Political life, Warren believed, called for "half-loaves" and compromises, while judicial opinions were based on principles. White argues that prior to the Warren Court, deference to legislatures was the rule. The Warren Court, however, seemed to view special interests and private concerns, rather than the public interest, as the usual basis for legislative action. The Court's negative view of legislatures and politics generally did not manifest itself in the overturning of congressional statutes, but rather in their interpretation; it was evident, however, in the Court's overturning of state law and bureaucratic practices at both the national and state level.[11]

The significance of polity principles and Warren's concern for "what is" can also be seen in his attitude toward the Founders. Warren rejected the deference to the Founders inherent in the theories that support judicial self-restraint, because of their belief that democracy would hurt the advantaged. Warren believed that legislative majorities showed little concern for the disadvantaged. This view not only indicated Warren's critical view of the pluralist polity, but also suggested that for him there was a nonoriginalism of polity as well as rights values—a view that would not be clearly articulated in constitutional theory until the 1970s.[12]

As to the place of the Supreme Court among political institutions, Leonard Levy reports that Warren viewed the Court as in a similar position to that of the president. At the ceremony in which Earl Warren retired and Burger was sworn in, Warren stated that the Court has "an awesome responsibility of speaking the last word 'in great governmental affairs' and of speaking for the whole American public. . . . It is a responsibility that is made more difficult in this Court because we have no constituency. We serve no majority. We serve no minority. We serve only the public interest as we see it, guided only by that Constitution, and our consciences."[13]

In the view of the Warren Court, the Supreme Court had not only the means to limit governmental injustice but also a mandate to eliminate inequalities by requiring affirmative government action. Here we see the Warren Court's ethical concerns and its less recognized critical polity values contributing equally to its expansive notion of this mandate. Funston argues that "the Warren Court came very close to establishing the principle that every socially perceived wrong should have a legal remedy."[14]

According to Archibald Cox, the Warren Court epitomized the "growing belief that government has an affirmative duty to eliminate inequalities and perhaps to provide opportunities for the exercise of other fundamental human rights," especially against governmental intrusions on personal liberty and privacy. Cox emphasizes that the Warren Court was unique in its acceptance of an expanded (safety valve) role—to accept "a wider responsibility for the open and democratic operation of our political system."[15]

In conclusion, it is important to note that each instrumental commentator on the Warren Court emphasizes that polity principles, that is, the institutional concerns of the Warren Court, were for the most part irrelevant to its jurisprudence. Rights and ethical concerns, as well as policy objectives, fully eclipsed polity principles, and the justices did not balance the two.

Legalist Criticism of the Warren Court

Critics of the Warren Court maintain that it sought to inject its ethical values into constitutional law. Their complaints focus on two dimensions of the

34   Court's performance: its lack of craftsmanship in its decisions and its assumption of "legislative" and "executive" powers. Critics feared that the Court's
poor craftsmanship combined with its expanded role would lead to a further
decline in the "rule of law" and public support for the Supreme Court as an
institution.

At the core of the debate was the issue of judicial craftsmanship: More precisely argued decisions built on precedent rather than decisions that read like
policy statements were important because they gave clear cues to lower courts
and to lawyers bringing or considering cases as to exactly what the Court had
stated as constitutional law. Specific criticisms leveled at the Warren Court included its failure to follow stare decisis and the will of the Founders; the quality of the theoretical base of its opinions; its tendency to make sweeping statements about past doctrine; inconsistency of approach within and among cases
dealing with similar doctrinal issues; results-oriented arguments rather than
precedent-based arguments and logical reasoning; and the insertion of justices' individual ethical values into opinions. These criticisms also reflected the
view of many legal scholars that the Court should aid, not mar, an incremental
policy process that was considered to work well.

Richard Funston, for example, criticizes the Warren Court for poor judicial craftsmanship and the lack of reason and reflection in its decisions.[16] Philip
Kurland asserts that the Warren Court did not pay heed to stare decisis, engaged in poor craftsmanship, which leads to the overruling of decisions, and
committed itself to positions prior to cases.[17] Funston argues that the Warren
Court no longer followed the history of the Fourteenth Amendment, but said
that the history and intent of the framers of the equal protection clause were
too ambiguous to serve as a guide for judicial decision. He accuses the Warren
Court of using "compelling interest" analysis, in the fundamental rights and
interests strand of equal protection, and privacy rights under the due process
clause of the Fourteenth Amendment to open the doors to a far wider nonoriginalism than previous courts.[18] While supporting the Warren Court's civil
rights decisions, Robert McCloskey criticizes the quality of their theoretical
base for "not confronting the task of intellectual architecture that is posed by
its modern jurisprudential claims in the field of civil rights."[19]

In a similar vein, Herbert Wechsler criticizes the Warren Court for its failure to employ neutral principles that transcend the immediate result. He argues that courts must decide cases upon grounds of "adequate neutrality and
generality tested not only by the instant application but by others that the
principles imply."[20] Principled decisions for Wechsler will limit courts from
being what he calls "naked power" organs, making choices based on outcomes which justices desire.

Henry Hart, the most prominent scholar of federal jurisdiction in the
Warren Court years, also attacks the Court on judicial craftsmanship grounds.

Alexander Bickel and Henry Wellington criticize the Court for too many *per curiam* decisions and for the tendency to overgeneralize—for sweeping, dogmatic statements not supported by reason. They criticize the Court's failure to explain conclusions, justify them, and relate them to past holdings.[21]

Anthony Lewis argues that Warren made no attempt, in opinions or otherwise, to propound a consistent theory of how a judge interpreting the Constitution should approach the task. Nor did Warren feel confined by precedent or by a particular view of judicial function. Warren "put aside . . . some of the qualities valued in the judicial process—stability, intellectuality, craftsmanship"—to search for "the just result."[22]

Archibald Cox of Harvard, who, like Anthony Lewis, is a supporter of the safety valve interpretation of Supreme Court decisionmaking, articulates robust support for Warren Court social change, even though it occurs at the expense of the quality of craftsmanship. The Supreme Court must cloak its opinions in the decisions of the past to gain legitimacy, he argues, while heeding the social, economic, and moral needs of the present.[23]

Another group of scholars attacked the Warren Court for basing legal choices on open-ended ethical values. Reflecting the concerns of Oliver Wendell Holmes and post–Civil War scholars who advocated a sharp separation between law and morals, many scholars favored choices based on principles rather than personal ethics, fearing the individual nature of ethical choices. According to White, scholars rejected what they viewed as outcome-oriented jurisprudence, especially when it was clear that Warren would tone down his language to get votes.[24]

Many scholars kept alive the pre–legal realist vision of clear differences among judicial, legislative, and executive powers. They criticized the Warren Court for acting like a legislature, that is, for policymaking, and for acting like the executive branch—intervening in the day-to-day affairs of the polity in the area of policy implementation. (This criticism is ironic because many of these scholars supported an instrumental policymaking interpretation of Supreme Court decisionmaking and doctrinal change.) Richard Funston argues that many viewed the Warren Court as a superlegislature, not unlike the Supreme Court in the *Lochner* era, and saw it as making substantive social and economic policy choices through the interpretation of open-ended langauge in the Constitution. The revival of the doctrine of fundamental, unenumerated rights in equal protection and due process cases vested the justices with "unlimited and ultimately unhealthy discretion in their decisions concerning American social and political problems."[25]

During the Warren Court years much was made of the view that there had been a decline in the rule of law and in the legitimacy of the Supreme Court as an institution. Kurland argues that the "political court" led to a crisis in confidence.[26] Drawing on the scholarship of Theodore Lowi, Funston argues that

36   the lack of craftsmanship by the Warren Court and the Court's assumption of superlegislative powers undermined the legitimacy of Warren Court decisions and the American political system. It led to a decline in the rule of law and principle and an increase in the power of bureaucrats and interest groups over more publicly accountable decisionmaking processes.[27]

At the core of these criticisms were differences over polity principles between the Warren Court, as evidenced by its doctrine, and legal scholars, who valued legal craftsmanship. These criticisms also reflected the view that the Supreme Court and federal courts were incapable of analyzing policy or managing social and political change. Richard Funston, for example, suggests that coupling egalitarianism with nationalism produces uniformity and conformity, not diversity and equality. He also fears that equality may repress blacks and women.[28]

Behind this fear of a Supreme Court that made national policy was a faith that state and local governments, voluntary organizations, and interest group politics were respectful of minorities. It was this faith in decentralized political forums and the pluralist political system that the Warren Court did not share. Rather than addressing this fundamental disagreement, however, critics of the Court addressed the managerial problems presented by Court action. Here again we see the Warren Court and its critics talking past one another. Where the Court resisted the academy's notion of polity, the academy greatly minimized the importance of polity principles in Warren Court decisionmaking and overstated the importance of equality as a value in its jurisprudence.

Fundamental Equal Protection Rights and Interests

The most dramatic example of the broad misunderstanding of the Warren and Burger Court eras is the way scholars employing instrumental interpretations have viewed cases involving the fundamental rights and interests strand of equal protection in general and wealth classifications. Many view these cases as the epitome of the Warren Court's pure vision of equality and efforts to expand individual rights; many see the Warren Court's decisions on voting, interstate travel, and differential access to judicial process based on wealth as a move to limit the political system when it makes policy choices that the Court opposes; and many see the Warren Court as making poverty classifications in the law subject to closer Court scrutiny—only to be stymied by the Burger Court.[29] Most importantly, many scholars argue that in *Shapiro v. Thompson* (1969), one of the last cases decided by the Warren Court, the Court was on the road to making wealth a classification in the law that was to be subject to close Court scrutiny under the equal protection clause, only to be stopped by the Burger Court in *San Antonio Independent School District v. Rodriguez* (1973), in which the Court refused to find that different levels of state funding for school districts with different numbers of poor people were a violation of the equal protection clause. Therefore the study of this doctrinal area is an excellent bellwether for understanding the constitutive nature of Supreme Court decisionmaking and doctrinal change in the Warren and Burger Court eras. Such an analysis, rather than mere bottom-line examinations of case outcomes, is necessary, for at issue is not only whether the Warren Court was actively considering wealth as a suspect classification under equal protection, but also the nature of the polity and rights principles used by these Courts in reaching their decisions, because these principles form the basis for future doctrinal innovation.

Pre–Warren Court Fundamental Rights and Interests Jurisprudence

In looking for the doctrinal roots of the equal protection innovations ascribed to the Warren Court, my objective is not to trivialize the Court's doctrinal innovations. In the areas of defendant rights, race relations, protection of voting rights, the right of privacy, and other civil liberty areas, the Warren Court was highly innovative. Many would argue that in the area of fundamental rights and interests the Warren Court was at its innovative best, seeking equality principles in Court review of welfare policies and other areas in which wealth differences among members of the population are the basis of unequal treatment before the law.

However, many years before the Warren Court, the Supreme Court had identified fundamental rights and interests in the Constitution in several important cases. In what has been called the *Lochner* era of the Supreme Court (from approximately 1905, when *Lochner v. New York* was decided, to 1937), the Supreme Court was willing to define liberty substantively in the due process clause of the Fourteenth Amendment and the Fifth Amendment. This resulted in the invalidation of federal and state wage, hours, and social welfare laws because the restriction on business activity was viewed as a violation of employers' and employees' right to contract their labor freely.

In the late 1930s, the Supreme Court overturned key *Lochner*-era cases in which it had invalidated legislation designed to counter the economic and social collapse of the Depression and limit the effects of economic declines in the future. No longer would the Supreme Court interpret liberty protected by the due process clause substantively with regard to economic and business legislation. Henceforth, the Court would analyze business regulation and social legislation designed to deal with the ravages of economic conditions under the rational basis test—the minimal level of scrutiny, which allows political institutions to regulate economic and social relations as they wish, accepting almost any possible rationale for such legislation. As long as the governmental regulations did not transgress specific rights and polity principles in the Constitution or were not patently capricious and irrational, the Court would not use judicial review to limit governmental regulation of business. However, during the

38   *Lochner* period the Court also defined liberty in the Fourteenth Amendment
       due process clause as including the rights to marry, procreate, bring up chil-
       dren and educate them according to parents' religious values, and protect fam-
       ilies. These rights were not renounced in subsequent Supreme Court eras.

The Carolene Products *Footnote*

The Warren Court was not the first to wrestle with the question of when it
should substantively read the due process and equal protection clauses of the
Fourteenth Amendment and the due process clause of the Fifth Amendment
in a way that limits government action. In the famous footnote 4 in *United
States v. Carolene Products* (1938) Chief Justice Stone tried to offer advice about
when social and economic legislation should be scrutinized at a level stricter
than the minimal level. Stone contends that a rational basis test is usually in
order in reviewing legislation: ''Prejudice against discrete and insular minorities may be a special condition, which tends seriously to curtail the operation
of those political processes ordinarily to be relied upon to protect minorities,
and which may call for a correspondingly more searching judicial inquiry.''[30]
In the *Carolene Products* footnote, Stone argues for judicial intervention when
specific prohibitions in the Constitution are violated or when the political
process does not offer equal respect to discrete and insular minorities, and that
the Supreme Court should be called upon to decide whether a particular law,
or a classification in a law, prevents the pluralist political system from being
open to all.

A good example of the Warren Court's building on earlier jurisprudence is
in the area of race discrimination. In addition to the *Carolene Products* footnote, the Warren Court drew on *Yick Wo v. Hopkins* (1886), in which the
Court examined the administration of a law prohibiting laundries in frame
buildings and viewed the law, as administered, an outlawed race-based classification because it had prohibited such buildings for all Chinese merchants but
for only one Caucasian merchant. It was, therefore, a violation of the equal
protection clause. Also, in *Strauder v. West Virginia* (1880) the Court held that
the denial of black membership in the panel from which juries were selected
was a denial of equal protection of the law, although qualifications other than
race, such as education and gender, were permissible. In *Korematsu v. United
States* (1944) the Court stated that all race classifications in the law were to be
subject to strict scrutiny. However, the race classifications that allowed Japa-
nese Americans to be moved from the West Coast during World War II were
permitted because of the compelling state interest to act quickly to ensure the
security of the nation during wartime.

Most important, the doctrinal roots of the landmark *Brown v. Board of Education* (1954) school desegregation case can be traced to cases from the previous Court that outlawed segregation in higher education. Before the Warren

Court, then, there were precedents for strict scrutiny of de jure race classifications, both in the law and in the discriminatory administration of laws.

Interstate Movement of the Poor: Edwards v. California

The idea of fundamental rights and interests is not an invention of the Warren
Court era. The Supreme Court had begun to shape the notion of fundamental
rights and interests as early as 1941, when in *Edwards v. California* (1941) it struck
down a California statute that made it a crime knowingly to bring or assist in bringing into the state a nonresident "indigent person." The Court viewed the statute
as an unconstitutional burden on interstate commerce.

Although the Court based its decision on the commerce clause, the notion
that laws cannot freeze population or economic conditions or chain people to
residence in a particular state suggests a right to travel. This right the Court
saw as a value within the commerce clause and, more generally, as a concern of
the Founders. Although the Court stated that it was not deciding the responsibilities of states to provide assistance to the needy,[31] it found that the power
to restrict indigent people is not within the police power of the state. Nor can
a state isolate itself from the problems of other states or the nation. The
peoples of the several states must sink and swim together. Justice Byrnes also
noted that indigent nonresidents, the real victims of this statute, were not in a
position to exert political pressure on the state legislature in order to change
the policy.

Justices Douglas and Jackson viewed the right to move interstate as a fundamental right of national citizenship to be protected under the rights inherent in the privileges and immunities clause of the Fourteenth Amendment.[32]
As with questions of the constitutionality of the public accommodations section of the Civil Rights Act of 1964, the Court in 1941 decided to rest this
case not on equal protection or due process grounds, but rather on commerce
clause principles and the Founders' desire to create one nation with regard to
economic movement and change. However, beneath the veneer of commerce
clause language lurked ideas about the individual liberty to travel linked to
commerce clause concerns about the absence of political processes through
which nonresidents of states that restrict their entry can seek protection and a
fair hearing. Thus, as early as 1941 the Supreme Court undertook an examination of polity principles and a structural view of inequality in suggesting a general right to travel. This decision became a strong precedent for the Warren
Court's later *Shapiro v. Thompson* (1969) decision.

The Birth of Fundamental Interests: Skinner v. Oklahoma

In 1942, the Supreme Court gave first form to an innovative concept of
fundamental rights and interests under the equal protection and due process
clauses in *Skinner v. Oklahoma*. The Court held unconstitutional an Oklahoma

statute that permitted sterilization of criminals convicted two or more times for felonies involving moral turpitude. Certain offenses were excluded from the statute—embezzlement, political offenses, revenue act violations, and other white-collar crime. The statute was viewed as a violation of the equal protection clause, and because it encroached upon the right to procreate and marry, a stricter level of scrutiny was in order. The Court decided not to rely on due process or cruel and unusual punishment grounds to decide the case. Instead it said that the law violates basic equal protection principles because a person could embezzle great amounts of money, habitually, and not qualify for sterilization, while another person could be sterilized for stealing chickens a few times or for repeated thefts involving small amounts of money. The law was both over- and underinclusive.

Justice Douglas's opinion for the majority identifies a substantive element in the equal protection clause that does not allow the usual deference to states where fundamental liberties are concerned or when minorities might suffer if public officials are allowed certain powers.[33] Douglas is concerned with both rights notions of liberty and procreation and polity issues about unequal access to political power for different classes and perhaps races. The majority opinion never says that sterilization itself is unconstitutional. But the fundamental rights underpinnings in this case would make sterilization for all criminals subject to a very close look by the Supreme Court, if states should pass such laws.

This case laid the cornerstone for analysis of the Warren Court fundamental rights and interests strain of equal protection because it suggests that certain fundamental rights and interests, such as marriage and procreation, require stricter scrutiny by the Court than does economic legislation. It also suggests that due process of law viewed in narrow procedural terms does not protect the fundamental rights of minorities or prevent their violation by the majority as effectively as strict scrutiny under equal protection. A due process standard would allow invasion of even fundamental liberty interests if states could show in individual cases that sterilization might be rational. This case also suggests that the Court will be careful to protect weaker groups, even those that are not racially based.

Therefore, *Edwards* does not rely merely on the process fairness aspects of the *Carolene Products* footnote, but also on concepts of individual rights and liberty that may be protected by the Court under the equal protection clause. It has within it many of the polity and rights rationales that form the centerpiece of equal protection analysis on the Warren and Burger Courts. This case, as with the other landmark pre–Warren Court cases, suggests that the level of innovation by the Warren Court in the fundamental rights and interests strand of equal protection may have been overstated.

Warren Court Fundamental Rights and Interests *41*
Access to Judicial Process

The Warren Court cases involving rights of access to judicial process and to counsel in processes of appeals by the poor build on *Carolene Products* polity malfunction ideas that were defined eighteen years earlier. These cases demonstrate the belief by a majority of the Warren Court that denying the poor, because they are poor, the right to defend themselves is the same as denying them the right to due process. But it is important to emphasize that the Warren Court viewed narrowly the polity malfunctions caused by the failure of indigents to pay court fees. It did not argue that the state must provide access and counsel in all stages of the appeals process, or even in all noncapital cases, but only at key stages of the process where a first hearing of cases is presented on appeal.

In its first fundamental rights and interests case, *Griffin v. Illinois* (1956), the Warren Court decided that denying a transcript of trial court proceedings in nonfelony cases because of the inability of the appellant to pay for a transcript is a denial of equal protection. Justice Black's majority decision emphasizes that the constitutional promise of a fair trial is worthless if the poor cannot have access to transcripts of trials. And since appellate review is an integral part of judicial process at all stages of proceedings, the due process and equal protection clauses protect persons from invidious discrimination. In criminal procedures "there can be no equal justice where the kind of trial a man gets depends on the amount of money he has."[34] Frankfurter in a concurrence says the right to appeal a conviction is today so established that it leads to the easy assumption that it is fundamental to the protection of life and liberty and therefore a necessary ingredient of due process of law. He scrutinizes the Illinois law in question on a rational basis test and views the state as authorizing the imposition of conditions that offend the deepest suppositions of our society. Frankfurter says the state need not supply the same quality lawyers, but it cannot use wealth through a fee to create different access to appellate process. These opinions of Black and Frankfurter are not the majestic equality pronouncements that many scholars ascribe to the Warren Court. They simply reflect the conviction, seen in other defendant rights cases of that Court, that one's wealth should not determine one's due process rights.[35]

In *Douglas v. California* (1963), the Warren Court decides that there is a right to counsel in the first appeal stage of state criminal cases. We note again that absolute equality is not required; the Constitution does not require a lawyer at all appeals but does require that the state provide lawyers for indigents at the first stage of appeal. Here the Court demonstrates its lack of trust in the capacities of state judges and the judicial process to determine fairly whether procedural or legal interpretations at the trial level were within the law. It also exhibits again a concern that different access to appeals for rich and poor will

42   undermine due process of law. However, as with *Griffin*, procedural due process had been viewed in the past as a fundamental right—in a way that a right to welfare without a one-year residency rule was not, prior to the Warren Court, viewed as fundamental to citizenship or civil rights.

Thus, in these cases the Warren Court falls short of advocating total equality in the right to appeal convictions. The majority does not require equally skilled lawyers for rich and poor; nor does it support the right to an attorney at all possible points of the appeals process. It requires only that the state not charge fees or deny lawyers to appellants at key points in the appeals process. *It is the total deprivation of any access to courts because of wealth* that the Warren Court seeks to prevent; it does not seek to guarantee equality of representation or a certain number of appeals. This, then, is hardly a deep structural view of judicial process inequality or of the effects of economic and social inequality in the nation on the rights of the accused.

The Right to Vote

There were two major innovations by the Warren Court in voting rights. The first involves the apportionment of votes and political power in state legislatures by district of different segments of the population, such as residents of urban, suburban, and rural areas, and the issue of whether district boundaries drawn on racial bases would be permitted. The second major innovation focuses on the creation of a right to vote in federal and state elections as a fundamental right and interest under the equal protection clause.

The Warren Court's first look at voting rights was in the area of how district boundaries affect black voting strength in the case of *Gomillion v. Lightfoot* (1960). Most importantly, the Warren court debated polity questions surrounding the proper role of the Supreme Court and federal courts as to voting before it considered the right to vote both in the areas of fundamental rights and interests and reapportionment. This is significant because it suggests that polity values—institutional views—are at least of equal interest with concerns about equality and rights. Therefore, the Warren Court was as innovative in its approach to the role of the Court as in its vision of rights. For example, the Court countered traditional polity arguments about deference to state and local government in *Baker v. Carr* (1962), overturning *Colegrove v. Green*'s (1946) reliance on the political questions doctrine, which counsels deference to political institutions on questions of rules about voting. After *Baker v. Carr* there are apportionment cases in 1963, 1964, 1966, and 1969. These polity-based decisions demonstrated the Court's concerns for equality in vote counting and had substantial impacts on the relative weight of urban, suburban, and rural representatives in state government. They also ensured that invidious race classifications would not be permitted in drawing up district lines—a major change in polity principles instituted by the Warren Court.

Yet these decisions did not substantially address gerrymandering, interest group politics, party bias in reapportionment, and other differences in economic and social power in our pluralist political system. Nor did the Court make substantive choices beyond outlawing clear racial bias in drawing district boundaries. As with the fundamental rights and interests cases, the Warren Court simply had less complex choices to make in its cases, given the formality of the inequalities that it identified.

The first voting case involving fundamental rights and interests did not occur until 1965—*Carrington v. Rush*, in which the Court invalidates a law requiring that servicemen vote in the county in which they resided when they entered the service. The Court says that a state cannot fence out voters because of their occupation. In dissent, Harlan opposes the "abstract justice" notions upon which the decision was based and the unleashing of such views on federalism, a key polity principle in the Constitution.[36]

In *Harper v. Virginia Board of Elections* (1966), we see a clear elaboration of fundamental rights and interests and of the idea that voting is a fundamental right. The Warren Court finds state poll taxes in violation of the equal protection clause and elaborates a fundamental right or, more precisely, a fundamental interest in voting. Some limits on voting, such as literacy tests, would be permitted, but lines drawn in state law between individuals who can and cannot vote are subject to close scrutiny by the Court. Wealth classifications that infringe on the right to vote are invidious; fee payments must not restrict citizens' ability to participate in the electoral process.

The significance of *Harper* is that Justice Douglas draws on the *Griffin, Edwards,* and *Douglas* decisions about wealth and access to politics and courts and that he links the fundamental right to vote with the wealth of citizens, though only through a consideration of whether the poll tax is constitutional. Douglas argues that wealth as a classification is capricious and an irrelevant factor and that lines drawn on the basis of wealth or property, like those of race, are traditionally held in disfavor.[37] Fee paying he views as an invidious discrimination between wealthy and poor like the earlier discrimination between chicken stealers and embezzlers in *Skinner v. Oklahoma* because it is not related rationally to the objective of the legislature, in that case to prevent criminal acts.

Justice Black, in dissent, argues that the interpretation of the equal protection clause in *Harper* is quite different from that of the Framers, who felt it was permissible for government to treat rich and poor differently—but not blacks and whites. States can decide they need poll tax revenues, or that those who pay poll taxes have a more intense interest in, and thus knowledge of, state problems and the candidates for public office than those who do not. Black argues that the concepts of natural rights and due process do not authorize the Court to view the equal protection clause as a means to put its policy

44　　wants into the Constitution. He argues that when the political theory of the Constitution is outdated, it is up to citizens rather than the Court to change it.

We see, then, very different views of the role of the Supreme Court in our political system for Black and for Douglas.[38] For Black, only Congress, not the Court, can pass laws to enforce Fourteenth Amendment principles. There is a law/polity dichotomy in Black's thinking: according to the Fourteenth Amendment, Congress, not the Court, has the power to enforce the principles in that amendment. The rule of law, for Black, requires that the Supreme Court not encroach on the prerogative of political institutions through adherence to natural law principles unknown to the Founders. Again, polity arguments, not merely views about equality, justice, or rights, inform Black's jurisprudence, as they do that of all Courts and justices to varying degrees.

Justice Harlan, joined by Stewart in dissent, argues that the states should decide whether to allow poll taxes in their elections. Harlan notes that only four states have poll taxes and that the Twenty-fourth Amendment eliminated them in federal elections. The equal protection clause requires only a rational basis test and that states treat their citizens equally. Unlike the majority, Harlan accepts polity arguments about federalism and deference to states on matters of voting.[39]

Throughout *Harper* there is little concern with the safety valve argument that voting protects rights and interests and the argument that unless the Court intervenes, the political system will not change. Raising these arguments would lead the Court deeper into issues of the relative political powers of the rich and poor and make linkages between political system and social/economic system inequalities. By centering its analysis on the individual citizen, with a primary emphasis on voting, the Warren Court could blur more controversial issues of the structural relationship in society between wealth and political power.

In *Kramer v. Union Free School District No. 15* (1969), the Warren Court finds unconstitutional a law that requires an individual to own or lease property or be a parent or custodian of children in schools in order to vote in school elections. Chief Justice Warren, in one of his last opinions, argues that when the vote is denied to citizens, a compelling interest must be shown by the state. Warren offers a full range of arguments: (1) voting preserves other rights; (2) the denial of the vote must be reviewed under strict scrutiny if vote dilution (through apportionment) is suspect; and (3) the denial of the vote requires court action and less deference to legislatures because there is no recourse politically. For Warren, a rational basis test is warranted only if we can assume that political structures can effectively redress an evil.[40] In vote denial or vote dilution cases, such an assumption is not warranted. Thus, Warren says that the Court will not make subjective choices about how important the vote is in specific institutions. However, he does establish the principle that the denial of the vote itself raises significant constitutional problems. As in *Brown v. Board of Education*, the Warren Court wants to consider only total denial of rights; it does not want to make determinations about the degree of power that a particular political institution will have in our political system. For example, the Court requires only "all deliberate speed" to implement *Brown v. Board of Education*, as stated in *Brown II* (1955).

The Right to Travel—Government Restrictions on Passports

The Warren Court defined a right to travel overseas based on a fundamental right to travel, a right to association and speech in the First Amendment, and a right to due process of law when government seeks to choose among those who wish to travel. The following travel cases illustrate the complexity of polity and rights principles in the constitutive decisionmaking process of the Warren Court. They also indicate important differences among the rights-oriented justices as to whether the right to travel is so fundamental that compelling state interests must be shown before it is denied.

In *Kent v. Dulles* (1958) the Warren Court says the right to travel is part of the liberty interest of citizens and cannot be abrogated by the federal government without respecting due process of law under the Fifth Amendment. Douglas writes in the majority opinion, "[Travel] may be as close to the heart of the individual as the choice of what he eats, or wears, or reads." Because the right to travel is a fundamental right, Douglas finds that unbridled delegation of power to the secretary of state to grant passports is not permitted.[41] Thus, in allowing free access to passports the Court cannot rely solely on interstate commerce and the one nation concept expressed in the *Edwards* case. Such presumptions about individual rights to travel must be considered in relationship to polity principles of foreign policy and the national security power of Congress and the executive when one questions the unbridled discretion of the secretary of state. The Court emphasizes that it is merely engaging in statutory construction, but in fact it is subjecting the statute to a stricter level of scrutiny. The Warren Court is not merely presuming that Congress and the secretary of state have legitimate, rational reasons to deny passports.

The Warren Court presents here what Laurence Tribe has called a "structural due process" argument. According to Tribe, the Constitution requires thoughtful consideration by the appropriate, knowledgeable, and legally responsible branches of government before decisions are made that impinge on a fundamental right or interest.[42] This is a developing polity-based argument, rather than an argument based on an individual right to travel interstate. Under this idea, as long as the proper governmental forum is used to decide whether to grant passports, the Court will not monitor the substantive policy choices that are made.

Presumably Congress could by law provide the secretary of state wide discretion to act on passports. Yet if Congress provided discretion so wide as to deny First Amendment association, its actions might not be permissible. Thus the Warren Court backs into a rights argument from a polity-based thesis, which suggests that the Court was thinking about polity principles—the role of the executive, courts, and legislatures—not just fundamental rights values, when it made its decision.

In *Aptheker v. Secretary of State* (1964) the Court moves from a general due process of law argument to a notion that the right to travel is fundamental, especially when it is linked to rights of association protected by the First Amendment. In this case, the government argued that leaders of the American Communist party could not travel overseas. The Court finds in *Aptheker* that this law constitutes a restraint on the right to travel and thereby abridges a liberty guaranteed by the Fifth Amendment. It also invades the freedom of association that was protected by the First Amendment in *NAACP v. Button* (1963). Here for the first time the Court argues that the right to travel and First Amendment rights are linked.

In *Aptheker* an individual rights analysis looms large, whereas it had merely hovered in the background in the *Edwards* and *Kent* cases. Note that the Court arrives at this rights-oriented position *through* a process of polity analysis extending through all three cases. The Court moves toward a position relatively distrustful of government's willingness to protect the freedom of travel and has thus elaborated, or "created," a framework of rights notions. Of course it continued to weigh in the state's need to make foreign policy and national security decisions.

In these passport cases, and in other fundamental rights and interests cases, one can see a progression from primarily polity-based arguments to more clear-cut definitions of fundamental rights, to principles by which the Court can make complex decisions about a fundamental right or interest. Here, and continuing into the Burger Court era, the structural complexity of the polity and its relationship to the denial of fundamental rights become more filigreed and complex. The depth and complexity of both rights and polity arguments and the relationship between concerns about the role of political institutions and fundamental rights grows with each new case and Court era. As one would expect in a constitutive decisionmaking process, the Warren Court added specificity to rights and polity arguments that lay buried in previous cases. In part this approach grew out of the necessity for the Supreme Court to react to new complexities in our society, but it is also due to changes in political structure and in what constitutes a right.

Zemel v. Rusk (1965), in many ways, is the archetypical Warren Court case. It reflects a debate about both polity and rights concerns and places Chief Justice Warren at the center of the Court in his views about the nature of individual rights as well as his views about political institutions. In this case involving a journalist who wished to visit Cuba, the Court finds constitutional the complete denial of all passports to Americans who want to go to countries with which the United States has broken diplomatic relations and forbidden travel to all under the Passport Act of 1926.

Chief Justice Warren distinguishes the issues involved in the *Aptheker* case from this denial of passports: Under this law, all were banned from travel; decisions to deny passports were not based on the political beliefs and associations of citizens. Warren argues that the balance between national security and the right to travel falls on the side of national security. He also argues that the right to speak and publish does not carry with it an affirmative right to gather information.[43] Here the *individual* quality of the right is less respected by Warren, and a majority of the Court than was the notion that the state may not decide whether to grant a passport on grounds of the applicant's political belief. Thus, the Warren Court relies on an equal access principle, not a guaranteed right to travel, and finds that there is no guaranteed right for citizens to enter foreign nations and to bring their acquired knowledge to our marketplace of ideas.

This decision has a pragmatic quality, a term normally applied to Burger Court jurisprudence. It is not a ringing endorsement either of an equality principle or of the fundamental right to travel. Instead, it is a balancing model, more like the intermediate level of scrutiny of the Burger Court years. Most significantly, the Warren Court does not even require the government to use the least restrictive means when it denies passports.

Black, in dissent, says that the president has no inherent power to make laws about who can or cannot receive a passport, and he uses a polity argument—the difference between congressional and executive power. Under a separation of powers doctrine, Black wishes to force congress to make specific the delegation of this power to limit travel. Therefore, inherent in the Black argument are both rights and polity perspectives.[44]

Douglas and Goldberg also dissent. They view the cases of *Kent v. Dulles* (1958) and *Aptheker* as based on peripheral rights—the right of travel as essential to First Amendment rights to know and consult. They view the ability of citizens to understand diverse ideologies and viewpoints as a prerequisite to protecting First Amendment rights and to ensuring a true marketplace of ideas. For them, because interests essential to First Amendment speech and study are threatened by government, legislative restrictions must be narrowly drawn. As in *Aptheker*, Douglas and Goldberg argue that limits on travel in wartime are permissible, but blanket restrictions based upon general fear of a communist government are not.[45]

Thus, rights-oriented justices, such as Goldberg, use both polity and rights arguments in their decisionmaking. They view the polity notion of sep-

48   aration of powers as relevant because it was placed in the Constitution in order to prevent the suppression of fundamental rights by a single branch of government. Chief Justice Warren, whom most scholars view as consumed by a concern for equality and fundamental rights, in this case supported the most restrictive use of government power—a total ban on travel. Other justices seen as supportive of individual rights and equality also expressed quite different opinions about how polity and rights concerns are to be balanced. The balance of polity and rights principles in the thinking of Warren and Goldberg is very different, which suggests that Warren's faith in pluralist politics was greater than that of Goldberg or Douglas. Goldberg (and Black) used a delegation and separation of powers argument, but not Warren. That Warren supported an equal access regime means that he was less of a fundamental rights advocate than other liberal justices.

Therefore, in important instances the Warren Court, and Chief Justice Warren himself, were not merely concerned about supporting fundamental rights and equality in the use of those rights. But rather, like the Burger Court, the Warren Court performed a complex balancing act, improperly labeled "pragmatism," in its case analysis. At work is a set of polity and rights values in the area of fundamental rights and interests that is more complex than most scholars of the Warren Court care to admit and different in substance and level of complexity from that of the Burger Court.

The Intent to Discriminate and the Fundamental Right to Marry

In *Loving v. Virginia* (1967), Chief Justice Warren writes a majority opinion that considers the following question: Does a statutory scheme that prohibits marriages between persons solely because of their race, even if applied equally to all races, violate the equal protection and due process clauses of the Constitution? Warren writes, "For reasons which seem to us to reflect the central meaning of those constitutional commands, we conclude that these statutes cannot stand consistently with the Fourteenth Amendment."[46] *Meyer v. Nebraska* (1923) and *Skinner v. Oklahoma* (1942) are the precedents used by the Court to justify its power to limit state regulation of marriages. The Court made special reference to the fact that because a fundamental right is at issue, concerns about federalism, state and local regulation of society, and the Tenth Amendment are not sufficient reasons to leave the regulation of marriage to the exclusive control of states.

Thus, again Warren addresses both the polity arguments used by the states and fundamental rights questions. Warren specifically emphasizes that because marriage is a fundamental right, and because race classifications are subject to strict scrutiny, laws involving them are assumed to be constitutionally suspect in and of themselves, as in the *Korematsu* case. States must demonstrate a compelling interest; the states' argument that these laws are applied equally to all races (assuming that the laws were written to deny intermarriage between persons of all different races) is not an allowable defense.[47]

The state argued that since scientific evidence is in doubt on the question of the effects of interracial marriages and because legislatures are better equipped than courts to decide questions of policy effects, under a rational basis test the law is permissible. That is, since there is no clear evidence that interracial marriages do not have negative effects on individuals or society, then the legislature should be permitted to outlaw them. Warren argues that the mere "equal application" of a statute containing race classifications is not enough to remove it from a Fourteenth Amendment proscription against race classifications, which are presumed to be invidious. The state must show that there is a permissible state objective independent of race discrimination. Since no legitimate, overriding purpose for the law exists, and since only intermarriages involving white people (not, for example, marriages between Native Americans and blacks) are prohibited, the Court must conclude that white supremacy is an objective of the law.[48] The Court also argues that intent to discriminate on the basis of race may be evident even when government interests other than race prejudice can be identified by the state.

This case was an easy one for the Warren Court, since only fifteen states still had antimiscegenation laws on the books. It built on *Brown, Meyer, Griswold, Skinner*, and a clear line of cases in the areas of race discrimination, fundamental rights to marry and procreate, and the emerging area of the right to privacy. Like *Brown v. Board of Education*, it involved clear de jure race classifications that treated white and nonwhite citizens in very different ways and clearly showed racial prejudice by the state of Virginia in the establishment of this law.

Residency Requirements, Welfare, and the Right to Travel:
Shapiro v. Thompson

Instrumental commentators of the Warren and Burger Courts have used *Shapiro v. Thompson* (1969) to argue that Warren Court jurisprudence was moving toward making wealth a suspect classification and, mistakenly, that the Burger Court led a hasty retreat in *San Antonio Independent School District v. Rodriguez* (1973).[49]

In the *Shapiro* case, the Warren Court held unconstitutional laws in Connecticut, Pennsylvania, and Washington, D.C., that denied welfare assistance to persons who were residents and met all other eligibility requirements except that they had not resided in these jurisdictions for at least one year prior to their applications for assistance. The Court ruled that the state laws violated the equal protection clause of the Fourteenth Amendment, whereas the Washington, D.C., residency requirement violated equal protection components of the due process clause of the Fifth Amendment.

Brennan's Majority Opinion

In the majority decision, written by Justice Brennan, the Warren Court concludes that the residency requirement denies equal protection of the law. Brennan argues that the law creates two classes of needy resident families based on the time spent in the state; this classification scheme constitutes invidious discrimination and denies equal protection of the law. The exclusion of the poor from states is impermissible, because in the *Edwards* case the Supreme Court had found that inhibiting the poor from migration was not a legitimate or compelling government interest.

The Court views the concepts of the federal union and personal liberty rights in the Constitution as closely related. Their union requires that all citizens be free to travel, uninhibited by regulations that unreasonably burden their movement. Brennan emphasizes that the right to move freely from state to state was a major impetus behind the Constitution, as was the vision of freedom of movement as a fundamental liberty.[50] Brennan also emphasizes that statutes such as the one challenged in *Shapiro* do not merely deter travel because of differences in welfare aid among the states; they retard movement by completely blocking welfare aid—the necessities of life—for one year. It is the *total* deprivation of aid that concerns Brennan. He is also concerned about the unrebuttable presumption that all who come to the state do so to get larger welfare payments. This assumption is merely implied and is not supported by any data.

However, Brennan's majority opinion does not rest on due process grounds. He writes, "A State may no more try to fence out those indigents who seek welfare benefits than it may try to fence out indigents generally."[51] This section of the majority opinion implies that consideration of the level of welfare benefits, like any other economic incentive by government (or nongovernment institutions), is permissible. The Founders established national control of commerce partly to encourage individuals who seek to move from state to state for economic reasons. Brennan argues that the level of welfare payment is not unlike the quality of schools as a reason people move. Both involve polity concerns.

Thus, both poor and wealthy people may consider quality of government programs and economic incentives for movement. It is clear that to Brennan, the right of individuals under liberal political and legal theory to maximize private economic and social interests and the right to travel are more important than the authority of state or federal governments to decide who gets welfare. This private-regarding ethic, together with the need for one union and limits on states' power to deny movement (a polity principle), forms the basis for the majority decision.

Brennan contends that the fiscal integrity of a government may not be achieved though invidious discrimination among classes of people. The constitutionality of such laws does not rest on a rational basis test, then, like most post-1938 economic and business regulation. Instead, a compelling interest test is used, because these laws allocate government benefits according to invidious classifications based on years of residence and impinge upon the right to travel. Any classification that impinges on that right is not allowed, unless the government can demonstrate a compelling interest.[52]

The Court here is taking a more structural view of the effect of state programs on individual decisions to move interstate. In the *Edwards* case the ban on the right of the poor to move to California was total. In *Shapiro* the allocation of state goods—welfare—to those who migrate is delayed one year, but the Warren Court decides that this delay is very close to a condition sufficient in itself to retard movement interstate. Thus, in the *Shapiro* case the Court comes close to stating that when the necessities of life are provided by government, a blanket deprivation of such programs is close to a restriction on movement and therefore on liberty itself.

It is important to note that the Warren Court never says the right to welfare is fundamental. It upholds a right to interstate movement, but not a right to welfare per se. Thus a state, or Congress, could pass a law that would require all applicants for welfare, old and new residents, to wait one year before they could get such aid. Would such a rule pass constitutional muster? It seems clear from this case that it would.

Warren's Dissent

The Warren dissent in this case, joined by Justice Black, is a crucial indication of his views of polity and rights principles, fundamental rights and interests, the roles of the Court and political institutions in our nation, and his place among the justices on the Warren Court. It also suggests that, counter to the interpretations of many commentators on Warren and the Warren Court, polity principles, not just a concern for New Deal policy outcomes, informed his choices.

Warren argues that Congress can impose a national one-year residency rule or authorize the states to do so. Here he places his faith in Congress, states, and elected officials to decide welfare policy, arguing that no individual right is violated by a one-year residency rule, because citizens can move from state to state. He views social security and welfare policy as efforts by Congress to encourage both increases in state funding for welfare and innovation by states in their welfare policies—a system of cooperative federalism.

As in the 1941 *Edwards* case, Warren views this case as involving the power to move interstate, as under the commerce clause. Here, however, Congress allows residency rules as part of public policy. In Warren's view, to say that congressionally mandated residency requirements violate the right to travel is to say that "Congress even under its 'plenary' power to control interstate com-

52   merce, is constitutionally prohibited from imposing residency requirements. . . . I reach a contrary conclusion, for I am convinced that the extent of the burden on interstate travel when compared with the justification
for the imposition requires the Court to uphold this exertion of federal
power."[53]

Thus Warren accepts both a balance between state and federal control of
welfare policy—a polity principle—and the fundamental right of interstate
movement. This disproves the view by many scholars that Warren and his
Court were dominated by equality as a central value. Warren views state rules,
and congressional acquiescence to such rules, in terms of Congress's power to
implement economic policy under the commerce clause. Warren is left, then,
trusting interest group politics to make choices about welfare policy and to
provide an adequate forum for demands from citizens about such policy.

Warren opposes the majority in his rejection of the applicability of an
equality principle and a definition of liberty interests at risk. He rejects the
linkage of welfare to equality of citizenship, First Amendment speech, and
other individual rights. He distinguishes this case from *Kent v. Dulles* (1958)
on the polity principle that in the *Kent* case Congress did not state its intention to give the secretary of state such discretionary power to limit movement.[54]

The right to move interstate is a more limited right for Warren than for
Douglas or Brennan. For Warren, a rational basis test, not a stricter level of
scrutiny, is all that is required when fundamental rights are not totally abrogated, so the Court should not look at the motives of Congress in deciding on
the constitutionality of its welfare laws. Warren does not treat this case as he
treated race discrimination cases, or cases involving the right to vote, as impli-
cating important fundamental rights.

Warren views the *Shapiro* case in pure polity terms—the power of Congress
over incentives to the political system to support a welfare system. Congress
can control interstate commerce; to do so is consistent with the constitutionally guaranteed right to travel. Warren castigates the Supreme Court for not
asking whether the Congress's enumerated powers support one-year rules.
For Warren, this case invokes the roles of the nation and the states in creative
federalism rather than the violation of fundamental rights, which places Warren closer to Harlan's vision of polity than most scholars perceive him to be.

Harlan's Dissent

Justice Harlan maintained polity principles that are deferential to state and
national political institutions to the waning days of the Warren Court. For
Harlan, all reasoning under fundamental rights and interest analysis is questionable as an "increasingly significant exception to the long-established rule
that a statute does not deny equal protection if it is rationally related to a legit-

imate governmental objective." He fears that "wealth" apparently was added to the list of "suspects" as an alternative justification for the rationale in *Harper*; he fears that the Court has added the right to interstate travel as a "fundamental right," subject to a compelling state interest test; and he also fears that all classifications that limit any fundamental right will be suspect. Harlan argues that only race classifications in the law are subject to strict scrutiny under the equal protection clause.[55]

Harlan argues that the due process clause is adequate protection against loss of constitutionally protected rights or traditional liberty interests. When a statute affects matters not mentioned in the Constitution and is not arbitrary or irrational, courts should not intervene. "I know of nothing which entitles this Court to pick out particular human activities, characterize them as 'fundamental,' and give them added protection under an unusually stringent equal protection test."[56] Rebutting the majority opinion, Harlan argues that the commerce clause is not a basis for creating a liberty of interstate movement to limit congressional regulation of such movement because Congress's power over commerce is plenary. Under the privileges and immunities clause, states are permitted to distinguish among the citizens of their state; they cannot, however, have different rules for citizens and noncitizens.

Both Harlan and Warren demonstrate a faith in pluralist politics and rest their dissents in the *Shapiro* case on polity arguments. Neither they nor those in the majority explore the deeper structural relationships among poverty, welfare, and redistribution of employment among the states and the relationship between receiving the necessities of life and individual and group autonomy and power in the economic, social, and political systems. These structural relationships will come to the fore in the Burger Court era (see Chapter 5).

The Inadequacy of Instrumental Views of Warren Court Decisionmaking

The Election Returns Approach

Does Dahl's election returns view of the role of the Supreme Court explain the decisionmaking of the Warren Court and doctrinal changes in its jurisprudence? To answer this question, we must examine the methodological problems with Dahl's approach, then two of his positions: his views on the relationship of the Supreme Court to the majority coalition in control of the national government; and his view of the place of internal Court deliberations and the polity and rights principles held by the justices as sources of doctrinal change.

Methodological Problems

Methodological problems seem to plague Dahl's election returns approach. The quantitative indicator used by Dahl to link Court choices to the

54   majority coalition—the Court's invalidation of national legislation—is a poor one.[57] Court invalidation of congressional statutes traditionally represents only a very small part of the Court docket and is thus a poor indicator of the overall place of the Supreme Court in the American political system. For example, under Dahl's counting method, the Supreme Court in the *Shapiro* case would be viewed as acting in concert with the dominant coalition. This incorrect assessment, along with a number of other factors and mistaken theoretical premises, lead me to question the validity of Dahl's election returns approach as a theory of doctrinal change.

Henry Abraham lists only sixty-two provisions of congressional enactments that were declared unconstitutional by the Supreme Court between the end of the *Lochner* era in 1937 and the summer of 1985—1.29 laws per year.[58] Thus, Dahl looks at only a very small set of Court decisions. Using this narrow set of data he then measures the effects of elections on changes in constitutional principles. Obviously this method is flawed. It assumes that the only significant act of the Supreme Court is to declare congressional legislation unconstitutional, and Dahl thereby overstates the place of the invalidation of congressional acts in overall Court jurisprudence.

In an article criticizing the Dahlian view of doctrinal change, Jonathan Casper also finds Dahl's view of Court–political system relations unpersuasive. He finds that from 1958 to 1974 the Supreme Court was more active than in the past and far more "decisive" than in earlier years. He criticizes Dahl for looking only at cases in which the Court declares federal legislation unconstitutional *within four years* of the passage of a statute, since the Court invalidated an additional forty laws more than four years after the legislation was passed. Casper also criticizes Dahl for considering only constitutional cases, not cases of statutory construction. The Court often "saves" statutes from unconstitutionality by interpreting them, as Casper notes. In doing so, it makes policy choices that are often at odds with the lawmaking majority. Casper views Dahl's listing of what Casper calls "winners and losers" between Court and political institutions as too narrow, because it draws attention away from the variety of ways the Supreme Court makes and influences public policy. The Court does not simply pick winners and losers, Casper argues; it (re)defines who has access to courts and the political system in the future. Court decisionmaking is in constant flux, with actions and reactions informing its choices.[59]

Even Richard Funston finds Dahl's data unpersuasive, because his measures do not offer a systematic view of the level of cohesion of a dominant coalition or the impact of critical elections on Court decisionmaking.[60] However, Funston's own reliance on declarations of unconstitutionality as the primary indicator of whether the Supreme Court follows the policy wants of the dominant coalition is similarly flawed. He, like Dahl, fails to discuss Supreme Court review of state law and actions by public officials, the constitutionality of

actions of the national bureaucracy, or the interpretation of national legislation where the invalidation of the entire law is not ordered by the Supreme
Court. Invalidation of statutes is a poor indicator of both Court power and
the relationship between law and politics, because legislators will write laws in
ways that prevent the Court from invalidating them or offering an alternative
interpretation. Thus the Court influences the majority coalition before legislation is even written.

Funston supports Dahl's view that the Court is seldom successful in
blocking the will of a lawmaking majority on important public policy questions and rarely protects minorities against majority will. However, Funston is
more open than Dahl to the thesis that the Supreme Court as an institution
differs significantly from Congress. He argues that the Court does act on principle rather than expediency and, unlike Congress, it is apt to consider long-
term needs. The Court is concerned about fundamental underlying values. In
contrast to Congress and the president, it looks at issues as matters of principle, not as momentary demands and electoral whim. The Supreme Court
led the civil rights revolution. For example, Congress reacted with the Civil
Rights Acts of 1964 and 1965, but only after an extraordinary set of assassina-
tions triggered by Supreme Court cases in the 1950s and 1960s. The Court,
Funston argues, can appeal to "our principled good sense, which may be for-
gotten in the heat of the moment." But Dahl admits to these points only
grudgingly and underestimates the degree to which the Supreme Court is different from electorally accountable institutions. In so doing, he undermines
the major premise of his approach to doctrinal change: that the Supreme
Court follows election returns.

Finally, Dahl's notion of a "dominant coalition" seems problematic.
Dahl's argument is built on the view that overall policy concerns of the governing coalition are united through agreement among its members, but Dahl
does not offer a precise definition of what he means by the terms "lawmaking
majorities," "national majorities," and "dominant alliance."[61]

The Election Returns Approach and Doctrinal Change

Dahl's overall argument assumes that there are no structural problems in
government, only a lack of properly placed political leaders to gain support for
the rights of blacks.[62] Thus Dahl rejects the notion that a major role of the Supreme Court is to overcome structural inequalities. He has great difficulty explaining *Brown v. Board of Education* (1954), though, as well as thirty years of
Court support of the rights of blacks. Nor does the Dahlian view of the
Court's role consider the effects of changes in polity and rights principles over
the years on the development of a more autonomous role for the Supreme
Court. But as a result of these changes, many scholars, other members of the
interpretive community, and the wider public do not expect the Court to fol-

56   low the policy wants of the majority coalition or enter into dialogue with political leaders. Instead they see it as the final arbiter of the Constitution.

This new role for the Supreme Court is accepted by many members of Congress as well as the public. As a result, a change in the majority coalition has a minimal effect on doctrinal change, as was seen with the Burger Court as compared to the Warren Court. This change in the Court's role may also explain the failure of most efforts by Congress to negate the effects of Supreme Court decisions on school prayer, abortion, busing, and race discrimination. Judicial finality has become an increasingly important polity principle in our nation.

The Supreme Court and the Majority Coalition

Contrary to Dahl's formulation, the evidence suggests that the Warren Court was very much out of kilter with the policy wants of the majority coalition during the Eisenhower presidency. In the area of fundamental rights and interests the Warren Court established important doctrinal innovations that were neither suggested nor favored by the Eisenhower administration. These included waiving transcript costs for the poor to allow appeals in *Griffin v. Illinois* (1956) and limitations on the power of the secretary of state to limit the issuance of passports on the basis of an applicant's political beliefs in *Kent v. Dulles* (1958). Nor can the Supreme Court appointments of Presidents Eisenhower, Kennedy, or Johnson explain the following doctrinal innovations in the area of fundamental rights and interests in the 1960s: the right to counsel at the key stage of the appeals process; support of the right to vote as fundamental to citizenship; support of the right to marry and procreate; and the finding that one-year residency requirements to receive welfare benefits are an unconstitutional encroachment on the right to travel interstate.

If the lag time between political eras, selection to the Supreme Court, and doctrinal change turns out to be far wider than Dahl's election returns approach would predict, and if the Supreme Court does not mirror the views of the dominant coalition, then we must also question the validity of the election returns approach on these grounds. Why were there so many landmark decisions that shocked the dominant coalition in the twentieth century? These include the *Lochner* era cases, *Brown v. Board of Education* (1954), and privacy rights cases in the 1970s, to name but a few. They certainly did not meet the policy desires of the dominant coalition. Even if Dahl explains Supreme Court cases in the 1930s that found some of President Roosevelt's social and economic legislation unconstitutional as based on Roosevelt's lack of opportunities to select Supreme Court justices, such an argument does not apply to the Warren and Burger Courts. Presidents Eisenhower, Kennedy, Johnson, Nixon, Ford, and Reagan made appointments to those courts, as did Presidents Bush and Clinton to the Rehnquist Court. *Brown v. Board of Education* and the Supreme Court's antisegregation decisions, its call to send troops to Little Rock, and the cases involving the rights of the accused clearly violated the policy wants of the Eisenhower administration, as did its fundamental rights and interests cases, which called for court intervention into the political and judicial systems.[63]

Dahl argues that the Court's support of the rights of blacks against the legislative aims of Congress and the states was caused by an instability in these political institutions with respect to these key policies. He argues that the Supreme Court's legitimacy is protected. It succeeds in establishing policy counter to the stated objectives of the dominant alliance "only if its action conforms to and reinforces a widespread set of explicit or implicit norms held by the political leadership, norms which are not strong enough or are not distributed in such a way as to insure the existence of an effective lawmaking majority, but are, nonetheless, sufficiently powerful to prevent any successful attack on the legitimacy powers of the Court."[64] In this quotation we see one of the few indications by Dahl that the pluralist political system does not work well, that it might have structural biases that elections and the majority coalition cannot eradicate. Dahl seems to be saying that the political leadership held values in support of ending race segregation and discrimination but could not, for some reason, make them into public policy.

Dahl, like most pluralist scholars of the 1950s, incorrectly assumes that there is free-floating coalition formation in pluralist politics and that the Court makes its choices in response to coalition formation rather than independently. But aren't there significant, perpetual conflicts between the president and Congress? And how can one maintain that the government consistently reflects the majority will, in the face of its clear responsiveness to "effective" single-interest groups that do not represent the nation's majority? Although presidential selection of Supreme Court justices influences the Court in the direction of the policy wants of the majority coalition, it simply does not explain why presidents cannot reliably predict the judicial policy directions of their appointees. More often than not, presidents have been able to secure opinions they agree with from their appointees; however, the "nots" have had an important effect on the development of constitutional principles.[65]

Dahl does not see the Court's constitutive decisionmaking process—with its continual rethinking of the nature of polity and rights principles and the relationship between them—as informing its decisions. When we look at judicial decisionmaking in the Warren Court we find that polity and rights values are more crucial to the debate within the Court than are the desires of the dominant coalition. The justices on the Warren Court did not dismiss the polity and rights elements in past Court cases or constitutional theory as the Dahlian view of Court role does. On the contrary, blocs of polity and rights-oriented justices disputed how to decide specific cases, both before and after Frankfurt-

58   er's retirement from the Court. We also see battles over polity and rights principles among rights-oriented justices, such as Warren's dissent in the *Shapiro*
case, and splits among polity-oriented justices in the area of the right to privacy.

Dahl's thesis simply cannot explain doctrinal changes brought about by
outside forces; internal principles of the law, precedent, and legal theory are
absent from his explanation, as are changes in the wider society caused by factors unrelated to changes in the majority coalition. If Chief Justice Warren and
the Warren Court had been representative of their age, or of the dominant alliance, or if they had adhered to Dahl's view of Court decisionmaking, they
would have been far more pragmatic, compromising supporters of the political system, which they would have viewed as well-functioning and in equilibrium. But as case analysis demonstrates, Warren believed the Court had an important mandate: to eliminate the inequalities caused by the dominant
coalition and pluralist politics, to protect public interests that could not be
protected by normal interest group politics, and to push political leaders to
end race and, in some instances, class inequalities even though the political
system and the majority coalition had neither the will nor the resources to do
so.

The Court did not undertake these changes incrementally like a group of
policymakers. Instead, it made structural changes in the political system,
changes that undermined the power of the majority coalition to make policy.
As Vincent Blasi argues, the Warren Court could have required a more incremental approach to reapportionment, for example, by favoring reform in only
one legislature in bicameral bodies—but chose not to do so.[66]

The Warren Court aimed to place into constitutional law polity principles
and visions of equality and fundamental rights that countered contemporary
views of Court power and judicial review. It rejected the ad hoc decisionmaking and compromises traditional to political institutions, but its view of equality was always tempered by polity principles that were different from the apologetic pluralist vision of Dahl.

The fact that the Warren Court found a number of state laws wanting is
not an affirmation of its partnership with the governing coalition. Rather it is
an indication of the failure of national government and the governing coalition to protect the rights of citizens at the state level. The national government's inaction on racial inequality before and during the 1950s and into the
1960s and the Warren Court's rejection of that policy of inaction are evidence
that the Court did not support the majority coalition. Thus we again see that
the Court's failure to overturn national legislation is a poor indicator of its participation in a majority coalition, because nonaction by the government produces no legislation for the Court to overturn.

There are also indications in Warren Court jurisprudence that the Court would have overruled Congress if it had passed legislation similar to that passed by the states. We see this in the *Shapiro* case. In the majority opinion, Brennan argues that even if Congress had wished to impose a one-year residency requirement for welfare, it would be unconstitutional under the equal protection components of the Fifth Amendment due process clause.[67] Finally, Dahl's view that the role of the Supreme Court is to legitimate the policy wants of the dominant coalition and political institutions is not supported by empirical evidence. In fact, as David Adamany argues, there is much evidence of the Court's *incapacity* to legitimate government action.[68]

The Policymaking Approach

Shapiro's policymaking approach assumes that outcomes rather than views about polity and rights inform the choices of justices. The outcomes of Supreme Court cases obviously have important policy implications, but as our case analysis demonstrates, justices make choices based on their individual views about polity principles, Court role, and fundamental rights and liberties. The polity and rights principles held by various justices prevent them, at important times in Court deliberations, from supporting policy outcomes that they personally favor; at key times justices may fail to support general equality principles or the allocation of goods or political power to members of the New Deal coalition. We see this in Black's and Stewart's dissents in the *Griswold* case on the Warren Court and in the abortion rights cases in the Burger Court. In other words, although justices may want more equality and the redistribution of education, economic resources, and status in our society, they may still oppose a specific policy outcome because it violates their views about polity, Court role, and fundamental rights and interests.[69]

In contrast, Shapiro views the Warren Court, like the *Lochner* Court, as unprincipled in making constitutional choices. The only difference between the *Lochner* and Warren Court eras is that the justices had different policy objectives and different clienteles—business and the New Deal coalition, respectively. Shapiro views debates over polity and rights principles between judicial activists and judicial self-restrainers as bogus. In contrast to G. Edward White, he sees no significant differences between the Frankfurter-Harlan (judicial self-restraint) and Warren-Brennan (preferred position) wings of the Warren Court. Both supported Court advocacy of personal and civil rights, which for Shapiro means acting "on behalf of those interests that carried the New Deal certificate."[70]

Shapiro's view that justices reflect fundamental ethical values and constitutional theories in making constitutional choices—because they are outcome-oriented policymakers—is a major problem in his theory of doctrinal change. By looking at polity, rights, and policy as separate entities, Shapiro trivializes

60 the role of constitutional theory and theories of polity in judicial decisionmaking.

Shapiro's misconception of Warren Court decisionmaking is seen in his analysis of *Shapiro v. Thompson*. He views the Warren Court as supporting the desire of the New Deal coalition for economic redistribution;[71] the Court had merely changed the set of interests it wanted to support from the *Lochner* period. The debates among the justices as to whether polity principles are violated in this important case are irrelevant, for Shapiro, to the explanation of case outcomes or the development of constitutional law.

In a similar vein, Shapiro argues that the Warren Court sought to serve the value of equality and the policy needs of blacks, the poor, and the left wing. He argues that the *Griswold* case was decided the way it was in order to make birth control as available to the poor as it was to the middle class.[72] Apparently the argumentation in that case—the differences among the majority and concurring justices—is not significant to Shapiro. If, as he suggests, only policy differences among justices govern their choices, then he must not take Justices Black and Stewart, who stated that laws that limit contraception were stupid but refused to support the Court's invalidation of the law on polity and rights principles, at their word. Clearly, these justices were not making choices on the grounds of their policy wants.[73]

Finally, we also see Shapiro's view of the decisionmaking process as one of policymaking, rather than one of constituting normative polity and rights principles, in his strong arguments that scholars engaging in doctrinal analysis should be "outsiders." He opposes scholars' use of political and constitutional theory to guide the Court in their doctrinal analyses.[74]

The Safety Valve Approach

Inherent in the safety valve position is the view that all legal theory—that is, all institutional and rights principles employed by Supreme Court justices and scholars—is based on one central principle: that the courts should generally mistrust majoritarian political institutions and protect minorities from raw majoritarianism.

The safety valve role—preserving individual rights—was an important one for the Court in the Warren and Burger years, but to view polity and rights principles in terms of one central role is to oversimplify the nature of the constitutive polity and rights principles at work on the Warren Court. To assume that the Supreme Court in general, or the Warren Court in particular, accepts in their entirety the political malfunction principles of the *Carolene Products* footnote, as the safety valve approach requires of us, is to oversimplify the basis of Court decisionmaking and to disregard the effect of complex external factors, such as the dialogue between the Court and the interpretive community, on doctrinal change.

The political malfunction principle alone tells us very little about what choices the Warren Court made, and most importantly, *why* the Court chose to oppose raw majoritarianism in a given instance. Nor does it explain why and when the Court performs, or chooses not to perform, this function. In this regard, this approach is little different than assumptions by scholars that the Court follows election returns or makes policy choices or makes choices because of the biographies of members of the Court. This generalization, like the others, obscures explanations of differences between doctrine in different Court eras and fails to offer a subtler analysis of why the Court makes doctrinal changes.

The safety valve approach is essentially ahistorical. It is a product of the Warren Court's first flush of enthusiasm with the *Carolene Products* footnote. During the Warren Court era this explanation of doctrinal change was not a carefully worked out theory of judicial decisionmaking and constitutional change, but the truism of an age.

A brief look at Warren Court doctrinal changes suggests the limits of this approach. It is possible to argue that the Warren Court's decisions on reapportionment, race segregation, defendant rights, and political questions indicate that a majority of the Court saw as its mission the overcoming of blockages and malfunctions in the political system. However, before we board this bandwagon, it is important to emphasize that the Court made these choices not because it sought to end blockages in the political system as an outcome. Rather, its concern for ending a malfunction is the end point of a more complex decisionmaking process in which constitutive polity and rights values are central.

Court choices cannot be explained by the safety valve view of Court role, because the Supreme Court did not always counter an institution that was not able to correct its own blockage. Nor does this theory help us understand the conditions under which political malfunctions are identified by the Court or why Supreme Courts in different eras have changed their definition of what constitutes a political malfunction and which malfunctions require new polity or rights principles. If the safety valve approach were accepted as valid in the *Shapiro* case, for example, all justices would have had to agree that denying welfare to residents of less than one year was a constitutional violation because it constituted a malfunction in the political system. However, the complexity of reasons given by the justices in that case and their different views of the rights and polity principles at issue reveal the false simplicity of the safety valve approach.

This approach cannot explain the votes of Warren and Black in opposing the *Shapiro* decision, because it does not explore the linkage of rights principles to polity malfunction principles, a relationship that is more complex than the safety valve approach suggests. A general polity malfunction approach to War-

62   ren Court jurisprudence does not explain the wide differences in the definitions of malfunction held by the justices. Nor does it explain when justices
choose to favor rights principles over polity malfunctions bases for their
choices.

The reapportionment cases concerned a rights principle: one person, one
vote—specifically the question of equal weighting of votes within and among
electoral districts. It applied to districts in which blacks had been gerryman-
dered out of political power for reasons of racial discrimination. The denial of
this right indicated a malfunction in the political system. However, the Warren Court chose not to outlaw other possible gerrymandering that might
result in less political power for a party, class, or group not defined by race. In
these cases there were multiple concerns: the right to vote as a citizen's right in
and of itself; the right to vote as a basis for ensuring other constitutional protections for citizens; and the right to vote as a means to reduce polity malfunctions. The safety valve approach simplifies reality by not seeing rights and polity principles as separate but related sources of judicial decisionmaking.

Polity malfunction is only one of the polity and rights considerations a
Court must take into account when it decides cases. It should not be viewed
as the primary polity principle among the many that the Court may consider.
Nor should it, by itself, be seen as at the core of Court jurisprudence, without
regard to important rights principles. For some scholars, it may constitute the
primary element in a process- or polity-based constitutional vision. However,
polity malfunction should not be viewed as Lewis does—as the primary principle at the core of Supreme Court jurisprudence.

The Biographical Approach

In advocating a biographical explanation of Supreme Court decisionmaking
White sees himself as taking an alternative position to those of most Warren
critics, who erroneously attack the Warren Court as outcome-oriented. Of the
four major approaches to Supreme Court decisionmaking explored in this
book, White's is the most complete, filigreed, and complex because his analysis of the Warren Court, at least prior to 1962, is based on reviewing the conflicts over polity and rights principles among the justices. White explores the
complexity of polity and rights principles held by individual Warren Court justices as they relate to rights principles at the core of Warren Court jurisprudence. To him, the Warren Court justices had quite complex and different
views of "the people," and he correctly views the Court as concerned about
competing attitudes as to what is "prudential." He does not view it as simply
informed by equality as an ideology, "functionally" ordained as in the safety
valve approach, or determined by the policy wants of the justices or the majority coalition.

White argues, in contrast to other instrumental views, that Warren believed that ethical imperatives deserved as much attention as constitutional language, "even if such an application resulted in a failure to achieve orthodox doctrinal consistency,"[75] and that visions of polity in contemporary constitutional theory and the Founding principles precluded justice for minorities. Here White points out the importance of polity principles to Warren.

Yet I think it is fair to say that White hardly transcended the limits of those very critics of the Warren Court that he criticizes. For example, it is significant that White emphasizes Warren's view of equality over his perception of institutional constraints. White argues that there was a direct link between Warren's discovery of ethical premises about justice and his opinions. In Eighth Amendment cases, he contends, Warren made no effort to analyze doctrinal history—that Warren bypassed judicial craftsmanship standards altogether. In reapportionment cases Warren made choices on the basis of principles of political theory about representation, which he then equated with specific constitutional rights.[76] For White, polity values are submerged beneath a general support of equality and fairness principles. However, the case analysis demonstrates that polity values were motor forces to Warren's constitutional choices, as in the *Shapiro* case, not merely post hoc justifications for his views of justice. Therefore, for White Warren seems to have done what the policymaking and election returns approaches argue he did—support the policy needs of the poor, minorities, and members of the New Deal coalition.

Because Warren held such strong polity principles in opposition to the dominant pluralist values of the day, views about polity and judicial self-restraint no longer informed Warren's specific constitutional choices, according to White. The problem with this formulation is that it overstates the place of moral values in Warren's decisionmaking. The fact that Warren's view of institutional role differed from the more consensual view of American politics is not to be discounted, as even White admits.

This argument, based on craft concerns, is similar to those of Funston, Kurland, and others discussed at the beginning of the chapter. The fact that Warren's views about political theory and polity principles informed his choices is obliquely indicated here by White. While White is concerned that Warren not be viewed as outcome-oriented, but rather as a person with lumpen moral and polity values, he nonetheless fails to engage in a sustained analysis of the relationship among polity principles, moral values, and craft issues in Warren's jurisprudence. Such an incomplete analysis does not place him very far above the formulaic evaluators of Warren who dominated the Warren Court era and, as we shall see, continue their influence today.

White joins with more conventional critics of Warren in emphasizing that the Court was out of step with public opinion. He argues that the Warren Court did not secure "ethical concordance" with public opinion as it should have in order to counter accepted notions of "analytical competence." Because of Warren's broad definition of "analytical competence," White argues, and because of a lack of craftsmanship and discipline in his judicial decision-making, a heavy burden is placed on ethical concords between the Court and public opinion.[77] White seems to suggest that when a Court does not play the judicial craftsmanship game, it has a particular duty to ensure that its views about what is just fit with those of the public. This view is essentially a judicial self-restraint argument and an argument for the Court's making choices on the basis of public opinion rather than in terms of the fundamental rights in the Constitution as interpreted by the Court.

However, White sees Warren as relying less on polity principles in his decisionmaking than did Frankfurter and Harlan. White argues that the institutionalists on the Warren Court did not have substantive liberal and rights values, while Warren tended to make constitutional choices on substantive moral value bases. But to formulate the question as one of institutionalists Holmes, Hand, Frankfurter, and Harlan versus moralist Warren, as White does, understates the amount of discretion in polity and rights principles available on both sides of the aisle. The focus on doctrinal consistency and craft in the institutionalist justices obscures the place of more complex polity and rights principles, and their interaction, in the specific constitutional choices Frankfurter and Harlan made. This formulation of Warren Court jurisprudence understates the fact that each of these "institutionalists" on the Court also had lumpen rights values in their jurisprudence. The mix of deference to institutions and ethical concerns was different from Warren's. Also, their views of polity were clearly different. White's concerns about legalism as mere form obscures the views about polity and rights that even these more pragmatic justices and scholars had.

The focus on substantive liberalism in Warren's jurisprudence understates the role of polity principles. After the legal realist revolution and the reaction to it, in which craft or procedure as law dominated the legal academy, one must unbundle the concept of craft into its more complex components: constitutive polity and rights principles. When one does this, the juxtaposition of Warren the moralist and the institutionalists becomes an oversimplification of both Warren Court decisionmaking and Warren as a jurist.

White's view also fails to underscore that at key points liberal justices like Warren made decisions based on their views about the institutional role to be played by legislatures, courts, and politics. Most important, when White concludes that there was a triumph of substantive liberalism over the polity principle process liberalism on the Warren Court after 1962, he dramatically misreads the nature of Warren Court decisionmaking. As we saw in the case analysis, Warren, and all members of the Warren Court, never gave up making constitutional choices on both polity and rights principles. Moreover, it was the dovetailing of mildly critical polity values with open-ended (and not always clearly defined) rights and justice notions that brought about the revolution in jurisprudence of the Warren Court era, not the victory of substantive liberalism, as White and other scholars would have us believe.

Finally, at the core of White's explanation of doctrinal change is the view that justices make consitutional choices in line with their biographies. However, White's argument that Warren Court jurisprudence and the differences in Court eras can be explained by biographical differences alone oversimplifies the causes of doctrinal change. As with the election returns and policymaking approaches, which view external factors as central to doctrinal change, the argument that the biographies of justices explain doctrinal change assumes that internal deliberations are irrelevant to Court choices. The biographical approach, like all the instrumental interpretations, fails to see that the interpretive communities of the day, and the interpretations of Court role in the American political system, have an impact on doctrinal change (see Chapters 3 and 6). The biographical approach assumes a direct linkage between biography and a justice's polity and rights principles and constitutional choices, choices unmediated by internal Court deliberations and changing views of the political and legal system in the legal and social science community.

Conclusion

Some argue that the romantic vision of the Warren Court as driven by a quest for equality is a product of *Brown v. Board of Education*, a case heard early in the Warren Court era that established the image of the Court and its chief justice as innovative and committed to equality.[78] A close look at the *Brown* decision (especially *Brown I* and *Brown II*, which implemented school desegregation under a call for "all deliberate speed") and the school segregation decisions in higher education prior to *Brown* suggests that polity principles, not just a concern for equality, informed Warren Court constitutional choices.

It is unfortunate that our image of the Warren Court generally arises from the *Brown* decision, the apportionment cases, and the cases in which the rights of defendants were given new life, because this vision of purity understates the degree to which political concerns informed the Warren Court's equal protection jurisprudence. Warren's jurisprudence demonstrates his rejection of the view of political institutions held by postwar pluralist and relativistic democratic theorists and interpreters of politics such as Robert Dahl and David Truman. For the Warren Court, including Justice Warren, did not see the pluralist political system as in equilibrium, ready to meet problems of unequal political power by trusting political institutions to meet citizen demands.

A more fruitful attempt to understand the Warren Court is to explore in more detail how the dominant instrumental explanations of doctrinal change and decisionmaking processes on the Supreme Court—the election returns, policymaking, safety valve, and biographical approaches—have tended to pic-

66   ture the Warren Court. The debate on polity and rights principles in the Warren Court, and the differing opinions among the justices as to what polity and
rights principles should be employed in deciding cases, suggests that Warren
Court justices did not use such principles instrumentally to support policy
outcomes that they desired.

Moreover, if there appears to be a purer equality principle at work in the
Warren Court than in the Burger Court, it is because of the formal nature, in
de jure terms, of the inequalities identified by the Warren Court, not because
rights principles were less central to the legal philosophies of members of the
Burger Court (see Chapter 5).

If one were to summarize the scholarly commentary on the Warren Court
by describing the major tenets of its jurisprudence as the primacy of ethical
premises; the unimportance of polity principles; the "pure" forms of its opinions; the lack of craftsmanship; an improper exercise of legislative and execu-
tive-type powers; or the decline in the rule of law, originalist constitutional
theory, and stare decisis, one would have only a one-dimensional sense of the
Warren Court. So if we were to end our analysis here, we would leave unex-
plored the deeper causes for our misunderstanding of the Warren Court—external factors and the process of doctrinal change. We would not understand
why the criticism of the Warren Court took the forms that it did. Nor would
we understand why Warren Court decisionmaking and doctrinal change were
viewed in instrumental rather than constitutive terms. To deepen our understanding, we need to place instrumental interpretations in the wider framework of the major ideational changes within social science and legal theory in
pre– and post–World War II America.

Chapter Three
Misperceiving the Warren Court:
The Limits of Instrumentalism

In Chapter 2 we saw that the instrumental election returns, policymaking, safety valve, and biographical approaches misconstrue the internal decision-making process of the Warren Court. In this chapter we will consider how instrumental interpretations have viewed the process of doctrinal change with regard to external factors, such as the majority coalition in power, the interpretive community, and political and constitutional theory. We will also consider why these approaches view the Warren Court as closely tied to political institutions, political elites, and electoral changes rather than as autonomous and why they seek direct "external" explanations of doctrinal change on the Warren Court. To address these questions we must examine the visions of the political and legal system that were held by political theorists and social scientists before and during the Warren Court era. (By clarifying the relationship of the interpretive community to doctrinal change, we can achieve a more sophisticated understanding of doctrinal change in the Warren Court era and have the foundations for understanding jurisprudence and doctrinal change in the Burger Court era.)

The Supreme Court's dialogical relationship to the interpretive community, contemporary polity and rights viewpoints, scholarly criticism, and longer-term developments in social, democratic, and legal theory explain Court definitions of constitutional questions, not policy outcomes, institutional functionalism, election returns, or biography. The interpretive community thus plays a larger role in the development of doctrine than do the policy wants of the majority coalition or of the individual justices, a finding that will be confirmed in our analysis of the Burger Court era.

Emphasizing Nonoriginalism

My analysis of the Supreme Court and the interpretive community in both Court eras centers on the dialogue between the Supreme Court and nonoriginalist, not originalist, constitutional theory. In order to understand the terms "originalism" and "nonoriginalism" it may be useful first to describe the terms "interpretivism" (which is like originalism) and "noninterpretivism" (which is like nonoriginalism). In *The Constitution, the Courts, and Human Rights* Michael Perry defines noninterpretive review "as a species of policy-

68   making, in which the Court decides, ultimately without reference to any value judgment constitutionalized by the framers." Most cases involving human rights, including *Brown v. Board of Education* (1954), First Amendment cases, and abortion rights cases, are noninterpretive decisions because "[they] reflect not value judgments, or interpretations or applications of value judgments, made and embodied in the Constitution by the framers, but value judgments made and enforced by the Court against other, electorally accountable branches of government. . . . The Supreme Court engages in *interpretive* review when it ascertains the constitutionality of a given policy choice by reference to a value judgments of which the Constitution consists—that is, by reference to one of the value judgment embodied though not necessarily explicitly, either in some particular provision of the text of the Constitution or in the overall structure of government ordained by the Constitution."[1] For clarity I use the terms "originalist" and "nonoriginalist" rather than "interpretive" and "noninterpretive."

If I focused primarily on the history of constitutional theory, rather than offering a revisionist interpretation of the Burger Court era, I would be obligated to argue normatively whether originalism or nonoriginalism is a more appropriate way to interpret the Constitution. But this is a different sort of book. My object is not to consider the pluses and minuses of originalism, nonoriginalism, and critical legal studies, of any particular theory, or of theory per se. Instead, I consider the validity of conventional instrumental interpretations of the Warren and Burger Courts and, most important, whether the most influential constitutional theories of the day, which were nonoriginalist in approach, offer adequate guidance to most of the justices on the Warren and Burger Courts, who also were nonoriginalist in their judicial philosophy.

I also am persuaded by Michael Perry's argument against originalism and for the importance of polity and rights principles in constitutional theory and practice. Perry argues that no one particular conception of democracy or Court role, such as the primacy of electorally accountable government, is axiomatic for the American political tradition. Nor is there one particular definition of the other central aspiration constituting constitutional theory: "liberty and justice for all."[2] Since all scholars, originalists and nonoriginalists alike, must choose among appropriate polity and rights aspirations in making constitutional choices, there can be no definitive answer to which is the better.

Perry favors nonoriginalist constitutional theory because it allows both polity and rights aspirations to be considered in making constitutional choices in a way that originalism does not. Originalism keeps faith only with the value of electoral accountability; but achieving justice as a value reflects the growth of morality in a way that a faith in majoritarianism "here and now" does not.

Originalism, *as a theory of constitutional interpretation*, is used by most justices of the Warren and Burger Courts neither as their primary theory of interpretation nor as the sole basis for defining their polity and rights principles. Nor is it the primary standard of evaluation among jurists, scholars, and practitioners in the interpretive communities of Warren and Burger Courts. Most of these justices choose, in different degrees, to apply nonoriginalist constitutional interpretations when they make constitutional choices. Close scrutiny of even those justices who claim to adhere to originalism reveals that a large degree of nonoriginalist jurisprudence enters their opinions as well. To criticize originalism as a method of constitutional interpretation because originalist scholars did not adequately guide the Warren and Burger Courts would be to set up a straw man, one attacked all too often and flippantly by nonoriginalist scholars.

Justices use insights from the Founders and the Civil War amendments in different degrees to formulate the polity and rights principles that inform their constitutional choices. However, these insights cannot be classified as originalist approaches to the Constitution as we usually think of such approaches. Most justices tend to be quite undisciplined in their use of Founding materials and arguments; thus their interpretations lie outside the expectations of most originalists about what constitutes a valid originalist interpretation. Also, most justices present their originalist insights along with many more nonoriginalist constitutional formulations, which drown out the former.

However, nonoriginalist constitutional theory is not above significant criticism. Nonoriginalist constitutional theory of the Warren and Burger Courts made it easier for moral values and social, economic, and political factors and ideas different from those of the Framers to inform constitutional practice; but the ability of these noninterpretive theories to be transformative and to aid the Court in its new definitions of constitutional law is severely limited by their failure to view constitutional questions through a prism consisting of fundamental, but changing, polity and rights principles, not all of which could be listed in the Constitution given its Lockean basis.

From Normative to Relativist Democratic and Legal Theory: The Rise of Non-Euclideanism and Scientific Naturalism

In his superb study of changes in democratic and legal theory in the twentieth century,[3] Edward Purcell argues that from 1900 to the 1930s the growth of respect for positivism and scientific naturalism undermined respect for traditional democratic theory, moral philosophy, and moral foundationalism as knowledge by attacking the view that moral principles, deductive and inductive logic, and higher law principles could be proved and thus justified rationally. Non-Euclidean geometry revealed that a priori reasoning and logic were not "real" knowledge. Scientific naturalism assumed that knowledge was verifiable only if it could be tested by scientific method. Non-Euclidean mathematics demonstrated the gap between deduction from principles as

70   knowledge in the same way that scientific naturalism and particularist objectivism implied an unbridgeable gap between induction and ethical principles as knowledge. Purcell writes, "The two approaches together, closely related both theoretically and practically, meant that no method of human reasoning could deal meaningfully with the problem of validating any set of ethical beliefs." Non-Euclideanism, as well as Einstein's relativity theory, demonstrated that deduction could discover or prove nothing and belief in synthetic, a priori knowledge lacked any scientific, geometric, or logical basis. Most important, non-Euclideanism robbed rational systems, including law, of their claim to be true unless they could be proved empirically. Knowledge about moral values could not be proven by use of natural science methods; therefore such matters lay in the realm of opinion—mere moral assumptions.

This view fostered a moral relativism that questioned the legitimacy of moral principles. Since scholars in the 1930s and 1940s argued that truth and ethical propositions could not be proven by either induction or deduction, moral ideals were left without a rational, theoretical basis. Empirical studies of American politics by scientific naturalists led to a questioning, and ultimately a rejection, of the three cardinal principles of democratic government: the possibility of a government of laws rather than men, the rationality of human behavior, and the practical possibility of popular government itself.

The question of how to justify democratic values and theory in an age of moral relativism and totalitarian atrocities became an unavoidable and essential one for social, political, and legal scholars. They asked, if moral values are not provable but merely relative, how can we explain democracy in America? How can we counter totalitarianism in Germany and the Soviet Union and remain true to scientific naturalist values? In the 1930s and after World War II, scholars had to find an answer to these queries.

By World War II many social scientists were at an impasse. How could they demonstrate the truth of a moral judgment that they accepted—that democracy was better than totalitarianism? From the late 1930s and into the 1960s, intellectuals continued to disagree on a philosophy of values. But they did begin, in the 1930s, to develop the outlines of a broadly naturalistic and relativistic theory of democracy. They began to sketch a pragmatic interpretation of the social consequences of absolutist versus relativist political theories.[4]

This new naturalist view of democracy was based on the insights of John Dewey, whose absolutist-relativist dichotomy framed the debate about democracy. Dewey argued that as long as all facts could be publicly and critically examined in light of their social consequences, people could freely make up their minds about the nature of truth; no authoritative ruling group was required, nor were epistemological dualisms necessary. Purcell writes, "American social theory [was left] with one controlling dichotomy: absolutism and authoritarianism versus experimentalism and democracy." This dualism, he maintains, became "one of the central *political* assumptions of most American intellectuals." Communism, fascism, and Nazism were totalitarian and absolute; American society, even with its restrictive capitalism, was nonabsolutist and relatively free. The "equation of philosophical absolutism with political authoritarianism," Purcell argues, "proved the linchpin of the developing relativist theory of democracy because it provided the one basis on which most American intellectuals could unite."

A majority of scholars accepted a relativist theory of democracy because it also preserved the intellectual dominance of naturalism. Purcell writes:

> Basing their approach on the powerful naturalist anti-absolutism, they assumed first of all the *de facto* connection between theoretical absolutism and practical authoritarianism. Second, they developed a corollary: only social theories that recognized all truths, including ethical truths, as tentative, changing, and uncertain, could support and justify democratic government. Finally, they argued that ethical theories by themselves were not in fact crucial to democracy, that they were important only to the extent that they were actually reflected in a society's cultural forms.

It is important to note that institutions were also viewed in terms of their flexibility and ability to compromise. Democracy was better than absolutism, not because anyone could prove in ethical, principled terms that it was better, but because it was more like scientific naturalism. It implied an open, diverse, democratic social order based on a rational and scientific attitude toward human understanding and political morality.

By 1945 the equation between intellectual relativism and democracy was widely accepted. Purcell describes the subtle shift from a logical problem of justification, through the relativist solution to that problem, to a growing concern for identifying what constituted a specifically democratic type of culture.

> The problem of justification thus led to an emphasis on the cultural bases of various political forms and later, in the postwar years, to the idea that a functioning democratic culture—and especially, American culture—was itself a normative phenomenon. . . . They [scholars] came to assume there must be a specifically democratic culture that underlay democratic political forms and equated that type of culture with an institutionalized relativism—a culture that denied absolute truths, remained intellectually flexible and critical, valued diversity, and drew strength from innumerable competing subgroups. From that assumption it was not difficult to jump to the conclusion that American society represented that specifically demo-

cratic type of culture and that it was in fact the norm for understanding the operative basis of democracy.

Now the question became, what kind of culture produces democracy? The dichotomy between absolutism and relativism characterized cultures as well as philosophies and explained in social terms why some countries were prone to totalitarianism. The absolutist-relativist dichotomy became central to American social, political, and legal theory and to our analysis of political and legal institutions and the law.

Relativist Democratic and Postwar Pluralist Interpretations of American Politics

A relativist theory of democracy was not only viewed as prescriptive logic, but also as an empirical theory of politics.[5] It was behind the major research paradigm in political science from 1944 to 1966. But in political science as well as the other social sciences, the relativist theory of democracy became the problematic. Scholars asked, what are the conditions for democracy? Where does democracy happen and why?

In the 1950s social scientists no longer claimed that complete value neutrality was possible, but studies of politics based on the relativist theory of democracy were still viewed as empirical and methodologically sound. Antiabsolutism took center stage in postwar scholarship. Purcell writes, "Hence radicals of the left and right [were viewed as] psychologically authoritarian, and liberals and conservatives of the center [were viewed as] tolerant." The middle represented an "emotional maturity" that was accepting of the compromising and bargaining that defined a working democracy.

In contrast to the absolutism of McCarthyism, established social institutions represented compromise, pragmatism, "market decision" intellectual complexity, and structural rationality. McCarthyism gave authority to the assumptions of a relativist theory because it encouraged intellectuals to look at established and presumably pluralistic institutions as bulwarks against the feared absolutist mass movement (of which McCarthyism was an example). Scholars argued that better-educated people would accept a sophisticated relativism and viewed elites with wider worldviews than the masses as a reliable source of democratic values. Comparing the United States with the Soviet Union, intellectuals assumed that American society was essentially relativistic and therefore pluralistic. Due to the country's pluralism, power relationships in America were seen as indeterminate and amorphous. Intellectuals viewed the nation as successful in the fundamental democratic tasks of balancing power; therefore they regarded "any serious disruption of the balance, any reform movement that went outside established institutions [as] harmful to the country's democratic achievement."

American Politics as Group Politics: David Truman 73

We see these qualities in the interpretations of American politics by the two leading political scientists of the Warren Court era: David Truman and Robert Dahl. They attempted to understand the prerequisites of democracy, assuming that American society, in both its public and private institutions, was pluralistic. This approach, along with an attempt to create a less dogmatic scientific rationalist framework, led to a revival in the 1950s of group-based theories of politics. Early in this century, Arthur F. Bentley's group theory sought to understand politics as the interaction of groups and eschewed the idea of "interest" groups as morally bad institutional forms that undermine the classical view of democracy and citizenship. This became the basis for seeking a relativist alternative to Marxist interpretations of politics.

David Truman's classic reinterpretation of Bentley's *The Process of Government*, titled *The Governmental Process*, was published in 1951 and reprinted nine times by 1964. It put forward a general theory of government based on the relativist theory of democracy and argued that the task of political science was to perpetuate a viable system. According to its "realistic" democratic theory, "reality" rather than an ethical ideal was the primary criterion of both theoretical validity and legitimate political action.[6] Since America was generally viewed as a well-functioning political system and pluralistic institutional forms were seen as central to our society, Truman's pluralist view of politics was based on complacent attitudes and overoptimistic evaluations of American politics. Democratic theory had lost its traditional moral, critical function and glossed over the glaring discrepancies of wealth and power that existed in American society.

Truman's relativist democratic theory did not accept the definition of the role of citizens in traditional democratic theory. The Truman book was a statement of why American politics was democratic even though elites, rather than the general citizenry, were the most active participants in the political process. He argued that groups, and the complex process of interest group politics, were necessary to democracy. He viewed government as a system with multiple access points through which a complex group process works.

Most political scientists equated group conflict with the dispersal of political power. They saw groups and their leaders as the key filters for citizen wants. Fearing loss of support, group leaders would ensure that the needs of organized minorities would be met. They were viewed as supporting democratic and civil liberties values if they played by the rules of this game; if they did not, they would suffer politically. Thus political change resulted from the flow of demands up through groups to government. The fear of the formation of new groups along with the fear of groups external to one's own group, led to a constant but incremental change, which was good for the overall society.

The key assumption—one that a majority of the Warren Court rejected—

74 was that normal group formation was not difficult in our society. Overlapping membership of individuals in numerous groups supposedly led to moderation because of cross-cutting cleavages. Agreement on "rules of the game," compromise, and an equilibrium among the groups seemed to demonstrate the wonderful, special working of American democracy. Political interest groups that made claims on other groups were not viewed as bad for the political system, because the overall system fostered moderation. The complexity of the governmental structure meant that the overall process would produce policies wanted by many in society, even if the wants of some groups were ignored.

Truman believed that the Founders' concerns for protecting the aggregate interests of the public and limiting the negative effects of factions were no longer valid. The public interest cannot be known. Therefore, all we can hope for is that the complex, easily accessible governmental process will produce policies that are not opposed by a significant minority. For Truman, Madison's desire for cross-cutting of interests to protect against faction was realized through overlapping group membership. Thus, it is the *process* that protects our nation and makes it democratic.

There was no traditional standard of evaluation external to the process by which Truman evaluated the workings of the polity. He opposed viewing the political system in separation of powers or "problem of faction" terms (as in *Federalist* no. 10), or along constitutional lines, for he felt that the reality is more open and less formal. Truman's group theory is a classic example of a relativistic theory of democracy prevalent during the Warren Court years. Having accepted the group politics process as good, his only concern was whether we should fear the pathology of class-based politics. He found that this is not likely in America because of group politics. His concern was for maintaining social control—order—and preventing mass movements.

Finally, for Truman the Supreme Court was more autonomous from direct politics than it was for Dahl—he argues that the Court does not just follow election returns. But Truman also contends that it is the elite's respect for the potential interests in rules of the game and constitutional values, not decision-making by the Supreme Court, that best protects the American political system.

American Politics as Pluralist Politics: Robert Dahl

"In *A Preface to Democratic Theory*, published in 1956, [Robert] Dahl rejected the descriptive accuracy and logical consistency of [democratic] theories based on constitutional checks and balances."[7] Instead Dahl viewed the United States as a nation where cultural conditions allow democracy: a nation with a cultural consensus and a number of competing minorities. For Dahl, minorities rule, not majorities or individual minorities. Society is pluralistic, open to new coalitions. "To assume that this country has remained democratic because of its Constitution seems to me an obvious reversal of the relation, it is much more plausible to suppose that the Constitution has remained because our society is essentially democratic."[8] Purcell writes, "Dahl assumed that American practice was the criterion for democratic theory itself."[9]

In the 1950s classical/normative democratic theory was attacked by theorists as overoptimistic about the role of citizens in a democracy. Voters were viewed as irrational, and few took part in politics. As a result, an elitist theory of democracy developed. Elites were praised as valuable protectors of society, as we saw in Truman's group theory. The consensus in America was within the elite. Elites represented groups better than members. While Truman argued that the private interest group process was a mini-government, allowing moderate policy change as it interacted with formal government agencies, Dahl emphasized that free-forming elites, dispersed inequalities, and public official fear of being replaced meant the American political system was democratic and *open* to all.[10]

Dahl argued that individual and group economic, social, and educational inequalities are somehow ameliorated (if not completely eliminated) by the American political system. Dahl, the pluralist, emphasized the positive benefits of federalism. He argued that federalism, local politics, and grass roots politics are good for our political system because they keep sensitive questions out of the national arena. This reduces the potential for political conflict, and reducing conflict is itself a positive end and primary goal of the pluralists. Dahl writes, "The importance of taking conflicts out of the national context can hardly be overestimated, particularly in a large country like the United States where there is great diversity of resources and local problems."[11] In Dahl's study of New Haven, he showed that most citizens were uninvolved and unconcerned about politics while elites were self-selected, broad in outlook and open to demands from below, and they moved freely among different issues.[12] Like Truman, Dahl believed it was not difficult to influence public policy. Both he and Truman sought to present realistic rather than normative theories of democracy. Because social scientists believed democratic procedures had been institutionalized in America, issues of stability and retarding the development of mass movements dominated political science.

Dahl does not have a deep fear that judicial review runs counter to the wishes of the governing coalition. This is not surprising, given Dahl's generally uncritical view of American politics, his failure to see significant structural biases in American federalism, and his views about the permeability of all institutions, including the Supreme Court, by the dominant elected political coalition of each historical period. Dahl contends that the judicial standards of justice, after some delay, will mirror the dominant political alliance. He argues against a stronger process of judicial review because he fears it would nationalize issues and raise the likelihood of conflict. Given this benign view of the

76 normal American political system, an active Court that allows wider citizen and group access on economic and social issues is not necessary. Like some process- *and* rights-oriented legal scholars, Dahl argues that on questions of state and local government power in areas other than race prejudice, the Supreme Court should not oppose the president and Congress; he sees only a limited role for judicial review. Dahl is more concerned than critical pluralists about the fact that the Supreme Court is not elected.[13]

Dahl's *Preface to Democratic Theory* was published in 1956, three years after the start of the Warren Court. Truman's classic work was published in 1951, two years before the Warren Court era began. Prior to the publication of these books, each scholar had outlined his realist position in articles. During this period in social science, "since ethical and empirical theory were conceptually though unconsciously fused, reality became the standard not only of systematic analysis but also of ethical behavior. That ambiguity created a fundamental reversal of roles. On an ethical level, reality became the standard to evaluate ideals, rather than ideals the standard by which to judge reality."[14] The relativist theory of democracy dominated American thought for two decades after World War II.

However, it is important to note that in the late 1950s and 1960s, during the heyday of relativist democratic theory, some scholars, such as Michael Rogin, Jack Walker, Grant McConnell, and Theodore Lowi, rejected realist democratic theory. Dahl himself questioned it in works written after 1964.[15] Their questioning of pluralist interpretations of American politics would form the intellectual basis for the reintroduction of traditional normative concerns into the systematic study of American politics and judicial process.

Non-Euclideanism, Scientific Naturalism, and Instrumental Interpretations of the Supreme Court

Out of the antiabsolutism and relativism of theories of democracy, non-Euclideanism, and newly redefined scientific naturalism grew our analysis of the Supreme Court in the postwar period—the election returns, policymaking, safety valve, and biographical approaches.

The acceptance of relativist democratic theory in the election returns approach can be seen in its key assumptions: a rejection of the autonomy of the Supreme Court from the wider political system; a rejection of differences between courts and elected bodies as policymaking institutions; a rejection of the independent effect of fundamental polity and rights values and precedent on Court choices; the view of natural rights ideas as anachronistic; a rejection of faith in constitutional principles as limiting politics; a belief in naturalistic, bottom-line views of Court action as a product of "interests," whether as supporters of the majority coalition, the New Deal, or the pluralist political system; the rejection of the possibility of neutral principles or the refusal to search for them as at the core of Court action or constitutional theory; the reinterpretation of the Madisonian principles of *Federalist* no. 10 from "thou shalt nots" to justifications for pluralist politics and a weaker Court role; a changing view of democratic theory from a set of future normative hopes for society and human participation; and support of popular sovereignty over fundamental rights in the Constitution as a basis for determining Court role.

The election returns approach is not only bad empiricism—in that it overstates the degree to which pluralist politics creates political change—but it also weakens constitutional theory by undermining polity principles, such as separation of powers and the autonomy of Court from politics. Likewise, it undermines fundamental rights principles in a way that does not occur in the writing of more legally oriented scholars.

We see similar linkages between relativist theories of democracy and the policymaking approach in the following characterizations of the Warren Court: the rejection of any significant differences between policymaking and legal institutions; the rejection of a separate place of principles and precedent as informing Supreme Court choices; the view that principles are used instrumentally to justify policy wants; the belief that the Court is, and should be, responsive to public sentiments and the general political climate rather than to constitutional values and precedent; the idea that Court choices are incremental variations of previous Court choices, viewed as policy choices; a rejection of the independent role of internal Court deliberations informing doctrinal change; the notion that preferred position and judicial self-restraint approaches to Court action are myths or ideologies to justify policy wants of the children of the New Deal, rather than judicial philosophies with neutral polity and rights principles; the idea that the primary objective of all Warren Court justices, whatever their philosophies, is to continue the redistribution of goods to those who benefit from the New Deal coalition; and, finally, the rejection of the Ninth Amendment view that all fundamental rights have not and could not have been written into the Constitution, and that these fundamental rights, rather than policy wants, inform justices' choices.

Like the election returns and policymaking approaches, the safety valve approach accepts the pluralist assumption that electorally based institutions function well. The Court plays a stronger role than in the election returns approach, and its objective is less directly policy-related than in the policymaking approach. The safety valve approach also views Court action in instrumental terms—as keeping the political system open. The relative democratic theory roots in the safety valve approach are evident in its rejection of a Supreme Court that would engage in a strong reinterpretation of individual rights based on acceptance of foundational polity and rights principles. Keeping the political system open, according to this approach, means that the Court should take a pragmatic look at our society and break down the most egregious barriers to access by citizens. There are no deep separation of powers, Tenth Amendment, *Federalist* no. 10, Reconstruction amendments, or other foundational principles at work in the safety valve approach. Instead it builds on the pluralist belief in the wonders of the American political system. The role of the Court is to help an already open, structurally unbiased political system operate in the few instances when blockages are identified.

Of the four major approaches to interpreting the Warren Court, the biographical approach relies least on a relativist theory of democracy and faith in the pluralist political system. It takes seriously the view that justices apply polity and rights principles in deciding cases, that precedent is important, and that deliberations and constitutional philosophies are not merely covers for justices' policy wants. Nor does this approach view the members of the Court as fulfilling the policy wants of the majority coalition or the constituents of the New Deal. It sees the Court as more independent of polity than do the election returns and policymaking approaches. Unlike the safety valve approach, the biographical approach identifies more than process liberalism—keeping the political process open—as the primary objective of the Warren Court. Both polity principles, such as process liberalism, and rights principles, such as substantive liberalism, inform Court choices. However, the biographical approach does tie into instrumental relativist theories of democracy and "interest" notions of Court action. It rejects the separation of law and politics and the autonomy of the Court from wider society by seeking to explain Court action by the "real world" personal histories of the justices. The constitutional text does not command the justice to follow its polity and rights principles. Nor should the justices follow such commands because *from an institutional effectiveness* perspective the Supreme Court must take judicial self-restraint seriously and be very craftsmanlike in its decisions.[16] Therefore, like the other three approaches, the biographical approach builds on assumptions fostered by the relative democratic theory predominant in the Warren Court era, but to a lesser degree.

From Normative to Relative Legal Theory:
The Rise of Legal Realism

The election returns, policymaking, safety valve, and biographical approaches were also significantly influenced by the legal realist movement at major law schools, which accepted non-Euclidean and scientific naturalist principles.[17] The battle lines between those who accepted foundational principles behind the law and those who did not were even clearer in legal than in social science circles. However, the influence of legal realism may have been greater among political scientists interpreting the Court, and legal scholars in areas other than constitutional law, than among constitutional law scholars.

Legal realists in the 1930s and 1940s argued that judicial decisions were not the product of impartial logic but rather of the personal values of judges. Their attack focused on the formalistic, deductive concepts of legal reasoning, natural law, and the use of precedent—syllogistic reasoning from rules and precedent to fact, to outcomes. They attacked the idea of judging as a process wherein the judge discovers analytically the proper rules and precedent and applies them in cases. They also took issue with the view that rules of law were founded on unchanging principles of rights and justice. By the mid-1930s the legal realists had labeled concepts of law as mere method and argued that the personal values of justices informed their decisions.[18]

Legal realists also questioned the fairness of judicial process. Sociological jurisprudence was at the core of this approach to the law, as legal realists studied the behavior of judges and courts. Jerome Frank, for example, argued that judicial opinions were rationalizations of judges' wants. For Frank, it was personal prejudice, subjective "facts," and jurists' concepts of justice as well as their social and political prejudices that decided cases. Borrowing from psychoanalytic theory, he showed that law as principle was a myth and that the judge was viewed as a father and infallible, whereas the citizen was a child. Lawyers and judges manipulated abstract concepts, precedent, and rules of law to get outcomes they wanted. The law had no independent force or moral basis, but was the result of this process of manipulation.

The realists shared the assumptions of the new social science—the empirical basis for knowledge. They questioned the idea of government as rule by laws rather than men; they viewed the administration of law as based on subjective beliefs of the judge. An intuitive sense of right and wrong, not legal absolutes, informed judicial choices. Purcell argues, "The rejection of the orthodox theory of judicial decision was the central point of the realist critique, and it relied heavily on non-Euclidean assumptions. . . . [The theoretical force of the realist critique] rejected any concept of higher law that could provide judges with objective, rational guidance to assure a just operative law."

Not all legal scholars shared these legal realist assumptions. Some argued that standards external to empirical facts were needed; others pointed out that by excluding ethical considerations and employing philosophical nominalism, the realists were destroying the ethical bases of law and democracy, leaving force as the sole arbiter of human affairs.[19] They argued that the rejection of natural law undermined the ethical bases of democracy—its moral foundations. Purcell identifies two problems created by the realists: "First, how could the idea of the subjectivity of judicial decision be squared with the doctrine that free men should be subject only to known and established law, one of the hallmarks of republican as opposed to despotic government? Second, if the acts of government officials were the only real law, on what basis could anyone evaluate or criticize those acts? What, in other words, was the moral basis of the legal system in particular, and of democratic government in general?"

80   Thus the scholars' objective became rethinking the theoretical and empirical bases of democracy and law in a way that defined the differences between democracy and totalitarianism. Like the social scientists, legal scholars attempted to demonstrate that democracy in general and in the United States in particular was superior to totalitarianism, and to do so in a way that did not return to discredited notions of faith in logic, absolutism, or moral foundationalism but supported scientific naturalism as a method of inquiry.

Legal Theory as Craft: How Relativist Theory
Worked Its Way into Legal Theory

In the 1950s scholars accepted legal realist opposition to doctrinal formalism, yet they sought, through better-crafted judicial opinions and more precision as to what is considered the "proper" jurisdiction and roles of courts and political institutions, to renew their faith in law and courts. Their emphasis on craft and rules included the following principles: formalistic rules in law are not possible; rules are not mechanical and self-executing; a proper legal education includes understanding the *purpose* of rules; one understands the purpose of rules by understanding that there is an agreement on common values and purposes for governmental and institutional roles; deference to legislatures is in order when they define purposes for legislation; law is not independent of social, economic, and political systems; and our political system works well.

A major concern of legal thought after World War II was how to react to legal realist attacks on the autonomy of law. The solution was that well-trained lawyers engaging in the adversary process, by employing their craft, would aid the pluralist political system. In the 1950s scholars argued that lawyers could learn a special form of legal reasoning and legal process that would allow legal institutions to meld easily with political institutions and would support the workings of the open pluralist political system. No longer could many legal scholars and jurists accept the legal formalism of the pre–legal realist era, with clear-cut general theory and principles to be applied by logical deduction. There were no self-executing legal doctrines.

The new kind of formalism was institutional, concerned with the appropriate role for courts, legislatures, and administration in a smooth-functioning political process. It emphasized the limits of courts' competence, federalism, and the benefits of having many points of access to the political system.

Bruce Ackerman has described the view of lawyering in the 1950s and 1960s as "reactive." Such lawyering does not question the economic and social foundations of law; it raises no questions of efficiency and justice of institutionalized practices; it views all legal arguments in terms of stable, accepted, prevailing practices; its norm is present social practice; original disputants, not others who are affected by the practice at issue in a lawsuit, dominate lawyers' concerns; and narrow problem definitions are the norm.[20]

Henry Hart's and Albert Sacks's unpublished textbook, "The Legal Process: Basic Problems in the Making and Application of Law" was unusually influential in the training of the Warren Court–era lawyers who would populate law firms and later positions of power in our society. In fact, Ackerman calls it "undoubtedly the most influential unpublished work in modern legal history." Hart and Sacks trained lawyers to understand how their clients' interests were mediated by the ongoing interaction between Court, bureaucracy, and legislature. According to Ackerman, "Courts were to be instructed elaborately upon their own lawmaking limitations compared with bureaucracies and legislatures." They were urged to "identify those legal functions better performed by other elements in the activist lawmaking system" and help institutions work together in a partnership for the public good.[21]

Ackerman argues that Hart and Sacks used inadequate models of the legislative and bureaucratic processes and failed to provide realistic, rigorous, and complex conceptions of these institutions. They viewed mistakes by institutions as isolated blunders rather than as systemic failures. Most important, the legal process scholars did not link views of process to power relationships and legal substance. Lawyers were trained to accept and support the pluralist political system, not to be critical of it or view the law as a means to secure rights and process changes when inequalities were identified. Hart and Sacks's assumption of coherence and stability was quite similar to Dahl's and Truman's analyses of equilibrium in the political system. Law became merely narrow problem solving within the view that all agreed on basic polity, rights, and legal principles.[22] This process view of democracy—democracy as method rather than a set of rights notions or standards that were to act as benchmarks for evaluating the political system—led to arguments over how each part of the political system was to do its different and special job to promote the whole.

Hart and Sacks emphasized the central place of procedures in a complex, interdependent society, the need for institutional settlements, a concern for justice, and the relationship of private decisions to public ones.[23] However, their definition of justice remained unclear, implicit in what lawyers and courts do. Legal academics were concerned about constitutional law, administrative law, procedure, and jurisdiction. Federal jurisdiction, craft orientation, and an emphasis on procedure dominated legal thinking (in a way that Sanford Levinson argues has occurred again in the 1980s).[24] Technical questions of whether a case involved a state or federal issue were central in law schools.

The institutional formalism and problem solving approach of Hart and Sacks, falsely labeled "nonideological," accepted to a degree the legal realist criticism of legal principles—that they were neither consistent nor above politics. However, it is important to note that Hart and Sacks differed in significant ways from the scholars who tried to explain doctrinal change on the Warren Court through the election returns, policymaking, and safety valve approaches. At least in Hart and Sacks's legal process approach, law and politics were somewhat separate and could be discussed in institutional terms. Also, injuries to particular clients or groups by regulators were seen as mistakes by government, even though there was not a strong antigovernment bias in the legal process approach.

The implications of the relativist theory of democracy and legal realism created the view that the Supreme Court is an institution that uses ideas and theory instrumentally to achieve policy outcomes. In the election returns, policymaking, and safety valve interpretations, and to a lesser degree in White's biographical approach, we see the transfer of central principles of the relativist theory of democracy to these instrumental interpretations of the Warren Court.

Uncritical Pluralism and Warren Court–Era Constitutional Theory

Hart and Sacks's view of legal theory did not constitute the entire landscape. A group of important constitutional scholars refused to accept the judicial process view of legal institutions. Three of the most prominent were Alexander Bickel, Paul Freund, and Herbert Wechsler, of Yale, Harvard, and Columbia law schools, respectively.

These three accepted the political theory of Robert Dahl, which stressed that the political system was quite open to political change. However, unlike Dahl and Truman, they could not reject the idea that it is the Supreme Court's role to interpret the fundamental rights and polity principles in the Constitution. In this light, they were the liberals of their day, for they did not fall back on pure craft and mechanics but agreed that rights values existed and needed protection. Ironically, the Warren Court was at the same time arguing that the failure of pluralism required that courts enter the political thicket in race and other areas.

These scholars did not reject rights-based choices. Nor did they, as Martin Shapiro argues, base their views on New Deal policy objectives. They had serious concerns about the nature of the American polity and of institutional needs of the Court within the polity, even when they approved the policy of the Warren Court. They were concerned about the relationship between polity and rights principles, even though they did not offer systematic constitutional theory as to how polity and rights values should inform constitutional choices.

Alexander Bickel

A review of Bickel's scholarship reveals a tension between rights- and process-based principles and action by the Supreme Court and a growing dislike for rights-based principles.[25] Although he never completely rejected the idea of rights-based Supreme Court choices, he always opposed rights-based theory and rights creation by the Court as a *usual* basis for its decisionmaking. At first Bickel sought to find neutral principles on which the Supreme Court could base its choices, although he never believed that the neutrality Wechsler advocated was possible. Central to his work was a concern for the nature of polity. In his early work he presented critical views about the political system, especially with regard to its ability to deal fairly with race issues.[26] In his later books we see a less critical view of political institutions in his impassioned opposition to rights creation and Court restructuring of the political process; at the same time, his support for pluralist politics increases. Bickel rejected the simple majoritarian populist view of polity that he saw implicit in *Baker v. Carr* (1962) and stated his opposition to the Warren Court principle of one person–one vote.[27] He also solidified his support for a Dahlian view of pluralism and his opposition to the ad hoc subjectivity of the Warren Court. He opposed broad rights declarations by the Court and the development of national norms. He saw localism and state choice of values as better for pluralism and judicial review as only one of many institutions of choice in the pluralist political system. He feared that support for the group process and its legitimacy would be undermined by the Supreme Court's usurping the place of other institutions in making public policy choices.

> It can be said, therefore, that the Warren Court's imposition of majoritarianism as the operative principle of political organization, and its conception of its own function were congruent. They met in the premise that the majoritarian process must, and perhaps if it works correctly will, produce certain results, which are given *a priori*. When it does not at the level of one constituency, it should be tried again at the higher level of another one. And when it doesn't at all, the Court will supply the deficiency.[28]

Bickel argued that we should trust the complexity of pluralist political institutions to make up for miscarriages of the majoritarian system.

In *The Morality of Consent* (1975), we see Bickel's most vehement opposition to a rights-based constitutional law and his support for pluralism and a limited role for judicial review. He seems to say that in the American theory of law the rights of individuals do not have an independent, theoretical existence apart from the institutions that citizens and leaders set up.[29] He believes in certain rights in the Constitution, such as property rights, but he fears conflict over abstractions, absolute egalitarianism, and usurpation by the Supreme Court of the role of political institutions in creating rights and making public choices. He supports state choices on right to abortion, that is, federal courts' supporting procedural but not substantive due process. He wants legislatures, not courts, to decide funding criteria, such as the right to welfare. He opposes

84   the contractarian rights view that the Warren Court had brought to its judicial
decisionmaking. Law is not a set of binding principles or rights, not an implied contract with citizens, but rather the result of institutional choice and
cross-checking in the Madisonian game of group and institutional politics.

What is significant in Bickel's jurisprudence is that it begins to explore the
tension between a rights-based, pro–judicial review type of jurisprudence and
a process-based, limited view of judicial review and rights creation by the
Court, a question that dominates modern constitutional theory. It was his
failure to maintain this early view of the tension between a rights- and process-
based law that led to a scholarship of expedience and policy choices in his later
works.[30] (This problem continues at a different level in modern commentary
on the Supreme Court.) Bickel's support for a pluralist concept of polity and
his faith in political institutions lead to his criticism of rights creation by the
Court.

As constitutional theory changed in the mid to late 1960s, scholarly interpretations of polity changed from pluralist to critical pluralist. Our comparison of the constitutional theory of Bickel, Freund, and Wechsler suggests that
while there is a variance in polity and rights values among these scholars, it
centers on a pluralist view of polity that triggers support for limited rights creation by courts: judicial self-restraint. But the variance among scholars in this
period is not as great as the variance that developed among the constitutional
theorists of the mid-1970s and 1980s, when a critical pluralist interpretation
of American politics dominated constitutional theory.

For Anthony Kronman, an important scholar of Bickel and postwar constitutional theory, "the distinction between prudence and its opposite—an
abstracted indifference to the intransigent complexities of the world—provides
the unifying theme in all of Bickel's work and represents the core of his political philosophy."[31] Bickel tried to resolve the tension between majoritarianism
and the need for enduring values by prescribing that the Court engage in
"prudence" and "passive virtues." Values promoted in Bickel's view of prudence were slow, gradual advancement of ideals; complex, historically evolved
institutions; modesty in institutional reform; high toleration for accommodation and delay; and acceptance of the final incommensurability among any
system of ideas, the world as given to us, and the need for the process of rational compromise. Prudence defined the needed skills of the judge and poli-
tician. Bickel viewed "impatient, uncompromising, and overly philosophical
insistence on principles, for their own sake, . . . as the antithesis of prudence
[and] a disabling vice in both statecraft and adjudication." Abstract theories
had a "tyrannical tendency"; Bickel believed that good practical wisdom, not
theory and ideology, should dominate politics.

Like Michael Perry years later, Bickel thought that the Court could legitimately postpone a decision that would cause fierce resistance. For Bickel, the

"colloquy" between the Court and the rest of society that the delay produces helps the Court better understand the issues involved. Partial solutions by the Court are also acceptable to Bickel. The internal aspect of decisionmaking must be principled. Bickel views the external aspect as a political process that requires not reflection or scholarly wisdom, "but skill in the arts of compromise" and knowledge of "muddling through." Kronman argues that Bickel's view of American democracy also reflected his prudential outlook. Bickel accepted the group as the unit of analysis of politics. For him, the formal system of checks and balances, malapportionment in the service of group representation, unit rule voting in the electoral college, and two-part government "form a complex scheme whose elements sustain, through a subtle interaction, the conditions required for a stable democracy." For Bickel, any attempt to reduce the political system's complexity to a single theoretical principle—such as one person, one vote—will leave out much that is of value in the existing arrangements and will "upset the balance produced by the scheme's mutually supporting parts."

In arguing for Bickel's prudentialism, Kronman fails to place his constitutional theory within the context of the dominant pluralist view of polity and democratic relativism of his age. Legal scholars today reject Bickel's view of the Court's role, and they also reject his view of pluralist polity because it does not see structural inequality. According to Kronman, Bickel was in awe of how well our political system was operating. He was training students, future lawyers and judges, to lead a double life—an internal life concerned with principles and an external life in which they limited the effects of the principled internal life whenever prudentialism required it. To make changes in the institutions and practices of government they would have to come back another day.

This split Bickel creates in the life of the mind undermines the fundamental rights values in the Constitution; it also provides a view of polity and Court role that is less critical of politics than the Founders wanted and it undermines the natural rights part of our tradition. There is no strong polity- or rights-based critical standard of evaluation in his theory; instead, Bickel's prudence argument makes the real world the standard of evaluation in each legal problem or decision.[32]

It seems clear that Alexander Bickel had a complexity to his jurisprudence not seen in the judicial process or craft views of his contemporaries. While Bickel accepted the apologetic pluralist polity principles of his day, he could not view the Court in the narrow policymaking framework of the election returns or policymaking approaches to doctrinal change. Though he did not like grand moral theory, he could not eschew the fundamental rights visions in the Constitution. Thus for Bickel rights and principles must inform the Court's choices, even if grand moral and constitutional theory is not at the center of his constitutional theory.

Paul Freund

To a greater degree than Bickel, Paul Freund acknowledged that the Supreme Court must demonstrate its concern for constitutive rights and polity principles when it makes constitutional choices. However, Freund cautioned about the need for craftsmanship, respect for group politics, and the balancing of concerns for principle with the specific policy outcomes and views of other institutions. "If the first requisite of a constitutional judge is that he be a philosopher," Freund writes, "the second requisite is that he be not too philosophical."[33] Freund believed that the Supreme Court should avoid making statements on absolutes—what is demanded of liberty or equality. It must be pragmatic, but not to the point of rejecting all principles behind its choices. He favored a balancing type of jurisprudence, in which cases would be decided on their particular policy factors. But he believed that the courts must do more than replicate political institutions; they should moderate conflict in society. All should realize, though, that the Court does have the power of judicial review.

Freund had great respect for judicial power and usually wrote in support of the Court when it chose to engage in judicial review. He was more concerned with the Court's method of action than with questions of its legitimacy, yet he wrote against unbridled scholarly criticism, always fearing a loss of legitimacy for the Court. Implicit in the Court decisionmaking method Freund advocated was opposition to a rights-based activism, because balancing requires limits on rights creation by the Court. Yet I see no opposition in principle by Freund to rights creation. He favored incrementalism when establishing new rights or constitutional principles.

> Can any discipline be more valuable today than one that teaches us to look through the great antinomies that present themselves like gladiators for our favors—individualism and collectivism, liberty and authority, secularism and clericalism—to look through them in order to discover the precise issue in controversy, the precise consequences of one decision or another, and the possibility of an accommodation by deflating the isms and narrowing the schisms? This is the task, and at its best, the accomplishment of the law, and particularly of the judges in constitutional law.[34]

His work, perhaps more than any other, shows the impossibility of a strict process- or rights-based constitutional theory, but Freund's commitment to the Court as a rights-based institution never wavered.

Like many scholars of his day, Freund saw the genius of American politics in our nation's lack of absolutism in political theory and process. But unlike Bickel, he did not see American pluralism threatened by Supreme Court action in the reapportionment of other cases. He opposed broad-based conceptualism as a basis for the law, while not opposing a "quiet" rights basis for constitutional choices. He saw a much more limited role for judicial process than that laid out by either the rights- or the process-based theorists of today. His scholarship suggests that he would oppose the conflict between process and rights principles as a method of approaching criticism of the Court, for they are based on absolutes. For Freund, it was essential that judicial choices be based on concern for both types of principle. However, in Freund's scholarship we do not see a clearly articulated tension between the two, for each decision and constitutional choice must be looked at in terms of the fact situation, expedience, rights protection, incremental imposition of change, and respect for, but not obeisance to, other political institutions in our society:

> The role of the courts in maintaining a working federalism is precisely this task of mediation between large principles and particular problems, the task of interposing intermediate principles more tentative, experimental, and pragmatic. The courts are the sub-stations that transform the high-tension charge of the philosophers into the reduced voltage of a serviceable current. . . . For judicial review is not merely a derivative from a society in agreement on fundamentals; in itself it is an educative and formative influence that, like the legal idea of a fair trial, may have consequences beyond its immediate application for the mind of a people.[35]

Herbert Wechsler

Herbert Wechsler is both representative of constitutional scholars in the 1950s and early 1960s and an excellent transition figure to modern constitutional theory.[36] Like later rights and process theorists, Wechsler hoped to develop a principled basis for the Court's choices rather than have them rest on policy ramifications and contextual factors. For Wechsler, the Court's constitutional action must be judicial rather than political. In order for the Court not to be an organ of naked power it must make its choices on the basis of neutral principles.[37]

This means that the Court makes value choices. Wechsler admits that it does. It also means requiring that the Court make each decision on the basis of principles articulated before it hears a specific case, rather than in the context of each case or in terms of policy wants. For example, in his analysis of *Brown v. Board of Education* (1954), Wechsler argued that the Court should have based its decision on the right to association rather than the right of blacks not to attend racially (de jure) segregated schools. A race-neutral principle for that case would not place the Court in the position of making "political" choices on the basis of the race of groups seeking Court action. It should simply prohibit laws that prevent citizens from associating with each other in public institutions.

Implicit in Wechsler's theory is the notion that Courts should not act like political institutions by making policy based on its fact, degree, and value choices *in each case*. In contrast to Bickel and Freund, who hoped the Court would seek accommodation with political institutions without causing egregious rights violations, the primary concern for Wechsler was that the Court not make constitutional choices merely because those choices would be politically acceptable to citizens, political institutions, or the justices themselves.

Unfortunately, implicit in Wechsler's jurisprudence is a method that severely restricts the role of the Supreme Court in our system of government: The Court cannot act until it is willing to make a principle applicable to many cases of injustice rather than choosing only to intervene to stop the worst instances of injustice. Ending de facto segregation and allowing affirmative action would not fare well under Wechsler's systems, since the Court would have to decide how many economic and social inequalities public officials should be allowed or required to alleviate through the use of their power. These are clearly consequentialist policy choices; they would undermine the legitimacy of the Court, Wechsler argued, by demonstrating that the Court made *specific* policy and value choices.

Wechsler also supported the dominant pluralist interpretation of the nature of the political system. But unlike Bickel, and to a lesser degree Freund, Wechsler believed in the rights basis of constitutional law and the need for the Court to make principled decisions. When the Court makes its decisions, it is to make them on a basis that would not open them to debates over what specific factors or consequences are to be allowed or not allowed by the Court. Unfortunately, the result of the method Wechsler advocated was similar to that of Bickel's method: great deference to choices made by the political system. However, the antagonism found throughout Bickel's scholarship to the idea of the Court's making rights-based choices is missing from Wechsler's work, as is the fear of absolutist rights bases of choices found in Freund's work. For to base judicial review and choices on neutral principles as defined by Wechsler, such as the right of association, would force the Court to intervene in the decisionmaking process and the substantive policymaking of electorally accountable political institutions to a degree that was not politically acceptable to the jurists and political leaders of the day.

Wechsler's jurisprudence was a reaction to the consequentialist balancing jurisprudence advocated by Freund and engaged in by Bickel. His neutral principles view of judicial decisionmaking opposed not only the craft view of his colleagues but also the result-oriented interpretation of doctrinal change and the Warren Court that is endemic to the election returns, policymaking, and safety valve approaches. It also was the start of the search that continues today for a more principled theory of constitutional law. Wechsler argued that if neutral, non-case-specific principles could be developed, then judicial review would be less "political." If a decision could be justified as neutral, non-case-specific, and principled, then the Court would be viewed as above politics and above making substantive policy choices in each case.

This approach would allow, in my terms, the Court to become a partner in the pluralist political process rather than simply identifying bases for conflict among groups, then being forced to make value choices about which groups are in unequal positions in the political system. It would further deny a conflict or inequality view of polity—a critical pluralist view—and reaffirm the principled nature of judicial decisionmaking and law, thus attacking a major criticism that the legal realists have leveled at courts and the legal process for many years.

However, in defining neutral, non-case-specific choices, the Court searches for consensus, not structural inequalities. It is not forced to decide which groups have power or to make fundamental substantive choices about moral values. But moral value choices must still be made. There is no way to deny the moral or value choices that are interior to a constitutional theory.

Wechsler's association notion was the most general level of argument one could make against segregation, for it had the least content. It did not address the intentions of political elites or federalism concerns. When an argument has content and makes choices about who is morally good and bad, it opposes the idea of a pluralist equilibrium. Therefore, legal theory and education in the 1950s had within them a deep program of social control whose objective was supporting the consensus about polity and law that they believed existed. When scholars assume that there is a consensus on values and institutional roles, they can avoid searching for those values. Consensus scholars of the 1950s agreed with *Brown v. Board of Education*, but they could not justify their agreement. To do so they would have had to make value choices about what is just and what the nature of individual rights should be, choices that violated their institutional and craft values, which were based on apologetic pluralist interpretations of legal and political institutions.

Explaining Misperceptions of the Warren Court Era: The Inadequacy of Instrumental Approaches

Our misperception of the Warren Court cannot be completely explained by exploring the effect of instrumental approaches on internal Supreme Court decisionmaking. We must also assess the relationship among the interpretive community, the Supreme Court, and instrumental approaches to doctrinal change and specify an alternative constitutive interpretation of that relationship. In this interpretation, the relationship of the interpretive community to

90   doctrinal change is important, as are the linkages between the interpretive community and the Supreme Court. I will argue that the Supreme Court does not use contemporary constitutional theory instrumentally to make its constitutional choices, but enters into a dialogic relationship with the interpretive community.

Because legal scholars, even in this age of apologetic pluralism, viewed the Constitution in terms of fundamental rights and polity principles, they could support the Warren Court as it worked out the fundamental polity and rights conflicts they had been trained to understand. In contrast to legal scholars, many political scientists continued to view the Supreme Court in lumpen non-Euclidean and scientific naturalist terms by converting the Court into a policymaking institution bereft of normative conflict over polity and rights principles.

According to Purcell, the emphasis on cultural agreement that lay behind the relativist theory of democracy led to the assumption that America enjoyed an underlying political consensus that stabilized society—a consensus rooted in common lives, habits, institutions, and experiences of generations, not in ideology. The belief in the existence of a cultural consensus informed the work of many political scientists and sociologists. It also led to the difficulty already mentioned that some scholars had in justifying the *Brown* decision. Furthermore, if the real basis of democracy was cultural consensus, intellectual diversity, and group competition, then the economic structure itself was of only subsidiary importance. Economic inequality was no longer a grave threat to democracy, because the cultural consensus accepted the capitalist economic system.

> Finally, and of the greatest significance, the relativist theory led intellectuals to assume that American society was not only good, but that it was itself a normative phenomenon. Accepting the relativist-absolutist dichotomy, they perceived America as pluralistic. The very idea of a science of society contained a normative implication; for, when social scientists thought they had discovered the social and cultural prerequisites for democracy, those prerequisites became a kind of norm—the conditions that must be present in order to sustain a democracy. Assuming that America was pluralistic they assumed that it fulfilled these conditions. Inheriting the prescriptive-descriptive ambiguity of the relativist theory, they came to assume that the country's pluralism represented both the empirically necessary foundation for democratic government and at the same time the institutionalization of the ethical relativism that justified democracy in theory. Under the pressure of the cold war and the unconscious conceptual fusion of the prescriptive and the descriptive, American society gradually emerged as an empirical and a moral norm for democratic government.[38]

Scholars who supported the instrumental election returns, policymaking, safety valve, and biographical approaches to doctrinal change for the most part accepted the view of the American political and legal system as a normative phenomenon. The prescriptive assumption of their empirical studies comparing legal and political institutions among nations or within the United States was that American law and politics were good. In so doing, they misperceived the Warren Court. Supreme Court justices and many legal scholars, especially the most influential constitutional scholars of the day, could not accept apologetic pluralist principles for reasons explored earlier. Because they could not, they could accept doctrinal innovations in ways that many political scientists could not.

The Warren Court could not accept America as a normative phenomenon. Chief Justice Warren and a majority of the Court represented the view that the polity was not operating as the pluralist equilibrium model had said it would, and they adopted this view before it was formalized by scholars in the late 1950s and early 1960s. The Warren Court's continuing debate over the place of relativist democratic views of polity and intuitive justice notions helps explain its accomplishments.

In the Warren Court era there was a mismatch between the view of polity held by the Court and that held by the nation and most of the interpretive community. To explain this mismatch we need to realize that polity principles *mediate* the ways rights issues are debated in the Supreme Court, the interpretive community, and the wider society. The genius of the Warren Court was not that it created rights, as most scholars argue, but that it placed into its jurisprudence a critical pluralist interpretation of politics and introduced political change while appearing to stay within a civil liberties paradigm that saw rights as individual, not group-based, and groups in equilibrium, rather than in conflict, when seeking to protect the interests of minority groups against majority prejudice.

Although the Warren Court's critical view of polity did significantly counter political and social inequality, it did not trigger radical change because it did not make manifest the effects of deep social, gender, and economic inequality. For example, in *Shapiro v. Thompson* (1969), views about the effects of Court extension of economic allocations to the poor were debated in terms of the right to interstate travel, not in terms of class position and political power.

It is important to note that the Warren Court's genius was not completely of its own making. The conceptions of politics and law in the wider interpretive community during the 1950s and 1960s, which came out of the struggle to define what constitutes democracy and law and to explain why democracy exists set the backdrop for the debate about the Warren Court. The introduction of a relativist theory of democracy and a redefined scientific naturalism helps explain the mismatch between the apologetic pluralist visions of polity

92 among legal and social science critics of the Warren Court and the critical views of polity by the Court itself.

This new relativistic view of polity and moral philosophy also helps explain why legal scholars of Warren Court doctrine supported the Court's actions. Leading constitutional scholars, such as Bickel, Freund, and Wechsler, kept alive the idea that law and the Court were independent of politics. In contrast to political scientists, who advocated the election returns and policymaking approaches, most constitutional scholars accepted the Supreme Court as a definer of fundamental rights. Even those who continued to adhere to pluralist, relativist views of polity and viewed law as craft understood the moral bases of Court choices, though they "fudged" the moral bases of law through procedural definitions of constitutional questions.

By interpreting law as craft, a pluralist view, legal scholars could support the existing political and legal systems while allowing moral values, not mere proceduralism, to enter their commentary on the constitutional choices of the Warren Court. Because the Court's critical view of government extended no further than formal access, it was not far outside the pluralist equilibrium model that the relativist view of democracy supported. Legal scholars supported the Warren Court not simply because they liked its decisions, as Martin Shapiro suggests, but because the Court's criticism of the polity was relatively incremental and formal.

Critics responded to the Court's critical view of polity and pluralism by arguing that the Court and the legal system must allow the cultural norms of democracy to operate. The activist Warren Court denied the polity principles of the pluralist-relativist view of democracy that dominated the legal and nonlegal academies.

Instrumentalism and Perceptions of Civil Liberties

Another issue that must be addressed is the perception of the civil liberties perspective by jurists, lawyers, and the Warren Court compared to that of members of the interpretive community who accepted instrumental interpretations of doctrinal change. Purcell explains scholars' acceptance of the civil liberties paradigm by pointing out that it was based on assumptions similar to relativist democratic and non-Euclidean values: the moral necessity of toleration, a rejection of absolutist and class-based visions of polity and political change, and a faith in pluralist political institutions. He argues that a belief in the primacy of toleration and compromise readily led to an assumption that was useful to determined defenders of the status quo. "The assumption that a 'reasonable' compromise was always possible within a given social structure made an opposition to established institutions appear politically illegitimate."[39]

However, Purcell's picture of civil liberties as an essentially defensive doctrine understates the possibility of political change through Court action. After all, the Warren Court did explore the relationship of wealth, rights, and polity, and it also rejected the notion of the society as an open, pluralist, compromising political system. Purcell's image also oversimplifies reality by viewing the civil liberties perspective in static terms and by failing to inform us of the important differences among social scientists, craft-oriented legalists, and constitutional scholars.

In one sense the pluralist system was working, for as the academy was praising pluralist politics, the Court was restructuring polity and rights to make pluralism work better. In another sense, however, the Court was limited by pluralist theory, as when it raised issues of the relationship between economic and social inequality and public economic policies such as welfare. Thus, the Warren Court was more radical in its views about polity than about rights, and its views about justice were more intuitive than systematic. It did not defend the status quo, but it clearly rejected a deep structural view of polity.

Purcell overstates the degree to which legal scholars continued to accept the pluralist view of polity and opposed doctrinal innovation; however, he accurately views social scientists as staying with a faith in pluralist political institutions. Moreover, Purcell fails to see that although political scientists and legal scholars were influenced by the same developments in intellectual history, they responded differently. Because views about fundamental rights still existed, though in a confused state after the rejection of pure scientific naturalism, legal scholars and many political scientists believed that the Constitution could not be viewed only through institutional or polity principles. Pluralist social scientists, in contrast, expressed unquestioned faith in the American polity. Many legal scholars and political scientists continued to emphasize that the idea of justice was important and that fundamental rights, not only polity principles, still informed the Court, though less significantly than before the age of legal realism. This position provided the Supreme Court and legal scholars a basis for questioning political institutions and the status quo. Also, because of the countermajoritarian premise in judicial review, legal scholars were never as apologetic of the pluralist political system as scholars of American politics were. As Purcell argues, few intellectuals consciously pursued the logical implications of the relativist theory. For this reason the prescriptive-descriptive ambiguity in the relativist view of democracy went unnoticed.[40]

However, the dichotomy in legal theory between prescription and description is sharper than that between polity and rights principles in constitutional decisionmaking. The prescriptive element also occurs on both the polity and rights sides of the aisle. Views of justice held by legal scholars, as articulated by the Warren Court, counter the pure trust of pluralism or faith in democracy; the views held by political scientists do not. Political scientists could no longer

94   use justice and fundamental rights values to counter the effects of apologetic pluralist assumptions about politics. Thus, Purcell's argument that civil rights and civil liberties are consonant with relativist theory still begs the more interesting question: What are the limits of that consonance? Degrees of difference are very significant, for on these bases the process of political change is established. The assumption that America was the norm of democracy, morally and empirically, caused the status quo orientation of the postwar decades. "If American society was unconsciously accepted as normative," Purcell writes, "then critical theory could only be peripheral and major change unthinkable. By what other standard could American society be judged?"[41] Purcell suggests that the "is" and the "ought"—the worlds of science and of morals—are merged. In American culture the "is" is the guide to the "ought," but in constitutional theory and practice this philosophy is simply not workable.

The Election Returns Approach

As we have seen, the Warren Court rejected the apologetic pluralism of political scientists, which was wedded to relativist democratic theory. Instead, it accepted a less apologetic process and the substantive fundamental rights values held by prominent legal scholars of the day. But it did not and could not range far outside the pluralist vision of the 1950s and early 1960s.

Political scientists and legal scholars who accepted the election returns, policymaking, safety valve, and biographical approaches to doctrinal change continued to rely on core values born of non-Euclidean and scientific naturalist assumptions, founded on relativist democratic theory and legal realist interpretations of the political and legal system. These core values led them to view the Supreme Court as a policymaking institution concerned primarily with securing policy outcomes rather than employing polity and rights principles and the evaluative standards fostered by the interpretive communities. In so viewing the Supreme Court, they undervalued the interpretive community as a significant factor in doctrinal change. They also underestimated the importance of the autonomy of law and the independent effect that constitutional theory, as compared to electoral politics, can have on doctrinal change.

Employing the election returns approach, Robert Dahl emphasizes that commentary on the Warren Court, legal theory, and the development of democratic theory are irrelevant to Supreme Court choices. He argues that "the elaborate 'democratic' rationalizations of the Court's defenders and the hostility of its 'democratic' critics are largely irrelevant, for law-making majorities generally have had their way." Dahl also argues that the role of the Supreme Court must not be derived from democratic and moral theory, because few Court policy decisions can be interpreted sensibly in terms of the majority versus the minority.[42] Thus he rejects the place of moral and democratic theory in influencing Supreme Court choices.

Dahl views the Supreme Court, like other government institutions, as a policymaking forum where bargaining secures policy wants. Dahl incorrectly assumes that the Court is part of the national coalition and not different from it and that justices make decisions and are motivated by the same interests and values as those that influence elected officials.[43] He also rejects the notion that the socialization of justices through legal training and their deliberations while on the Supreme Court affect their thinking and Court doctrine.

It is impossible to accept this view because in both the Warren and Burger Court eras the debate about which polity and rights principles to employ and how to apply them was far more textured and sincere than the elections returns (or policymaking) approach suggests. It is also impossible to accept the view that the interpretive community is epiphenomenal to Supreme Court decisionmaking. The case analysis in Chapter 2 suggests that the Warren Court was aware of the apologetic pluralist definitions of American history, politics, and legal institutions—the hegemonic ideas in that era—but refused to accept them. The Court needed this awareness for its legitimacy and discipline, even as it rejected central tenets held by members of the interpretive community.[44]

Dahl believes that the interpretive community mirrors the policy wants of the majority coalition. However, Dahl's argument that the role of the Court is to confer legitimacy on the majority coalition suggests that the interpretive community is not a source of critical theory for the Court. Dahl assumes that the Court accepts the apologetic pluralist views of polity dominant in the Warren Court era, since he sees no process by which the Court learns from the interpretive community. Having rejected natural rights and fundamental rights principles as significant bases for Court action, Dahl clearly believes that Court choices based on such theory are outside the purview of doctrinal change.

There is evidence that Dahl's (and Funston's) view of the Court's role as legitimating policy actions of the majority coalition rather than the interpretive community has its roots in Dahl's acceptance of tenets of the relativist theory of democracy and legal realism. He wants the Court to legitimize public policy through its role of symbolic legitimacy, which he sees as a positive element of the pluralist political system. Dahl takes for granted the legitimacy of acts of Congress and the president.[45] Thus he views the Court as supporting what Theodore Lowi has called "interest group liberalism," and its role as essentially "symbolic." However, as the case analysis suggests, the Warren Court (and Burger Court) did not view its role as symbolic.

Members of the Supreme Court may choose to reject or accept these hegemonic polity and rights principles in different degrees, which suggests that there is a dialogic relationship between the Supreme Court and the interpretive community. The Court is autonomous of the *direct* influence of electoral politics and the interpretive community, but when it makes its choices it is fully cognizant of the boundaries of the debate within the interpretive community and within the wider, informed society as well. Its decisions are not the result of following the policy wants of the majority coalition.[46]

The Policymaking Approach

Martin Shapiro argues that to most justices, conventional legal scholarship and criticism are insignificant. "No member of the current [Burger Court] cares much about legal scholarship. . . . There is no reason not to say openly what the justices care so little to disguise, that they make their decisions on the basis of seat-of-the-pants predictions of the immediate and direct policy benefits of the various alternatives available to them. . . . Earlier Courts may have been no better. The goal of equality may be more important than the niceties of legal reasoning. Whatever defenses may be offered, it was pretty clear that by the late 1960s nobody in the Warren-Brennan majority really cared much about anything but the policy outcomes of the cases."[47] According to Shapiro, it was only when commentators became a cheering section for New Deal policy wants in the late 1960s that what they said concerned the Supreme Court.[48]

Shapiro goes even further in rejecting theory and principles as a source of Court decisionmaking. He argues that like Supreme Court justices themselves, commentators on the Warren Court do so merely to get the Court to support their policy wants. The role of the interpretive community is to offer grist for the mill, in the form of constitutional theory, to help the members of the Court and their clerks support specific outcomes. Thus, whether constitutional scholars view polity and moral principles in neutral, results-oriented, or democratic process terms, their arguments are merely instrumental, according to Shapiro, driven by their policy wants.[49]

Therefore, Shapiro's argument in baldest terms, leads to the conclusion that no constitutional or moral theory is better than any other, since the merit of a constitutional theory is not linked to polity and rights principles in the Constitution or to precedent. If the justices do not consider contemporary constitutional theory when they make constitutional choices, then there is no role for the interpretive community or constitutional theory in influencing doctrinal change. For Shapiro, the relationship between the Court and the interpretive community cannot explain *why* the Court makes specific choices, for these factors lie outside of the interpretive community. Unlike Dahl, Shapiro argues that the relationship of the Supreme Court to scholarly commentary is of some importance, but only when the commentators support the policy wishes of the Supreme Court. This relationship may explain the success of a Court in translating its policy wants into doctrine—as long as the Court and contemporary scholars agree on policy wants.

The most significant problem with Shapiro's analysis is that he views the theory and ideas held by the interpretive community as merely instrumental to outcomes in New Deal terms. He writes,

> A jurisprudence of values is a poor one if the proper function of commentators and justices is to rationalize the case law—that is, to organize the Court's decisions into consistent patterns. . . . Moreover, the gap between generalized statements of value and actual policies is so great that two persons alleging the same values may come to conflicting policy conclusions. If, on the other hand, the job of commentators and justices is to arrive at good public policy, a jurisprudence of values does have one great advantage over its predecessor. At least so long as the Court is dedicated to action, it seems more sensible to argue about what the Court should do than about whether it should do it and to praise it when it does well rather than yearn for the good deeds to be done by someone else.[50]

The problem with this formulation is that the role of commentary and constitutional theory is not to rationalize case law but to create constitutional theory that can act as a guide to constitutional choices. Mere consistency, after-the-fact analysis, is less important to constitutional scholars than is the creation of proactive polity and rights theory that can speak to the nature of political institutions and rights in light of the realities. Furthermore, Shapiro is arguing that debate over Court role, over polity principles, is not what the game was about in the post-1962 Warren Court and the Burger Court, when in fact polity principles were important to the development of constitutional law in both Court eras and continue to be important to this day.

Shapiro is on target in suggesting that moribund judicial self-restraint, nonelected Courts and democracy notions, and craftsmanship as central values were not that informative about Court role and constitutional theory. He is also correct in seeing this craft view as being overwhelmed by alternative concerns by the Warren Court. However, the cause for this lack of concern by scholars for the craft view was not because they sought specific New Deal policy wants, as Shapiro suggests. Rather, it was because many of the most influential scholars, such as Bickel, Freund, and Wechsler, saw that the Court was interpreting fundamental rights principles, and complex polity principles, principles that they valued.

To dismiss polity concerns, whether of the Supreme Court or of its commentators, as trivial compared to equality values is to misunderstand the bases of Court choices. Also, to say that constitutional theory and the interpretive community are epiphenomenal to Warren Court action, except when they act as cheerleaders for the policy wants they favor, it to trivialize the importance of constitutional theory and changing polity and rights principles held by the in-

98   terpretive community. Such a view also does not allow us to understand the place of the interpretive community and theories of doctrinal change that they hold as causes of our misperceptions of the Warren (and Burger) Court era.

The Biographical Approach

Unlike the election returns and policymaking approaches, White analyzes the Warren Court in terms of the constitutional theory of its day. He argues that Chief Justice Warren and a majority of the Court were not socialized into the dominant constitutional theory and view of the Court role of their era. Instead, he views Warren as reacting to the interpretations of American politics and legal theories of his day, which focused on the questions of craftsmanship, stare decisis, ethical values, and outcome-oriented jurisprudence. White argues that we see Warren viewing constitutional theory as in a tortured state. Warren "rejected the constraints of doctrinal consistency and institutional deference, often encapsulated in the phrase 'principled adjudication,' when he felt that those constraints served to divert attention from the ethical imperatives of a case."[51]

Warren believed that blacks, suburbanites, indigent criminals, atheists, and Communist sympathizers were not protected by the passive theory of judicial review, a theory that some scholars said was advocated by the Founders and that many contemporary constitutional scholars accepted. White views Warren as concerned with ethical imperatives and opposed to institutional principles of deference to political institutions.[52] Justices should be viewed as participants in an interpretive community and era, White argues, and his point is significant. The fact that a justice chooses to support or reject the dominant constitutive polity and rights values of an era is evidence that the interpretive community does influence Court choices and definitions of constitutional problems.

White analyzes the commentators of the Warren Court as products of their socialization into constitutional theories and judicial roles through their training and professional life. He argues that many commentators on the Warren Court sought a return to a Supreme Court that was independent of direct involvement in politics and policymaking—a Court that trusted political institutions. But it was Warren's independence from the corpus of judicial wisdom that many feared—especially as a general statement of Court decisionmaking power because the "rightness" of a decision based on personal ethical principles turned on intuitive perceptions of morality and justice rather than "technical or recondite learning."[53]

Such criticism of Warren was an outgrowth of what White called a theory of judicial "good sense," most famously argued by Harvard Law School's Henry Hart and Albert Sacks. This theory, which held that judging should be an exercise of "reasoned calibration," was equated with judicial self-restraint, cautious exercise of judicial power vis-à-vis other lawmaking branches, and suspension of judicial "bias" in favor of principles, rationality, impartiality, and intelligibility.[54]

White's theory of judicial "good sense" oversimplifies the nature of legally based constitutional theory; the most highly regarded scholars, such as Wechsler, Freund, and Bickel, did not accept its premises. The theory is based on faith in the polity, which it sees as a moral good, and on the relativist democratic and moral theory of the postwar years. The support of compromise, the good sense of the populace not to be involved in "isms," the cultural diversity without conflict over fundamental values, and most importantly the faith in pluralist politics all inform White's theory of judicial good sense.

White argues that Warren's view of judging was more complex than that envisioned by his critics, who emphasize Warren's lack of craftsmanship, intellectuality, and analytical skill. White and critics of the Warren Court in the 1950s and 1960 cogently argue that the rejection of doctrinal and institutional good sense does not entail an acceptance of result-oriented jurisprudence.[55] However, White does a poor job of expressing this point. Insofar as he mischaracterizes the Warren Court as dominated by moral and ethical values, he only reinforces the stereotype of the Warren Court as outcome-oriented. White fails to see that his own view—that ethical values predominate over polity values—deflects our attention from the central role that polity principles played in Warren Court decisionmaking.

In the nomenclature of the non-Euclidean and relativist world in which they lived, scholars and jurists, who like White clearly opposed the legal realist positivistic view of law and courts, were viewed by legal realists as having "buried" rights and polity values. Pure craft and legalism were impossible. A pure "finding of the law" and doctrinal consistency were not possible. Moral and polity values informed the choices of all of these justices and scholars; it was in the breadth of moral values and polity principles that they differed with Warren, not in the presence of rights values in Warren's thinking versus the presence of polity or institutional values in that of Frankfurter and Harlan. Even though White tries to maintain that the distinction between polity and rights principles is important, and that principles inform Court choices, he seems to have fallen into the instrumentalist tendencies of the Warren Court era.

With regard to the relationship between Supreme Court decisionmaking and the interpretive community, White argues that Warren's perspective as a jurist was formulated outside the dominant academic perspective of the twentieth century. He argues that Warren responded to the doctrine of "neutral principles" by viewing them as a "fantasy" and stating that the Court cannot be neutral as a defender of the Constitution.[56] White's point obscures the relationship of constitutional theory and practice as a general explanation of con-

100   stitutional change and, more particularly, with regard to Warren and the War-ren Court.

Warren was not *outside* the dominant academic perceptions or assumptions. He had considered such perceptions and rejected them, as had Douglas, Brennan, and a majority of the Court. But as the cases demonstrate, this rejection did not mean that the Warren Court rejected polity principles or viewed all cases only in equality terms. It meant that the Court had two reasons—polity principles and rights principles—not to accept the formulation of judicial good sense.

Warren's progressivism, his upbringing in California politics, his reform ethos, his concern for principles over private interest politics, and his view of polity—none of these fell within the dominant pluralist academic perspective in the twentieth century. Those values so dear to Warren declined in stature in the nation in the 1950s, 1960s, and into the 1970s, as a public philosophy of what Theodore Lowi calls "interest group liberalism" became dominant among political scientists, public officials, and citizens. It is based on a faith in the operations of private interest groups working with public officials to make policies. It is liberal because it calls on government to do more things, such as reduce the risk of private economic interests. However, Lowi argues that this public philosophy was born of the acceptance of pluralist, noncritical interpretations of polity. For Lowi, interest group liberalism is a pathological public philosophy because it is not based on the principles of *Federalist* no. 10 questioning the power of factions or private interest groups, it does not call for laws to meet public interests, and it is not based on any foundational principles in the Constitution, such as equal protection before the law. Interest group liberalism is based on pluralist principles that praise private interest groups and view public policy and politics as the summation of private wants.[57] In addition, Warren's progressivism, concern for public rather than private interests, and formal separation of the public and the private reflected a relationship between polity and rights values that are at the core of constitutional principles such as separation of powers and political accountability of the rulers to the ruled, principles that were rejected by apologetic pluralist interpretations of polity and relativist democratic theory. It was the particular relationship of polity and rights principles in the apologetic pluralist vision of government that Warren rejected, not the importance of institutional vision in constitutional theory and practice.

Constitutional theory in the 1950s and 1960s did not help resolve this dilemma, not even the work of Bickel, Freund, and Wechsler, the less narrowly procedural and legalist scholars of their day. This lack of clarity in the work of constitutional scholars as to moral values and polity values suggests that their views of polity and rights values were more complex than the raw pluralist institutional view. It may be that polity and rights values combine to produce the jurisprudence of the age in the way polity and rights values countered social welfare in the *Lochner* era. The commentators accepted a pluralist view of Court role and political system. The open, ethical language of the Court was a way to obtain decisions that rectified malfunctions in the political system identified by the Warren Court, without requiring the Court to articulate a fully articulated "critical pluralist" interpretation of American politics. Such an interpretation would be available to the interpretive community in the late 1960s with the publication of Grant McConnell's *Private Power and American Democracy* in 1966 and Theodore Lowi's *The End of Liberalism* in 1969.[58] As I shall argue in Part Two, the Burger Court era must be understood in part as a product of the institutionalization of a critical pluralist view of polity in constitutional theory and practice.

Conclusion: Hegemonic Principles and Constitutive Doctrinal Change

Judicial decisionmaking in the Warren Court era cannot be understood by looking only internally within the Court. The justices' views about polity and rights must be considered first in light of interpretations of political institutions and Court role by political theorists and social scientists and then in light of the conceptions of democratic theory that dominate the age. Justices write opinions in consideration of the debate within the interpretive community. Their reactions to the hegemonic ideas of their era are also important to their judicial decisionmaking and to how it is evaluated. They consider these ideas in light of their training, political philosophy, experience in politics and law, and basic views about the role of law in society and justice. They also consider where these views are to be found in previous Court cases, how the words and principles of the Constitution have been interpreted in the past, and their interchanges, by word and draft opinion, with fellow justices.

Lawyers trained in constitutional law and theory tend to be less relativist and more rights-oriented than scholars of American political institutions. No matter how much the legal realist ethic is present in law training and thought, the ideas that all rights are not listed in the Bill of Rights and that some language in the Constitution needs interpretation are central. This is not always the case for many political scientists trained in relativist democratic theory with its implicit assumption that the political system is in equilibrium.

Legal scholars could not completely accept the relativism in democratic theory and faith in political institutions and interest group politics that dominated political and social science interpretations of American politics. Although they did accept, at some level, a pluralist interpretation of politics because it was the hegemonic view of the day, many legal scholars had less faith in pluralist politics and more belief in the autonomy of law and politics than did the positivistic social scientists. Their training and socialization as lawyers prevented them from easily dismissing the idea that the Constitution contained open-ended rights language, a concept that had been accepted by constitutional scholars and jurists even before the *Lochner* period.

The craft view of law among legal scholars was a way to respect polity values under relativist interest group theory and still allow some new individual rights, such as the right to attend schools that were not segregated. For the Warren Court the debate centered on whether judicial decisionmaking should respect the prerogative of political institutions to make constitutional choices, or whether it should employ a more robust fundamental rights—moral values behind the law—view of judicial decisionmaking. Both positions involved views about the role of courts and political institutions and rights in the Constitution.

Ultimately, the Warren Court rejected the balancing of polity and rights values through craft, incrementalism, and judicial self-restraint that the more conventional legal scholars advocated. The Court favored a more open-ended consideration of rights and moral values and justice as well as critical pluralist polity values that were neither as relativist nor as approving of American politics as views held by scholars of American political institutions. The Court also rejected the apologetic pluralism of the day and placed within its jurisprudence a more critical view of the American polity. Thus it was not only the Warren Court's view of equality and rights that explains its jurisprudence, but also its critical view of polity.

In an era when pluralist views about polity predominated but no *developed* critical pluralist theory of political system blockage yet existed, a critical pluralist viewpoint meant that the Warren Court criticism of polity blockage centered on the formal denial of access to the political system. Neither the Warren Court nor the interpretive community had developed a view of structural inequality built on informal economic, social, and political inequality. Equal protection doctrine in the Warren Court era centered on inequalities of access to the political system by blacks—denial of the right to vote and to have that vote count the same as any other vote, denial of equal access to schools, courts, and bureaucracies, and other forms of invidious discrimination. It did not grapple with more complex views of informal discrimination and inequality. An attack on unequal access for blacks was not far outside the pluralist view of polity that dominated the scholarship of the 1950s to 1960s.

Ironically, the craft, election returns, and policymaking approaches furthered the decline of our faith in the courts as venues for political change. Only the safety valve and the biographical approaches reinforced our faith in the legal system as a means to keep politics in check. With the loss of a bright-line separation of the public and the private, which was replaced by a continuum of complex choices about what is public and private, our view of the autonomy of the courts declines. The idea that the state can be bad is lost in pluralist views of the state as good—with no standards of evaluation outside the process itself. The idea that Court decisionmaking is different from legislation or policymaking—that law and politics are different—is lost. Legal realists led us toward a loss of faith in institutions, courts, law, and formal principles. Then the legal scholars who followed and the major constitutional theorists of the age sought to renew our faith in the law and the courts.

Within our own era, we cannot predict how the polity values in the Court, the academy, and the nation will intersect. That intersection is far more complex than is indicated by saying the Court follows the election returns, institutional functionalism, biography, or policy outcomes in making its choices. For these ideas about polity and rights principles and how they should intersect are mediating ideas, built from past Court choices and Court roles, views about rights and moral values in the Constitution, and rejections of trusting polity.

In the 1950s, a national concern for civil liberties supported faith in the pluralist political system. Pluralists did not attack the structural bias of the polity—as built on social and economic inequality—in the same way that a more structural critical pluralist view of polity did. Even pluralists have traditionally been concerned about whether normal pluralist politics works in race issues. In *Who Governs?* Dahl said it did. David Truman feared stasis in race and class terms but gave us a theory built on equilibrium. The Warren Court got away with reforms because scholars accepted the equilibrium view of government and society. However, the Warren Court's view of polity and its linkage of this view of polity to social inequality precluded, to some extent, viewing the political system in apologetic pluralist terms. Thus, the more interesting question is to what degree the Warren Court was working from inside or outside the pluralist framework.

One could argue that the Warren Court was working within a pluralist interpretation of American political institutions because the structural changes that the Court advocated were in the formal process of the political system: the right to vote and to have individual votes count equally, the end of segregation so blacks could participate in the political system, and the protection of fundamental rights and interests so citizens could vote, move interstate, and secure access to criminal courts. All of these could be seen as a way to ensure that politics remained open to all citizens in a diverse nation. Thus, political scientists in the Warren Court era did not confront in a systematic way basic value questions about moral foundationalism and constitutional theory. They saw legal realism as a positivistic view of law, which most constitutional scholars rejected.

In contrast to many political scientists who accepted instrumental relativist theories of democracy, legal scholars took two paths in their analysis of the Supreme Court. The craft-oriented scholars attempted to cover over deep issues

104   of moral foundationalism and Court role by emphasizing that the quality of constitutional adjudication was based on the legal craftsmanship and prudence in Court action as one nonelected institution in a complex pluralist political system. Bickel, Freund, and Wechsler accepted the idea of natural rights and fundamental rights in the Constitution and accepted the independence of judges from politics. (This was a view alien to Dahl's election returns approach.) They could not accept the notion that judges were merely outcome-oriented or that they inserted their personal policy wants into their constitutional interpretations. They wrestled with the fact that the Constitution had within it open-ended fundamental rights language, not just polity principles or apologetic pluralist visions of the political system.

It is through the debate within the interpretive community over these polity and rights principles, and through the Warren Court's rejection of them, that we can explain the Warren Court. In so doing, we get a better picture of the nature of doctrinal change in the Warren Court era, the process of Supreme Court decisionmaking, and why we misperceive the Burger Court.

Part Two

The Burger Court: A Constitutive
Interpretation

Chapter Four

Constituting the Separation of Church and State

I continue to explore why the Burger Court has been misunderstood by testing the validity of the "no counterrevolution" interpretation of the Burger Court era, which views the major accomplishment of the Burger Court as not undertaking a counterrevolution to Warren Court jurisprudence.[1] This interpretation continues many of the assumptions about Supreme Court decisionmaking and the process of doctrinal change that were found in the instrumental approaches to interpreting the Warren Court. In this chapter I test the validity of the no counterrevolution thesis by offering a constitutive interpretation of Burger Court decisionmaking in interpreting the First Amendment prohibition on the government's establishing religion, with an emphasis on cases involving aid to parochial education. In chapter 5, I will use a constitutive interpretation of Burger Court equal protection jurisprudence to test the validity of instrumental policymaking approaches to Burger Court decisionmaking and doctrinal change.

In this chapter I will consider establishment clause cases, primarily in the area of aid to sectarian education, and how they demonstrate the constitutive decisionmaking process of the Supreme Court justices. I have chosen this doctrinal area for analysis because it generated a large number of cases in the Burger Court era and because some scholars argue that the doctrine and decisionmaking process in this area epitomize Burger Court jurisprudence.

In comparing Warren and Burger Court jurisprudence, Vincent Blasi writes on the financial aid to sectarian school cases, "Those decisions reflect no deep-seated vision of the constitutional scheme or of the specific constitutional clauses in dispute . . . the line drawing aspect of the process of doctrinal formulation has come to dominate the endeavor. The justices have crafted some significant practical compromises, but have not exerted any kind of moral force either by legitimating nascent aspirations or by reinvigorating dormant ideals."[2] Martin Shapiro uses an instrumental approach to interpret the Burger Court and explain both the internal decisionmaking process and the effects of external factors on the process of doctrinal change. Like Blasi, he views the aid to parochial education cases as attempts by justices on the Burger Court to permit a policy of government aid to traditional religions without hurting their autonomy.[3]

Instrumental Interpretations of the Burger Court Era:
The "No Counterrevolution" Thesis

The Burger Court has never been accepted on its own terms. It has never been viewed as a Court with a vision of polity and rights principles or the creator of a unique body of constitutional law. Most scholars believe that the Burger Court merely responded incrementally to innovative constitutional principles established during the Warren Court era rather than engaging in a counterrevolution against its doctrinal innovations.

This "no counterrevolution" theory is most cogently articulated in Vincent Blasi's collection *The Burger Court: The Counter-Revolution That Wasn't*. Blasi and Martin Shapiro wrote the book's major theoretical essays; other contributors—Thomas Emerson, Norman Dorsen, Robert W. Bennett, Yale Kamisar, Robert Burt, Paul Brest, and Ruth Bader Ginsberg—apply this approach to different areas of constitutional law. The no counterrevolution theory is also the primary thesis in books on the Burger Court by Bernard Schwartz, Richard Funston, Francis Lee, William Thomas, and Herman Schwartz and in a recently published book of essays on each of the Burger Court justices.[4]

This thesis holds that the Burger Court lacks the Warren Court's sense of mission on behalf of equality before the law. Blasi argues that "the distinctive hallmark of the new [Burger Court's] centrist activism has been the powerful aversion to making fundamental value choices." In contrast to the Warren Court, the Burger Court is viewed as "inspired almost exclusively by discrete, pragmatic judgments regarding how a moderate, sensible judicial accommodation might help resolve a potentially divisive public controversy." Blasi contrasts Warren and Burger Court decisionmaking to establish that Warren Court jurisprudence was directed "by principle, a rooted activism"; Burger Court decisionmaking he describes as "rootless" activism. The Warren Court, we are told, invalidated fewer congressional acts than did the Burger Court.[5]

As I have emphasized in the first part of this book, this vision of the Warren Court is simplistic; it does not show the complexity of Warren Court jurisprudence. Nor does it give enough emphasis to the place of polity principles in Warren Court decisionmaking or reveal the limits of Warren Court doctrinal innovation. It makes the salient error of many scholars who view the Warren Court through the election returns, policymaking, safety valve, and biographical approaches: It does not show Warren Court justices balancing polity and rights principles.

The "Centrist" Justices and the Justices at the "Extremes"

The no counterrevolution thesis emphasizes the importance of centrist justices to the development of constitutional principles. Blasi argues that a pragmatic, intelligent, moderate, nondoctrinaire, and dedicated centrist majority consisting of five justices—Potter Stewart, Byron White, Lewis F. Powell, John Paul Stevens, and Harry A. Blackmun—was the intellectual center and the dominant force on the Burger Court—the force that prevented it from engaging in a counterrevolution against Warren Court principles and landmark decisions.[6] Unlike the justices at the right and left poles of the Court, the justices in the middle were pragmatic, considered cases "on the facts," and had no "defined juristic *Weltanschauung*."[7] They oscillated between the polar blocs and saw themselves as holding the center.

Blasi views the "ideological" wings of the Burger Court as weaker, less influential, and more doctrinaire than the "centrist majority." He argues that neither Brennan nor Marshall was well suited to the role of dissenter (on the left) because they could not articulate in "pure and compelling form the liberal theory of the Constitution" with the "elemental force and vision of a Holmes, or Brandeis, or Black, or Douglas, or Warren." Blasi calls them "pragmatic men, more clever than profound" and views Brennan as performing the role of a centrist justice "to perfection during the heyday of the Warren Court," but not during the Burger Court era. On the right, Blasi characterizes Justice Rehnquist as "more a debater than a thinker, more a lawyer than a statesman. He has not even approached his predecessors Frankfurter, Jackson, and Harlan in articulating a conservative constitutional philosophy."[8]

Bernard Schwartz, another proponent of the no counterrevolution theory, argues that "the actions of the polar justices were based upon more or less fixed juristic principles that served as the foundation for the jurisprudential edifices they sought to construct. They adhered rigidly to those principles in most cases." The two justices on the left, Brennan and Marshall, "saw it as their duty to preserve, and if possible extend, the Warren Court's liberal jurisprudence." The two justices on the right, Burger and Rehnquist, supported the opposite political agenda, which was "not only a halt, but a rollback of much of the Warren jurisprudence."[9]

For Blasi and Schwartz, justices at the right and left extremes of the Burger Court lacked the intellectual credentials to develop coherent scholarly visions. The no counterrevolution approach, like the election returns, policymaking, safety valve, and biographical approaches, views Burger Court justices as furthering (or not furthering) specific policy objectives of others—in this case, the policies of the Warren Court era.

Burger Court Activism as "Rootless" and "Pragmatic"

Scholars supporting the no counterrevolution interpretation of the Burger Court argue that justices decide cases without much deliberate consideration of polity principles such as the proper role for the Supreme Court. The activism of the Burger Court, Schwartz holds, reflected a new, post-Warren consensus against judicial restraint.[10]

The no counterrevolution thesis emphasizes that, unlike the Warren Court and its quest for equality of the races, of rich and poor, and of prosecutor and defendant, the Burger Court never consciously used the law to change society or its values but simply rode society's wave, "letting itself be swept along by the consensus it perceived in the social arena." It moved along, for example, on gender discrimination only when it became "fashionable" to be for women's rights.[11] This thesis corroborates Dahl's premise that the Court followed the majority coalition and agrees with the idea that law and politics were interdependent.

For Blasi, the Burger Court's "rootless" activism can be explained as a direct consequence of the divisions among the justices—the strength of the center and the weakness at the wings. The Court's activism was both generated and moderated by the pragmatic men in the middle, who were "inspired not by a commitment to fundamental constitutional principles or noble political ideals, but rather by the belief that modest injections of logic and compassion by disinterested, sensible judges can serve as a counterforce to some of the excesses and irrationalities of contemporary government decision-making."[12] Thus, Blasi explains Burger Court activism along contextual lines—the Burger Court, for some reason, countered the structural limits of the political system.

The no counterrevolution interpretation of the Burger Court continues the methodological and normative assumptions, and the assumptions about the American political system, that are found in the election returns, policy-making, safety valve, and biographical explanations of doctrinal change and Supreme Court decisionmaking. These include accepting non-Euclidean and scientific naturalist notions that justices use polity and rights principles instrumentally to secure policy wants; belittling the role of the interpretive community and changing interpretations of American politics in doctrinal change; viewing justices as policymakers not significantly different from elected or other appointed officials; rejecting the idea of the Court as autonomous; viewing polity principles as secondary to rights principles in Court decisionmaking; viewing the Supreme Court as legitimating the policy wants of others; and believing that the Court is not principled in its jurisprudence.

Identifying Polity and Rights Principles
in the Establishment Clause

In analyzing issues of separation of church and state I will focus on various disputes among justices and factions *within* the broader liberal ideological framework of law, at the micro- rather than macrolevel ideology.

The establishment clause involves both a general (public) polity value—that the state must not establish religion—and a (private) rights imperative, that the individual be allowed free exercise of religion uninhibited by state action.[13] Both depend on a contrived public-private split in liberal thought that has caused an enduring dilemma.[14] This split has allowed for much leeway in judicial policymaking and generated a surprisingly wide spectrum of ideological disputes in modern judicial interpretations of church and state doctrine. Absolute state neutrality toward any religion—the "wall of separation" judicial view—has had prominent proponents on the Court, and the Court generally adheres strictly to the prohibitions imposed on government by the establishment clause. Some justices see this principle of hermetically sealed, exclusive spheres that belong either to church or to state as unrealistic in the light of modern complexity; others see it as the only means of maintaining the integrity of religious practice and principled adjudication by the Supreme Court.

Polity arguments in church and state cases are balanced against the substantive rights interests of individuals, religious minorities, or nonbelievers who cannot count on institutional support for protection. Rights protection requires the courts to take a more positive, interventionist role, at least potentially. Hence, conflicts over dual obligations are at the heart of the First Amendment religion clauses.[15]

The free exercise rights central to questions of government establishment of religion are either external or internal to a religious institution or activity. The religious atmosphere of society and government *external* to the institutions in question is at issue; free exercise rights for believers and nonbelievers in a generally hospitable political and cultural environment is the ideal. But how shall the state encourage such an environment without invoking the clear prohibition against the government's favoring one religion over another? The rights principles in church and state cases also involve what I shall label an *internal* right to individual free exercise of religion within particular institutions.

The question before the justices has not been whether to sanction individual rights or guarantees but how best to integrate and accommodate the general logic of the doctrine of separation of church and state and free exercise rights within modern society. Thus, the religion clauses ask the Court to look at polity (institutional separation) and substantive rights (free exercise) principles. Justices' choices of polity or substantive rights definitions of constitutional problems result in both a bounded discipline in Supreme Court decisionmaking and a movement to process-based choices, with a resulting breakdown of the separation between law and politics. An analysis of the interplay of process and substantive rights values, and of the justices' ideological interests in support of different concepts of process and rights values, indicates that under our liberal tradition, rights are precarious because of their linkage to process values, which are subject to the justices' views of institutional relationships in society. Thus, the liberal legal tradition, with its concern for religious freedom and the separation of law and politics, also contains the seeds of decline in these values.

112   Justices decide cases by fitting them into their continuing process and substantive rights values rather than by deciding outcomes and then making any
argument they can in support of the outcome. Justices are ideological in that
these process and rights principles provide *definable limits* on the range of values that individual justices can use in development of more innovative Court
doctrine. The volatility of such principles does not indicate, in my view, a tendency for the Court to engage in simplistic bargaining but rather an "ideological jurisprudence" that is highly motivated and highly competitive, with certain ends clearly in sight. Through the analysis of cases I will determine the
extent to which each justice has a set of process and rights priorities. From
such analysis we can see differences in the way various justices make principled
choices, and the implications of different types of principles for the justices'
constitutional choices for the development of constitutional principles. In
particular, this approach allows us to pinpoint differences among the justices
as to the degree to which they view constitutional law as prescriptive of public
official and citizen action, and whether they trust political institutions or
other venues, such as churches, to make choices of constitutional significance.

This kind of inductive analysis allows us to identify turning points and la-
cunas in a given justice's values and thereby explore the possibilities for constitutional change in the future. Unlike traditional voting bloc analysis, this
method does not place an undue quantitative weight on case outcomes as indicators of a justice's ideology, nor does it simply average agreement scores
among justices. This approach allows the comparison of the rights- and process-based constitutional principles held by each justice and group of justices
so we can see what cross-cutting values exist and are in conflict in Supreme
Court decisionmaking.[16]

If it is correct that different ideological currents are present within the
Burger Court, the differences among the justices should manifest themselves
in the following ways: (1) at crucial times justices will make clear statements as
to past and future directions of the Court and trigger turning points where a
continuation of doctrine would undercut long-held process and rights values
(for example, Blackmun in *Committee for Public Education and Religious Liberty
v. Regan* [1980] case); (2) groups of justices will differ consistently as to
whether and to what degree process and rights values are to be considered in
each case, although the actual decisions may vary; (3) justices will differ as to
whether and to what degree strong notions of individual freedom of religious
conscience are the guiding norms for establishment clause doctrine, as opposed to reliance on process values such as the entanglement between church
and state or political divisiveness.[17] Therefore, consistency alone proves insuffi-
cient to determine whether ideology informs judicial choices, given the complexity of process and rights values inherent in the religion clauses. Internal

questions of value (process and rights) must be posed, rather than an exclusive structure being imposed by desires for consistency in *policy* questions.[18]

The findings below challenge those scholars who argue that Burger Court justices are primarily pragmatic in their choices.[19] Their formulation confuses an increased *complexity* of constitutional values as bases for Court choices with pragmatism. My objective is to make sense of this new complexity and demonstrate consistency in the principles applied by Burger Court justices. By rooting scholarly analysis of constitutional law once again in values I will also respond to what might be labeled a rebirth of the relativism and empiricism of postwar scholarship (see Chapters 6 and 7).

Burger Court Voting in Aid to Religious Education Cases: Ideology and Outcomes

In fourteen aid to religious education cases (see Table 4.1), there were two major groups on the Burger Court: one consisting of Justices Brennan, Marshall, Stevens, and Blackmun (the Brennan group) and another consisting of Justices Rehnquist, Burger, and White (the Rehnquist group). Marshall and Brennan voted the same in all choices, joined by Stevens in all but one case. Blackmun voted with Marshall and Brennan in all choices from 1980. Rehnquist and White disagreed in only two of eighteen choices; they disagreed with Burger in five choices, but in only one since 1973. (see Tables 4.2 and 4.3).

The statistics shown in the tables suggest that the composition of the pragmatic middle block (Blackmun, Powell, White, Stevens, and Stewart) was not constant over time. Justices Blasi considers to be members of the moderate and pragmatic middle appear at *all* points on the list by percentage of dissenting votes from majority opinions (Table 4.2). Between 1970 and 1985 the justices can be grouped into those voting against the majority less than 10 percent of the time (Harlan, Powell, Stewart, and Blackmun); 25 to 36 percent (Black, Douglas, Stevens, Brennan, Marshall, and Burger), and 50 percent and over (O'Connor, Rehnquist, and White). Moderate "middle" justices appear in all three groupings. White has the highest percentage of dissents of any justice on the Burger Court. Stevens represents a median. Powell, Stewart, and Blackmun did tend to vote with the majority position most of the time.

To argue, however, that three members of the Burger Court impose a coherent and overriding influence on Court jurisprudence oversimplifies the judicial choices on church and state issues. It is especially difficult to talk about a coherent middle after 1980, when Stewart retired, because then only two justices, Powell and Blackmun, can be considered to be in the middle. Finally, after 1980, Powell and Blackmun voted opposite to each other in two of the four relevant cases, *Mueller* and *Regan*, and they disagreed on two of the five policy choices made in these cases.

Table 4.1. Burger Court Aid to Religious School Cases, 1970–1985

Case Number	Date Decided	Case
1	4 May 1970	*Walz v. Tax Commission of New York* (397 U.S. 664) Permits property tax exemption for church property
2	28 June 1971	*Lemon v. Kurtzman* (403 U.S. 602) A. No reimbursement to nonpublic schools for teacher salaries and instructional materials B. No 15 percent state salary reimbursement directly to church school teachers for teaching secular subjects
3	28 June 1971	*Tilton v. Richardson* (403 U.S. 672) Permits federal aid for secular buildings at sectarian universities
4	25 June 1973	*Committee for Public Education and Religious Liberty v. Nyquist* (413 U.S. 756) A. No aid for maintenance and repair of nonpublic schools, including parochial grammar and secondary schools B. No tuition reimbursement for low-income parents of parochial school children C. No income tax benefits to parents of children attending nonpublic schools including parochial schools
5	25 June 1973	*Levitt v. Committee for Public Education and Religious Liberty* (413 U.S. 472) No aid for direct payment to parochial schools for test grading, including teacher-prepared tests
6	25 June 1973	*Sloan v. Lemon* (413 U.S. 825) No reimbursement for tuition to parents of children attending nonpublic schools, including parochial schools
7	25 June 1973	*Hunt v. McNair* (413 U.S. 734) Permits states to secure less expensive financing of sectarian college building through state bonding power
8	19 May 1975	*Meek v. Pittenger* (421 U.S. 349) A. Permits aid to parochial school children through the loan of secular textbooks B. No direct aid to parochial schools for instructional materials/remedial teaching
9	21 June 1976	*Roemer v. Board of Public Works of Maryland* (426 U.S. 736) Allows annual state fiscal subsidy to nonpublic schools, including sectarian schools, colleges, and universities

(Continued)

Table 4.1. *Continued*

Case Number	Date Decided	Case
10	24 June 1977	*Wolman v. Walter* (433 U.S. 229) A. Permits state aid to parochial schools for textbook loans and testing/scoring of state-provided tests B. Permits aid for out-of-parochial-school (off premises) remedial, guidance, and therapeutic services by staff hired by public school officials C. Forbids aid to parochial schools for instructional materials even if loaned to students and parents D. Forbids aid to parochial schools for field trips
11	20 February 1980	*Committee for Public Education and Religious Liberty v. Regan* (444 U.S. 646) Allows direct payment to parochial schools for salaries of teachers for attendance record keeping and state standardized tests, including tests that have subjective element in grading
12	29 June 1983	*Mueller v. Allen* (463 U.S. 388) Allows parents of children in all nonprofit public and nonpublic schools, including parochial schools, to deduct expenses for tuition, textbooks, and transportation
13	1 July 1985	*Grand Rapids School District v. Ball* (473 U.S. 373) A. Forbids a shared-time program: state-provided secular classes and guidance services in parochial schools to parochial school children B. Forbids a community education program: state-provided classes after school for students and adults in parochial schools
14	1 July 1985	*Aguilar v. Felton* (473 U.S. 402) Forbids use of federal funds to pay for public school teachers to teach remedial reading and math courses in parochial school buildings to economically disadvantaged children attending parochial schools, even when close state supervision of content is provided

Note: Important post-1980 cases involving spheres of state and religious authority but not involving state aid include *Wallace v. Jaffree* (1985), overturning an Alabama "moment of silence" statute when it was ascertained that the legislature was not content-neutral in its religious choice; *Lynch v. Donnelly* (1984), upholding the constitutionality of including a creche in a city-sponsored display at Christmas: and *Marsh v. Chambers* (1983), upholding the right of prayer in state legislative chambers.

Table 4.2. Dissents from Majority Opinions in Aid to Religious Education Cases

Justice	Number of Choices	Number of Dissents	Percentage of Dissents
Harlan	4	0	0.00
Powell	18	1	5.55
Stewart	18	1	5.55
Blackmun	21	2	9.52
Black	4	1	25.00
Douglas	12	4	33.33
Brennan	22	8	36.36
Marshall	22	8	36.36
Burger	22	8	36.36
O'Connor	4	2	50.00
Rehnquist	18	9	50.00
White	22	13	59.09

It is also incorrect to argue that the right and left wings of the Court take similarly extreme positions on church and state issues. Simply put, Blasi's liberal justices (Brennan and Marshall) seemed more likely to go along with the majority position than those he labels conservative (Rehnquist, Burger, O'Connor). White, whom Blasi calls a pragmatic centrist justice, took the most extreme positions on these cases. Moreover, coherence between the middle justices, Blackmun and Powell, declined after 1980, and Blackmun's voting with the majority declined after 1980, when he voted with the majority in only two of four cases.

Between 1980 and 1986 on the Burger Court there was increased bloc voting. Blackmun voted most often with Marshall, Stevens, and Brennan. White, Rehnquist, and Burger usually voted together. O'Connor voted with the Rehnquist group in three of the four cases since 1980 and in two of the three major establishment clause cases that did not deal with aid to education, *Marsh v. Chambers* and *Lynch v. Donnelly*.[20] She voted against her bloc, however, in *Wallace v. Jaffree*, invalidating Alabama's moment-of-silence law, and in *Grand Rapids School District v. Ball*, a case involving parochial school personnel teaching secular subjects after school hours. Only Justice Powell voted with the majority opinion in all aid to education cases after 1980. These data suggest that the Burger Court after 1980 had a "pragmatic middle" of only *one* justice, who is now gone from the Rehnquist Court.[21]

These statistics raise serious questions about the Blasi thesis, especially the notion that "modest injections of logic and compassion by disinterested, sensible judges [in the middle] can serve as a counterforce to some of the excesses and irrationalities of contemporary governmental decisionmaking,"[22] or that

Table 4.3. Burger Court Voting on Aid to Religious Education Cases

																	Case Number					
Justice	1	2 A	2 B	3	4 A	4 B	4 C	5	6	7	8 A	8 B	9	10 A	10 B	10 C	10 D	11	12	13 A	13 B	14
Harlan	M	M	M	M																		
Black	M	M	M	D																		
Stewart	M	M	M	M	M*	M*	M*	M	M*	M	M*	M*	D	M	M	M	D	M				
Powell				M*	M*	M*	M*	M	M*	M*	M	M	M*	M*	M*	M*	M*	M	D	M	M	M
Blackmun	M			M	M	M	M	M	M	M	M	M	M	M	M	M	M	M	D	M	M	M
Stevens										D	M	M	D	D	D	D	M	D	D	M*	M*	M*
Douglas				D	M	M	M	M	M	D												
Marshall	M	M	M	D	M	M	M	M	M	D	D	D	D	D	D	D	D	M	D	M	M	M
Brennan	M	M	M	D	M	M	M	M	M	D	M	M	D	D	D	D	D	D	D	M*	M*	M*
Burger	M*	M*	M*	M*	M	M	D	D	M*	M	M	M	M	D	D	D	D	M*	M	M	M	M*
Rehnquist				M	M	M	D	D	M	M	D	D	M	M	M	M	M	M*	M*	D	D	D
White	M	D	D	M	D	D	D	M*	D	M	M	M	M	M	M	M	M	M	M	D	M	D
O'Connor		D	D	M				D	D	D								M*	M	D	D	D

Note: Case numbers and column headings refer to Table 4.1.
*Justice writing majority opinion
M represents a majority vote.
D represents a dissent.

judicial excesses came solely from the extreme right and left of the Burger Court. Rather, all justices manifest nonrandom ideological interests in their jurisprudence. Such interests are informed by a tension between fundamental process and rights principles in their choices, and this trend is likely to continue in the future.

The Burger Court reacted to the establishment clause in a variety of ways. As we predicted, inconsistency in specific policy outcomes does not necessarily indicate inconsistency in judicial perspective. In fact, we can identify a markedly ideological bent in all of the justices, with one notable exception, Justice Powell. (His process and rights values are present but seem less controlling.) More specifically, the Burger Court justices expressed a variety of judicial outlooks, including process emphasis absolutism on the part of Rehnquist, White, and Burger; process and rights tension on the part of O'Connor and Powell; and substantive rights emphasis (with clearly defined process underpinnings) by Blackmun, Brennan, and Marshall. All of these perspectives are ideologically informed and reflect greater or less degrees of tension between process and rights values. It is useful to chart, in a preliminary way, some of these perspectives.

Justice Powell voted with the majority in all cases. This record implies that he takes each case on the merits and is swayed by particular contexts and by the opinions of both his process- and rights-oriented colleagues on the Court. This style can lead to contradictory outcomes (see Table 4.1). For example, in 1973 Powell wrote the *Nyquist* opinion disallowing aid for facility maintenance as well as tuition reimbursement and tax benefits for parents of children attending parochial schools. Ten years later, he voted with the majority in *Mueller*, which allowed parents of parochial school children virtually the same thing—tax deduction benefits for tuition, textbooks, and transportation. Justice Powell was, at base, willing to honor legislative determinations before his own consistency of rulings.[23] Justice Powell based his judicial view on process norms requiring that legislative outcomes be respected in all cases and that parochial schools have a right to be helped, or to have "benevolent neutrality" extended to them by the state.

For conservative Justices Rehnquist, White, and Burger there is no such tension between polity and rights principles in the establishment clause. These justices feel it is the state's prerogative to extend aid to religious institutions and, despite the rights of such institutions and their members to be left undisturbed, to support legislative action in the establishment clause area short of establishing a state religion. After 1973, Burger no longer showed concern for a stringent entanglement standard.

Justice O'Connor, in the Burger Court era, shared the initial presumption of good faith on the part of the state to get in and then out of church affairs (or to keep the scope of the interaction constitutional in even longer relationships, as in *Mueller*). She did, however, uphold individual rights of free exercise more strongly than did her process-oriented colleagues.

Justice Blackmun's voting record in the establishment clause cases reveals the most abrupt change, with the exception of Burger's. Like Powell, Blackmun voted with the majority in every one of these cases prior to *Mueller v. Allen* and with the process-oriented bloc prior to and including *Wolman v. Walter*. Fearful that he had gone too far in subscribing to the majority's flexible reading of the *Lemon* standard (a three-part test involving political divisiveness, effects, and entanglement that will be explored in the next section), and wondering about the future implications of that choice, Blackmun dramatically joined the rights-oriented bloc in dissent in *Regan*. Although his past voting record clearly indicates his support for process determinations about the church-state relationship, Blackmun consistently refused to accept *direct* aid to parochial schools. After 1983 he voted consistently to stop indirect state and Court support of the religious enterprise and to return to a more forceful application of the *Lemon* standard.

Perhaps Blackmun finally heeded Stevens who, as in other areas of constitutional law, embarked on a crusade to reintroduce watertight principles in establishment clause adjudication. For Stevens there is no tension involved in guaranteeing religious rights and practices for citizens. After joining the Burger Court in 1976, Stevens authored typically terse opinions advocating the reintroduction of an inviolable wall of separation and lamenting the decline of the *Lemon* standard as a guide for stringent scrutiny. However, in *Wolman* he ruled against a "package plan" of aid to parochial schools in all provisions *except* that which would afford parochial school children remedial, therapeutic, and guidance services off school premises rendered by employees who were not parochial school teachers. For Stevens, this exception to his rigid rule could be justified on the grounds that it furthered universal state and private goals of better health and adjustment for society's children.[24]

In the "liberal" bloc, Justice Brennan relies to a greater extent than Justice Marshall on the major process prong, or polity principle, of the *Lemon* standard—that the Court must not allow the entanglement of church and state and the possibility of political divisiveness. Brennan abides more by a criticism of current process practice than explicit rights protection, as he might in other areas of First Amendment doctrine. We see this tendency most clearly in his opinion in *Aguilar v. Felton*, in which process norms served to bolster rights protection. But this approach is not overtly instrumentalist; the *Lemon* standard itself is a tool designed to achieve the same end through an overlay of both process and rights guarantees. Brennan reflected in his jurisprudence the importance of polity-based prohibitions on the entanglement of church and state and concerns about political divisiveness found in the *Lemon* standard with protections against the violation of what I have called the internal and external individual rights of believers and nonbelievers respectively. Many other justices did not do this. Brennan tried, ironically, to give establishment clause doctrine a push in a substantive direction by building a wall around it. He opposed allowing legislatures the right to determine the degree and nature of mutual jurisdiction with the parochial institutions in their boundaries. In a twist of logic, Brennan and Marshall asserted that religious institutions are best helped by not helping them at all, a position seemingly close to that of Madison and many of the Federalists.

Polity and Rights Values in the *Lemon* Standard

In an attempt to provide clarity by disassembling general establishment clause principles, the Burger Court in *Lemon v. Kurtzman* (1971), in which the Court banned state reimbursement for parochial school teacher salaries and instruction materials, offered what has since become known as the *Lemon* standard. This standard, as applied, turned out to be a set of loosely defined scrutiny rules that accommodate the justices' process and rights values. For a statute or government action to pass muster under this standard (1) it must have a secular legislative purpose (the secular purpose test); (2) its primary effect must be one that neither advances nor inhibits religion (the primary effects test); and (3) it must not foster an excessive government entanglement with religion (the no excessive entanglement test).[25]

The terms "pluralist" and "critical-pluralist" may be used to indicate differences among the justices with regard to process values. Support of pluralist process values suggests a trust of legislatures and electorally accountable political institutions to make choices about aid to parochial schools and other issues relating to the separation of church and state. Holding critical-pluralist process norms, on the other hand, suggests an underlying distrust both of these majoritarian institutions and also of other forums such as religious organizations as protectors of establishment clause principles.[26] I will use the terms "rights," "weak rights," and "nonrights" to differentiate among the levels of concern among the justices for establishing a wall around parochial schoolchildren and those external to religious institutions, including nonbelievers, to protect their right to free exercise of religion.

Qualitative analysis of the cases along these dimensions shows that the members of the Burger Court possessed a variety of judicial outlooks that complement the voting alignments reported above. They ranged from a pluralist process-nonrights emphasis by Rehnquist, White, and Burger, to pluralist process-weak rights values by centrists O'Connor and Powell, to a critical pluralist-rights approach by Blackmun, Brennan, Marshall, and Stevens. A strong belief in free exercise rights was the basis of the Brennan group's call for a wall of separation between church and state. Every justice with strong rights values also had strong critical-pluralist process values. Process values in the es-

tablishment clause, however, operated as separate from the free exercise rights   *121*
values. Justices with pluralist process values, usually trusting of the political
system, had quite different views about whether free exercise rights of children
were violated by government aid to parochial schools. These differences
proved decisive in the development of the line of separation between church
and state.

Process Value Tensions in the Lemon Standard

Given the shifting nature of rights guarantees in the structurally oriented Constitution, it makes sense that the Supreme Court should come up with sche-
mas to accommodate its many views of church and state issues and even that it
should overestimate its ability to make consistent decisions in these areas by
forging loosely defined scrutiny guides like the *Lemon* standard. Rather than
focus on the well-documented decline of the *Lemon* test's judicial guidelines, I
will evaluate its internal structure to show the relevance of process principles
found in establishment clause choices. Once we have examined these guidelines, we are in a position to explore some of the more subtle, underlying processes and tensions among process and rights values at work in the justices'
logic.

Entanglement

The prong of the *Lemon* standard most debated in establishment clause
cases was the entanglement of political and religious pursuits through state involvement in sectarian affairs. Sharing of textbooks by public and religious
schools and reimbursement of religious elementary schools for the cost of pur-
chasing secular textbooks were upheld by the Court in *Board of Education v. Allen* (1968) and *Meek v. Pittenger* (1975), but not the establishment of longer
lasting and more intricate church-state financial relationships. In *Lemon v.
Kurtzman*, Chief Justice Burger articulated the fears that had prompted his
subscription to this prong of the *Lemon* test, warning against the "self-perpetuating" and "self-expanding" tendencies of annual government appropriations, which had the effect of entrenching the state in religious affairs—a sort
of institutional and fiscal momentum.[27] Questions of political divisiveness—itself a process norm—were central in this argument, but the case also concerned the degree of state supervision of the church-state relationship that
would result from teachers' salary supplements and general subsidies for instructional materials. Burger believed that only so much state monitoring
could occur before the "variable barrier" would be breached and the state
would intrude. If direct fiscal arrangements made him uneasy in *Lemon*, he
gave no indication of it in *Committee for Public Education and Religious Liberty v.
Regan*, in which a bare plurality vote endorsed direct payment to parochial

122   schools for teachers' time in the administration of standardized tests and routine state-required attendance and record keeping.

In *Meek*, the Court split its decision on entanglement grounds, arguing that the loan of secular textbooks directly to parents was acceptable in the *Allen* tradition, but not the direct loan of instructional materials and equipment to the schools. Given the religious mission of the schools, the latter could be constitutionally permissible only if it relied on an *unconstitutional* policing process. Justice Stewart wrote: "It would simply ignore reality to attempt to separate secular educational functions from the predominantly religious role performed by many of Pennsylvania's schools. Such aid cannot be considered as beneficial to the secular without providing direct aid to the sectarian."[28] In this case, Justices Brennan, Marshall, and Douglas opposed even the loan of the textbooks to parochial schools on entanglement grounds, a conflict that would eventually lead Marshall, in *Wolman*, to call for the overruling of *Allen*.[29]

Process entanglement has been referred to as a "tightrope," and indeed it presents a difficult problem for state legislatures. Justice White described it in *Lemon* as "an insoluble paradox. . . . The State cannot finance secular instruction if it permits religion to be taught in the same classroom; but if it exacts a promise that religion not be so taught . . . and enforces it, it is then entangled in the 'no entanglement' aspect of the Court's Establishment Clause jurisprudence."[30] Nevertheless, in every case involving elementary and secondary parochial schools—as opposed to the collegiate institutions awarded aid in *Tilton*, *Hunt*, and *Roemer*—the Court applied strict scrutiny for political entanglement with important consideration given to political divisiveness, religious permeability, and rights principles.

The clearest example of the Burger Court's reevaluation of entanglement occurred in *Lynch v. Donnelly*, in which the Court allowed a creche as part of a city's holiday display. Justice O'Connor advocated a clearer *Lemon* test that emphasized the entanglement prong in response to the Court's increasing dissatisfaction with the *Lemon* standard after *Regan*. This test relied on proof of entanglement rather than the potential for political divisiveness—a measure that she believed is too difficult to gauge. In her view, an after-the-fact policing of abuse of free exercise rights by the Court was more important than prohibiting activities that might infringe on those rights.[31] A strict reading of the entanglement provision better ensures that the institutional strength afforded to religious institutions by state participation in their affairs will not tip the balance against similar process rights shared by nonadherents.

Political Divisiveness

This process argument, first articulated by Justice Harlan in *Walz*, has become the focus of rights-oriented justices on the liberal wing of the Court in their effort to bolster the *Lemon* standard against unprecedented state encouragement to religious institutions. By asserting the potential for political divisiveness resulting from competition among various religious bodies for state funds, Justices Brennan, Marshall, Stevens, and Blackmun hoped to reintroduce some of the prohibitive aspects into the establishment clause that they felt the loose application of the *Lemon* standard had helped to erode.

Direct subsidies to parochial institutions, like those afforded in *Regan*, tended to promote unhealthy competition among religious groups for state funds, particularly when the religious institutions were the sole beneficiaries. For example, in *Nyquist*, the Court feared that direct aid to parents would result in political strife over maintaining levels of aid in the future and the growth of constituencies for and against such aid, resulting in conflict within the interest group structure. In that case, polity principles weighed heavily against direct state aid.[32]

In the *Wolman* case, we see Justice Powell's views concerning the political divisiveness prong of the *Lemon* standard fully articulated for the first time. There he stated that in the modern era we need not fear religious control over democratic processes or deep religious divisions in politics.[33] Powell did not demand a neat analytic tidiness from the establishment clause cases, but he supported aid to parochial education as sound judicial policy when there were not serious intrusions of the state into parochial schools or specific evidence of political divisiveness. Accordingly, Powell concurred with the majority in favor of the aid.

However, in a dramatic reversal eight years later in *Aguilar v. Felton* (1985), Justice Powell reasserted the "political divisiveness" standard of the *Lemon* test, indicating a reevaluation of his traditional position in these areas. Concerning a New York program in which public school teachers taught secular subjects in parochial school classrooms, Powell stated:

> This risk of entanglement is compounded by the additional risk of political divisiveness stemming from the aid to religion at issue. . . . I do not suggest that at this point in our history the Title I program or similar parochial aid programs could result in the establishment of a state religion. There likewise is small chance that these programs would result in significant religious or denominational control over our democratic processes. . . . Nonetheless, there remains a considerable risk of continuing political strife over the propriety of direct aid to religious schools and the proper allocation of limited governmental resources.

In contrast to the other members of the *Aguilar* majority, Powell did accept *indirect* aid to parochial schools through evenhanded assistance programs for the parents of both public and parochial school children. However, he had clearly reconsidered his position in reaching the conclusion with Brennan that

124 these programs do not constitute the "indirect and incidental effect beneficial to [the] religious institutions that we suggested in *Nyquist* would survive Establishment Clause scrutiny."[34]

The process value of deterring political divisiveness, in the *Grand Rapids* and *Aguilar* cases, received at least a temporary lease on life, even though Chief Justice Burger's use of the *Lemon* standard in *Lynch v. Donnelly* became consequentialist enough to render legitimate any state government action toward religion. Under Burger's application of the watered-down *Lemon* standard in *Lynch*, states were guaranteed the presumption of secular purpose and good faith in all actions directed at religious institutions, short of establishing a state religion as the Framers would understand it. In a concurrence, but displaying a more subtle analytical twist, Justice O'Connor abandoned the political divisiveness prong of the *Lemon* standard in favor of a more stringent "no entanglement" test. In *Lynch*, she found that the city creche display did not violate any of her modified *Lemon* criteria, and she voted with the majority. Justice Brennan, however, dissenting in that case, warned about the perils of "religious chauvinism" and that political antagonism might come from minority dissident religious groups.[35]

Ideological tensions were rife on the Burger Court at this time and were reflected in the reshaping of Court coalitions in establishment clause cases, not merely in process terms but on rights and free exercise grounds as well. The *Lemon* standard, for so long a principled standard for establishment clause cases, but flexibly applied in the *Lynch* case, may at least provide for its own resurgence in the future.[36]

Secular Purpose and Deference to State Authority

All Burger Court justices acknowledged that state legislatures have a legitimate secular interest in ensuring a hospitable environment for religious institutions. Broadly defined, this interest involves the services that sectarian schools provide as educational alternatives for many school children and the resulting alleviation of tax burdens on society; wholesome competition with public schools, resulting in the overall betterment of a pluralistic society; and a general state interest in seeing that its children are properly educated.[37] The scope of that interest, however, was the source of heated debate.

This secular interest, and its effective implementation through statute, lay somewhere between the two poles of judicial deference to process determinations (as advocated by conservatives Rehnquist, White, Burger, and to a lesser degree O'Connor) and outright distrust of those same processes on the other (with liberals Brennan, Marshall, and to a lesser degree Stevens and Blackmun as the main proponents). Polity principles of the most fundamental sort came into play when justices were asked to what extent a government should be trusted to intrude into religious enterprises, even when it may benefit from such intrusions. The question of state neutrality was in turn reflected back on the Court's role in determining such neutrality. Thus views about the Court's role must inevitably underlie any choices made by justices about who has authority to intervene in which situations.

This question of decisionmaking authority—that is, whether state legislatures, federal courts, or school systems can be trusted to make choices about aid to parochial education—was crucial to the substantive outcomes in the cases and is a polity-oriented question. Justices' views about American political institutions, and whether they, rather than courts, should be trusted to decide the relationship between church and state, range from pluralist interpretations of the American political system as "open" and vigilant to violations of values in the Constitution to critical pluralist views that only courts, using strong polity and rights principles to establish a wall of separation, can be trusted to protect against government establishment of religion and denial of free exercise rights.[38] Justices Brennan and Marshall favored the prohibitive constraints on state action that they found in the establishment clause. Their bloc emphasized a hermetic seal between church and state, with the Court as a proscriptive body policing the integrity of that relationship *preventively*. Justices Burger and O'Connor, on the other hand, emphasized an initial presumption of good faith on the part of agents of the state in dealing in church affairs. In O'Connor's dissent in *Aguilar v. Felton* she declared her support for the ability of public school teachers teaching remedial reading and math in sectarian classrooms to prevent the *potentials* of indoctrination, relying on the record in the case to support the assertion.[39]

Justices White and Rehnquist—in the center and on the ideological extreme, in Blasi's view—shared the process value of Court deference to legislatures in these cases. Characteristically to the point, Justice White said in *Lemon v. Kurtzman*, "It is enough for me that the States and the Federal Government are financing a separable secular function of overriding importance in order to sustain the legislation here challenged. That religion and private interests other than education may substantially benefit does not convert these laws into impermissible establishments of religion."[40] White favored dismantling the *Lemon* standard in favor of such a deferential outlook.[41] Justice White should be credited for acknowledging his predispositions outright, but he implicated himself as well when he attacked the majority in *Lemon* for banning the Rhode Island and Pennsylvania statutory aid schemes, saying that they substitute "presumption for proof" of potential state abuse.[42] The majority may have been overly proscriptive of state action in expectation of state abuse, but White failed to see that he was equally presumptuous in his *denial* of the potential for such abuse. Thus the consensus that the state had a secular interest in acknowledging religious institutions breaks down once we try to define that interest. The Court balanced standards of state neutrality toward religious

126   institutions, on the one hand, with the process principle of the Court's stance toward majoritarian political processes, on the other.

The most crucial views of the Burger Court concerning church-state relations and the institutional role of the Court in the polity were found at the center. In this regard, Blasi is right but for the wrong reasons. The votes of justices in the center were crucial to case outcomes, but not because they were pragmatic and unprincipled. Nor were most justices on the right and left, whom Blasi labels "extreme," more principled or extreme. Justice Blackmun seriously reevaluated the ideas in contention in church and state cases after he wrote for the majority in *Roemer v. Board of Public Works* that "it has not been the Court's practice, in considering facial challenges to statutes of this kind, to strike them down in *anticipation* that particular applications may result in unconstitutional use of funds."[43] He retreated to more principled, if less flexible, grounds in establishment clause cases after *Regan*. The general trend on the Burger Court was toward less fixed ideas about key process principles in church and state cases; thus, Justices Powell and O'Connor also cast crucial votes against the conservative coalition with which they were usually associated.

The Effects Test: Accommodative versus Proscriptive Jurisprudence

The justices' views varied a great deal on the question of what actually constituted a detrimental effect upon the religious enterprise. Questions of process entanglement, political divisiveness, and religious pervasiveness were figured in to the extent that the "no entanglement" tier of the *Lemon* test was a redundancy of the "effects" test. Instead of wanting the three prongs of the *Lemon* test to be separate, some justices wanted to conflate them into a quite general primary effects standard—that the primary effect of a law must be one that neither advances nor inhibits religion. In his concurrence in *Roemer*, Justice White stated:

> Today's plurality leaves the impression that the [*Lemon*] criterion really may not be "separate" at all. . . . In affirming the District Court's conclusion that the legislation here does not create an "excessive entanglement" of church and state, the plurality emphasizes with approval that "the District Court [found that the religious institution is] capable of separating secular and religious functions." Yet these are the same factors upon which the plurality focuses in concluding that the Maryland legislation satisfies the second ["effects"] part of the *Lemon* I test.[44]

The internal redundancies among the standards of the *Lemon* test gave justices sympathetic to aid to parochial schools considerable leeway in determining how far any authority can be entrusted. In the *Tilton, Hunt,* and *Roemer* cases, and in the parochial school cases after *Meek,* the *Lemon* standard ceased to be a forceful tool for constraints on legislative action. On the contrary, *Lemon* was invoked loosely to accommodate ideologically conservative process norms of deference to legislative bodies.

The saving grace of the property tax exemption permitted to churches in *Walz v. Tax Commission of New York* was that money was not *directly* provided by state government, but rather was only passively endorsed as part of a general tax exemption for nonprofit institutions and that historically such an exemption had been allowed. As a rule, in the early establishment clause cases of the Burger era, direct grants—be they salary supplements, provision for instructional materials, test grading, tuition reimbursement, or tax deduction schemes—were disallowed (*Nyquist, Lemon, Levitt*). But state legislatures responded to Court prohibitions with increasing persistence and ingenuity, forcing the Court both to inject their tests with a greater amount of broad applicability to the new legislative schemes and to reevaluate the limits individual justices were willing to impose on state actions that several of them perceived as clearly legitimate and justifiable.

Perhaps the criterion that served to qualify the process guarantees of the *Lemon* standard to the fullest degree was the *breadth* of the aid that was offered by state legislatures and the federal government. In *Walz,* an instance in which the property tax exemptions were offered to all nonprofit institutions, the Court found it difficult to reject aid on narrow establishment clause grounds. Conversely the statutory schemes in *Lemon, Nyquist,* and *Sloan v. Lemon* were all invalidated because of the advantages that were offered solely to sectarian schools or to the parents of children attending them. The Court was most amenable to aid in those instances when it could look to past precedent—in particular, the *Everson v. Board of Education* and *Board of Education v. Allen* cases, which allowed for general state subsidies for bus rides and secular textbooks for parochial school children in support of state subsidization of a number of nonprofit needs.

Another widely disputed aspect of government aid to religious institutions concerned permeability, that is, the incorporation of secular values into parochial schools as a byproduct of state aid. The dilution of "religious atmosphere" as a consequence of "benevolent neutrality" on the part of state legislatures was connected in kind, but not in scope, to the free exercise rights of *individuals.* Justices on the rights-oriented bloc used process- or polity-based nonentanglement arguments to support free exercise rights of sectarian school children as well as nonbelievers. After *Walz,* liberal justices feared that the decision might be used to support other demands for aid to religious schools. The permeability problem was addressed in a string of rulings disallowing direct aid to sectarian schools (see Table 4.1). In *Walz,* Justice Douglas emphasized the importance of severing the private and public domains of the church and state relationship.[45] Similarly, in a

128   concurring statement in *Lemon*, Douglas, joined by Black, termed the religious enterprise as a whole entity within itself—an "organism" that could suffer irreparable damage if its internal equilibrium were altered. Entanglement might dilute both the religious environment and the controlling sectarian purpose, he contends. "The intrusion of government into religious schools through grants, supervision, or surveillance may result in establishment of religion in the constitutional sense when what the state does enthrones a particular sect for overt or subtle propagation of its faith."[46]

Many of these process and rights distinctions turned on the differences between individual and institutional forums of rights protection. As in other aspects of the *Lemon* standard formulation, the justices carried predispositions toward state efforts to discourage active intervention and guarantee the integrity of religious pursuit. Statistical determinants of adverse effects on parochial schools were given more or less credence by individual justices, depending upon the *ideological* result he or she desired. In an important footnote White mentioned that "our prior cases demonstrate that the question of whether aid programs satisfy the 'excessive entanglement' test [like the broader "effects" test] depends at least to some extent on the degree to which the Court accepts lower courts' findings of fact."[47]

In sum, the "effects" standard of the *Lemon* test was used as often to justify state aid to parochial institutions as to prevent its expansion. How it was used in a given case depended on the nature of the aid itself: whether it was indirect or direct; whether it involved buildings; whether the immediate recipients of the aid were individual parents or institutions; and finally, the diffuse nature and broad applicability of the aid. The Burger/*Lemon* "effects" approach was geared toward policy outcomes and a flexible attitude toward the majoritarian process rather than toward principles focused on rights. The wall of separation theories and benevolent neutrality and flexibility norms that prompted the coalitions on the Court were appended by the appropriate justices onto the *Lemon* standard in specific cases to further the justices' own process and rights ideologies. Their pragmatism was premised "more on experience and history than on logic" in establishment clause cases; it was fueled by readily perceptible ideologies.[48]

These differences among the justices over polity and rights principles resulted in the patterns of decisionmaking I have identified. These patterns cannot be explained by justices' seeking to secure policy objectives, as the instrumental policymaking approach would have us believe. Nor are these patterns based on the policy objectives of the majority coalitions, as the election returns approach would argue.

Process Value Dominance in the Lemon Standard

The prevailing *Lemon* standard was a process-oriented and process-accommodating measure of judicial scrutiny based on arguments about the safeguarding of religious minorities, institutional entanglement, the political divisiveness that could occur as a result of state favoritism, and the nature of the institutional benefit that churches can or should receive under state auspices. It has tended—the 1985 cases excepted—to vary with the legislatures that challenge it, resulting in the flexible establishment clause jurisprudence that characterized the late Burger era. This coupling of deference to legislative bodies with a concern for the institutional or policy implications of aid to parochial education in Court decisionmaking served to unite and divide different justices in the process of bloc formation and group voting.

That these developments should be attributed to ideological considerations rather than a disinterested pragmatism is clear. In fact, the genuinely centrist Justices, Powell and O'Connor, displayed the most innovative responses as their concepts of the proper balance between process and rights values changed. In *Lynch*, O'Connor redefined the *Lemon* standard by strengthening the entanglement prong and thereby revealed, as we shall see, considerable sympathy for the free exercise rights of both believers and nonbelievers. Similarly, Justice Powell displayed a willingness to reevaluate the process principle of political divisiveness in the *Aguilar* case.

Process-oriented justices on the conservative wing used the flexibility afforded by loose application of the *Lemon* standard to further their ideological ends within their larger constitutive polity and rights visions. The center was in ideological flux and rejected a disinterested pragmatism. Each of these indicate a profound refutation of Blasi's "pragmatic middle" thesis.

Pluralist and Critical Pluralist Process Values

The Brennan Group: Critical Pluralist Process Values

Between 1980 and 1986 Justices Brennan, Marshall, Stevens, and Blackmun invoked process values—political divisiveness, religious or secular effects, and entanglement—to argue their critical pluralist position. They argued that the government was not capable of ensuring the separation between church and state, the paramount requirement of the establishment clause. The prong of the *Lemon* standard that was most debated in establishment clause decisions was the entanglement of political and religious pursuits through state involvement in sectarian affairs. A concern for political divisiveness then became the focus of critical pluralist/rights-oriented justices in their effort to bolster the *Lemon* standard against state support for religious institutions. Dissenting in *Lynch*, which allowed a creche in a city holiday display, Brennan warned that the "religious chauvinism" in this excessive entanglement could cause political antagonism from minority dissident religious groups.[49] The Brennan group sought to reintroduce the prohibitive aspects of the establishment clause that the loose application of the *Lemon* standard by the Burger Court had helped

130   erode by asserting the potential for political divisiveness and expressing their fear of religious groups vying for state funds.

Justice Blackmun's voting record in the establishment clause cases and his move to the Brennan group revealed an abrupt change. (This is an example of how our methodology highlights strategic turning points in individual justices' jurisprudence.) Blackmun had voted with pluralist, weak rights-oriented justices Powell and Stewart through *Wolman v. Walter* (1977), a case that had allowed state aid for textbook loans, off-school therapeutic services, and the administering of state-provided tests for parochial school children. Fearful that he had gone too far in subscribing to the majority's flexible reading of the *Lemon* standard in *Hunt v. McNair* (1973), a case that upheld state financial support of parochial school construction, Blackmun dramatically joined the rights-oriented group in dissent in *Regan*, a case that allowed direct payment to parochial schools to pay teacher salaries for "secular" tasks such as taking attendance.[50] Blackmun stayed with the rights values group thereafter. Justice Stevens embarked on a crusade to reintroduce watertight rights principles in establishment clause adjudication. Thus the Brennan group leaned toward a strict separation between church and state, with the Court policing the integrity of that relationship *preventively*.

The Rehnquist Group: Pluralist Process Values

Justices Rehnquist, White, and Burger supported Court deference to legislatures and to the pluralist bargaining arena generally. White wrote in *Lemon*, "It is enough for me that the States and the Federal Government are financing a separable secular function of overriding importance in order to sustain the legislation here challenged. That religion and private interests other than education may substantially benefit does not convert these laws into impermissible establishments of religion."[51]

The Rehnquist group worked to do away with a stringent *Lemon* test, especially the part that sought to ensure that the primary effect of government aid was not to advance or inhibit religion. They rejected the notion that parochial schools had a pervasive religious atmosphere, and they determined that almost all effects of government aid were incidental when considered within the broader context of a complex society in which religion plays an integral role. They did not view aid to education in prescriptive constitutional process or rights terms. They did not fear entanglement—that the state might corrupt the church or vice versa. Nor did they fear that their views would result in a denial of the free exercise rights of parochial school children or of believers and nonbelievers in the wider society.

Beginning in 1973, Chief Justice Burger no longer displayed concern for a strict entanglement standard. His consequentialist application of the *Lemon* standard in *Lynch*, the creche case, was representative of the Rehnquist group's presumption of secular purpose and good faith in state actions directed at the support of religious values, drawing the line only at the establishment of a state religion.[52]

The Centrist Justices: O'Connor and Powell

We also see ideological interests rather than a disinterested pragmatism when we consider Justice O'Connor's innovative, adaptive, but quite coherent responses to religious questions before the Court. Justice O'Connor emphasized an initial presumption of good faith on the part of government in dealing in church affairs. Evidence for this is provided in O'Connor's dissent in *Aguilar v. Felton* (1985), in which she declared her belief in the ability of public school teachers to keep the potential of indoctrination out of the sectarian classroom.[53] In the Court's reevaluation of entanglement in *Lynch*, O'Connor advocated a more rigorous entanglement test than that found in *Regan*. She contended that there must be *proof* of entanglement rather than merely fear of it, the position advocated by the Brennan group. Nor did she support the Brennan group's standard of *potential* political divisiveness. Entanglement problems that encroached on students' free exercise rights were, according to O'Connor, to be policed after the fact.[54] She sought to separate process from rights values, thus undercutting a strong rights-based jurisprudence.

Justice Powell voted with the majority in all cases. To some this implies that he considered each case on its merits, but a closer look at his opinions reveals that Powell was influenced by particular contexts and by the opinions of both his process- and rights-oriented colleagues on the Court. These influences led to contradictory outcomes. For example, in 1973 Powell wrote the *Nyquist* opinion disallowing aid for facility maintenance, tuition reimbursement, and tax benefits for parents of children attending parochial schools. Ten years later, he voted with the majority in *Mueller*, which allowed parents of parochial school children virtually the same benefits—tax deductions for tuition, textbooks, and transportation. In the *Wolman* case Powell also rejected the political divisiveness standard, arguing that in the modern era we need not fear religious control over democratic processes or deep religious divisions in politics.[55] In a dramatic reversal eight years later in *Aguilar*, however, Powell reasserted the "political divisiveness" standard, indicating a reevaluation of his position. O'Connor, more than Powell, was interested in developing consistent process norms, but even Powell took as his starting point a range of process and rights values. Unlike the Brennan group, Powell did not support only process norms that would result in a wall of separation.

Rights Principles: The Wall of Separation

We now turn from process values to consideration of those substantive rights principles embedded in religious provisions of the First Amendment. As

132   might be expected, these principles center on rights of individuals and groups more than on broader institutional arguments. Without downplaying the process value protections afforded by the establishment clause, the liberal wing of the Court consistently relied on rights arguments to bolster its call for a "high and impregnable" barrier between church and state. That the opinions of Justices Douglas, Brennan, and Marshall in support of the notion that the right of free exercise of religion for believers and nonbelievers alike were influential in the development of doctrine is indicated by the addition of adherents to the rights-oriented camp during the Burger Court era, namely Justices Blackmun and Stevens, and by Justice O'Connor's acknowledgment that free exercise rights constitute limitations on the involvement of church and state. In addition, polity and rights principles of the *Lemon* standard continue to inform contemporary Rehnquist Court establishment clause jurisprudence (see Chapter 8).

Compared to the process principles at work in the establishment clause cases, rights-based principles produced greater rigidity in the Supreme Court's stance on state aid to religious institutions. In fact, denial of all aid to religious institutions was seen as preferable in the long run to benevolent neutrality. The prohibitive aspects of the establishment clause therefore were invoked to supersede any aid that the Court might wish to offer on the basis of a magnanimous reading of the free exercise clause (a reading to which primarily those justices on the process-oriented block subscribe). Relying upon principled separation arguments, the liberal justices sought to use the strong process orientation of the establishment clause to their best advantage in protection of free exercise values. Accordingly, unprincipled adjudication—as indicative of a general Court leniency toward political bodies—did not fit their stance well.

These process and rights predispositions of the liberal bloc on the Court determined the outcome of many of the subtle choices of degree that must be made in exploring what constitutes legislation or government action whose primary effect advances or inhibits religion, which is outlawed by the effects prong of the *Lemon* test. The liberal justices hoped to keep these flexible choices at a minimum by creating a principled separation that would permit fewer questions about the church and state relationship in the first place.

The Brennan Group: Protecting Believers and Nonbelievers

The external and internal components of the free exercise clause were most clearly articulated by Justice Brennan in his majority opinion in *Aguilar v. Felton* (1985):

The principle that the state should not become too closely entangled with the church in the administration of assistance is rooted in two concerns. When the state becomes enmeshed with a given denomination in matters of religious significance, the freedom of religious belief of those who are not adherents of that denomination suffers, even when the governmental purpose underlying the involvement is largely secular. In addition, the freedom of even the adherents of the denomination is limited by the governmental intrusion into sacred matters.[56]

The external free exercise rights of sectarian institutions and nonadherents were forcefully articulated in Justice Brennan's "symbolic union" thesis in the majority opinion in the *Grand Rapids* case, in which the Court forbade state-provided secular classes and guidance services in parochial schools. The symbolic union premise was based on a concern that state and federal programs not be perceived by adherents of the denominations involved as an endorsement of their religious beliefs or by nonadherents as disapproval of their individual religious choices. Brennan wrote, "Government promotes religion as effectively when it fosters a close identification of its powers and responsibilities with those of any—or all—religious denominations as when it attempts to inculcate specific religious doctrines. If this identification conveys a message of government endorsement or disapproval of religion, a core purpose of the Establishment Clause is violated."[57]

Questions concerning the integrity of religious atmosphere for denominations and their individual members also touched on the free exercise right of individuals to support no particular religion and the right of atheists to support none at all. In a passionate defense of the external rights of nonbelievers, Justice Douglas, dissenting in *Walz*, argued that these people should not be asked to support churches with their tax dollars. If the dictates of pluralism applauded by the majority of the Court in this case are to be properly followed, then nonbelievers deserve just as much financial support as believers. In short, he asserted, independence for religious institutions is the price of liberty, and state aid is the sacrifice.[58] Implicit in Brennan's arguments in both the 1985 *Aguilar* and *Grand Rapids* majority opinions was a concern for the individual child's *internal* free exercise rights. Any form of state support of schooling could very easily passively indoctrinate a child into believing his particular sect was superior to those of his friends across the block, or perhaps even the views of his agnostic relatives.

The Brennan group's objective was to keep Court discretion at a minimum by creating a principled separation between church and state. Clear principles would reduce the factors to be considered, factors that might permit accommodation between church needs and majoritarian state interests. The rights principles of the Brennan group promoted a rigid stance toward state aid to religious institutions and worked against benevolent neutrality. Relying on principled separation arguments, the Brennan group sought to use the clear prescriptive process and rights values in the establishment clause to protect

134   specific religious thought and practice. Accordingly, adjudication based primarily on consequences—as in Court leniency toward political bodies supporting religious holidays such as Christmas—did not fit their stance. These process and rights predispositions of the Brennan group, more than the open-ended *Lemon* test, provided definitive answers to many subtle choices that had to be made in exploring what constitutes the establishment of religion.

Centrist Justice O'Connor and the Rehnquist Group

Discussion of free exercise rights for sectarians and nonsectarians, and their internal and external rights, pervaded the liberal bloc's wall-of-separation arguments. The conservative wing of the Court—Rehnquist, Burger, White, Powell, and O'Connor—tried to transform the process guarantees from a prescriptive separation of church and state to a *positivistic* one in which all state and church interactions were considered constitutional unless they were shown *by the facts* to result in unconstitutional state indoctrination. But just as Powell asserted his independence from this bloc over the issue of political divisiveness, O'Connor also displayed some nonpragmatic innovation in her depiction of free exercise rights principles.

O'Connor was concerned with protecting "internal" free exercise rights. In her concurrence in *Grand Rapids*, she relied in substance on Brennan's "symbolic union" thesis. She determined that when parochial school instructors teach secular subjects after school in their regular classrooms, there was a significant chance that they would infringe on the free exercise right of children to make up their own minds about religion. O'Connor's fear was that identification of children with their parochial school teachers, furthered by being in regular classrooms, would lead to a mixing of secular and religious messages and thus to a constitutionally impermissible belief that the state endorses the students' religion. Furthermore, she feared there would be no way of monitoring this situation without entangling the state deeply in religious school activities.[59] Unlike the Brennan group, O'Connor did not view the use of state funds in religious school surroundings as a violation of the establishment clause per se. Also, in *Wallace v. Jaffree* (1985), a case that struck down an Alabama law authorizing a period of silence for "meditation or voluntary prayer" in public schools, O'Connor, in a concurrence, strongly supported the idea that children's free exercise rights would be infringed if there was implicit state encouragement or favoritism for prayer in a state's moment-of-silence law.

O'Connor opposed the Rehnquist group's view that free exercise principles should be evaluated on the basis of the Framers' preference for prayer and religion. She argued that the *Lemon* standard should not be applied ahistorically, noting that public education was nonexistent in the eighteenth century.

But she also took issue with the Brennan group's wholesale removal of questions of state support of religion from Court scrutiny by erecting a wall between church and state. For O'Connor, the effects of state policy need not be religiously neutral or exclusively secular, but the policy must be free of religious content—a requirement, the record confirmed, that Alabama's actions could not meet.[60] To her, content choices by states warrant Court vigilance, but she did not favor wholesale support of state aid to religion, as Burger and Rehnquist urged, or the "wall" that her liberal colleagues urged.

It is clear, however, that O'Connor supported a consequentialist case-by-case *Lemon* test in the interest of free exercise. This flexibility was more characteristic of the conservative bloc with which she is usually associated. She trusted in the Court's ability to differentiate between sham and actual secular purposes in state laws and, as shown in her concurring opinion in *Lynch*, she favored a scrupulously monitored system of state support for religion that respected both believers and nonbelievers. Also, the rights component in O'Connor's thinking was clearer than that of her fellow centrist, Justice Powell.[61] O'Connor's centrism was not a search for pragmatic policy determinations but rather a search for process and rights guides to a principled jurisprudence in light of her interpretation of the Constitution, precedent, and allowable rights definitions under the Court's power of judicial review.

Constitutive Decisionmaking on the Burger Court

The case analysis demonstrates four points: (1) that the "pragmatic middle" thesis is not borne out by the evidence from establishment clause cases prior to 1980 and is clearly not a useful way to describe post-1980 Burger Court decisionmaking; (2) that the substantive basis of judicial choices—the polity and rights principles on which the establishment clause cases were decided prior to 1980—informed the bloc voting in the post-1980 cases; (3) that an "ideological jurisprudence" methodology is particularly suited for analysis of Supreme Court decisionmaking in general; and (4) that the Supreme Court is primarily constitutive rather than instrumental in its decisionmaking.

Blasi's description of the pragmatic middle, which he claims was central to a disinterested and balanced Burger Court jurisprudence, does not fit the facts. The Court never acted in the way he describes. If one were to attempt to identify such a center, one might argue that it consisted of Justices Stewart, Powell, and Blackmun before 1980, because those justices seldom dissented from the majority opinions. But one third of the Court does not make a coherent center. Nor can it perform the tasks and inculcate the values described by Blasi. The other members of the pragmatic middle identified by Blasi—White and Stevens—often dissented from the majority. In fact, they were ranked higher in percentage of dissents than many of the justices Blasi labeled as extreme.

Moreover, these middle justices viewed the principled basis for judicial

136   choice in cases involving aid to parochial education as declining in the late 1970s. For that reason they could no longer support the movement away from rights-based decisions and toward process-based decisions. Thus Blackmun, and to a certain degree O'Connor and Powell, refused support for the unprincipled, narrowly policy-oriented choices made by the Court's right wing. Most important, the only justice on the Burger Court who consistently voted with the majority opinion in religion cases after 1980 was Powell.

Thus the Burger Court, because of its reliance on a tension between long-standing process and rights values in the religion clauses of the First Amendment, did not surrender to the attempts by religious fundamentalists to place schools and government in a position of advocating religious beliefs. However, the nose of the camel was under the tent, so to speak, in the creche case and cases involving general programs of aid to parents of school children. In essence, the Burger Court endorsed religion as part of our general societal values and religious education as part of a general system of public, tax-supported education. However, it stopped short of allowing schools and legislatures to affirmatively support religious fundamentalism as a right of children in secular schools. In so doing, the Burger Court emphasized that religion is an important value in our liberal society, but not one that should replace the objectives of our schools to educate in a secular, rather than a sectarian, manner. The creationism cases confirm these findings.[62]

Inevitably, the pragmatic middle thesis leads us to view the Supreme Court and its process of decisionmaking as similar to electorally accountable, instrumental policymaking institutions to a degree that is unwarranted by the evidence. By contrast, a constitutive approach to Burger Court decisionmaking in this doctrinal area asks us to analyze and document tensions among polity and rights values in the jurisprudence of justices and blocs of justices. It also asks us to elucidate differences in constitutional principles over time so we can better understand the process of doctrinal change. Finally, it asks us to consider normative issues concerning the roles of law, courts, and rights in our society—questions that have become clouded.

Underlying ideology and values provide the key to each judicial era, as we have seen in the case of the Burger Court. The reconstitution of doctrine, rather than a reaction to precedent, continues into the Rehnquist era. Court decisionmaking reflects justices' continuing process and rights values as they decide cases that arise out of modern political tensions in society. Hence, law does not stand above politics or mimic power relationships of society. Process and rights principles act as filters for Court decisionmaking and ensure that the Court's choices as it encounters political tensions in society reflect long-standing constitutional values.

There is no universal judicial stance. Justices animated by clear positions form groups in support of different process and rights values, revealing that the institutional momentum provided by the Supreme Court is fueled by a timely *convergence* of views. This changing dynamic of Court jurisprudence is a sliding scale of sorts, in which process or rights values, or a combination, captivate a dominant coalition of individual members on the Court for sustained periods of time. The distinction between valueless pragmatism and the convergence of value hierarchies of like-minded justices may appear small, but it is a factual and theoretical difference of the greatest magnitude. It is around this convergence that Supreme Court decisions revolve and doctrinal change centers, with differing values providing the problematic elements of specific cases rather than stare decisis or precedent.

The conflict and, perhaps more important, the *relationship* of polity and rights principles that inform judicial choices are strongly manifest in First Amendment cases in which rights guarantees mesh in an uneasy equilibrium with the structural or process guarantees of the Constitution. Justices who hold strong convictions about a particular mix of values will try to stretch the common ground or, in another case, will try to erect a permanent barrier in the law. Ultimately, some accord must be reached to keep the shifting alliance intact.

I am forced to disagree with Anthony Lewis, who, drawing on the words of Justice Holmes, described the Burger Court era as "that period of dry precedent which is so often to be found midway between a creative epoch and a period of solvent philosophical reaction."[63] While reflecting societal debate about the proper institutional role of the Supreme Court, the Burger Court did more than refine Warren Court doctrine in an activist but rootless manner. It was, in Justice Holmes's terms, reactive and creative in forging a new—if complex—ideological course. This reconstitution of doctrine, rather than merely a reaction to precedent, continues into the Rehnquist era.

This more complex view of judicial activity reflects a diminishing consensus on the controlling principles of political and legal theory. It is also a product of the dilemma facing legal theory in a liberal democracy: how to achieve equity without undermining the autonomy of law from "politics," a goal that has been called into question repeatedly by scholars and activists alike.[64]

Unfortunately, scholars of rights or process orientations often fail to recognize the central *interrelationship* of process and rights values in the development of constitutional principles. Because values are often viewed as irrelevant or arbitrary, it is not surprising that the values that inform judicial choice should themselves come under attack as an inadequate measure of judicial perspective. Although values are admittedly difficult to categorize and next to impossible to quantify, recent scholarship has taken a path that is too easy by abandoning the study of values altogether. We must instead *qualify* in a positive sense, using qualitative and quantitative data in the establishment clause cases, the statement "A jurisprudence of values is a poor one if the proper

138   function of commentators and justices is to rationalize the case law—that is, to organize the Court's decisions into consistent patterns. For in the contemporary world, individual value systems are both internally inconsistent and inconsistent with those held by others.''[65] Rooting scholarly analysis of constitutional law once again in a debate over values can also serve as a response to what might be labeled a rebirth of the relativism and empiricism of postwar scholarship. The scholarly debate that pits pluralist theories of access and participation against theories emphasizing structural inequalities and elite rule in our polity cannot have been lost on the Court, which has the capability to enforce and enact such positions in law.[66]

Vincent Blasi's analysis begs this question: To what end has the Court been active? It is at this level of values that critical analysis must take place. By refusing to make prescriptive statements about the nature of judicial choices in Burger era activity, Blasi overlooks those elements of political theory that serve the reservoir of values upon which justices inevitably rely in their decision-making.[67]

Ultimately, the core value of Blasi's work and of most instrumental interpretations of Supreme Court decisionmaking—nonideological political compromise—is antithetical to the fundamental presence of a constitutional legacy in society. Political scientists have lost track of an entire range of ideologies—a range that, as argued here, can be delineated into either process or rights principles. Analysis of such "intersubjective" dimensions of the legal environment moves justices onto common ideological ground, away from predictable responses based on expectations of what Court policy outcomes should be.[68] In sum, we must understand that Supreme Court justices are moved by ideological interests just as are other political officials in the policy processes.[69]

Analysis of constitutive process and rights principles in Supreme Court decisionmaking allows for the systematic organization of judicial choices in specific areas of constitutional law and can account for group momentum in the shaping of constitutional doctrine. It points us to *definable limits* on the range of values that individual justices use in developing innovative Court doctrine. Such principles in flux do not indicate simplistic bargaining as the hallmark of the Burger Court's activity, but instead reveal an "ideological jurisprudence" that is highly motivated and highly competitive—justices who hold principles as essential to an informed interpretation of an increasingly complex polity.[70]

Chapter Five

Equal Protection on the Burger Court

We continue to test the validity of instrumental, or utilitarian, assumptions about internal Court decisionmaking. However, in this chapter emphasis is placed on testing the validity of Martin Shapiro's policymaking interpretation of Supreme Court decisionmaking in the Burger Court era rather than Blasi's instrumental no counterrevolution thesis.[1] The fundamental rights and interests strand of equal protection is used to test the validity of Shapiro's approach because Shapiro has emphasized that fundamental rights and interests doctrine is the best exemplar of both the differences between the Warren and Burger Courts and the validity of his approach to Supreme Court decisionmaking and doctrinal change.[2]

Instrumental Assumptions in the Policymaking Approach

Shapiro's policymaking approach, especially as it is applied to the Burger Court era, is the instrumental interpretation that most forcefully argues that justices use constitutional law pragmatically, in an unprincipled way, to make policy choices that they desire. It claims that justices use constitutional theory and polity and rights principles to support their own policy wants: "We have come to expect five or six opinions in major cases, none of which does more than state the author's policy preferences dressed up in cursory and pro forma legal argument. There is no reason not to say openly what the justices care so little to disguise, that they make their decisions on the basis of seat-of-the-pants predictions of the immediate and direct policy benefits of the various alternatives available to them."[3]

As is typical of instrumental interpretations, Shapiro views precedent as mere fodder for what is essentially a justice's choice of policy outcomes: "Whether one agrees or disagrees with the substantive policy outcomes achieved by the Burger Court, it is surely fair to say that the Burger Court's style mirrors the reality of its decision-making. No member of the current Court cares much about legal scholarship."[4] Shapiro emphasizes that, in contrast to the jurisprudence of the Warren Court, there is no definable, predictable pattern or coherence in Burger Court jurisprudence. However, he also argues that *autonomy* (individual, group, and institutional) is a more important value to the Burger Court than it was for the Warren Court. But it is the ad hoc policy wants of the Burger Court, not deeply held polity or rights principles, that inform its decisionmaking. Autonomy values, polity principles, or rights principles are not analytically, functionally, or otherwise legitimately distinct from a justice's policy wants, according to the policymaking approach. Nor do such principles explain which value—autonomy or equality—is chosen as the primary value in a case.

We see this emphasis on the policy wants of justices in Shapiro's analysis of several important Burger Court cases. For example, he argues that in *Eisenstadt v. Baird* (1972), in which the Court decided to view unmarried and married persons alike with regard to the sale of contraceptives, there was a valid policy reason to treat married and unmarried people the same way. To treat them differently would imply Court intrusion into sexual behavior. Similarly, Shapiro labels the case of *Roe v. Wade* (1973) the archetypical Burger Court opinion. "The prize of the Burger Court is surely the *Abortion* cases, which range over a truly amazing variety of medical, psychological, and sociological data in order to construct a social policy that is totally the Court's own invention and rests totally on considerations of social and political prudence that cannot possibly be subsumed under any constitutional principle."[5]

Shapiro's standard of evaluation for the Burger Court is a flawed vision of the Warren Court. Shapiro argues that the Burger Court did not announce a general rule and then balance it with other values as the Warren Court did. Instead, it more often retained the power to make case-by-case decisions, refusing to delegate implementation powers to subordinate branches. Shapiro emphasizes that the Burger Court made choices about degrees of a value rather than using clear, ringing language to define a value. For example, Shapiro, like fellow instrumental scholar Blasi, offers the questionable proposition that the Burger Court was not principled in its church and state cases because it would not condemn entanglement, but only "excessive" entanglement, with the justices deciding how much entanglement is too much.[6]

Shapiro views the Burger Court as similar to the Warren Court in having equality as a major, but quite muted policy objective. He contends that the Burger Court, unlike its predecessor, did not make its choices on pure equality principles but instead engaged in a type of balancing that was not seen on the Warren Court. This balancing, Shapiro argues, resulted in less protection of individual rights and equality and less attention to economic and social redistribution than in the Warren Court era.

Shapiro's view is clearest in his analysis of the bellwether doctrinal area of equal protection of the law and the important fundamental rights and interests strand of doctrine. The policymaking approach argues that the *Rodriguez* case is significant because it put a halt to two major Warren Court emphases: equality and the right to subsistence. Shapiro also argues that because some of the Burger Court justices hold different policy views from their predecessors, the Burger Court will sometimes find reasonable classifications that the Warren Court found unreasonable.[7] As I will argue in this and the next chapter, different case outcomes and innovations by the Burger Court are the result not of the specific policy wants of the justices but of the application of more complex polity and rights principles and standards for evaluating what constitutes individual rights, standards born of developments in constitutional and political theory in the interpretive community.

Fundamental Rights to Education and Other Government Benefits: A Constitutive Interpretation

San Antonio Independent School District v. Rodriguez

Powell's Majority Opinion

In the 1973 *Rodriguez* case, the Burger Court had to decide whether grossly different school funding levels in school districts with different levels of taxable property and varying racial makeup violated the equal protection clause of the Constitution. The Burger Court majority found that the laws should be given minimal scrutiny, since strict scrutiny is to be reserved for laws that disadvantage suspect classes or interfere with fundamental rights and interests. There was no suspect classification in the law because the financing scheme did not discriminate against any definable class of people. Even if the financing system disadvantaged those who lived in comparatively poor districts, the resulting class could not be viewed as suspect. Nor did the Texas system impermissibly interfere with the exercise of a fundamental right or liberty. Though Justice Powell quoted *Brown v. Board of Education* in emphasizing that education is perhaps "the most important function of state and local governments," it was not within those limited categories of rights recognized by the Burger Court as guaranteed by the Constitution.[8]

The complexity of the analysis in *Rodriguez* goes far beyond any analysis articulated by the Warren Court. It involves consideration of both polity and rights, for the relationship between the Court's view of its historical institutional role and its approach to future cases is at issue in this case. In rejecting the finding of a constitutional violation, the Burger Court opens itself to a more searching look at structural characteristics of society and education—at poverty, education, and the role of citizenship—than that expressed in the Warren Court's *Brown v. Board of Education* or *Shapiro* decisions. Also, when the Court says that receiving some education may be essential to securing other fundamental rights of citizenship, it accepts the general premise of a Marshall-type peripheral rights argument—that education is a nexus to other fundamental rights. Inequality here is structural. Yet the Burger Court looks at structure in a different way from the Warren Court. For example, in the *Goldberg* case the Burger Court expressed a fear that bureaucracies are not fair to individuals when they terminate welfare payments and created a right to a hearing to ensure that governments would not take away welfare payments ar-

142   bitrarily. However, issues of school politics and state funding choices do not, the majority argues in *Rodriguez*, arouse parallel fears. Thus, the Burger Court differs in its trust of state and local governing bodies, which are open to citizen demands in *Rodriguez*, but not in *Goldberg*.

A polity argument is at the core of the *Rodriguez* case. Justice Powell writes that the Texas school finance law "should be scrutinized under judicial principles sensitive to the nature of the State's efforts and to the rights reserved to the States under the Constitution."[9] He makes the following polity arguments for the majority: (1) the rational basis test is in order because the Court traditionally defers to states and localities on school issues; (2) fiscal and tax policy is up to states; (3) justices lack the expertise and familiarity with local problems to make wise decisions about the allocation of resources; (4) all tax schemes have a discriminatory impact, and therefore mere impact is not enough to trigger strict scrutiny; (5) a standard of scrutiny that is too rigorous will force all local tax schemes to become subjects of Court intervention under the equal protection clause; (6) fiscal matters involve the most persistent and difficult issues of educational policy—another area in which the Court lacks specialized knowledge; (7) experience counsels against premature interference with informed judgments made at state and local levels of government; and (8) there are many constitutionally permissible ways for legislatures to tackle problems. The view of polity here is different from that of the Warren Court. For the Burger Court, polity concerns about institutions and rights concerns take center stage in a way that a narrower examination of fundamental rights and interests would not permit.

Powell argues that the Texas system allows a large measure of local participation in the control of schools, which counters an overly centralized government (*Wright v. Council* [1972]). This concern for polity principles and prudence, that is, the concern for deference to state and local government, court role, and a trust of experts, is evidence that polity and rights considerations at work in Court decisionmaking. The balancing occurring in this case was also evident in the Warren Court's *Shapiro* decision and in Warren's dissent. Thus, one can argue that either principles or pragmatism were at work in both Courts. However, a more valid premise is that both Courts rested their choices on *both* polity and rights principles and decisions about the relationship of these principles. This kind of judicial analysis can be clearly seen in landmark decisions, when Courts decide to change the mix or definitions of basic polity and rights principles in or across doctrinal areas.

The implications of the *Rodriguez* case are not national. Schools of uneven quality, unlike the denial of welfare, do not in themselves constitute a denial of interstate movement. More importantly, the hint in *Rodriguez* that a total denial of education might raise similar questions to those found in *Shapiro* and *Plyler v. Doe* (1982), in which the Burger Court said that the state of Texas cannot charge tuition to illegal aliens seeking to attend public schools, suggests that *Rodriguez* did not end Court concerns about the right of citizens to government programs, as the policymaking and no counterrevolution interpreters of the Burger Court suggest. Justice Powell, for example, suggests that a complete denial of a fundamental right—not that education per se is a right—but that without education other fundamental rights are threatened or lost. He writes, "Even if it were conceded that some identifiable quantum of education is a constitutionally protected prerequisite to the meaningful exercise of either right [speech or vote], we have no indication that the present levels of educational expenditures in Texas provide an education that falls short."[10]

Therefore, the view that *Rodriguez* is the end of the line for fundamental rights and interests analysis is misguided. A majority of the Court respects the complex relationship between education and individual rights but refuses to place itself in the position of deciding the degree of difference in educational resources that should trigger Court intervention in state and local educational institutions.

So did the Warren Court, however. The claim that the Burger Court merely filled in the gaps of Warren Court principles is false, because in *Rodriguez* the Burger Court indicates that there may be a fundamental right to education as a nexus to fundamental rights in the Constitution, but that absolute denial of education would be required to mandate Court intervention. The Warren Court's analysis of education was quite narrow, concentrating on whether race classifications can be used in the law to separate black and white children. Given the pre–Warren Court precedents in graduate and professional school segregation cases, and in *Shelley v. Kraemer* (1948), *Korematsu v. United States* (1944) and other cases, for the Warren Court it was the presence of a race classification, not consideration of a right to education, that triggered strict scrutiny. This point was confirmed in the relatively short period during which segregation laws were declared invalid in nonschool settings.

Powell argues that there is a special need for judicial self-restraint when educational issues are involved because of their complexity and the need for experimentation, which can be fostered by respect for federalism. He writes that (1) education presents a myriad of "intractable economic, social, and even philosophical problems"; (2) experts disagree over the relationship between education spending and the quality of education; (3) "in such circumstances [debate among experts], the judiciary is well advised to refrain from imposing on the States inflexible constitutional restraints that could circumscribe or handicap research and experimentation"; and (4) the relationship between state power and local school board power is an important issue. "It would be difficult to imagine a case having a greater potential impact on our federal system than the one now before us, in which we are urged to abrogate systems of

144 financing public education presently in existence in virtually every State,'' Powell concludes.[11]

Conceding that action to prevent violations of fundamental rights or other clear principles of the Constitution come first, Powell argues that it must be balanced with polity considerations and judicial prudence. He concludes that a rational basis test is met by the Texas system: Districts differ on taxes paid for schools because of differences in land values, and higher salaries provide the major difference between wealthy and poorer school districts. Thus the Texas system is like most other systems because it allows for more support of schools in the districts where the residents want to support schools. It also ensures basic education where the ratable taxes are low.

In this case there is far more discussion of the role of states, localities, and the Court's role as umpire in the federal system than appeared in the important cases that followed.[12] Thus, the *Rodriguez* case is a landmark because of the sophistication of its polity and rights analysis, not because it eliminated wealth as a classification subject to heightened scrutiny.

Justice White's Dissent

Justice White, joined by Douglas and Brennan, argues that if Texas had ensured minimal educational expenditures and allowed school districts to tax themselves beyond these minimal levels, then the law might have been upheld under a minimal level of Court scrutiny (also called a rational basis test), on the premise that a state finance law with local options for taxation does allow community participation as a key value in school board decisionmaking.[13] White argues that the Texas law does not provide a meaningful option for local participation in school districts with a low per-pupil tax base because there is a limit to the property taxes that can be collected for schools. Therefore, property-poor districts cannot make the choice to meet the school funding levels of property-rich districts.

White asks: Is the state meeting its objective—local control of education? His is not a fundamental rights analysis in the sense advocated by Brennan and Marshall. White uses a *polity* argument to undermine the law; he does not posit a fundamental right to education. While White's heightened rational-basis argument is polity-oriented, it actually involves more scrutiny than most Warren Court equal protection cases. By referring to *Reed v. Reed*, a gender rights case decided in 1971, to make the argument in *Rodriguez*, White shows that he is asking for a more imaginative equal protection analysis than that of the Warren Court. The Warren Court favored equality and rights arguments, rather than polity arguments, to end the denial of formal access to government. It did not, as Justice White does here, question whether the process established by a state denies a certain allocation of specific goods.

This is an excellent example of how nonoriginalist interpretations of polity principles in the Constitution, not just rights principles such as the fundamental right to liberty in the Fourteenth Amendment due process clause, can have important implications for the redistribution of power, status, and government resources. I say this even though to date polity-based constitutional theories, like that of John Hart Ely, have not been redistributive in the degree found in constitutional theory based on fundamental rights values. A constitutional theory built on both polity and rights principles can both be more critical of politics and act as a more thoughtful guide to what the Court is actually doing.

Justice Brennan's Dissent

The complexity of Burger Court jurisprudence is also indicated by Brennan's and Marshall's acceptance of nexus theories—theories of equal protection analysis similar to those used by centrist justices in gender and race areas. Brennan, in dissent, agrees with White that the Texas statutory scheme is devoid of any rational basis and thus violates the equal protection clause. He also records his disagreement with the Court's assertion that a right may be deemed fundamental for purposes of equal protection analysis only if it is explicitly or implicitly guaranteed by the Constitution. Brennan agrees with Marshall that prior cases stand for the proposition that fundamentality is in large measure a function of the right's importance for carrying out other rights that are constitutionally guaranteed.

Brennan argues that education is linked to the First Amendment rights of free speech and association and to meaningful citizen participation in the political process. Therefore any classification in the law affecting education must be subject to strict scrutiny. Since the state admits that its finance scheme cannot meet the strict scrutiny test, Brennan finds the scheme constitutionally invalid. He quotes from Marshall's dissent: "As the nexus between the specific constitutional guarantee and the non-constitutional interest draws closer, the nonconstitutional interest becomes more fundamental and the degree of judicial scrutiny applied when the interest is infringed on a discriminatory basis must be adjusted accordingly." He accepts a sliding scale view of how to review government programs that Chief Justice Warren refused to accept in the *Shapiro* case.[14]

It is this *relative* nexus theory of the liberals, compared to the total-deprivation nexus theory of the moderates, that differentiates the majority from the dissenters. Insofar as the relative nexus theory encompasses polity concerns for the future, one could argue that liberals are more pragmatic than the centrists. However, to do so would not grant enough credit to the place of rights and polity principles in the jurisprudence of all Burger Court justices.

Justice Marshall's Dissent

The Marshall dissent has become a classic in equal protection analysis because it predicts the intermediate level of scrutiny that the Burger Court

146   would formalize in later gender rights and equal protection cases.[15] (It is important to note that *Frontiero v. Richardson* [1973], the case in which the Court discusses the level of scrutiny warranted for gender classifications, was decided the same year as the *Rodriguez* case, thus indicating that in 1973 there was ferment on the Court as to how to undertake equal protection analysis.) The central doctrinal consideration was whether a two-tiered system of minimal and strict scrutiny is possible in the complex modern world.

Marshall approaches the constitutional questions in *Rodriguez* by asking what constitutes a disadvantaged class. He argues that if the discrimination is against individual interests, then the constitutional guarantee of equal protection is applicable because it is based on group characteristics, as the apportionment cases showed. Marshall argues that the Texas law had discriminatory impacts on children and that there is no need under equal protection analysis to precisely identify particular individuals who compose a disadvantaged class. He argues that all the Court must do is define the basis of discrimination and test it against the state purpose given for such discrimination.

Marshall then asks whether the discrimination against children in property-poor districts violates the Fourteenth Amendment, and his answer is yes. He argues that if a classification in the law affects a fundamental interest, strict scrutiny is in order. He opposes a two-tiered equal protection analysis, stating that the Supreme Court already applies a spectrum of standards in reviewing issues of discrimination that violate the equal protection clause. The spectrum is based on the constitutional and societal importance of the interest adversely affected by the classification and the recognized invidiousness of the basis on which a class is drawn. The classification of the law is to be measured against the relative importance of the governmental benefits a citizen is deprived of. For Marshall, the concept of fundamental rights goes beyond those rights established or implied in the text of the Constitution itself.[16]

Marshall argues that the Court must make choices about what fundamental interests citizens must have in order to protect fundamental rights, as defined by the Constitution and the ideas that inform them. The Court must decide the extent to which constitutionally guaranteed rights are dependent on interests not mentioned in the Constitution (e.g., the vote, procreation, privacy). As the nexus between the specific constitutional guarantee and the nonconstitutional interest becomes closer and more fundamental, the degree of judicial scrutiny applied when a state infringes on the interest must be increased accordingly.

Through this reasoning Marshall tries to get the Court to expand its view of nexus to encompass more complex causation. The debate over nexus in the Burger Court was a far more difficult one than the polity and rights formulations of the Warren Court era. The equality principle that Marshall seeks is more expansive than that sought by the rest of the Burger Court or the Warren Court. Unlike the majority, Marshall cannot stand to leave the fate of Texas school children to the vagaries of the political process. The Texas legislature has failed to act, he believes, because the strong vested interests of property-rich tax districts in the existing finance scheme pose a substantial barrier to self-initiated legislative reform in education financing.

Marshall's dissent suggests that in *Rodriguez* the Burger Court was going beyond Warren Court polity and rights principles, not because all the justices accepted Marshall's version of the sliding scale, but because most justices used it as a point of reference for more complex polity and rights principles. That the Court did not go all the way in *Rodriguez* to make differences in school spending by district a violation of equal protection of the law leads some commentators to conclude, wrongly, that the relationship between wealth and fundamental rights and interests was no longer of constitutional significance. Scholars employing the policymaking approach and those accepting the no counterrevolution view argue that the Burger Court merely responded to the polity and rights principles of the Warren Court and did not create new constitutional principles or visions.

The debate about nexus and the intermediate level of scrutiny in which the Burger Court engaged was not merely a clarification of Warren Court equality principles. Equality principles did not win out in all cases on the Burger Court; formal equality and access to government did tend to win out in the Warren Court, largely as a function of history: the cases involving clear denial of equal access were submitted to the Warren Court.

The Maturation of Fundamental Rights and Interests after *Rodriguez*

In post-*Rodriguez* cases, the Burger Court demonstrated a willingness to innovate in fundamental rights and interests jurisprudence with regard to the right to government benefits. We see a complexity of polity and rights values; ideology, not mere pragmatism, is at work. In *Dunn v. Blumstein* (1972), *United States Department of Agriculture v. Moreno* (1973), and *Memorial Hospital v. Maricopa County* (1974), the Burger Court shows its more complex equal protection analysis at work. It goes beyond the confines of both *Shapiro* and *Rodriguez* and lays the groundwork for a process of constitutional decisionmaking that is more rights protective than the Warren Court, while appearing to be conservative and pragmatic.

In *Dunn v. Blumstein*, Justice Marshall, writing for the majority, rejects arguments against durational residency requirements for voting even though there was no evidence that such requirements actually deterred travel.[17] In this case Marshall gets the Court to agree to his argument in *Rodriguez*—that it was the right to an opportunity for education, not the suspect classification itself, that was at issue in the state's finance scheme; therefore no specific group of

148   victims needs to be identified. In *Dunn v. Blumstein* it is the right to travel interstate, not evidence that traveling is limited by this law or durational residence requirements for voting, that is protected by the Court. In *Shapiro*, there is more of a concern that the necessities of life (welfare payments) are a "but for" condition—that is, "sufficient condition in and of itself"²—for moving. This difference between a psychological or chilling effect and a right is another important indication that the Burger Court sees a more complex view than the Warren Court of the relationship of government and the economic and social structures.

The Court reached different conclusions in decisions involving necessities—food and medical care. The Food Stamp Act of 1964, amended in 1971, denied food stamps to any household containing an individual who is unrelated to a household member. In *United States Department of Agriculture v. Moreno* (1973) the Burger Court finds this classification irrelevant to the stated purposes of the act and is not rationally related to furthering any other legitimate government interests. It will not hurt those who are likely to abuse the program but those who need the aid but cannot afford to alter their living habits.

Brennan's majority opinion in the *Moreno* case, joined by Douglas, Stewart, White, Marshall, Blackmun, and Powell, states, "For if the constitutional conception of 'equal protection of the laws' means anything, it must at the very least mean that a bare congressional desire to harm a politically unpopular group cannot constitute a *legitimate* governmental interest."[18] Here, Brennan has gone beyond a rational basis test in claiming that the law indicates the government's real interest—a constitutionally impermissible interest. The Court does not accept the reason given by the government. Because the food stamp program involves the necessities of life and because the realities of home costs means unrelated people double and triple up in lodging, the Burger Court uses strict scrutiny to protect those who need better nutrition—those the law was intended to serve.

The constitutive decisionmaking process is evident here, in that Douglas now sees within the rational basis test more discretion for the Court to decide what is rational. He sees the banding together of poor people as an "expression of the right of freedom of association that is very deep in our traditions."[19] Thus, there is a connection between poor people living together, freedom of association, and government programs that support such associations. This proposition, if accepted by other members of the Court, generally would allow more Court intervention to ensure equality of government benefits. Therefore, Douglas and Marshall seek a more open-ended Supreme Court review of government aid. These peripheral rights arguments, while not totally accepted by most members of the Burger Court, are of far greater significance in Burger than Warren Court jurisprudence.

The court dealt with another survival issue, health care, in *Memorial Hospital v. Maricopa County* (1974). The justices decide that a county cannot impose a one-year residency requirement on indigents who need nonemergency hospitalization and medical care. The Burger Court finds that the law includes a classification that impinges on the right of interstate travel by denying newcomers the necessities of life. The Court draws on *Shapiro* and *Dunn v. Blumstein* to find that the state must demonstrate a compelling interest when the right of interstate movement is involved. None of the arguments put forward by the county meets the compelling state interest test: saving money, inhibiting the migration of indigents, deterring indigents from receiving the hospital care benefits of residents, protecting long-term taxpayers, maintaining public support of hospitals, providing administrative convenience, eliminating fraud, or improving budget predictability.[20]

The Court rejects arguments that county residence requirements retard only intrastate, not interstate, travel.[21] What is unconstitutional for the state is no less unconstitutional for the county. There is no polity notion of local control here, unlike in the education cases, *Rodriguez* and *Milliken*. States cannot impose limits on interstate movement by saying they seek to limit intercounty movement. Basic to the *Maricopa* case is the Court's rejection of the notion that different classes of residents—new and old arrivals—may be treated differently, especially when necessities of life are allocated. In a principle that will be extended later to nonnecessities in the *Zobel* case, the Burger Court says that a state may not employ an invidious discrimination among classes of residents to lower the cost of medical aid—because a fundamental right exists.[22] This right is not a direct right to welfare, but rather a limit on states' ability to create different classes of citizens based on length of residence in the state.

The Court also says that the move to Arizona for people with respiratory illnesses may allow them to work and get relief from unemployment and poverty. It is not a right to medical aid but a right to move interstate that would be impeded if this law were allowed. There is a peripheral right here but one different from Douglas's link to the First Amendment. The link is directly to fundamental rights in the *Corfield v. Coryell* (1823)[23] privileges and immunities tradition—interstate movement. This rights notion is important because it suggests that the interdependent causes of individual action—when one moves and the contributions one makes—are so complex and so thoroughly incorporated into social and economic structures that government cannot arbitrarily decide who gets benefits without undercutting the fabric of the nation. The nation thrives on unencumbered interstate movement and equal rights of citizenship. Under the fundamental rights and interests strand of equal protection analysis, the Burger Court, more than the Warren Court, sought to force states and the federal government to treat all citizens equally when basic and essential government services are given.

In both *Maricopa* and the abortion funding cases the Court identifies fundamental rights, the right to interstate movement and the right of privacy as it applies to a woman's choice whether to bear a child, respectively. It must then consider whether continuation of a government benefit—access to hospitals and abortions at government expense—is necessary to protect the fundamental right. However, in the abortion funding cases the Burger Court rejects the idea of linking government benefits to the right to abortion choice. Note also that the polity basis of that choice is important, because Congress specifically chose not to allow federal payment for abortions. For example, in *Harris v. McRae* (1980)[24] the Burger Court considers whether the federal government and states that pay the medical costs of maternity and the birthing of indigents may decide not to pay for indigents' abortions. Although tangential to fundamental rights and interests analysis, the Burger Court's rejection of such payments is based on a view of the right to abortion choice that considers the state's interest in potential life as well as the health of the mother as defined in *Roe v. Wade* (1973). Those concerns are balanced against the rights of abortion choice and procreation as well as the presumption that the state can provide what benefits it wants.

The majority of the justices agreed that since an indigent person is not poor because of state action, the state is not required to provide aid merely because a person is poor. The dissent made telling arguments about the nexus between abortions and liberty interests. There are, however, cases where the poverty of citizens is a concern of the Court in regard to meeting fundamental rights (such as in *Bullock v. Carter* [1972], which concerned filing fees and the ability of the poor to have an equal chance to run candidates in primaries). These cases involve fundamental rights and voting and "but for" effects on interstate travel, as with welfare in the *Shapiro* case and *Maricopa*, that the Court does not see in the case of payment of abortion fees.

Thus, in *Rodriguez, Dunn, Moreno*, and *Maricopa* the Burger Court builds on and goes beyond the *Shapiro* rationale under fundamental rights and interests analysis in that it deals with programs beyond welfare and not subject to federal-state relations, including schooling and nonemergency hospitalization.

Residence Years and State Benefits—Zobel v. Williams

In 1980 the state of Alaska decided to distribute annually a portion of its Permanent Fund from Mineral Income. Each adult citizen was to receive one dividend unit for each year of residency between 1959, the first year of statehood, through 1978. Residents who came after 1959 brought suit against the state, saying the law denied their constitutional right to migrate to Alaska and enjoy the full rights of state citizenship (*Zobel v. Williams* [1982]).[25]

Justice Burger writes the majority opinion in this case, joined by Brennan, White, Marshall, Blackmun, Powell, and Stevens. O'Connor concurs and

Rehnquist dissents. The Burger Court finds that this law denies equal protection. To get this benefit does not require waiting a period of time or meeting some test of bona fide residence. Thus, the issues are different from many fundamental rights and interests cases because wealth is not a factor in the classification. Also the benefit is not remedial or compensatory, but rather it is an affirmative good the state wishes to give to those who came years ago to Alaska to settle.

The Court says that it uses a rational basis test because the Alaska law concerns an allocation of funds. This law fails the rational basis test because Alaska shows no valid state interests that are rationally served by the distinctions it makes between residents arriving before and after 1959. Neither a state incentive to get people to maintain residency nor its claimed interest in prudent management of the oil fund are rationally related to this distinction. The Court actually applied a level of scrutiny higher than a rational basis test. The Court could rationally find that a state might wish to offer a reward to those who took risks and moved to Alaska in early years, but the Court fears that Alaska's reasoning could open the door to state apportionment of other benefits and services according to the length of residency and permit states to divide citizens into an expanding number of classes—results that would be clearly impermissible. The Court takes from *Shapiro* its concern about residency rules, yet its concern here cannot be as active, because no fundamental right is at issue. Also, the money from oil revenues is allocated after all other state needs are satisfied. There is no "but for" condition relating this government program to a loss of rights or to a fear that future discrete and insular minorities will be hurt. The deterrent effect on travel is not very great. By definition those who came to the state many years ago are few in number relative to the rest of the population.

Brennan concurs, joined by Marshall, Blackmun, and Powell. These justices see constitutional concerns of somewhat larger proportions than the right of travel and the effects of residency rules. Brennan views the right of interstate travel as an "unmistakable essence in that document [Constitution] that transformed a loose confederation of States into one Nation. A scheme of the sort adopted by Alaska is inconsistent with the federal structure even in its prospective operation." Brennan argues that states can attract industry, give benefits in public service to citizens, or lower taxes. But states cannot compound their offers of direct benefits in this manner, for if a person leaving the state lost his or her accrued seniority, the mobility so essential to economic progress of our nation would be undermined. Here we see a complex view of the nation, of interstate travel, and of citizenship. States can make classifications among citizens, but not based on length of residence unless there is a valid state interest independent of the discrimination itself.

Justice O'Connor agrees with Brennan that a right to travel is at issue. A

152   federal government interest in free interstate migration is clearly, though indirectly, affected by this law. However, for her the violation is found in the commerce clause or the privileges and immunities clause, a violation of the constitutional purpose of maintaining a union, as explored in *Edwards v. California* (1941). Her view is based on polity. The Alaska law establishes one definition of citizenship and then hands out benefits on a different basis. The plan denies non-Alaskans settling in the state the same provisions afforded long-term residents, assigning them an inferior status, and thus is a violation of the privileges and immunities clause. O'Connor wants a test like the one in *Baldwin v. Montana Fish and Game Commission* (1978): A state may not discriminate in essential services or rights when they bear on the vitality of the nation; however, it may discriminate on nonessential matters between residents and nonresidents, such as fishing and hunting licenses. For differential treatment to be legitimate, nonresidents must be a source of evil or hurt to the state; the classification in the law must bear a substantial relationship between the evil and the discrimination practiced against the noncitizens. Thus, we see O'Connor using an intermediate level of scrutiny. This law infringes on a fundamental right—the individual right to establish a residence in a different state. New residents are not the peculiar source of any evil addressed in this case; even if they were, Alaska did not choose a cure that bears a "substantial relationship" to the malady.

In *Zobel* we see a classic debate among justices who wish to view issues in polity terms and those who prefer rights terms. The rights-oriented justices wish to view the cases as one of equality before the law. All residents, they believe, have a right to equal treatment in all programs, as long as they are similarly situated with regard to the hurt the state wishes to repair. For the polity-oriented O'Connor, the right to move interstate in one nation, with regard to the effect on residents and on nonresidents who come to a state—a one union notion—is central to the decision. Again O'Connor articulates an intermediate level of scrutiny in which states could argue that important state interests would be met by treating residents of different durations in different ways. Thus, there is less of an equality principle operating for O'Connor than for Brennan. The Brennan position may operate to limit irrational allocation of benefits, but it also allows less possibility for argument by states to the Court. In both positions the Court must make fact, degree, and value choices as to whether either the polity- or rights-based requirement has been met by a state. In either approach, decisions are based more on equality principles than polity issues, yet equality as seen by the Burger Court is more open-ended, more complex, and less geared to formal entry than during the Warren Court era.

The Fundamental Interest or Right to Education: Plyler v. Doe
The decision in *Plyler v. Doe* (1982) followed through on the suggestion in *Rodriguez*; the Court agreed that elimination of education for a group could

trigger judicial action, whereas mere inequality could not. In *Plyler* the Burger
Court considers whether a state may refuse to pay for the education of undocumented alien children.[26] A 1977 Texas law said that no state funds were to be
provided for the education of children who had not been "legally admitted"
into the United States. These children theoretically retained the option of attending public schools and paying full tuition. The Burger Court found this
law in violation of the equal protection clause of the Fourteenth Amendment.
It was a 5-4 decision, with White, a Warren Court veteran, among the dissenters. Only two of the five majority votes (Marshall's and Brennan's) came
from former members of the Warren Court.

In *Plyler*, the Court finds that illegal aliens are "persons" in any normal
sense of the term under the equal protection clause. They are within the
state's jurisdiction, even if they entered it illegally. The analysis is not based on
a belief that resident aliens are a suspect class or that education is a fundamental right. Instead, the Court uses classes of uneducated children who may
form *future* discrete and insular minorities as its focus of concern and analysis.[27]
The Court finds that the Texas statute imposes a lifetime hardship on a discrete class of children who are not responsible for their disabling status.

Brennan views the illegal entry of these undocumented aliens and children
as a structural phenomenon caused in part by actions of the United States government. Its inability to keep out undocumented aliens and its lax enforcement of immigration and employment laws results in what Brennan calls a
"shadow population." He raises the specter of a permanent caste of undocumented resident aliens, encouraged to remain here as a source of cheap labor
but nevertheless denied the benefits offered to citizens and lawful residents.
The Court also finds that public education is now unlike any other government benefit; it is pivotal in maintaining the fabric of our society and in sustaining our political and cultural heritage. Even though the Court is aware of
the different status established by Congress for aliens, it finds no rational basis
for states to deny alien children benefits they provide to other residents.

Plyler shows the Court's view of basic rights. The state can withhold benefits to those who, because of their own actions, require censure, but not to
children who are here because of their parents' actions. To make children suffer because of parents' misconduct "does not comport with fundamental
conceptions of justice." Thus, for Brennan and a majority of the Court scrutiny must go beyond the minimal level. In fact, the Court's analysis nearly
leads it to declare a right to education for all.

What is extraordinary about this case is that not only does it rest on a *near-
right* of individual undocumented alien children to an education, but that this
near-right is based on a structural notion—the fear of inadvertently creating future groups with limited political power. This case goes far deeper in its analysis of factors that affect political power than *Shapiro*, for the Burger Court here

154   rejects a mere equal citizenship notion and requires the Court to speak directly to the rights of children as future citizens. The negative polity implications of state inaction on immigration and schooling trigger a heightened scrutiny.

Is this mere pragmatism? Or is it a more subtle view of polity and rights principles? It is clear that a balancing act occurs in which polity principles, one of which is the fairness of the future structure of politics, are in conflict with the more open-ended notions of nexus and peripheral rights articulated by Justice Marshall in a concurring opinion. The polity and rights values of the Burger Court are less static, but no less principled, than those of the Warren Court. They allow a more complex view of constitutional questions, which opens the way for formulations of constitutional issues and rights not conceived of by the Warren Court.

Brennan explains why the denial of education increases the level of scrutiny by the Burger Court. Public education is neither a right granted to individuals by the Constitution, nor "is it merely some governmental 'benefit' indistinguishable from other forms of social welfare legislation. Both the importance of education in maintaining our basic institutions, and the lasting impact of its deprivation on the life of the child, mark the distinction. . . . Denial of education to some isolated group of children poses an affront to one of the goals of the Equal Protection Clause: the abolition of governmental barriers presenting unreasonable obstacles to advancement on the basis of individual merit."

However, while the denial of education to individual children means they cannot achieve at a level commensurate with their abilities, it is the polity effects, not the individual's right to education, that the Court emphasizes in *Plyler*. The Court employs both a critical-pluralist view of polity and the concept of the right of each citizen to be judged on his or her own merits. In both respects this law is invalid. The right to education is based on the structural effects of denial, given the polity goal of government *not* to create discrete and insular minorities and on the rights principle that individuals should not suffer for situations not produced by their own actions. The polity argument creates a right to education, showing that Burger Court polity arguments were not inherently conservative or pragmatic.

Plyler joins two types of principles, polity and rights, in a new way. In Warren Court jurisprudence, the nature of individual rights was never linked to a complex structural effects argument. The Burger Court, by contrast, applied structural analyses to the gamut of equal protection issues, to questions of poverty, illegal entry, and individual punishment, as it did to questions of the separation of religious institutions and the state. The Warren Court came closest to such structural analysis in its apportionment cases, in which it spoke of the fundamental right to vote. It also saw that the effects of malapportioned legislative districts made some individuals' votes less valuable than others' and

gave certain groups of people (city residents, suburbanites) votes with dispro-
portionately weak political effect. That type of structural analysis, however,
addressed a right to formal access, not peripheral rights for individuals and disadvantaged groups concerning their future power in society. This is a complex
view of the place of individuals and groups in society. It is not a simple matter
of the relationship of welfare to the right to travel interstate, an argument rejected by Chief Justice Warren in *Shapiro*. It is a deeper view of the interdepen-
dency within society of education and general social, economic, and psychological well-being.

Polity concerns in *Plyler* center on the state's affirmative limit on government and its production of future discrete and insular minorities, as they did
on race segregation's producing such minorities in *Brown v. Board of Education*.
However, in *Brown* the structural relations among the races under segregation
were a predicate or basis of action for the denial of rights, while in *Plyler* and
other Burger Court cases, the future unequal structural relationship of undocumented children to the society is the direct hurt to society. Thus, in *Plyler*
polity principles take center stage and prove more effective in supporting individual rights than a direct rights argument, because an open-ended rights argument makes the Court appear undisciplined in its principles and raises fears
of uncontrolled and uncontrollable Court intervention in the political system.

Brennan asks what state interests might exist to deny these children an education. He finds none that can counter the individual and societal interests
outlined: (1) illegal aliens do not impose a big strain on state resources; (2) illegal aliens underutilize state services while they pay taxes; (3) denying education is an ineffective way to stem the tide of illegal immigration—prohibiting
employment to the parents would be far more effective; (4) reducing expenditures for education by barring some children from schools is unacceptable; (5)
excluding aliens will not improve the overall quality of education in Texas; and
(6) encouraging the child's departure from the state is not a permissible reason, as many aliens remain in the United States despite state pressure against
their doing so. This is a structural notion of causation—one that suggests a
more searching review than merely an intermediate level, since traditionally
states may choose how to attack a problem. Brennan writes, "It is difficult to
understand precisely what the state hopes to achieve by promoting the creation and perpetuation of a subclass of illiterates within our boundaries, surely
adding to the problems and costs of unemployment, welfare and crime. It is
thus clear that whatever savings might be achieved by denying these children
an education, they are wholly insubstantial in light of the costs involved to
these children, the State, and the Nation."

For Brennan, the key issue is the link between denial of education and the
creation of discrete and insular minorities, not the link between education and
First Amendment rights. Thus, Brennan may feel that a structurally based

nexus is more solid than a linkage based on loss of rights, which is a more open-ended nexus argument. This distinction is important to the outcome in this case because it allows Blackmun and Powell to support the finding of the unconstitutionality of the Texas law, even though their long-standing polity and rights principles force them to reject more open-ended fundamental rights and nexus arguments.

The Burger Court may appear pragmatic here because of its dry approach, which appears to be a cost-benefit analysis of education. However, the Court rejects arguments that only the total deprivation of a fundamental right anchors equal protection cases. The Court will look at each case to decide the individual rights and interests in question, the societal effects of their denial, and the implication of discrete and insular minorities in the denial of a benefit.

In supporting the basic arguments used by Brennan, Justices Blackmun and Powell, in concurring opinions, distinguish their votes in *Plyler* from their votes against a finding of constitutional violations in the *Rodriguez* case. Blackmun asserts that he does not believe that the *Rodriguez* formulation of constitutional rights and economic and social legislation fits every issue of fundamental rights arising under the Constitution. To the contrary, *Rodriguez* implicitly acknowledges that certain interests, though not constitutionally guaranteed, must be accorded a special place in equal protection analysis. Drawing on Marshall's dissent in *Rodriguez*, Blackmun argues, "Classifications involving the complete denial of education are in a sense unique, for [unlike housing and welfare] they strike at the heart of equal protection values by involving the State in the creation of permanent class distinctions . . . relegat-[ing] the individual to second class social status."

Though this may appear to be mere pragmatism on their part, it results from the further development of complex polity arguments found in *Rodriguez* and throughout Burger Court equal protection analysis. Through a constitutive decisionmaking process the Burger Court establishes a more complex view of inequality different from that of the Warren Court. The Burger Court could not accept the two-tiered scrutiny system of the Warren Court; to do so would mean that it could neither counter polity inequalities found in pluralist politics, nor define new individual rights to correct polity malfunctions.

Justice Marshall also concurs, but he argues that the Court should decide whether there is a fundamental right to education, because of the close relationship between education and basic constitutional values. He wants a sliding scale method of analysis that views class-based denial of public education as incompatible with the equal protection clause of the Fourteenth Amendment.

Had education itself been made a fundamental right, or had an open-ended rights argument been used by the Court, Blackmun and Powell might well have joined the dissenters. Brennan fashioned an opinion consequentialistic enough not to scare Powell and Blackmun into thinking that the Court's future choices are too rigidly limited. But in doing so he has changed the nature of polity principles by expanding the importance of the interrelationship between social and economic inequality caused, in this case, by lack of education and individual and societal disequilibrium. Marshall prefers to stay within a rights framework, perhaps thinking that it will open the door to a greater redistribution of resources to blacks and the poor. Both of these approaches, which are based on polity and rights values different from those held by other justices, place the framework of analysis in this case, and for future courts, in a more complex light. This kind of intricate analysis is the contribution of the Burger Court to jurisprudence. *Plyler v. Doe* is at the heart of Burger Court sliding scale analysis. At that point, nearly every member of the Burger Court except Rehnquist and perhaps Burger had accepted a more complex view of law and society than had the Warren Court. It is this kind of analysis that Marshall had argued for in *Rodriguez* and *Dandridge*.

The Court has never formally adopted the sliding scale analysis Marshall promoted in *Dandridge* and *Rodriguez*; it gives much more weight to structural questions, such as the societal effects of the denial of education, than Marshall's model encourages. However, it is clear that the Court uses more than a rational basis test in *Plyler*. Also, by not making education a fundamental right or illegal aliens a classification subject to strict scrutiny, the Court allows itself to make choices protective of long-standing equal protection principles without fearing that if it makes a strong rights protection decision, it and future Courts will be forced into a too-activist intervention whenever education programs or illegal aliens or benefits to children are the subject of judicial inquiry.

Burger's dissent, joined by White, Rehnquist, and O'Connor, seeks invalidation of this law, using primarily polity arguments. He emphasizes his disagreement with the Texas law, but argues that the role of the Court is not to eliminate bad laws. "We trespass on the assigned function of the political branches under our structure of limited and separated powers when we assume a policymaking role as the Court does today." Thus, Burger views the polity questions as involving separation of powers and federalism principles, not fear of future discrete and insular minorities created by the denial of education to illegal alien children. He argues that it is not for the Court to make up for the lack of effective congressional policy on illegal immigration: "The Court's holding today manifests the justly criticized judicial tendency to attempt speedy and wholesale formulation of 'remedies' for the failures—or simply the laggard pace—of the political processes of our system of government."

Note that the difference between the views of justices in the majority and the dissenters is not that one group relies on polity arguments and the other does not, but rather that they look at American political and legal institutions and issues of causation in significantly different ways. For Burger, the question

158 is whether in allocating resources a state has a legitimate interest in differentiating among persons who are and are not lawfully within its borders. He finds this distinction, which Congress places in national laws, permissible. Burger sees the Court piecing together quasi-suspect classifications and quasi-fundamental rights analysis into a theory custom tailored to the facts of the case. He argues that the equal protection clause protects only against arbitrary and irrational classifications and invidious discrimination stemming from prejudice and hostility. "It is not an all-encompassing 'equalizer' designed to eradicate every distinction for which persons are not responsible." This view, however, misreads the majority opinion of the Court. Although the Court says that neither a traditional suspect class nor a fundamental right exists, it finds a violation of long-standing polity and rights principles because this law will help create a discrete and insular minority of uneducated children and future adult citizens.

A comparison with the *Shapiro* case suggests that pragmatic considerations and views about polity were also important to all members of the Warren Court. Thus, the Burger Court should not be viewed as returning to a more pragmatic, less ideological jurisprudence. The Warren Court was not making decisions on the basis of pure equality principles, as the conventional wisdom would have us believe. Wealth was never to be a suspect classification or equality of benefits a fundamental right. Likewise, Warren Court cases involving defendant rights and access to lawyers and judicial process were incorrectly interpreted as a call for equality of government benefits, rather than simply establishing a right to access, with some counsel at crucial stages of the judicial process.

The Burger Court era was not one in which pragmatism dominated or one which merely worked out Warren Court principles. It had its own mix of polity and rights values. But to make the argument that the Burger Court was just fulfilling the Warren Court's vision of rights and polity, one must be willing to argue that the seeds of fundamental rights and interests talk in the Warren Court era, not the political, economic, or social forms, or most important, contemporary constitutional and democratic theory, gave rise to the particular and unique strains of polity and rights principles of the Burger Court. An analysis of fundamental rights and interests doctrine in the Burger Court era demonstrates the degree to which the conventional comparison of Warren and Burger Court jurisprudence is misguided.

Other Equal Protection Doctrine
in the Warren and Burger Courts

Other important areas in which equal protection analysis exploded in new doctrine in the two Courts include race discrimination in schools, race discrimination in settings other than schools, racial classifications in the law and affirmative action, race discrimination and the structure of government action, and classifications other than race that are subject to stricter than minimal levels of scrutiny—such as aliens, illegitimate children, women and men, and individuals with varying lengths of state residence and levels of state taxation.

Race Discrimination in Schools

The Warren Court authored the landmark decision in *Brown v. Board of Education* (1954) that outlawed segregation of the races in schools and led to the end of race segregation in other public bodies.[28] The Warren Court also supported the constitutionality of the Civil Rights Acts of 1964 and 1965. However, not until the Burger Court era did the Supreme Court lead the lower federal courts in ending racial segregation of schools in the South; and only through a novel definition of the intent to discriminate did the Supreme Court support integration of the races in the North, where segregation by law had not occurred. Scholars of the Burger Court tend to emphasize the *Milliken* case, which outlawed busing across school districts where there was no finding of discriminatory action by suburbs. But the Burger Court, not the Warren Court, made *Brown v. Board of Education* a reality.

Race Discrimination in Settings Other than Schools

The Warren Court, mainly through per curiam decisions, desegregated public parks, beaches, and other public lands and outlawed racial classification on ballots. The Burger Court added to this legacy with more complex formulations of the intent to discriminate than those that arose in the Warren Court. Starting with *Griggs v. Duke Power* (1971), the Burger Court defined the intent to discriminate to allow both formal findings of either discriminatory *intent* by public officials or discriminatory *effects* on blacks that could trigger stricter scrutiny of government action than had been present in the Warren Court.[29]

Most important, it was the Burger Court that considered whether government can affirmatively aid blacks to achieve racial equality when there are no formal findings of specific discriminatory intent. Affirmative action cases offer additional evidence that the Burger Court was far more willing than the Warren Court to view issues in complex structural terms. These cases, as well as cases involving race separation in northern schools, indicate that the Burger Court no longer considered its only objective getting rid of de jure race discrimination in the law and in clearly biased government action. It sought to end de facto race discrimination, that is, to root out racism even when inequality of outcomes between the races cannot be traced to specific wrongdoers. Not only individual blacks and individual whites, but black citizens as a group became the unit of analysis for the Supreme Court.

Intent to Discriminate through Changes in Political Process

The Warren Court led the way in demonstrating that changes in political processes involving issues important to blacks can indicate an intent to discrimi-

160 nate. However, in this area the Warren Court considered only formal process changes, such as requiring a referendum for open housing laws when there was no such requirement for other legislation. The Burger Court had to consider whether there was an intent to discriminate when changes in process and outcome patterns were more subtle. Also, while the Warren Court in *Loving v. Virginia* (1967) made a strong statement that equal application of race classifications in the law is not a sufficient basis for minimal levels of scrutiny, the Burger Court would have to deal with more complex cases of intentionality. Laws would have to be analyzed to see whether there was either intent to discriminate or discriminatory effects. Even the rejection of equal application of race classifications in the law is an easier decision, for one does not have to confront the question of how to counter the effects of de facto action as a cause of race inequality. The Burger Court would confront these issues with a new view of polity and rights.

Classifications in the Law Subject to Heightened Scrutiny

That the Burger Court redefined equal protection thinking, rather than merely working out Warren Court principles, is most evident if we consider the number of classifications in the law that the Burger Court made subject to a stricter than minimal level of scrutiny. The most dramatic example lay in the area of gender classifications. The Warren Court rejected a heightened level of Court scrutiny for such classifications. The Burger Court made gender a classification in the law subject to an intermediate level of scrutiny. To be legitimate, gender classifications had to be shown to meet important government interests and to be substantially related to those important interests. The Burger Court also considered de facto, as well as de jure, discrimination based on gender, supported affirmative action policies for women, and redefined, through statutory interpretation, the areas in which Congress and states may treat men and women differently.

Polity Principles in Burger Court Standing and Separation of Powers Cases

Warth v. Seldin (1975), *Immigration and Naturalization Service [INS] v. Chadha* (1983), and *United States v. Nixon* (1974) are three cases in which the Burger Court was called upon to make fundamental decisions about the sources of constitutional authority and its limits for various levels and branches of government. The Court was confronted with claims that the judicial branch of government should remove itself from a case involving the executive branch's authority in criminal matters, that the Court should refrain from interfering with a political compromise between the other two branches, and that the rights of individuals to move to a town of their choosing required the Court to strike down local zoning practices. The Burger Court's response to these claims and its handling of basic questions about which level of government is properly equipped and constitutionally authorized to exercise power over polity and rights questions tell us much about how the Court views our constitutional system and how it believes power should properly be distributed within that system.

A narrowly divided Burger Court refused to allow the federal courts to become involved in matters of residential segregation by race and income when only a generalized grievance could be raised about the alleged unconstitutional conduct. In *Warth v. Seldin* (1975), the Supreme Court considered a challenge by various organizations and residents of the Rochester, New York, metropolitan area, who alleged that a zoning ordinance enacted by the nearby town of Penfield prevented minority and low- and moderate-income people from moving to the town.[30] The complaint alleged that it was "practically and economically impossible" to construct sufficient low- and moderate-income housing because of regulations concerning "lot area, set backs, . . . population density, density of use, units per acre, floor area," and so on. Justice Brennan, in a dissent joined by Justices White and Marshall, concluded that "the portrait which emerges from the allegations and affidavits is one of total, purposeful, intransigent exclusion of certain classes of people from the town, pursuant to a conscious scheme never deviated from." Brennan would have allowed such "pattern and practice" claims to proceed to trial, since the plaintiffs properly alleged that because of the exclusionary practices they could not live in Penfield and thus suffered harm. He recognized that merely relying upon the apologetic pluralist view that the outsiders would somehow be represented in the political process failed to acknowledge the structural barriers that insulated Penfield from participatory input.

Despite plaintiffs' allegations, the majority opinion, written by Justice Powell, focuses on the doctrine of standing and the "concern about the proper—and properly limited—role of courts in a democratic society." Invoking constitutional requirements that those seeking standing to sue in federal court have been subject to personal injury, Powell questions whether the plaintiffs (various nonresidents of Penfield, home builders, and housing and taxpayer organizations) had alleged a sufficiently personal stake in the controversy's outcome to warrant the invocation of federal jurisdiction and the exercise of federal remedial powers. Powell referred to prior court decisions to support his view that "when the asserted harm is a 'generalized grievance' shared in substantially equal measure by all or a large class of citizens, that harm alone does not warrant exercise of jurisdiction."

Powell also emphasizes that plaintiffs must assert their own legal rights and interests and cannot make claims for relief based upon the rights of third parties. The majority opinion goes on to consider each class of plaintiff and concludes in each instance that no sufficiently personal stake in the controversy

162   was established. For example, with respect to individual plaintiffs who alleged exclusion from Penfield on the basis of income, race, or ethnic status, the Court holds that "petitioners must allege facts from which it reasonably could be inferred that, absent the respondents' restrictive zoning practices, there is a substantial probability that they would have been able to purchase or lease in Penfield and that, if the court affords the relief requested, the asserted inability of petitioners will be removed."

By establishing a high threshold for plaintiffs who seek to air grievances based upon exclusionary zoning practices, the Court effectively sanctions broad-based practices that create discrimination in effect so long as individualized, intentional discrimination is not alleged. The purported rights of individuals who sought to live in Penfield are subordinated to the view that local zoning decisions that are reached in a political context are entitled to substantial deference. Although Powell invokes standing and justiciability principles, the effect of *Warth* is to insulate locally elected officials from comprehensive scrutiny of regulations that serve to exclude outsiders. The political process is seen as sufficient to address generalized grievances. The Burger Court in *Warth* declines to question the pluralist assumption that local political actors will look out for the interests of all relevant constituencies—even those that may not be directly represented. The standing doctrine as applied by Powell reinforces local majoritarian preferences, but those who exist on the margins do not find constitutional vindication in the majority's calculus.

In contrast to the Burger Court's deference to political decisions in *Warth v. Seldin* (1975), the Court in *INS v. Chadha* (1983) rejected arguments that it should defer to the legislative process with respect to alien deportation policy. The federal statute challenged in this case authorized either house of Congress to invalidate the decision of the executive branch to allow a particular deportable alien to remain in the United States. The Supreme Court, in an opinion by Chief Justice Burger, rejected arguments that foreign citizens lacked standing to challenge the legislative veto provision and held that a "case or controversy" under Article III existed. The Court held that the congressional veto provision was unconstitutional because separation of powers principles requiring passage of a bill by both houses were not adhered to. Therefore the veto provision conferred legislative power upon a single house of Congress. The majority opinion's treatment of justiciability issues (standing, "case or controversy," and the political questions doctrine) clearly rejects the argument that the dispute over Chadha's deportability status properly belonged to the nonjudicial branches.

The Court's analysis, animated by a deeply held concern about upholding the proper roles of the legislative and executive functions and the core constitutional procedural arrangements for lawmaking, curtly dismisses arguments based upon justiciability. In only four sentences, the majority opinion rejects the argument that Chadha lacked standing because his position would support the executive branch in a separation of powers dispute with Congress. The Court noted that Chadha had demonstrated the necessary "injury in fact." It also determined that the "case or controversy" requirement of Article III was satisfied even though the attorney general and INS agreed with Chadha's contention that the legislative veto provision was unconstitutional. The Court indicated that the controversy was "concrete" because if the veto provision were upheld, Chadha would be deported.

Finally, the *Chadha* decision rejects the view that the powers of Congress with respect to naturalization established by Article I of the Constitution render the issue of Chadha's deportability status a political question that the Supreme Court is not authorized to address. Although the Court acknowledges that the matter presented issues related to legislative authority, Chief Justice Burger notes that the political questions doctrine (which traditionally has led the Court to defer to elected bodies on questions that justices consider have been left to these bodies by the Constitution or that raise concerns about the prudence of Court action) does not mean that the executive and legislative branches acting in concert "can decide the constitutionality of a statute; that is a decision for the courts."[31] The majority opinion in *Chadha* clearly rejects calls for the invocation of prudential concerns and efforts to characterize the dispute as one properly belonging to the political branches. The Court repudiates the apologetic pluralist view that would have left in place a wide array of existing statutes containing legislative veto provisions.

Seven justices of the Court make it clear that deference to popularly elected officials would not be sanctioned in a matter involving basic constitutional structures relating to the legislative process (i.e., the presentment and bicameralism clauses of Article I) or the right of an individual facing deportation to be treated pursuant to these Article I dictates.

A dramatic conflict between judicial authority and the asserted power of another branch of government occurred in a case in which a sitting president challenged the authority of the Supreme Court to order the release of documents he held. In *United States v. Nixon* (1974), a special prosecutor investigating wrongdoing by President Nixon's aides and campaign staff sought to require the president to release various papers, memoranda, and tapes relating to an ongoing criminal investigation. Nixon, an unindicted coconspirator, released edited versions of some conversations and sought to quash the subpoena for the actual tapes. A unanimous Burger Court[32] rejected the president's arguments that the dispute between a prosecutor and the president was not justiciable and that separation of powers principles prevented adjudication of the dispute. The president's counsel argued that since the executive branch has the exclusive authority and absolute discretion to decide whether to prosecute a case, the president's decision is final in determining what evidence may

164   be used in a criminal case. Since the dispute was between the president and an inferior executive officer, the case was characterized by the president's counsel as a "political question," not subject to resolution in a judicial proceeding.

The Burger Court, relying in part on the unique authority of the Watergate special prosecutor, rejected the justiciability argument. The Court noted that the prosecutor was invested by the attorney general with powers to seek evidence and that the evidence was deemed to be relevant and admissible in a pending criminal case. The case was deemed to be justiciable because the "concrete adverseness" standard was satisfied. The Court also unanimously rejected Nixon's claim of executive privilege. The Court noted that it was necessary to "interpret the Constitution in a manner at variance with the construction given the document by another branch." Invoking "the basic concept of separation of powers and the checks and balances that flow from the scheme of a tripartite government," the Court rejected the argument for an absolute, unqualified presidential privilege of immunity on the grounds that, if it were to accept such a claim, the Court would renege on its own "primary constitutional duty . . . to do justice in criminal prosecutions."[33] If it allowed the president's claim to stand, the "workable government" created by Articles I and III, consisting of three branches responsible in a sovereign way for certain basic functions, would be eviscerated.

Although *United States v. Nixon* represented only the penultimate step in a tale of political corruption, the Court's opinion was a breathtaking affirmation of the judicial role in a constitutional system of divided powers. The Court refused to affirm the assertion of executive privilege in the context of a legal and political crisis which, largely because of the Court's decision, led to the resignation of a president for the first time in U.S. history.

The Burger Court's defense of "workable government" in *Chadha* and *Nixon* is not based on an abstract notion of the relationship among various parts of government. Its premises are those of constitutional text, structure, and principle. *Chadha* was decided by a Court that reinvigorated basic constitutional structure precepts despite the claim that the other branches had struck a workable compromise in a complex administrative society. In the *Nixon* case, the Burger Court also demonstrated its commitment to the polity values represented by separation of powers principles and the constitutional limitations on executive power inherent in the creation of an independent judiciary.

The Burger Court aggressively pursued a course of defining and defending the proper functions of the legislative, executive, and especially the judicial branch in *Chadha* and *Nixon*. Its task in *Warth* was different in many respects. Although Justice Brennan recognized that the rights of individuals were at stake as the result of the exclusionary practices in that case, the majority held that plaintiffs' grievances were too remote. The Court deferred to the local majoritarian preference and declined to view the conflict as one involving regional and perhaps national ramifications. While the Court vigorously defended constitutional mandates relating to the proper authority of various branches, it hesitated to take on the enduring legacies of social inequality. The Burger Court had far more filigreed polity principles than a simple notion of autonomy of institutions.

The Complexity of Burger Court Visions of Polity

The Burger Court had to make complex and difficult choices about classifications that, unlike race, were not clearly the concerns of the Fourteenth Amendment's equal protection clause (such as gender, nonmarital children, the aged, retarded people, and illegal alien children). Therefore, its response to those classifications was more varied than is possible under a two-tiered classification scheme that considers race under strict scrutiny and economic legislation under a minimal level of scrutiny. It also had to deal with more questions involving structural causation of inequality. Thus the Burger Court simply had more discretion and more chances *not* to support Court intervention than the Warren Court with its less problematic agenda.

Because of the more complex structural basis of inequality in gender and other areas and because these areas do not have the historical impetus for action that race does, they require members of the Court to make more choices about fundamental fairness and equality. They also offer more possibilities for ways that laws and public officials can relate public policy to inequality in the social and economic system. More choices about what constitutes inequality, intention, official action and inaction, and stigma based on classifications in the law are inevitable, as is a wider range of responses to them by the Court. In such a complex setting, ringing, clear-cut statements about equality and the correctness of Court intervention are not possible. Thus the view of the Burger Court as merely pragmatic and less concerned about pure principles of equality arises, in part, from the kind of cases it considered.

The Warren Court went no further in its equal protection analysis than seeking to ensure that similarly situated people were treated equally. It tied arguments about equal protection to whether there was prejudice in the political process or whether formal laws denied fundamental rights and interests necessary to citizens to participate in the political process. It did not address questions about the failure of government to classify persons who for equal protection purposes should be considered differently. For example, it was the Burger Court that defined gender as a semisuspect classification, which allowed the state to permit different treatment of men and women, but only in those cases in which men and women were not similarly situated with regard to a government interest—for example, the right of pregnant women to medical benefits and the rights of men and women to work near toxic substances.

166   The Court must consider questions of social, economic, and political inequalities—structural inequalities—in determining whether gender classifications are
to be permitted—questions that are more complex than in matters of race. In
addition, the Burger Court had to consider the constitutionality of affirmative
action programs—the question of what race or gender classifications are to be
allowed to make up for past political, social, and economic inequality, when
there has not been a finding of intentional discrimination.

In the apportionment cases the Warren Court did make structural arguments claiming that political institutions cannot change because those in
power do not want to give up power. However, malapportionment was so
great that the Warren Court did not have to make subtle arguments about
whether effects of voting systems on races and other groups were intentional.
In the vote dilution cases of the Burger Court era,[34] the causes of vote dilution
were not as clear, which meant that this Court had to make more choices and
decisions that appear more pragmatic.

In equal protection analysis, as in other areas of Warren Court jurisprudence, we do not see the intensity of debate or the number of concurrences
and dissents found on the Burger Court, whose arguments involve differences
in the substance and intensity of belief in polity and rights principles. With
the establishment of more systematic constitutional theory and a clash of
deeper polity and rights arguments, the Burger Court justices apparently believed there was a need for more elaboration of the polity and rights bases of
their constitutional choices. The Court era was characterized by more textured and nuanced elaborations of polity and rights principles, not more pragmatism. With Brennan, Marshall, and Rehnquist on the Burger Court playing
similar roles to those of Douglas and Harlan on the Warren Court, the Warren
Court should not be considered more principled and dominated by visions of
equality than the Burger Court. Neither Court was merely pragmatic in its
making of constitutional choices.

Coherence and Uniqueness
in Burger Court Jurisprudence

Scholars supporting the no counterrevolution thesis argue that the Burger
Court reacted to changes in the wider society rather than making fundamental
moral choices. They also assert that the "rootlessness" of the Burger Court
can be explained by differences in its internal decisionmaking process. Bernard
Schwartz argues that the increasing number of concurring, plurality, and dissenting opinions on the Burger Court can be explained by Chief Justice Burger's weaknesses as a leader. He also contends that the Court's rootlessness was
caused by the fact that direct oral interchanges among justices about principles
were less frequent on the Burger Court because of the expanded role of law
clerks, a greater reliance on written interchanges, and the rise of an institu-

tional mentality—the idea that nine "law offices," not justices, were crafting "individual" judicial decisions.[35]

Proponents of the no counterrevolution approach make valid points when they argue that the Burger Court responded to the effects of a more complex bureaucracy and malfunctions in the political process due to single-issue politics. However, their failure to identify the polity and rights principles that the Burger Court valued and to explore how the relationship of polity and rights principles led the Burger Court in doctrinal directions quite different from those of the Warren Court severely limits the validity of their conclusions. Nor does this approach place Burger Court decisionmaking in context in terms of changes in the visions of polity and rights in political theory, interpretations of American politics, and constitutional theory within the interpretive community and the wider societal context.

The Burger Court should be viewed as groups of justices with pluralist, critical pluralist, and structural critical pluralist views about society and politics. The justices differ in the depth they seek within constitutional practice— the depth of critical questioning about the political institutions they believe is needed to protect individual rights and to meet separation of powers and other structural limits on political power. To define the Court as right, left, or middle, or to view the Court as consisting of middle-centrist justices and the extremes, is to misperceive the dance of polity and rights principles that is the core of judicial decisionmaking. The Burger Court had middle justices who were not merely pragmatic but held varying views of political institutions and the importance of branching out to social and economic relations; the depth of their critical thinking mirrored the complexity of the analysis they undertook. They differed in how open- or closed-ended their views were of the fundamental rights and moral values in the Constitution, and of their authority to interpret such language.

Views about polity are not case specific, but show continuities among cases, as seen in *Rodriguez, Dunn, Moreno, Maricopa, Plyler*, and *Zobel*. Both "liberals" and "centrists" must consider structural inequality—the relationship between fundamental rights in the Constitution and polity principles— and the social and economic factors that structure life chances, rather than only cases of formal blockage by the political system. The Warren Court could, in principled terms, stop formal blockage and inequality and be perceived as innovative and even radical. The Burger Court is not a mini-Warren Court because the configuration of polity and rights values is different from both the 1950s and 1960s Warren Court and is a product of its own age.

There is a coherence in Burger Court jurisprudence, suggested by fundamental rights and interests cases, that flows from agreement among groups of justices about polity and rights principles and values. We can see it in a similarity of viewpoint in many cases by Brennan and Marshall and differences be-

168   tween them and other groups of justices. These are analogous to differences among Frankfurter/Harlan and Douglas/Brennan and, to a lesser degree, Warren on the Warren Court as to basic views about polity and fundamental rights. However, while adding up agreement among dissenters and opposition to the rest of the Court may suggest the amount of dissent, it does not show how constitutional choices are made. For example, Brennan, whom Blasi had characterized as an extreme justice concerned about articulating an ideological position, in key cases played the role of centrist—coalescing other justices' opinions around the majority opinion.

What do Blasi and other scholars mean by arguing that the Burger Court is less principled than the Warren Court? Do they mean that the Burger Court made less ringing rights statements? Such a definition of principle is substantively uninteresting. Only if "less principled" means that the Burger Court, compared to the Warren Court, moved more slowly in arriving at major changes in doctrine, or that it decided more cases before it was willing to make major innovations in Court policy (as in the *Reed, Frontiero*, and *Craig* cases) can the Burger Court be so labeled. However, Blasi's definition of what is "principled" is wanting, for it suggests that the pace of doctrinal innovations, not their substance, is the primary standard of evaluation. Also, in contrast to the no counterrevolution view, the "isms" of the right and left, or the presumed lack of "isms" by centrist justices are not the primary bases for Burger Court choices. Scholars and jurists have shown that society has deep social, economic, and political imbalances; they must now find a way to create constitutive polity and rights principles that reflect that complexity.

The Burger Court, even when it chose to rely primarily on polity arguments, could be more reformist than the Warren Court because it no longer accepted the political process in apologetic pluralist or equilibrium terms. (In the next chapter we will trace the impact on Burger Court jurisprudence of following critical pluralist views among nonoriginalist rights theorists and process theorists, such as John Hart Ely, and scholars of American political institutions, such as Grant McConnell and Theodore Lowi.) As the Court moved toward more deeply structural arguments, as it had to do to consider issues of gender, affirmative action, and the creation of additional suspect classifications, it could no longer enjoy the safety of the less critical view of American politics found in the Warren Court era.

Blasi's assessment of the Burger Court as not principled enough in its jurisprudence ignores the complexity of both the equal protection cases and the other complicated questions the Burger Court had to face. It also fails to address the increased complexity of constitutional theory and the changing public expectations about political institutions and fundamental rights in the 1970s and 1980s. For when the Court must decide what rights different groups are to get and who has been discriminated against under the Fourteenth Amendment equal protection and due process clauses in complex organizations and social settings, choices are complex. They appear pragmatic, but they are not. Complexity and the appearance of pragmatism are built into the *group* nature of the inequality in these cases, requiring a balancing of majority and minority inequality and de facto social and economic factors.

Recognition of social and economic facts and the realization that the political system by itself does not have the means to correct itself mean that even moderate justices must make more complex choices about when and when not to trust politics and whether the Court should act to protect fundamental rights principles in the Constitution. That the Warren Court, in such cases as *Baker v. Carr* (1962), *Griswold v. Connecticut* (1965), and *Shapiro v. Thompson* (1969) and the defendants' rights cases, opened American constitutional law to more nonoriginalist jurisprudence should not obscure the coherence and innovations of Burger Court jurisprudence.

Ironically, because polity and rights principles and their intersection with social and economic factors in society are more complex on the Burger Court than the Warren Court,[36] there are more instances both of additional rights protection under the equal protection clause and of failure to support additional individual rights. This anomaly is built into the Burger Court's expansion of the factors that need to be considered in constitutional theory and practice. It is in the nature of the rule of law, the existence of differences in polity and rights values, and the efforts of jurists and those in the interpretive community to develop new definitions of rights violations that there will be limits—starts and stops—on the growth of equality, ironically, resulting from significant Court protections of wider numbers of groups in our society.

Constitutional theory in the 1970s and 1980s enriched the issues to be considered in constitutive choices by justices to a far greater degree than the more passive, incremental, constitutional theory of the 1950s and 1960s (see Chapter 6). The constitutional theory of the latter era did have open problematics but was bounded enough to cause a debate among scholars. The important point is that a majority of the Burger Court viewed questions of polity and causes of action and omission of action by public officials in relation to providing equal protection of the law as far more complex than formal denial of the vote or access, or of clear intentionality as expressed through the words of laws.

A critical pluralist, rather than the apologetic pluralist, equilibrium model of the 1950s became the conventional wisdom among justices of the Warren Court. The Burger Court also became more critical, even though principles such as equality could not be articulated in such clear or pure terms. This questioning of public officials with regard to rights and their use of constitutional polity authority did not result from the attack on relativist democratic theory in the 1960s and 1970s—that is, it was not caused by complete accept-

170 ance of ideological polity views, that public officials are never to be trusted because the Framers' view of political institutions was mistrusting of it or that rights in the Constitution demand that we not trust public officials. Therefore, the Burger Court's polity views about autonomy principles for states, families, and legislatures were a change from the weak critical pluralist views of the Warren Court in the 1960s, which sought to limit only formal denial of access to individuals. Ironically, although the Burger Court chose not to use a rhetoric of deep mistrust of public officials, it accepted a far more expansive Court intervention into public officials' decisionmaking than the Warren Court. The difference in the tone of the rhetoric should not cause us to understate the far greater activism of the Burger Court.

It is not only that activism has become institutionalized, but that a mistrust of polity has been institutionalized by all but the most conservative of justices. Liberal, moderate, and even conservative justices raise deep questions about polity and social and economic structures. In such a complex context, viewing issues in policy outcome terms is irrelevant, because justices must get their views of institutional trust accepted before their views of fundamental rights will be respected. Justices can no longer get away with merely defining a right and offering a remedy, as the Warren Court did. The difference between the two Courts is not merely, as Shapiro argues, that the Burger Court views the world in group terms rather than the individual terms of the Warren Court. The Burger Court's rejection of a trust in interest groups and interest group liberalism means that its arguments must be made in terms of the social, economic, and political realities that prevent interest group and political processes from functioning as they should in the pluralist model of equilibrium and incremental change.

Because of the more complex view of polity, the lack of a simple individual view of rights, civil liberties issues take on a more structural, polity type resonance. All issues are no longer simply issues of "individual" rights but are to be viewed as questions of the rights of individuals in a more complex structural reality. Moreover, discrimination can no longer be viewed simply in group terms, even though groups attempt to do so. It must now be viewed in terms of complex social, economic, and political causes of inequality and not necessarily as a result of bad intentions of public officials.

For example, in First Amendment cases and cases involving separation of church and state, the Burger Court makes complex structural determinations about whether freedom of speech can occur in a specific setting.[37] Part of the reason that more complex polity and rights principles are needed is that actions of the bureaucracies and legislatures are criticized and result in lawsuits that create new ideas of fairness. The Burger Court addressed the problem of bureaucratic stasis in the 1970s with what Richard Stewart has called a reformation of administrative law, the expansion of access to bureaucracies, and

Court review of agency actions.[38] Also, in the Burger Court years, public interest groups tried to ensure, through Court action, wider access to agencies.
They sought more access to policy review to ensure that agencies follow the
law and the rules they create. As the Burger Court got closer to influencing
the substantive choices by public officials rather than merely securing process
openness, it backed off from advocacy of increased Court intervention in
agency affairs.

Public interest administrative law was pointed in this new direction by the
Burger Court. How can this new direction be explained? The Court was not
merely being pragmatic or fulfilling the rights and polity principles established
by the Warren Court, for the major cases involving changes in administrative
law are products of the early Burger Court years. The change can be better explained as the Burger Court viewing the polity in critical pluralist terms—that
is, questioning whether political institutions are as open as the pluralist equilibrium model suggests. At one level, administrative law can be seen as within
the pluralist polity gestalt, for the Court sought only to assure direct access to
government. However, in its language about procedural due process, the
Burger Court articulated fundamental rights values that were not found in
Warren Court jurisprudence. At another level, administrative law can be
viewed as counter to the Warren Court acceptance of questions of administrative law in individual and economic interest terms.

The Burger Court looks at administrative law in political structural terms,
mistrusting interest group politics, which it views as allowing the best-orga-
nized interests to prevail. The creation of increased due process rights, opportunities for more class action suits, and more ways for citizens and courts to
question whether bureaucrats followed the law indicates that the Burger
Court was more critical of government than the Warren Court. These new
rights and opportunities—known as "new property"—give citizens and groups
the ability to limit governmental action where the Court has determined that
government entitlements are close to being property.

A Critique of Instrumental Interpretations
The "No Counterrevolution" Approach

The fear of modern critics of the Burger Court, among whom Blasi looms
large, is that the Court would be "counterrevolutionary" to the changes
made by the Warren Court. Note here the juxtaposition: the Warren Court is
defined in terms of its struggle to secure equality, a rights value, and the
Burger Court is viewed as considering issues primarily in polity terms.

Blasi offers a contrast of Warren and Burger Court decisionmaking that
characterizes the Warren Court jurisprudence as directed "by principle, a
rooted activism," while the Burger Court activism was defined as "rootless."
Blasi views the Warren Court as unconcerned with separation of powers or

172   with overturning laws passed by Congress. As evidence he cites the fact that the Warren Court invalidated fewer congressional acts than the Burger Court.[39]

However, another explanation lies within the Blasi thesis: that Burger Court "pragmatism," rather than the "ideology" of the Warren Court, is the major difference between these two Courts. This institutional functional argument, like that of Lewis, assumes that Courts must or will respond to changes in political structures. Although the growth of what Lowi calls "interest group liberal" politics epitomized the 1970s and the 1980s, this alone cannot explain Burger Court politics, since Courts are not required to respond to needs felt in society. For example, in the *Lochner* period the Supreme Court's view of liberty—substantive due process—countered needs expressed by citizens and invalidated New Deal legislation designed to meet those needs. The assumption is that the Supreme Court merely meets functional needs in society—that it is an intellectual tabula rasa. This according to Blasi explains the lack of a counterrevolution.

This explanation for why the *Lochner*-era Court did not allow more citizen rights as government got larger is weak. Why did the Administrative Procedures Act come in the late 1940s and 1950s? Why did the Burger Court start to reduce access to federal courts in the 1980s? The answer has to do with changes in process and rights values in the 1980s Court, which had an important effect on how rights and polity were viewed. The independent effect of constitutional theory on judicial decisionmaking and views about the Supreme Court must be analyzed. This argument about the parochialism of single-issue electoral politics is interesting. It suggests that polity values were central to the activism of the Burger Court. Similarly, the Dahlian view that the Supreme Court reflects beliefs of the dominant political coalition, with a lag time of several years, clearly is not an automatic explanation for Court action. It simplifies rather than explains the relationship of politics and law.

Implicit in Blasi's thesis that the Burger Court is responding to Warren Court principles is the concept that there is a staying power to ideas that remains after changes have occurred in the larger society. This is counter to the Dahlian view about the plasticity of change in the development of constitutional law with changes in the majority alliances. Blasi and other scholars of the Warren Court agree that when the Supreme Court makes decisions in terms of moral values such as equality, its jurisprudence should be defined in these terms. When a Court makes decisions based on both polity *and* rights principles, then the explanation for constitutional developments must come from changes in their concept of polity. For some reason, moral values are viewed as ideological while polity values are viewed as pragmatic. Blasi thus operates on two perverse but common premises: a Court in which equality principles loom large must necessarily have *no* concern for polity questions, and a Court in which polity questions are central will *never* be innovative or progressive, only pragmatic.

The Burger Court did allow a more public debate about polity, which does not mean that the Warren Court did not have polity values behind its choices. The critical pluralist views about polity held by justices other than Frankfurter and Harlan resulted in polity values being a less important problematic for them after Frankfurter retired. In the Burger Court era moral and polity visions abounded for all the justices and were the basis for their constitutional choices. *Frontiero v. Richardson* (1973), a case in which four justices favored making gender a suspect classification, with a definition of moral vision about women in society behind it, provides an example. It was Powell and the center who supported making gender a semisuspect category under the equal protection clause and thus requiring an intermediate level of scrutiny of all laws with gender classifications. The left wing of the Court supported a stricter level of scrutiny than the middle. In other words, there were differences on the Court over how far the Court should go in creating equality principles. The middle justices were not pragmatic. They were not nonideological. They simply had a different view of polity and rights. That is, the middle justices had a less critical view of polity and structural inequality than justices on the left. They gave half a loaf, not because they were pragmatic, but because they were not as convinced that polity limited women's rights or called for Court intervention. They also did not believe that Court role and the equal protection clause precluded action by the Court on gender rights.

In the area of equal protection of the law and benign gender discrimination, Justice Brennan expressed a concern that the Court not help women in the short run only to undermine equality in the long run. Did the center have new ideas in this regard? I believe the center was reacting to the left on the Court, which had created a new statement of polity inequality and moral vision of equality beyond formal limits on voting and access to a more structural view of inequality. The benign gender rights cases show this, as do the affirmative action and church and state cases, in which a conflict about rights and polity principles rather than a mere pragmatic response to the facts and issues in each case set the stage for the decisionmaking.

Additional data to counter the no counterrevolution view of internal Court decisionmaking can be gained through a comparison of the dockets and the numbers and patterns of opinion writing on the Warren and Burger Courts. David M. O'Brien offers the following data on the increasing size of the Supreme Court's docket: 1950, 1,750 cases; 1960, 2,100; 1970, 3,750; 1980, 4,750; and 1985, 5,250. He suggests many reasons for the growing number of cases, including the increase in government legislation and regulation. He also identifies an increase in the amount of discretion exercised by the Supreme Court in whether to take cases, in part due to case load and in part due to the loss of any distinction between original and appellate jurisdiction.[40]

His data offer evidence of the growing complexity and uniqueness of the constitutive decisionmaking process in the Burger Court compared to the Warren Court. Gaining standing became much easier in the Burger Court era.[41] *Warth v. Seldin* (1975) did not signal an end to increasing citizen access to the Supreme Court or to new definitions of rights of access. The *Rodriguez* case did not mean an end of the protection of fundamental rights and interests or of new polity and rights principles in support of those rights. Nor did *Everson v. Board of Education* (1916), the case on which the Warren Court rested its relatively few religion decisions, explain Burger Court doctrinal innovations and the constitutive decisionmaking process in the area of the separation of church and state.

In addition, as seen in the *Chadha* and *U.S. v. Nixon* cases, the Burger was far more critical than the Warren Court in opposing the powers of Congress and the president, respectively, when they violated polity and rights principles, which were seen now in far more complex terms. The definition of political questions was narrowed by the Burger Court as it restricted the power of the national government.

The Burger Court's power to pick and choose its cases meant that it was even more of a "superlegislature" than the Warren Court. Most importantly, the invalidity of the no counterrevolution thesis is supported by comparing the data on the subject matter of opinions before the Supreme Court. O'Brien reports that in the Burger Court era there was a significant increase in the number of decisions regarding the Bill of Rights, the constitutionality and construction of federal legislation and administrative actions, the rights of the accused, and Court jurisdiction.[42] But numbers alone reveal nothing about the significance and direction of decisions, whether they were landmark cases or not. Only the qualitative analysis of constitutive decisionmaking patterns used here can inform these questions.

Perhaps the most telling sign of the uniqueness of the Burger Court and the structural nature of changes in the Supreme Court's constitutive decisionmaking power is the startling increase in the number of decisions by the Court. Between 1969 and 1980, the Burger Court averaged 331 signed opinions per term. The Warren Court averaged well under 250 signed opinions. Of particular note are O'Brien's dramatic data on the increasing number of concurring, plurality, and dissenting opinions in the Burger Court era compared to the Warren Court. O'Brien also emphasizes that ideological differences among justices do not have a bearing on issuing concurrences.[43] He presents data that suggest that the no counterrevolution approach overstates the differences among justices in the center and extremes and the importance of these differences to Court decisionmaking. Between 1969, the first year of the

Burger Court, and 1988, two years into the Rehnquist Court, the most frequent dissenters were Douglas at 38.5 percent—an extreme justice in Blasi's eyes—and Stevens at 21.2 percent—a "centrist" justice. Justices in the 10–15 percent range include "extreme" justices Brennan (13 percent), Marshall (15.4 percent), and Rehnquist (13.8 percent), and "centrist" justices Stewart (10.8 percent), Blackmun (10.7 percent), and White (10.6 percent). Powell, at 9.9 percent, and Burger, at 6.7 percent, had the lowest percentages of dissents of those justices with long tenure on the Burger Court.[44]

David O'Brien, Vincent Blasi, and Bernard Schwartz argue that changes in internal Court processes are a primary reason for the increasing numbers of concurring and dissenting opinions on the Burger Court. Factors highlighted by these scholars include the expanded number and role of law clerks, the rationalization of the certiorari process, and a reduction in the role of oral argument and collective meetings in Court decisionmaking. These changes have unquestionably occurred. Yet the increase in the number of concurrences and dissents and the dispersion of Court views can be explained better as a product of the expansion in the kinds of issues decided by the Court, the complexity of those issues, and the greater complexity of polity and rights principles viewed as at issue in a case.

Chief Justice Burger's failure to engage in this debate over polity and rights principles reduced both the respect that his peers and the wider interpretive community had for him and his influence on the Court. However, his failings as a leader do not support the no counterrevolution thesis, as its instrumental proponents, especially Bernard Schwartz, argue.[45] Cases such as *Bakke, Chadha, Rodriguez, Plyler, Donnelly, Casey*, and the equal protection suspect classifications cases of the Burger Court years, with their greater number of concurrences and complexity than the decisions of the Warren Court, are excellent examples of the unique constitutive decisionmaking process of the Burger Court. As we shall see in Chapter 6, we must look beyond the internal workings of the Court to explain why the no counterrevolution thesis is wanting and to explain the uniqueness of the Burger Court decisionmaking process. Burger Court jurisprudence involved a structural change in constitutional adjudication as a response to the complexity of constitutional questions and the causes of inequality and a response to the interpretive community.

The Policymaking Approach

Shapiro argues that for the Court there are only three possible avenues to constitutional law: requiring equality among individuals and classes, valuing liberty and autonomy over equality, or letting politics make the choices. There is some truth to Shapiro's claims about the value and outcome-orientation of commentators, but this formulation oversimplifies the complexity of constitutional decisionmaking. In each case the Court must look at all three ap-

176   proaches and more. Each case is not a decision to favor equality, liberty, or politics, but rather requires a balancing of process and rights values.

The differences between the Warren and Burger Courts for Shapiro lie not in a switch from activism to self-restraint, but rather in differences over policy choices. Thus, the Burger Court accepts the Warren Court view of judicial power. Shapiro argues that the pre-1937 Court presumed that free enterprise was the rule and regulation was the exception. The Burger and Warren Courts presume that governmental action is the rule and freedom from government the exception. Both these assumptions fit the general ideology and general stance toward government of their day. The problem is that there is no problematic about Court power and other polity principles in Shapiro's view. There may be no one-to-one relationship of polity and rights values to specific policy choices. However, there is an important consistency among Burger Court justices' polity and rights values that is displayed in their policy choices. While justices with similar value choices about polity and rights may disagree on specific outcomes, agreement on values and outcomes is the rule.

Like many scholars, Shapiro argues that the 1973 *Rodriguez* case "put a halt" to the Warren Court's flirtations with establishing a right to subsistence. He asserts, moreover, that the case stands as a landmark in the decline of the Warren Court's concern with equality. Shapiro views the Burger Court's refusal in the *Frontiero* case to make gender a suspect classification and its refusal to create additional evidence as stopping the thrust toward equality that began with the New Deal coalition.[46] This view, which denies the importance of polity and rights values and argues that principles and constitutional theory are not significant sources of constitutional development, understates both innovations in equality as a principle on the Burger Court and the impact of changes in the views about polity from the Warren to the Burger Court. It also denies that the Burger Court employed a more critical pluralist view of polity than the Warren Court, although it is that view that allowed Burger Court equal protection doctrine to go beyond improving formal access to the political system. The Burger Court's complex structural view of polity paved the way to judicial scrutiny in many new areas and heightened judicial scrutiny in other areas. Shapiro's instrumental assumptions also fail to acknowledge the fact that views of polity are not by their nature conservative. The explosion of systematic polity- and rights-based theory at the end of the Warren Court era made it impossible for the Burger Court and its commentators to view issues as fulfilling the need for equality in only policy terms.

Shapiro assumes that all Court choices are instrumental to that justice's policy wants. This view presumes that the Court does not consider its role in our constitutional system and what liberty interests mean today, given their meaning in the past. For Shapiro, the right to travel and polity considerations, such as the nation as one economic union, are mere window dressing for the

Court to establish in constitutional law the policy wants of the justices, the New Deal coalition, and commentators. Shapiro's failure to see the change in definitions of polity by the Court undermines his ability to see differences between Courts.

While Shapiro is correct in pinpointing that substantive choices as to liberty and equality are made by the Court today, as in the past, his transmogrification of concerns about rights into concerns about economic theory misstates how the Court thinks about these issues. Education, race discrimination, and gender rights are not merely cases of economic redistribution; for the Court they involve issues of status and institutional inequality as well as difficult questions about which groups in our society fit which constitutional definitions of equality. As our case analyses suggest, Shapiro, in viewing the Burger Court as working at the margins of the Warren Court equality principles, overstates in structural terms the Warren Court's move to equality and understates the significance of doctrinal innovations by the Burger Court in equal protection and other doctrinal areas. For example, in *Frontiero* the Burger Court did not stop the development of major rights in the area of gender discrimination but simply refused to label gender classifications suspect.

The folding together of polity and rights aspects of Burger Court choices by Shapiro in *Roe v. Wade* (1973), viewing the case in bottom-line terms as supporting the value of individual autonomy, oversimplifies the dimensions of the Burger Court decisionmaking process and the place of polity and rights principles in the making of its constitutional choices in general. For example, as we saw in Chapter 4, the *Jaffree* and *Grand Rapids* decisions cannot be explained as concerned only with autonomy. Does the Burger Court's protection of established religions but not more recent sects in *Wisconsin v. Yoder* (1972), in which the Court said the Amish did not have to attend school beyond the eighth grade, explain this case? Or does the Burger Court use different polity and rights values than those used by the Warren Court? The juxtaposition of rights values, such as the free exercise of religion and the polity principle of group autonomy, explains this case. As our case analysis demonstrates, Shapiro's analysis of Burger Court religion cases underestimates the place of rights values, which along with polity values inform establishment clause cases.

If Shapiro is correct in asserting that the autonomy value is not wedded to an absolute, then it undermines his theory of the Burger Court as influenced by the autonomy principle. If in equal protection, the most significant area of constitutional doctrine, Shapiro maintains that the Burger Court holds primarily an equality value and that the Court must look at equal protection issues in complex group conflict terms, how important can an autonomy principle be as an organizing principle for the Burger Court?

The trichotomy of liberty, politics, and equality as bottom-line notions

178 cannot be the explanation of those choices but only the outcomes of process and rights values held by the Court. To view each as causative forces one to argue that justices think only of outcomes and do not have both polity and rights principles as part of their theoretical baggage and that in equal protection cases judges base their decisions only on autonomy, liberty, or equality principles rather than on all three. Shapiro's distinction between a jurisprudence of values and one of institutional roles is too sharp. Polity and rights values informed the judicial choices of both Courts. The shorthand of discussing the dominant value oversimplifies what was going on in each era and the nature of judicial decisionmaking.

Chapter Six

The Burger Court and Constitutional Theory

In this chapter we return to the question of why scholars have misperceived the decisionmaking and doctrinal change processes of the Supreme Court by drawing on a constitutive analysis of the Burger Court. In Chapter 3 I argued that doctrinal change in the Warren Court era can be explained by exploring that Court's relationship to the interpretive community of its day and its rejection of apologetic pluralist visions of polity that dominated the interpretive community and our society in the 1950s and early 1960s. The Warren Court, however, did not range far outside this pluralist vision in stating the nature of malfunctions in the political system as a basis for Court intervention. The interpretive community had not yet provided a coherent critical pluralist vision of polity, nor had constitutional scholars developed a complex moral theory of individual rights to justify Court intervention beyond securing formal access to the political system and remedying the arbitrary denial of government benefits.

Misperceptions of the Warren Court, and of the processes of Court decisionmaking and doctrinal change, were caused by the acceptance of instrumental approaches to Supreme Court decisionmaking and doctrinal change, which were based on apologetic pluralist visions of the political system and legal realist interpretations of Supreme Court decisionmaking. These were born of non-Euclidean and scientific naturalist views of knowledge in social science and law, and the rejection of moral values as knowledge or the basis of legal principles. The Supreme Court was viewed as synchronous with a political system that was in equilibrium and self-correcting as part of the wider society. As a result commentators overstated the level of innovation in Warren Court doctrinal change.

In this chapter I argue that the Burger Court's more complex view of polity blockage and innovations in individual rights under the Fourteenth and First amendments (see Chapters 4 and 5), can, like Warren Court doctrinal change, be explained by viewing the Supreme Court as in a dialogue with the interpretive community. In the Burger Court era, the incorporation into constitutional theory of critical pluralist visions of polity as conceptualized by political scientists such as Grant McConnell and Theodore Lowi and political theorists such as William E. Connolly, and the introduction of moral theories of individual rights into constitutional theory,[1] led to very different views of

180   political system blockage in the Burger Court era than in the Warren Court era.

If the constitutional theory of the Burger Court era was more critical of polity and had more complex visions of individual rights, was any constitutional theory of that era up to the task of providing guidance to Burger Court decisionmaking? There was a significant break between the scholarship of the Warren Court years and that of the 1970s, when scholars attempted to offer more systematic theory on the relationship of polity and rights principles. Frank Michelman, Jesse Choper, and Laurence Tribe sought more systematic theories of constitutional law, taking their cues from legal philosophers such as Ronald Dworkin and John Rawls.[2] Especially after the publication of John Hart Ely's classic polity-based theory, *Democracy and Distrust*, constitutional scholars began to take a stand on whether to support open-ended rights and moral choices behind the law or to view the Constitution as consisting primarily of polity values and concerns.

The major thrust of constitutional theory in the 1970s was the creation of a framework of principles that would guide jurists and scholars in the making of constitutional choices, particularly in the area of human rights. There was a faith, after the impact of legal realism and the *Lochner* era, that somewhat neutral constitutional principles were possible through nonoriginalist constitutional interpretation. These efforts culminated in the publication in 1978 of Laurence Tribe's *American Constitutional Law*, which emphasized rights values in constitutional theory and practice, and in 1980 of Ely's *Democracy and Distrust*, which argued for a process- rather than rights-based constitutional theory and practice. The debate raged as to whether constitutional choices should be based on non-originalist rights or process principles.

As a result, constitutional theory bifurcated into two major camps. Some theorists took pluralist rather than strongly critical pluralist polity visions. Others, such as Tribe and other rights-oriented theorists rejected polity visions and moved to a more consequentialist rights theory directly based on the economic, social, and political facts of life facing women, economic classes, and other groups subject to inequalities from the economic, social, and political system. This bifurcation added to the criticism of the Burger Court. Scholars in each camp criticized the Burger Court for the impurity of its constitutional choices. Meanwhile, the Burger Court did what all Supreme Courts have done—based its constitutional choices on both polity and rights principles. The constitutional theory of the Burger Court era is complex in its vision of polity malfunction and individual rights, but disappointing because of its inability to provide an integrated constitutional theory in which both polity and rights principles play an equally important role. Thus, during both decades of the Burger Court, as in the Warren Court years, constitutional theory failed to inform the justices' choices. However, the reasons for the failure of constitutional theory in the 1970s and 1980s are different. Ironically, both the polity- and rights-based constitutional visions are informed by a realization of a more complex social and economic reality than in the Warren Court era.

Burger Court jurisprudence can be explained by the Court's taking part in a colloquy about the nature of American political institution and causes of inequality. Its vision of society stemmed from social unrest in the 1960s and views about pluralist politics among scholars of American political institutions, and legal scholars, which were far different than those that predominated in our society and the academy in the Warren Court years.

What constituted being a conservative or a liberal both on the Court and in the academy had changed in significant ways. There is a process of development in the law and among the justices that resonates with the age in which they function. None of the instrumental explanations—election returns, policymaking, safety valve, or biography—offers enough respect for the change in the terms of debate in society, on the Court, and in the interpretive community of legal and moral scholars and jurists.

A Constitutive Interpretation of the Supreme Court, the Interpretive Community, and Doctrinal Change
Critical Pluralist Interpretations of American Politics

In order to understand why the Burger Court had more complex views of polity malfunction and more innovative definitions of individual rights than the Warren Court, we need to look first at the critical pluralist interpretations of American politics developed in the late 1960s and 1970s. These interpretations of American politics rejected the relative democratic theory and apologetic pluralist interpretations of the American polity that were dominant in the Warren Court era. Along with advances in moral theory by Dworkin and Rawls, who also employed critical pluralist interpretations of American politics, the critical pluralists significantly influenced the constitutional theory of the Burger Court era. Their interpretations were the stimulus for the change in the standards for evaluating the Burger Court and its constitutional law and principles.

The questioning and rejection of apologetic pluralist interpretations of the American polity that formed the basis of Warren Court–era constitutional theory and the introduction of a complex view of American politics can be explained as a backlash among social scientists and legal scholars. These scholars viewed government and society as not in equilibrium and saw institutional functional definitions of causation as self-satisfied and simply wrong. They also questioned the adequacy of the relativist democratic theory that had spawned pluralist views of polity and a faith in interest group politics.

In an attempt to counter the apologetic pluralist visions of polity, a new generation of political scientists sought to develop a critical pluralist interpretation of the American political system and the Supreme Court's role. Critical pluralists were not content to criticize the built-in inequities of our American polity without offering at least the basis for alternative plans for its improvement. Their theory suggests a set of hypotheses about our political system that can be explored through empirical study. For this reason the term "critical-pluralist" may be a misnomer, for this theory is not just a rejection of pluralist theory; it is an analytic statement in its own right, a theory of how our political system operates and *should* operate. It could be accurately described as a structural inequality approach, which suggests both the positive analytic aspects of the approach and the potential for wide applicability of critical pluralist theories in studies of politics and law.[3]

Unlike pluralist scholars, critical pluralists question whether the American political system is sufficiently open to political change and to the influence of wide segments of the population in many areas of public policy. Critical pluralists link the presence of small-constituency decisionmaking arenas to deeper problems of economic, social, and political inequality in our nation. They center their analyses on the relationship between the boundaries and constituencies of decisionmaking arenas and the types of values, policies, and interests that are optimized in different arenas. Drawing upon insights from the boundary-setting notions of E. E. Schattschneider, critical pluralist scholars argue that localism, federalism, grass-roots politics, and free enterprise tend to narrow the scope of conflict and make political change and political equality more difficult.[4] The interpretations of American politics by Grant McConnell and Theodore Lowi are the most comprehensive critical pluralist interpretations of American politics, established to question and replace pluralist models of politics and institutional functional interpretations of government and society. Each of these scholars raises critical questions about the nature of polity and political institutions and the role of law, courts, and legal principles in the public philosophies and operations of political institutions.

Grant McConnell and the Rebirth of Federalist *No. 10 Principles*

For Grant McConnell, American government is dominated by hundreds of small decisionmaking arenas. He argues that there is an orthodoxy in America, which political actors accept, that favors both small-constituency policymaking and private power, imbuing them with the myth of grass-roots democracy.[5] A major theoretical contribution of McConnell is his critique, based on empirical data, of small-constituency politics. He argues that as we move decisionmaking arenas away from the presidency, with the largest constituency, and the Supreme Court, with its purported bird's-eye view of issues, toward the most local and decentralized decisionmaking units, we view several negative consequences for the democratic character and quality of decisionmaking in our polity. First, the *smaller* the decisionmaking arena, the greater the chance that social and economic power will prevail; second, the more *informal* the style of decisionmaking, the less likely it is that issues will become politicized and the distinction between private and public values will be weakened; and third, the greater the *autonomy* of the decisionmakers, the less diverse are the interests represented in the decisionmaking arena.[6]

In McConnell's view, the boundaries of American political institutions are the best predictor of the types of decisions that will be made in them. When decisionmaking moves to political institutions with wider constituencies, open conflict, the visibility of issues, and concern for the interests of wider publics increase. For the most part, however, McConnell sees the American polity as a myriad of small geographically and functionally defined decisionmaking arenas that make public policy for narrower, private interests. Consequently, he does not believe that interests or power in one decisionmaking arena can usually cross-check interests in another. Instead, private interest groups and local interests are generally headed by like-minded elites and usually have common material interests.[7] Rather than true compromise based on clash of interests, logrolling among leaders of different narrow constituencies becomes the rule, producing wasteful policies. Fragmentation of congressional decisionmaking into more narrow functional units makes it difficult for unorganized or less powerful groups to gain enough political influence to produce a redistribution of values and goods or for substantive rights questions to arise in political debate. Likewise, federalism serves to increase the local power of interest groups and the inequalities in our political system by limiting our ability to redress wrongs by restricting access to the political process. For McConnell there is not one wider public interest; the tragic reality of American politics is small-constituency politics.[8]

In contrast to Robert Dahl and David Truman, McConnell stresses the *cumulative effects* of our decentralized political system and the oligarchy of power within private interest groups in our polity. Such effects involve economic burdens on minorities who suffer other disadvantages, such as race or gender discrimination, and on all minority dissidents who lack the resources and influence to promote political or economic change. In McConnell's view, pluralism tends to produce stagnation in our polity by allowing economic injustice to remain institutionalized. Narrower public decisionmaking arenas place severe constraints on political change, aid social inequality, and result in conformity of values within these narrow constituencies and in the making of public policy itself. Finally, McConnell sees formality in the law and in bureaucracies and universal concepts of equal protection and due process as means to overcome inherent biases in the pluralist political system.[9]

To remedy the effects of small-constituency politics, McConnell argues that the presidency, the Supreme Court, and the national party system as deci-

184 sionmaking arenas with large and broad constituencies should increase their power within the American political system, whereas cities, states, congressional committees, and congressional districts should have reduced decisionmaking power. Most importantly, McConnell seeks an interpretation of American politics that reintroduces the normative and structural insights of *Federalist* no. 10 to counter the attack on its principles by relative democratic theorists such as David Truman and Robert Dahl.[10]

Theodore Lowi and the ''End of Liberalism''

Theodore Lowi also emphasizes the negative aspects of small-constituency and interest group politics as they are played out in Congress, bureaucracies, cities, and in our practice of federalism. Lowi argues that the system of federalism and grass-roots politics has been a particularly significant barrier to political change and equality in our nation. He sees post-1960 America as embracing a public philosophy of ''interest group liberalism,'' in which the political system is open to all who seek access. However, because of the control of public policies by bureaucracies, subcommittees in Congress, and private interest group clienteles, public collective values and legal-moral principles such as equal protection of the law are not placed into public policy or even considered by elected officials.[11]

Lowi argues that interest group liberalism obliterates lines between public and private power, and law and politics, with the dire result of a decline in our faith in the political system. The result is the loss of an institutional forum in which questions about what is equal or unequal can arise. For Lowi, the concept of equal protection is violated by the Court's rejection of formal separation of powers principles, such as the concept of delegation of powers. He also blames the structure of pluralist politics and the public philosophy that has dominated American politics since World War II for limiting normative consitutional values—such as liberty, racial tolerance, and public rather than private control over property. Political science and political theory have added to interest group liberalism by providing the relativist ideas that make ''what is'' dominate what should be. The idea of public interests and the public as being different from the sum of private wants is lost in such a public philosophy.

In his classic study *The End of Liberalism*, Lowi calls for a juridical democracy—the imposition of a rule of law in our political institutions—so that the informal power that economic and social elites have gained by the capture of small decisionmaking arenas can be overcome by the imposition of clear legal principles and lines of authority above and beyond bureaucratic action.[12] In the scenario Lowi describes, delegation of authority to bureaucracies, local governments, and states would be clarified by Congress. Through its power of judicial review, the Supreme Court would make sure that there are limits on the authority of public officials in order to accommodate a more open decisionmaking process. Lowi states that this measure would reduce the power of the organized interests.

In sum, critical pluralists like McConnell and Lowi favor federal court intervention because they see that it may result in the expansion of the range of issues under discussion to include questions of rights, due process, and equal protection. Therefore it would signal a retreat from the narrow, economic issue formulation that dominates small-constituency politics and decisionmaking. In contrast to Dahl's positive view of federalism, the critical pluralists stress how federalism and narrow state and local decisionmaking lead to inequality in resource collection and allocation (in the gerrymandering of voting and tax districts, for example). An active federal court system, headed by the Supreme Court, is called upon to deal with inherent and fundamental structural inequalities in our political system.

Segmentation of the Interpretive Community into Polity and Rights Camps

Theories and outlooks of pluralist and critical pluralist scholars find parallels in the scholarly studies of constitutional law issues, and it is to the convergence of these institutional arguments with those rooted in the law that we now turn. As an organizing principle, the debate over pluralism serves as a center around which issues of modern constitutional theory can be analyzed. If we agree that the relationship between the Supreme Court and the interpretive community is a dialogic one, as I have argued, we can then inquire into the nature of constitutional theory in the Burger Court years and, more pointedly, whether such theory provided an adequate basis for the constitutive decisionmaking process of the Burger Court.

As we saw in Chapter 3, the liberal constitutional scholars of the Warren Court era made a final attempt to respond to the growing criticism articulated by the pluralists about the fairness of political institutions. Scholars such as Wechsler and Freund tried to find a rationale for Court power in a reconfigured pluralist polity through advocacy of greater formal equality of access. They asked: Should constitutional law protect formal access to the political system? Their support of *Baker v. Carr* (1962) was part of their response to this question.

Burger Court–era constitutional scholars sought a principled constitutional theory, but not one requiring such a high level of neutrality of principles as Wechsler had advocated in the 1950s. Given the increased complexity of the economic and social system, even the most neutral principle in theory could not be neutral in effect. Modern scholars realize that nonprincipled constitutional law leads to less legitimacy for Court action, not to less support for Court intervention into the political, economic, and social systems. More Court intervention was a goal of increasing significance in both process- and

186   rights-based theories after 1965, in contrast to the constitutional scholarship of the previous generation.[13]

In the 1970s constitutional scholars sought a more principled constitutional theory than is found earlier in the work of Freund and Bickel, more flexible in principle than that of Wechsler. Modern scholars could not accept the degree of separation between law and politics Wechsler had advocated. At the same time they felt the necessity of avoiding the mildly reformist judicial principles of Freund. In the 1970s the critical pluralist critique of American political institutions was accepted by most of the major nonoriginalist constitutional scholars of the Burger Court era, including Laurence Tribe, John Hart Ely, Paul Brest, Frank Michelman, and Jesse Choper.

There was an explosion in constitutional theory in the 1970s as well as a quest for a more systematic constitutional theory. The explosion centered around a debate among constitutional scholars, led by John Hart Ely and Laurence Tribe, about whether the Constitution should be viewed as consisting primarily of polity values—keeping the pluralist political process open to all discrete and insular minorities—or whether constitutional theory should be based on natural rights and open-ended language about rights in the Constitution. This debate made problematic the place of moral choices in constitutional decisionmaking and, at another level, what values informed the jurisprudence of the Warren Court.

Thus, in the late 1960s and the 1970s, with the rise of a new wave of constitutional scholars who sought a more principled constitutional theory, the process-rights distinction grew through the effort to find a clearer basis of justification for Court action than formal access rules.[14] It also led to a debate not prominent in the previous decade of scholarship: To what degree should constitutional law take economic and social inequalities into account when deciding questions about citizen, group, and political elite power and the role of courts in society? This debate grew out of the critical pluralist attack on the pluralist system and the politics of despair in the middle and late 1960s. Critical pluralists, such as Lowi and McConnell, questioned the notion of the separation of the political system from the economic and social system that was embedded in the pluralist interpretation of American political institutions. At the same time they searched for a principled way to bridge the gap between economics and politics. The question for the young constitutional scholars was how to secure a fair distribution of outcomes for citizens while still upholding a distinction between law and politics, for only with such a distinction could the legitimacy of an activist Court be sustained. This was an especially acute problem, since faith had declined in an open political process as an institutional solution to the problems of pluralism.

Modern constitutional scholars have accepted the critical pluralists' description of the workings of American political institutions. However, they have not built into their theories of judicial review the conflict between political structure and rights that is central to the incorporation of a critical pluralist analysis of American politics into constitutional theory. Such a constitutional theory must be critical, not apologetic, and must make a renewed effort to address the Framers' concerns about the relationship between political structure and individual rights. Instead, modern constitutional scholars seek a theory of judicial review and a system of justification for constitutional choices that rests either on a theory of rights specification or on a set of rules about the polity. Each camp of modern constitutional scholars is myopic when it comes to the relationship between polity and rights. Because they do not keep this conflict alive, they lose the opportunity to make more credible arguments in support of the changes in constitutional principles they desire.

Polity-Based Constitutional Theory

John Hart Ely, the most distinguished modern process theorist of constitutional law, accepts notions of polity that are more critical than those of the pluralist scholars, but less critical than those of rights-oriented constitutional scholars. He believes that on most issues the American political system is quite open to political change through electoral and interest group politics. Like pluralist scholars, he does not recognize that there are deep structural biases against political change. Process theorists see malfunctions in the political process, such as its denial of access to some citizens, as rare occurrences that are usually related to our history of race prejudice.

Ely argues that judicial review and judicial activism should be limited to enforcing specific requirements of the Constitution (such as the commerce clause or free speech provisions); prohibiting discrimination against discrete and insular minorities (usually racial in nature); preventing the denial of voting or other formal rights of citizenship; and correcting instances in which political leaders insulate themselves from being formally accountable to citizens. On most federalism issues and questions of local and state governmental power, Ely, like other process theorists, argues that the political system, not the courts, should make policy choices. Like pluralist scholars, process theorists fear repression of insular minorities by majorities but are not concerned about inequalities of political, economic, and social power implied in small-constituency decisionmaking. They also view the power of judicial review in most cases as problematic because federal judges are not elected. This fact is significant to them because of their faith in political change through electoral, congressional, and interest group politics—a faith they share with the pluralists. For these reasons, process theorists do not favor the use of judicial review to overcome economic and social inequalities in the political system. Rather, the role of constitutional theory is to keep the political system open.

Most important, Ely deplores the creation of fundamental rights by the

188   Court, such as in *Roe v. Wade* (1973). He views the Constitution as a means to ensure equal rights to participation in the political system and to provide each citizen equal respect in the process of public policymaking. Ely admits to the open-ended nature of the Constitution, especially as seen in the privileges and immunities clause and the Ninth Amendment. However, he argues that judges should not make choices on the basis of natural law, neutral principles, reason, tradition, consensus in the nation, or predictions of progress. Any of these bases for choice will allow values of the justices and their policy wants, rather than principles, to dictate Court choices.[15]

Scholars have criticized Ely for reading all parts of the Constitution as related to protecting access to the political process rather than granting substantive rights; for his failure to recognize that moral and value choices must be made in order to find malfunctions in the political process; for his failure to discuss the presuppositions used to find a denial of equality of access to the political process; for his instrumental notion of process rather than viewing participation as a good in and of itself; and for the choices that he makes in deciding when a discrete and insular minority exists.[16]

Another major problem with Ely's process theory is that it separates the political system from the social and economic systems and assumes that mere "channel-clearing" is enough to ensure equal protection in a complex society. The fact that, for Ely, being poor or a woman cannot be the basis for a suspect classification in equal protection law indicates his relatively narrow view of malfunction in the political system. It also indicates that his theory is based on an uncritical pluralist view of polity. For, like Dahl, he sees noninterpretivism as permitted in race cases but trusts pluralist group politics to protect other subgroups in our society. Ely says little about problems of federalism with regard to small constituencies and state and local autonomy.

What is most problematic in Ely's process theory, however, is that it fails to acknowledge the tension between process and rights protection. In this view it contrasts both to the way the Framers viewed questions of where political power should lie and to the beliefs of critical pluralists who see systematic relationships between political issues and size of constituency.[17] Ely presents a formalistic view of the structure of government. He has not included in his theory of polity a concept of power that will produce the process enhancement he desires. Perhaps a process theory of greater complexity, one that has within it principles that respond to the critical pluralist criticism of American politics and its relation to society, would be a better aid to constitutional theory.

Ely's theory is a critical response to the faith in pluralism that dominated the Warren Court, in which race was the most important suspect classification and wealth was a factor only when fundamental rights were concerned. Ely does pose a more searching set of questions about what constitutes a denial of equal concern and respect than was evident on the Warren Court. However, unlike rights- and moral theory-based constitutional theorists, he, like the Warren Court, still requires that there be a close link between constitutional concerns about inequality and concerns about the political system as the primary cause of limits on access. Ely asks us to consider whether the majority is treating the minority unfairly. Linking inequality, majoritarian values, and access to the political system, he argues for ending invidious discrimination against blacks, religious groups, and gays. Women, he argues, do not need protection by courts, because unlike religious groups, they do not have rights that are specified in the Constitution, they are a majority of the population, and they have no formal structural limits on their participation in politics. To declare oneself a woman publicly does not bring the opprobrium and personal hurt from the majority that was found with respect to gays.[18]

Thus, Ely's approach does not consider, or allow jurists to consider, deep structural inequalities in society that cause economic and social inequality. Rather, it looks at inequality of access in majority and minority terms. Nor does it allow the filigreed analysis of the causes of equality that the Burger Court's intermediate level of scrutiny permits. Ely's acceptance of protection for blacks and gays and his rejection of it for women is unsupported. All three groups suffer significant social inequality and are hurt economically if they try to advocate their interests in society. Differences in numbers should not be the determinant of whether classifications are suspect. Other scholars, such as Laurence Tribe, do not rest their constitutional theories on the numbers of individuals in a group but on the strength of prejudice caused, in part, by social values and past economic inequality.

Ely's theory goes only part of the way in criticizing pluralist politics. It does not include prejudice caused by inequality in the interest group structure or in relationships among individuals and social groups other than the majority-minority prejudice writ large. Ely claims that justices who were umpires in the political system would make less free-wheeling claims for the law than justices who made decisions on social inequality grounds. Like Lowi and McConnell, Ely believes that if judges think deeply about fairness in the political process and help those who truly cannot help themselves, the political system can fulfill the objectives of the Constitution.

Because Ely attempts to link public authority prejudice with classifications in the law beyond race, he proposes a more critical view of polity than the Warren Court and pluralist scholars, who trusted formal political process as long as no formal barriers to voting and access were present. However, Ely's rejection of open-ended rights notions, not related to polity malfunctions in the Constitution, suggests a major theoretical flaw in his constitutional theory: It does not consider fundamental rights principles and moral values along with process reinforcement principles in the constitutive decisionmaking process.

190   The introduction of critical pluralist interpretations of American politics and the rejection of relativist theories of democracy strongly influenced the constitutional theories developed by John Hart Ely, Laurence Tribe, and Frank Michelman in the 1970s, as they did the work of political scientists Theodore Lowi and Grant McConnell in the 1960s and 1970s. However, analysis that relies solely on polity principles as a basis for evaluating either American political institutions or constitutional principles is of only limited usefulness, if constitutional theory and interpretations of American politics are to provide adequate guidance to the constitutive decisionmaking process of the Supreme Court.

Lowi and McConnell are deeply critical of the polity notions that have developed since World War II, when relative democratic theory replaced more substantive rights talk and standards of evaluation in our public philosophy. However, like pluralists Robert Dahl and David Truman, Lowi and McConnell rest their hopes for a just society on political structure reforms, not on the introduction of substantive visions of individual rights into a theory of political reform. Both McConnell and Lowi assume that if all groups got "pieces of the action" and access to politics and decisions were centralized, society would be good and fair. But the nature of the access and the outcomes each group gets vary so greatly that mere access reveals little about fairness or equal protection of the law. If the only standard of evaluation is formal access, then the concept of equal protection of the law as ensuring fundamental rights such as liberty, property, and equal respect can be easily undermined.

Thus, it is not clear what place fundamental rights and natural rights hold for Lowi. He hopes that through institutional change, principles can be employed over politics to reduce self-interested policy choices and limit private and support public bases for governmental choices. He has faith in congressional limits on private power, if structural changes are made to clarify what general principles of policy are, so that political actors in less public roles (such as in bureaucracies) cannot dictate private rights and public policy. Therefore, Lowi seeks to reintroduce institutional separation and complexity as a limit on private power. He is faithful to the *Federalist* no. 10 system but argues, as McConnell did, that embedded within that system is a concern for public interests and public normative values, rights and fairness and equal protection, that gets undermined in the operation of the political system. He rejects mere access as a protector of rights and a preventer of inequality. But with the Federalist Founders Lowi seeks structural changes as a means to better public-regarding choices. The vague part of his theory involves equal protection notions, fairness to all groups, and the way that fairness is undermined by the decentralized political system, both vertically—from national to state government—and horizontally, among the institutions and agencies of the national government.

Lowi's interpretation of American politics is a structural counterpart to Ely's polity-based constitutional theory; neither scholar starts his analysis from a fundamental rights perspective nor asks more searching questions about the social and economic bases of inequality and the denial of equal rights. While their critical stance toward pluralist politics and institutions is supported by social science data about inequality in social and economic relationships, the degree to which data can become the basis identifying structural incapacities and defining reform strategies is limited by each scholar's faith in the reform of political structure along *Federalist* no. 10 principles.

This type of analysis, although very critical of political structure and the equilibrium model of politics dominant in the Warren Court era, is neither affirmative enough of the equality notions nor searching enough of moral theories and values, such as liberty, equal concern and respect, freedom of speech, and rights to education. The Burger Court decided cases on complex polity principles, and on rights values, that were not envisioned by critical pluralist scholars such as McConnell, Lowi, and Ely. The Burger Court allowed more questioning by federal courts of deeper pathologies in the political system than envisioned by these conventional critical pluralist interpreters of politics while, ironically, appearing to be pragmatic and proceeding slowly in countering those pathologies.

Critical pluralists are brilliant at showing how the idea of equilibrium and the self-satisfied love affair with pluralism and interest group politics was not in keeping with *Federalist* no. 10 and present-day constitutional polity notions. These concepts share a substantive element—a concern for public interests. However, these scholars did not build into their theories an argument for the need for structural bases as justification for Court action. There is a limit to the degree to which polity arguments alone permit the Court to support the fundamental rights and polity arguments in the Constitution. The same problem exists for Ely's theory. To reject fundamental rights principles, or to bury moral values and principles of justice behind polity principles and arguments, leaves the Supreme Court, other jurists, and constitutional scholars in the lurch. The Supreme Court, as evidenced by the constitutive decisionmaking process in the Warren and Burger Court eras, decides cases and establishes constitutional principles based on both polity and rights principles.

Rights-Based Constitutional Theory

Naturalistic Rights Theory in the 1980s
In the 1970s, fundamental rights–oriented scholars offered an analysis of constitutional theory that held assumptions about the American polity similar to those of critical pluralist interpreters of American politics, but they refused to rest their constitutional theory on polity principles alone.[19] Like the critical

192   pluralists, they saw political inequality as inherent in the present American regime. They successfully pointed out the insensitivity of process theorists to the relationship between social and economic factors and political inequality. They argued that process theory cannot be value free, no matter how much process theorists attempt to make it so, and they criticized the process theorists for their pluralist assumption that the American political system normally functions smoothly and democratically. They shared with the critical pluralists the view that process theorists fail to recognize that potential majorities who are economically and socially weak have great difficulty in influencing public policy.

Richard Parker, like McConnell and Lowi, argues that process theorists skew their concerns about American politics to fears of potential majorities and conflict rather than stressing the more significant dilemma of the American political arena—the control of public policy by narrow oligarchic elites. He contends that process theorists such as Ely and Choper tend to be little concerned with the fact "that powerful minorities can get the state to act in ways that disregard or undervalue interests of non-mobilized majorities and that, in any event, legislative majorities often fail to champion the interests of passive popular majorities."[20] Parker endorses the most significant critical pluralist conclusions about the American polity and makes a careful, articulate statement of why process and pluralist analysis is unrewarding as a basis for constitutional law theory. Like McConnell and Lowi, Parker believes that concepts of polity are implicit in most works of political analysis and that such concepts determine the behavior of actors in the American political system. Given his critical pluralist value structure and criticism of interest group politics, it is easy to understand why Parker also accepts a more significant role for judicial review as a vehicle for political change. For him, judicial review would do more than merely protect insular (usually racial) minorities and those denied formal participation in the political system.

Laurence Tribe, perhaps the foremost nonoriginalist constitutional litigator of our times, argues for a rights-based constitutional theory.[21] He favors wide-ranging noninterpretivism by the Supreme Court. The Constitution consists of open-ended substantive rights and an overall structure to protect rights; rights creation is implicit in the open-textured language of the Constitution to a degree not envisioned by process theorists. In the 1970s, Tribe's arguments for the use of judicial review for rights creation were based on his views about rights and process values in the Constitution. He sees the structural inequality in American political institutions as a major problem in our society. In contrast to Ely, he believes that inequality is caused not only by lack of formal access or by prejudiced choices against discrete and insular minorities; it is also the result of economic and social inequality in our society. Therefore the Court, through its power of judicial review, must expand rights and equalize the social and economic resources available to citizens, thus reducing structural inequality.[22]

Tribe rejects the argument that judicial review is inherently less democratic than legislative and administrative actions.[23] He cautions against the Court's using the *Lochner* era to justify avoiding rights creation and value choices. The problem with that Court, he asserts, was not that it made choices about the economic and social systems, but that its views of those systems were antiquated.

This view of a wide power of judicial review is seen most clearly in the way in which Tribe and Frank Michelman, another rights theorist, analyze the case of *National League of Cities v. Usery* (1976).[24] Although they were asking only "what if" the Court were thinking in terms of substantive rights theory, their case commentary offers an example of the rights approach and how it differs from that of the process theorists. Tribe and Michelman read *Usery* as leading toward a *right* to essential services for citizens of the states. In that case the Burger Court said that Congress could not require the states to pay minimum wages to state workers because to do so was an intrusion on the states' right to determine their essential services. Based on the *Usery* decision, Tribe and Michelman argue that the delivery of those services must be implicit in some concept of sovereignty or state obligation. Therefore, the citizens of the states, as the recipients of services, must have a right to welfare and services because it is inherent in the nature of statehood and their role as citizens in the states.

In contrast to the process theorists, the rights theorists refuse to look only at the system of representation. They do not accept the position of Jesse Choper and Michael Perry, explored below, that states should not have the right to bring suit against congressional limits on their power. Nor do they see the formal participation of representatives from states in the House and Senate as a justification for depriving states of access to federal courts. They look at the substantive outcomes of the political system and the relationship of those outcomes to the structure of political power. They believe that the regime of constitutional law must create rights so inequalities of economic and social resources will be considered by the Court in such areas as equal protection and the First Amendment. Tribe writes, "The time will come when constitutional law will answer the scholar's question, 'Why education and not golf?' with the only reply that makes human sense—'Because education is more important'—and when this answer, however odd it will seem to some lawyers, will seem convincing to those who take their lessons from life itself.'"[25]

Tribe's sensitivity to the relationship between political structure and rights is exemplified by his early argument for structural due process. In reviewing *Hampton v. Mow Sun Wong* (1976) Tribe argues that the Court should not simply assume that the substance of a governmental rule or policy is in accord with constitutional principles or ask whether the application of the rule is procedurally acceptable in due process norms; it should ascertain whether the structure through which the policy is formed and applied is consistent with the due process of law. The Court must decide whether the power to make choices is vested in the agency with the knowledge and authority to make the broader policy choices in a subject area. If it is not, then there is a chance that the government is making choices not related to its broader legitimate goals. With reasoning similar to Lowi's juridical democracy notion, Tribe argues that government should not allow decisions involving foreign policy to be made by the Civil Service Commission, which has no foreign policy expertise. Citizens deserve policy made by proper agencies.[26]

Implicit in Tribe's notion is the old delegation doctrine: that choices should be made by institutions that have, in principle, both the authority to make the choices and the know-how to do so. Like the critical pluralists, Tribe makes an effort to show how the boundaries of a particular institution influence the types of issues discussed within it. Tribe hopes to protect individuals and groups from arbitrary decisions about whether they could be employed by a specific agency by having courts enforce what he calls "structural due process." Under this polity principle only an official in an agency in which a position exists, and staff have thus engaged in a careful consideration of whether aliens or other groups can perform the tasks of the position, may determine whether certain groups are to be banned from employment. To allow an independent agency, like civil service commission, to determine what groups may be denied employment is arbitrary under the structural due process concept.

Of constitutional scholars in the 1970s, Tribe proposes the most sophisticated view of the relationship between polity and rights. In addition to introducing the concept of structural due process, Tribe makes a process-based role-allocation argument in support of *Roe v. Wade*. There he argues that decisions about whether to have an abortion are similar to an individual's religious or ethical choices; they should not be made by electorally accountable institutions.[27] But in the end, Tribe admits that seeking to protect individual rights by securing new polity-based principles, such as substantive due process and role-allocation theory, requires constitutional scholars and jurists to make choices based on some theory of justice or moral values, not strictly on neutral principles about the proper role of political institutions alone.[28] Tribe admits that role-allocation choices for institutions, and theories in support of them, are based on values regarding what is important for society and its citizens today.

Therefore, institutional competence arguments such as we see in the work of Ely, Perry, and Choper, at their base, require substantive value choices about what aspects of life need to be protected from government. Tribe writes, "The process theme by itself determines almost nothing unless its presuppositions are specified, and its content supplemented by a full theory of substantive rights and values—the very sort of theory the process perfecters are at pains to avoid.''[29] Deciding what constitutes a group, which groups are to be protected, who shall vote, what constitutes discrimination, what interests are at stake, and whether a procedure is just requires substantive value choices regarding how well the polity operates and what rights are needed for citizens.

In contrast to Ely, Tribe advocates the creation of rights to affirmatively compensate for physical, economic, and class differences in society.[30] Here the Court must make choices about inequality and create rights to redress the balance of power between men and women, rich and poor, and majority and minorities, even if neutral principles are not possible. Tribe argues that, under the First Amendment, efforts to secure content-neutral categories, to make distinctions between speech and action, to create different rules for obscenity, commercial, and libelous speech and in public and private forums, and to secure equal versus guaranteed access principles lead to grossly inadequate protection for the poor, the politically weak, and those with unconventional, unpopular viewpoints. The Court must instead make choices based on the resources available to groups.[31]

In the area of abortion rights, Tribe has all but given up on the process-based rationales found in his earlier attempt to base the right to abortion choice on religious and ethical values best left to the individual.[32] Tribe favors basing equal protection and other rights on what I call a new naturalistic approach to individual rights. He argues that constitutional theory must consider the differences between men and women, the poor and the wealthy, and other important distinguishing groups and ask: What are the effects on groups' or individuals' liberty interests of allowing those differences to continue without affirmative Court intervention? The right to abortion choice must be viewed in terms of systemic norms concerned with structuring power relationships to avoid the creation or perpetuation of hierarchy in which some perennially dominate others. To view the right of abortion choice as relational and systemic is to see it as necessarily inalienable, says Tribe, since individuals cannot waive it, for individuals are not the sole focus. It is the relationship of women to men that constitutes inequality under the law: men have the right not to use their bodies against their wills, while women are forced to use their bodies when pregnant. Thus, for the state not to pay for poor women's abortions is to treat men and women as unequal with regard to their use of their bodies and to treat rich and poor with regard to their liberty interests as if they were equal.[33]

More than any other scholar we have discussed, Tribe in the 1970s saw the interplay between polity and rights values and the need for a complex structural inequality concept of polity in a theory of constitutional law and judicial review. However, his concern for the relationship between process and rights values, and for process values in all human rights areas, seems to have declined in his later scholarship. The problem with his theory now, with its movement to naturalistic differences as a basis for rights, is that polity inequalities are secondary and rights are too much based on sociology, resulting in an increase in ad hoc, case-by-case analysis. No longer does he search for enduring process and rights principles as a basis for constitutional choices; thus he fails to provide future scholars or jurists with principles on which to base arguments for rights and their protection over the long-term. Unfortunately, the imbalance in his theory—the favoring of substantive rights over polity principles as a basis for judicial decisionmaking—occurs at a time when the Court seems more interested in guidance on how the allocation of power between institutions in our society should be balanced with constitutional rights than in a philosophy of rights creation.

Tribe understands both political and social/economic structures and their interface with politics. Yet he does not advocate a full program of structural reform. He tends to seek only a better allocation of goods so that citizens might be more powerful in the polity of structural inequality. Focusing on the individual or group rather than the political structure leads us to a deficiency in Tribe's rights theory of judicial review. His new contextualism, or legal realism, builds relational rights from naturalistic distinctions defined almost on a case-by-case basis and fosters an implicit attack on the search for enduring rights and process values. Tribe's method of interpretation and his denial of a general theory in which process and rights principles are considered in a disciplined relationship to each other, leads to criticism by scholars who ask why Tribe's values are better than anyone else's. Unfortunately, he can offer no theory or sustained, disciplined analysis to answer that question.

Rights Scholars Who Argue for Judicial Self-Restraint

Jesse H. Choper and Michael Perry are also rights-oriented theorists. However, unlike Laurence Tribe and Frank Michelman, they have developed formulas to restrict the jurisdiction of federal courts in some areas of public law and arguments for caution by the Supreme Court in engaging in nonoriginalist interpretation.

Choper argues that states should not be allowed to oppose congressional actions because they have representatives within Congress. He also argues that federal courts should not decide constitutional questions concerning the respective powers of the president and Congress.[34] Both of these proposals are based on the assumption that the political system is a better forum than courts for such choices. Choper argues that avoiding issues of federalism and separation of powers in the national government would allow federal courts more time to do what is really important: secure racial equality, protect the rights of the accused, ensure freedom of expression, ensure equal apportionment in representative bodies, and protect rights of privacy. Choper is not opposed to rights creation by the Court, but he fails to tell us how to choose the principles on which federal courts should decide individual rights under the open-textured parts of the Constitution.

Choper accepts the formal representation of states in Congress as a reason for not allowing the power of states to be issues before federal courts. He accepts the uncritical pluralist trust in the group process to decide questions of institutional power, a trust not found among rights theorists. Choper assumes that questions of institutional power and individual rights are somehow separate and that state representatives in Congress can protect the interests of their minority communities or their own interests when a state's values differ from those of the majority in Congress. On issues of federalism and separation of powers he assumes that the political system can be trusted to illuminate the needs of all segments of society.

The stark, simplistic separation between issues of rights and of polity is a problem in Choper's theory because it narrows too much the domain of federal courts. His theory is founded on a mildly critical pluralist impulse to protect individual rights, a pluralist concern for judicial self-restraint, and a belief in the lack of legitimacy of courts because they are not electorally accountable. Under Choper's approach, the federal courts would no longer be a forum to ask questions about the range of interests that would be protected in a given instance of institutional power. Raw politics would be trusted with the answer, and decisions that resulted would replicate the political power already present in our national politics.

By limiting questions of institutional power to issues of individual rights or procedural fairness, rather than addressing questions of substantive power and access to the political arena by wider sets of interests, Choper narrows the scope of constitutional law as a system of political accountability. Line drawing between states and the federal government or between institutions of the national government allows us as a society to decide the nature of our institutions and the role of groups and citizens in those institutions. Such decisions are related to the protection of rights and must not be thought of as merely ones of process. This is the type of formalism the critical pluralists rejected, arguing that mere formal representation of states in Congress would not protect the interests of groups in those states, given the functional segmentation of Congress. It is an even grosser kind of formalism to assume that since the Supreme Court is not electorally accountable it will have less legitimacy in deciding questions of institutional power and that a loss of legitimacy will result in a deterioration of its role as an interpreter of individual rights. As is argued in *Federalist* no. 78, deciding questions of institutional power necessarily involves raising questions about the process of rights protection. To decide questions of individual rights is to decide issues about the power of political

198   institutions. A constitutional theory that attempts to separate the world into issues of rights or issues of polity oversimplifies the relationship between them.

Like Choper, Michael Perry accepts a wider role for noninterpretivism for the Supreme Court and rights creation than Ely.[35] Perry also believes that on questions of federalism and separation of powers, political processes can usually be trusted to make decisions. Perry centers his analysis on the role of the Supreme Court in the protection of First Amendment freedoms, equal protection of the law, substantive due process, and the protection of human rights. Deciding moral issues cannot be left to the vote of the people or to public officials who will follow the short- and long-term conventional morality of the majority of citizens.[36]

Perry accepts both the federalism principle of Choper and the view that the legitimacy of Supreme Court action in all matters is suspect because of the Court's lack of electoral accountability. He sees extending Congress's power to limit the jurisdiction of federal courts as the only means to increase the legitimacy of Supreme Court actions. The amending process, political selection of Supreme Court justices, and public opinion are inadequate means of ensuring the accountability of the Supreme Court. There is a need to limit the rights creation process and to trust the political system over the Court on controversial issues.

The institutional formalism in Perry's theory undercuts his goal of establishing the Supreme Court as moral leader of the nation. It allows conventional wisdom and interest group politics to be the ultimate bases for the definition of rights. A constitutional theory that keeps the tension between rights and polity alive, introducing a more precise analysis of what to expect from interest group politics into our choices about institutional competence to decide rights and other constitutional issues, would meet Perry's goal of protecting human rights and answer the dilemmas of the American political system as outlined by the critical pluralists. A more complex structural inequality theory of polity in areas of human rights *and* federalism, one with a more comprehensive view of the relationship between concepts of polity and rights, could reduce Perry's defensiveness about the power of judicial review. Yet once the power of judicial review is seen as legitimate, one would still need a constitutional theory that would link issues of rights and polity in making specific choices.

Why We Misperceive the Burger Court:
A Critique of Instrumental Approaches

As we saw in Chapter 3, a major problem of the instrumental interpretations of doctrinal change is that they do not sufficiently respect the impact of the terms of debate in society, on the Court, and in the interpretive community.

Instrumental approaches tend to simplify the causation of doctrinal change. Most importantly, they undervalue the constitutive nature of the debate in the interpretive community by assuming that direct policy wants of scholars inform the development of constitutional theory. This problem will be brought into focus by exploring Martin Shapiro's instrumental policymaking view of doctrinal change, as well as the influence of the interpretive community on doctrinal change in the Burger Court era.

There is a significant anomaly in Shapiro's analysis of the relationship of the Burger Court to the interpretive community. Shapiro emphasizes that no member in the Burger Court cares much about legal scholarship. Unlike Vincent Blasi, the major advocate of the no counterrevolution approach, Shapiro seeks to "draw some parallels and contrasts between the Burger Court's behavior and styles of contemporary commentary, without imputing causal relations in either direction."[37] He argues that Warren Court commentators could not praise the Warren Court because they were brought up on institutional role principles antagonistic to Warren Court activism and its rejection of craft arguments. These commentators rejected the Court's policy agenda, which Shapiro incorrectly identifies as fulfilling New Deal policies and the Great Society program of President Johnson.

Shapiro argues that for the new generation of commentators—a generation that includes Brest, Blasi, Ely, Fiss, Grey, Choper, Tribe, Michelman, and Van Alstyne—*Brown v. Board of Education*, not the New Deal, was the consciousness-shaping crisis. Thus, "their central problem was not whether the Court can or should act, but how it ought to act." Shapiro argues that the foundation of the new commentary was broader movements in philosophy and legal theory rather than polity principles.[38]

There is a significant problem in Shapiro's view of constitutional theory and the place of the interpretive community in the process of doctrinal change. Like his view of internal Supreme Court decisionmaking, it is instrumental, not constitutive, in its assumptions. Shapiro argues that the major role of constitutional and moral theory is to tell courts what public policies to make and to praise good choices and oppose bad choices. The problem here is that a constitutional theory that is linked directly to outcomes—to policy choices—rather than to the theory and principles behind the choices, has quite limited transformative possibilities.

Criticism at the policy level accepts the value premises of the polity and groups already in power as the end point of power relationships. Shapiro's view that all courts are policymaking institutions rejects fundamental values and constitutional theory in "should" or "ought" terms; that is, his view that such values are not part of the problematics faced by the Supreme Court is a major problem in his theory of doctrinal change. By looking at polity principles, rights values, and policy as separate entities, Shapiro trivializes the role

200   of constitutional theory, theories of polity, and changing visions of the political system and citizen participation in Supreme Court decisionmaking. He writes, "The post–New Deal generation of commentators is unlikely to achieve the elegance or the professional sense of superiority of the generation of judicial restraint, for it is going to be down with the rest of us in the dirty pit of public policy. It may, however, have more interesting things to say about what is really going on in the world and in the Court than did the generation that devoted itself to self-restraint."[39]

This argument also has problems. To the degree that commentators stay in the "dirty pit of public policy" they will do what they did in the Warren Court era: stay out of touch with the polity and rights values that inform Burger Court decisionmaking. Simply discussing policy does not mean one has explained it or its causes. When constitutional theory becomes merely utilitarian, not substantive in polity and rights values, it automatically loses legitimacy. Ironically, we may be better able to understand what is going on in society by examining the complex polity and rights values on the Court and then asking why issues are viewed by scholars and the wider community in narrow policy terms rather than in terms of theories of rights and community. The development of these theories, as a counter to "what is," will ensure that equality and other values in the Constitution will be protected. Praise of empirical study of "what is," as in Laurence Tribe's naturalistic view of equality, ultimately does have a transparent case-specific, not deeply principled quality that Shapiro alludes to—like the equality value in the Warren Court. The problem with this formulation is that it moves from general equality and general self-restraint arguments to policy and back to theory arguments without stopping to consider the complex community and rights values that inform both judicial and commentator choices.

A major problem with Shapiro's view of Burger Court–era scholarship is that he tends to fold together theories that are quite different. There are important differences between Ely-type theories and those of Brest, Tribe, Michelman, Dworkin, and Rawls. Tribe and others reject the moral skepticism of Ely. The fact that Ely's theory rests on polity principles and that the other scholars' theories rested first on rights and polity grounds, then on naturalist rights principles, suggests that there are significant differences in these scholars' theories and their implications for guiding the Court's constitutive decisionmaking process. The failure to take commentators' principles seriously and to accept the constitutive, not utilitarian, basis of constitutional theory underlies the central problem of instrumental analysis: it is too willing to view both Court eras as operating under a general and simplistic vision of equality.

The word "equality" loses meaning when instrumental interpreters do not view polity and rights values in constitutional thought and action as separate and important analytic categories, and when they are more interested in offering bottom-line conclusions about case outcomes than in analyzing the polity and rights principles employed in the constitutive decisionmaking process. This deeply legal realist bent in the instrumental policymaking approach limits its usefulness in explaining the constitutive Burger Court decisionmaking process.[40]

This limitation is evident when Shapiro argues that "the Supreme Court always has intervened, and continues to intervene, in the economic policymaking process guided by its own assessments of what constitutes reasonable economic and social policy."[41] He appears to view Ely's constitutional theory based on polity values, Perry's view of polity and rights, and Tribe's view of rights-based constitutional theory as superfluous to explaining judicial decisionmaking. Shapiro seems to view issues of constitutional theory as secondary in the Court's deliberations, because commentators merely support the poor, blacks, government workers, and ethnic groups in a welfare state.

Shapiro's view of 1970s scholarship as merely outcome-oriented is simplistic. It does not take seriously the idea that views about polity and fundamental rights inform constitutional theory and at times produce choices that a scholar might not want in raw policy terms. Shapiro's argument that the scholars of the 1970s and, I presume, the 1980s have developed a "jurisprudence of values rather than institutional roles" and that "their central problem is not whether the Court can or should act, but how it ought to act" understates the place of polity principles in the new constitutional theory.[42] All constitutional scholars have a view of institutional role; they differ on the amount and nature of nonoriginalism in which the Court should engage.

Tribe's and Michelman's work in the 1970s shows a concern for redistribution, as did their work on the *Usery* case and *Shapiro v. Thompson* (1969). However, in the 1980s Michelman's concern for institutional roles shifted to a new concern for the relationship of the polity and individual rights. This concern is sincere and deep and not designed just to produce New Deal outcomes. So when scholars pursue what Shapiro calls a "jurisprudence of values," they find that the values employed by scholars of the Burger Court era include views of institutions that range from critical pluralist to pluralist. They show different ranges of trust for politics and view the Founders and the Court as having accepted different levels of trust in the past. Shapiro assumes all such theory and arguments are window dressing for policy agendas.

In viewing the new constitutional theory as a jurisprudence of values rather than of Court roles, Shapiro does what many commentators of the Court in all periods do: he overemphasizes the role of moral values in Court choices and commentary and underemphasizes the role of institutional or polity principles, when in fact they are interrelated. In the 1970s, constitutional scholars such as Tribe and Michelman related polity to rights values in seeking

202 constitutional theory—in their treatment of *Roe v. Wade*, for example. Tribe replaced this approach in the 1980s with a more lumpen equality-based constitutional theory, but other scholars continued their consideration of institutional roles. For Shapiro, institutional role theory seems to encompass only conservative judicial self-restraint theory, rather than suggesting that institutional roles and principles need not be limited to a formulaic opposition to nonoriginalism.

Contemporary nonoriginalist constitutional scholars take seriously the criticism that judicial review is undemocratic and respond to it in their theory, endorsing the view that the Supreme Court must counter majoritarianism in support of individual and minority rights. To dismiss them as merely seeking to extend the New Deal's welfare state without the qualms about judicial activism is incorrect.[43]

Ely does attempt to improve the theory of "interest group liberalism" by seeking to define conditions under which the majority does not accord equal respect and concern to minorities and by identifying policy outcomes that cannot be explained except as discrimination by the majority against a minority. However, Shapiro misreads Ely when he fails to understand that Ely espouses a set of moral values regarding when to intervene and for whom. Interest group liberalism includes no such set of values.[44] The proceduralism in Ely's work is a more thought-out proceduralism, more to the pluralist than critical pluralist side of the ledger, but it is not a simple faith in pluralism; it questions pluralism in a most critical sense.

Shapiro argues that in the heyday of the Warren Court, the Court was activist and the commentators were not. In the Burger Court era the Court was activist and so were the commentators. Yet the Burger Court commentators were unhappy with the Burger Court, and the Warren Court commentators were happy with the Warren Court.[45] The reason for this puzzling reaction is that Warren Court commentators held to pluralist Dahlian values about political institutions: Process was at the center of their concern. In the Burger Court era, views about polity changed: The Burger Court internalized critical pluralist values beyond the area of race. The internalization of the dilemma of interest group liberalism by constitutional scholars of the Burger Court, not the Court's rejection of equality as a principle, is what differentiates Burger Court constitutional theory from that of the Warren Court. The dilemma is that governmental authority is viewed as illegitimate because its laws are perceived by the public as meeting the needs of private interests rather than as the result of a public process of deliberation based on public values and interests.

Individual versus Group Rights

Shapiro makes an interesting argument as to why the Warren Court could view the individual as the unit of analysis and why the Burger Court had to view groups in conflict as its unit of analysis: "Because of the precise stage of American social and political development in which the Warren Court operated, it could combine the quest for equality with individualistic values and so both build and profit from a value consensus." He notes that the potential conflict between individual freedom and equality was finessed by treating the problem as one of distribution rather than redistribution.[46] The Warren Court got away with this sleight of hand, Shapiro maintains, because the Supreme Court reflected the American consensus in the 1950s, which glossed over the fundamental value problems and differences among the groups in the New Deal coalition. During the Warren Court era institutional change was seen as less conflictual and problematic in terms of hurting others than in the Burger Court years. Shapiro writes:

> The extent to which the Warren Court was already an anachronism can be seen in the chief justice's cavalier rejection of the by then standard political analysis of the varying influence of various constituencies, groups, and locales. In response to this essentially group analysis of electoral politics, he could respond that it was people (he meant individuals) not trees who voted. He could still cling to the earlier vision of politics as revolving about the individual choices of individual voters rather than admitting that politics was a matter of groups and constituencies of unequal strength. The eventual triumph of polyarchy as the orthodoxy of modern political analysis has made this kind of one man–one vote synthesis of equality and individualism intellectually untenable. The Warren Court exited just as this change in political theory became so striking.[47]

Shapiro argues that the Burger Court viewed politics and social life differently than the Warren Court. He argues that the Burger Court did not choose to move the egalitarian tendencies of the Warren Court to the next stage: dealing with the conflicts between individual autonomy and social justice—conflicts that were suppressed in the Warren Court era. Had the Burger Court only done this, it could have developed a consistent value position compatible with recent developments in political and legal theory and the popular idea of compensating the underdog until equality is reached.[48]

Shapiro believes that no significant increase in individual rights protection occurred in the Burger Court era. He argues that the Burger Court chose the value of autonomy against equality and that the Court combines "separation of powers, federalism, privacy, and individual freedom aspects into something close to a conservative political philosophy." It sought "to reassert the presumption against government action" and emphasized the integrity of groups and families as buffers between government and individuals.

Shapiro sees *Roe v. Wade* as reflecting this shift from equality to autonomy.

204   Here the evil is government intervention into privacy choices, not unequal distribution of services. Family autonomy, not individual autonomy, is the primary value in *Moore v. City of East Cleveland* (1977) and *Village of Belle Terre v. Boraas* (1974). In *Wisconsin v. Yoder* (1972), autonomy of traditional religions is the central value. In the religion cases, the principle of no entanglement is another autonomy value. Shapiro argues that the Court also sought autonomy for local school districts in the *Milliken* case and for states in the *Usery* case. The autonomy value was not primary in search and seizure cases. The Court rejected autonomy for pornographers, war protesters, welfare recipients, those following nontraditional religions, and the business community. In equal protection cases, race and sexual equality were more important than autonomy of political units, private organizations, and individuals. The Burger Court carried autonomy values into areas, such as affirmative action and gender rights under the equal protection clauses where the conflicts between individual and group theories of equality are not easily resolved.[49]

It is significant that Shapiro must allude to changing interpretations of American politics among political theorists and constitutional scholars to make sense of doctrinal changes in the Warren and Burger Courts—particularly because he claims that justices do not listen to the interpretive community. Moreover, he misinterprets the way the Warren Court related to the relative democratic theory and group politics theories of the day. As the case analysis in Chapter 2 demonstrates, the Warren Court viewed the pluralist political system critically in a period when the consensus was that the system was operating smoothly. It was this critical view of the pluralist political system, not the Court's ability to finesse the interest differences among groups and individuals that made the Warren Court reformist.

Why has the synthesis between individualism and equality achieved by the Warren Court disintegrated? What changed after the Court corrected the problem of formal denial of access? Did the definition of what constitutes denial of access to political institutions change? By emphasizing the disintegration of the synthesis of individualism with the growth of equality values but failing to suggest the presence of a more complex view of polity both in empirical and normative views, Shapiro's argument falsely assumes that only conflict in society produces new theory and practice in constitutional development.

The problem of simplicity versus complexity was not just that the Court acted as if all rights and issues of equal protection dealt with *individual* rights versus the *group* interests in questions of redistribution of status, government benefits, and political power, as Shapiro suggests. Rather, the level of inquiry on the Warren Court stopped at the question of what is fair at the stage of formal denial of access or gross racial inequality rather than considering more subtle factors that cause denial of equal protection. The Warren Court had more basic questions of justice to consider than those that faced the Burger Court.

Also, the individual view of justice that Shapiro says the Warren Court got away with incorrectly assumes that there were not important differences about fundamental rights and polity principles on the Warren Court that informed its choices—conflicts that spoke in both individual and group terms. The failure of the group consequences of equal protection doctrine to become manifest in the interpretive community and the wider society is a result of the uncomplicated and unsystematic nature of constitutional theory in the Warren Court years.

Differences in polity and rights principles with regard to the Burger Court were caused by both an emerging critical pluralist interpretation of American politics by political theorists and political scientists that was later accepted by constitutional theorists and structural changes, such as the growing place of bureaucracy in American government. The growth of critical pluralist interpretations of American politics and the resulting loss of respect for government in the new world of interest group liberalism placed the Burger Court in a very different intellectual and political environment.

As we have seen in Chapters 4 and 5, the Burger Court could not duck the prescriptive-descriptive ambiguity that was prevalent in the Warren Court; while the Warren Court rejected pluralism, it took advantage of the nation's belief that pluralism worked. But in the Burger Court era, pluralism was no longer accepted. In this new setting the general trend was to question government, even if creating new rights was not required of the Court. The debate over polity and rights values is the key to seeing the rejection of the prescriptive-descriptive ambiguity today. While civil rights may be supportive of pluralism if viewed in formal polity terms, as Purcell suggests,[50] the Burger Court could no longer view rights in individual terms or polity in individual or simple interest group liberal terms. The Court rejected the prescriptive element of the 1950s both in polity and in rights terms and understood that polity could no longer be viewed in simple process terms and rights could no longer be viewed in simple natural rights terms.

Legal theory in the 1970s addressed the prescriptive-descriptive ambiguity by giving resonance to the problematic of polity. John Hart Ely tried to add a prescriptive element to polity while staying within a mildly critical pluralist stance. Yet, he rejected big fundamental rights questions as central to constitutional inquiry, allowing moral concerns and values to enter by the back door. Rights-oriented theorists rejected polity and process values as the sole or primary bases of constitutional choices and tried to develop theory that melds critical pluralist and natural law rights values, rejecting Ely's apologetics for polity. These legal scholars attacked implicitly, and sometime explicitly, Dahl's pluralist view of polity. They clearly did not accept the pluralist equilibrium system as good.

The Burger Court rejected the election returns view of Court role to an even greater degree than did the Warren Court. It also rejected an institutional functional or safety valve approach because such an approach does not explain what values go into judicial choices. Nor does pure biography explain justices' stances, because each person's biography is mediated by legal training, concern for stare decisis, legal scholarship, view of Court role, and notions of the autonomy of law from politics and of the collective process of Court decisionmaking.

The Burger Court does have natural rights principles that inform its choices, as we saw in the separation of church and state cases analyzed in Chapter 4. However, clear-cut rights principles, like clear-cut pluralist and critical pluralist views of polity, no longer are possible, even though constitutional scholars may want them.

Conclusion: The Supreme Court, the Interpretive Community, and Doctrinal Change

In both the Warren and Burger Courts the relationship of law and politics turns not so much on the election returns or policy wants of justices as on the response by the Supreme Court to constitutional theories and formulations of polity rights principles developed in the interpretive community.[51] The interpretive community consists of many individuals: constitutional scholars, political scientists, and journalists who comment on the Court; constitutional scholars who attempt to systematize constitutional thought and principles as guides for future judicial decisionmaking; judges, public officials, and leaders of private institutions of many kinds who must wrestle each day with the impact of Court decisions; and the many informed citizens who consider the numerous issues of justice, individual rights, and American institutions that are sparked by Supreme Court decisionmaking. Thus, when the Court acts, it does so before a complex array of audiences that wield both direct and indirect influence on the Court.

The constitutive approach contends that the Supreme Court is influenced by the interpretive community instead of election returns. Most important, it emphasizes that legal principles and theories are not used instrumentally by the Supreme Court to justify predetermined policy wants; rather the process of individual justice and Court decisionmaking constitutes the development of the law itself.

Instrumental approaches are inadequate because they do not take seriously the idea that justices make choices based on polity and rights principles that are central to their political philosophies; they understate the autonomy of the Supreme Court from electoral politics; and they do not view the Court in a dialogue with the interpretive community of legal scholars, political scientists, and political theorists who are creating standards of evaluation for Court choices and interpretations of the political system.

Court choices are a response to changing factors in the wider society. From the Warren Court era to the Burger Court era, the political system was viewed by each passing generation as more complex and potentially damaging to individual rights. However, while the Supreme Court responds to political and social events, there is no direct relationship between political events in the real world, changes in political party and dominant coalitions, and the development of constitutional law. Constitutional and political theory serve as filters, as foils, for Court decisionmaking that influence constitutional change.

Standards of evaluation of the performance of the Court and political institutions have changed as views of the American polity evolved and the desire to ensure individual rights grew. Unfortunately, perceptions of the polity and rights principles of the previous Court often obscure our understanding of subsequent eras. The vision of the Warren Court as one dominated by a concern for "equality" set a standard of evaluation for the Burger Court that reified the moral values side of Warren Court decisionmaking and underemphasized the significance of polity principles in informing the Warren Court's constitutional choices.

Each Court creates new doctrine, yet each also must react to past cases, not only in terms of formal precedent but also in terms of changes in the complexity in the way political and social reality is considered. The Burger Court, in contrast to the Warren Court, was more complex in its view of pluralist politics and more critical and more structural in its view of the political system, in part because the protection of fundamental rights and polity principles in the Constitution in the 1970s and 1980s required moving beyond considering only formal blockage of the political system. The nature of constitutional issues, as our nation becomes more heterogeneous and our government more complex, forces courts to view discrimination and the necessity of rights protection in different ways than in previous Court eras.

Also, the standards for evaluating Court doctrine change with the evolution of constitutional theory. Our visions or images of the Supreme Court are shaped by constitutional scholars and social scientists, as well as those in the wider community. I concentrate on the Court and the interpretive community, realizing that such a look, at one level, oversimplifies reality, for the Court is addressing real problems and does not just respond to commentators about the Court. The commentary may or may not fit with the actual polity and rights principles emphasized by the Court itself. However, the Court takes such views of polity, rights, and Court role into account even as it sometimes chooses to reject them.

My second major concern is to consider whether the constitutional theory in the Warren and Burger Court eras acted as a sufficient guide to Supreme Court decisionmaking, whether the dominant constitutional theories of each Court era helped the Court to confront the constitutional questions before it.

In Chapter 3, I argued that less prominent Warren Court era legal scholars failed in their role as guides to the Court because they narrowly viewed judicial craftsmanship as their standard of evaluation. More prominent constitutional scholars of the Warren Court era, such as Paul Freund, Herbert Wechsler, and Alexander Bickel, were for the most part supportive of Warren Court doctrinal innovations. They recognized that the Constitution included fundamental rights, which needed interpretation, as well as polity principles, some of which were countermajoritarian and thus counter to apologetic pluralist interpretations of the American political system. However, unlike the constitutional scholars of the 1970s and 1980s they did not develop full-blown constitutional theories that would guide Court choices.[52]

In the Burger Court era the interpretive community bifurcated over whether to accept John Hart Ely's brilliant nonoriginalist constitutional theory, which argued that the Constitution and all constitutional questions should be viewed as concerning polity principles, with the role of the Supreme Court as primarily keeping the political system from malfunctioning. Also, the constitutional theory of rights-based scholars such as Laurence Tribe and Frank Michelman[53] in the 1970s was a quest to secure an intricate meld of polity and rights principles in constitutional theory. However, in the early 1980s, Tribe eschewed the attempt to meld polity- and rights-based principles in favor of a rights-based constitutional theory that linked constitutional principles to the bodily and sociological differences (economic, gender, and others), while Michelman seeks to reinvigorate civic republican-polity principles and theory.[54]

The separation of modern constitutional theory into advocates of distinct rights and polity theories is artificial. It denudes constitutional theory of the important and legitimating vision of the Founders of the Constitution, both Federalists and Anti-Federalists, and of the Civil War amendments, that the reciprocal relationship among polity and rights principles is the best protection of individual rights, even as we may redefine what those principles mean. This separation produces a failure to fully explore the relationship between polity and rights concepts in Court decisionmaking and to consider the consequences of choosing either polity or rights concepts as a basis for constitutional choices.

Part Three
*Constitutional Theory and
Future Doctrinal Change*

Chapter Seven
The Limits of Civic Republicanism

In Chapters 3 and 6, I explored the relationship between doctrinal change in the Warren and Burger Courts and developments in constitutional theory and interpretations of American politics. I found that to understand doctrinal change the Supreme Court should be viewed as in a dialogue with the interpretive community. This dialogue may result in the Court's rejecting major assumptions about polity and rights principles enunciated by members of the interpretive community, as the Warren Court did, or accepting most of them, as the Burger Court did. I also found that although constitutional theories and interpretations of American politics in the Warren and Burger Court eras were wanting in major respects, the polity and rights assumptions enunciated in these theories and visions of polity were important to how the Supreme Court approached constitutional questions.

Of equal importance, I found that constitutional theories and interpretations of American politics were important to the standards used by justices, the interpretive community, and the wider public to evaluate the Supreme Court. Constitutional theories and instrumental interpretations of Supreme Court decisionmaking in the Warren and Burger Court eras led to serious misperceptions of these Court eras. The degree of innovation in individual rights protection by the Warren Court has been overstated; innovation and uniqueness of approach to constitutional questions in the Burger Court era has been understated.

Now I ask whether we can expect constitutional theory in the future to offer better guidance to Supreme Court decisionmaking than was found to be the case of constitutional theories in the Warren and Burger Court eras. I ask whether attempts to establish new constitutional theories based on the reestablishment of civic republican values will do a better job of guiding decisionmaking by the contemporary Rehnquist Court, and future Courts, than did the constitutional theories of these earlier eras. Will the dialogue between Court and interpretive community be more fruitful in the future in terms of the development of constitutional law than it was in the past? I focus the examination on civic republican constitutional theory because it is the most important new approach to constitutional theory since the polity-based constitutional theory of John Hart Ely and naturalistic rights-based constitutional theories of the Burger Court era.

Michael Perry, Sanford Levinson, and Mark Tushnet, the first wave of civic republican scholars who in the late 1980s went deeply into the scholarly questions and polity and rights principles at issue in establishing a civic republican constitutional theory, seek a return to a more deliberative, decentralized system of constitutional choices to combat self-interested politics.[1] These scholars center their work on whether judicial review, nonoriginalist and originalist constitutional interpretations, and civic republicanism can be justified in an age of moral skepticism and self-interested politics, and whether the Supreme Court or elected political bodies should be trusted to make constitutional choices.

Though scholars differ significantly about what constitutes civic republicanism, they generally agree that it connotes a politics not dominated by raw power and preference, concern for protecting the public good as opposed to meeting private wants, a belief that government actions must be responsive to something other than private pressure, and a desire that politics not merely reconcile but transcend the different interests in society in the search for the common good through a process of collective self-determination. Thus, civic republicanism is a communitarian concept, less suspicious of government than Tribe's naturalistic rights-based principles or Ely's polity-based constitutional theory of the Burger Court, and built on the possibility of awakening in its citizens a concern for public values.

Civic republicans respond to developments in political theory, moral philosophy, and literary interpretation that have drawn on hermeneutics, analogies to the place of sacred text in religious communities, and deconstructionist insights. Moreover, they reject both moral foundationalism and moral skepticism. Though each scholar takes a different approach, all consider the following questions: Is our faith in the Constitution and constitutional adjudication justified in an age of moral skepticism? Does the acceptance of moral skepticism preclude the success of the liberal political, philosophical project to establish neutral principles of law and government? Do modern philosophical and legalist approaches to constitutional theory provide the neutral principles demanded by liberal thought? Are there tensions between liberal and civic republican values in constitutional theory? If there are, can they be resolved by modern constitutional theory, the process of constitutional adjudication, and the wider political system? Does originalist or nonoriginalist interpretation meet the need for neutral principles in a liberal society? More generally, what are the justifications for originalist and nonoriginalist approaches to constitutional interpretation?

The central finding of this chapter is that civic republican scholars have introduced a vision of polity far less complex than is warranted by polity problematics in our Constitution and the social/economic structures in society. In doing so, they have created a situation that can undermine the necessary ten-

sion between polity and rights values in the Constitution, which has traditionally made constitutional theory a set of questions that are critical of politics, usually in the name of rights and reduction in the abuse of governmental
authority.

Thus, constitutional theory has been only partially successful in helping
us, and the Court, understand the complexity of polity, society, and rights. I
fear that constitutional theory in the 1990s will truncate into two camps, one
based on a continuation of naturalistic rights visions (such as Tribe's) and the
other based on civic republican theories grounded in interpretations of American politics that share an undue faith in the political system not unlike the assumptions about politics found in the apologetic pluralist interpretations of
the Warren Court era. Such a theory fails to provide a coherent and complex
analysis of the relationship among structures of the American political, social,
and economic systems as a basis for individual rights and polity principles in
the future.[2] I do not mean to provide here a definitive analysis of civic republican constitutional theory, for I will analyze only the first wave of such theories.

Moral Foundationalism and Liberal Political Philosophy

For Michael Perry, Mark Tushnet, and Sanford Levinson, the search for neutral moral principles and law, required by liberalism to achieve a politics that
transcends the deep, pervasive, persistent differences among us, has failed. All
three scholars reject moral foundationalism—the idea that a specific set of
moral and polity principles can constitute authority for constitutional choices.
All three accept modern hermeneutical principles in viewing the Constitution
as having no fixed meaning in the following way: as a document that is not
purely procedural or positivist, as lacking a self-referential ranking of constitutional provisions; as part of a historical narrative of society blending the past
with the present; and as part of culturally shared truth rather than self-evident, immutable, or eternal creed to be followed blindly. The instability of the
language adds to the life of the text. Thus principles are indeterminate prior to
judges' decisions, which moral foundationalists view as highly discretionary
and tied in important ways to wider political discourse. Because there is no
necessary connection between constitutional choices and good moral values,
each choice must be analyzed with regard to moral theory and outcomes.[3]

Perry's Rejection of Moral Foundationalism

Michael Perry, in *Morality, Politics, and Law*, does a masterly job in arguing
against both moral foundationalism and moral skepticism, the idea that there
cannot be moral knowledge. Therefore, the moral and constitutional theories
of John Rawls and Ronald Dworkin cannot be neutral, for no one can be neu-

tral about the basic moral differences among individuals and moral subcommunities. Perry questions moral foundationalism because to accept one moral theory violates the process of deliberative, transformative politics by which moral subcommunities mediate their deeply held values with the aspirations in the Constitution, allowing moral development to occur in society. We get moral knowledge from the religious and other moral subcommunities in society, but given the pluralistic nature of moral communities, no one moral perspective should be viewed as transcending all others. Such definitions of moral values preclude moral discourse among members of society and thus hinder the development of the deliberative, transformative politics that Perry desires. Utilitarian theory also fails as a basis for constitutional theory because we cannot assume that individual choices will lead to satisfaction or human good.

Given the range of possible moral goods, Perry argues that the state should be tolerant, not coercive. States can never make neutral choices and individuals' conscientious disobedience is to be allowed, for no absolute rules of conduct are possible, given the moral choices that officials must make in applying the law and given the centrality of moral ideas to the constitutive nature of the individual. Like Levinson, Perry contends that procedural arguments for following the law cannot work because an unjust law can ultimately be passed, even with democratic procedures. For Perry, epistemological differences between the naturalists and foundationalists are of no consequence at the level of moral discourse on particular issues. However, epistemological differences between moral skeptics and naturalists are important at that level, for moral skeptics refuse to engage in moral discourse because they view all thought as only individual self-interest. Perry argues against moral skepticism, admitting that no one neutral moral truth exists. If the person is constituted by moral conviction about how to flourish, and part of that conviction is acceptance of the need to accommodate differences among moral communities, then there might be a justification for constitutional adjudication, even though liberal thought as neutral principles is dead.[4]

First we shall consider why Perry chooses not to base his argument for nonoriginalist constitutional adjudication as a form of deliberative and transformative politics on respect for the rights and process values in the liberal American constitutional tradition. Perry believes that the search for neutral moral principles and law, required by liberalism to achieve a politics that transcends the deep, persistent differences among us, has failed. Particular constitutional theory preempts deliberation. For Perry, moral foundationalism—reliance on principles first as a basis of moral knowledge and constitutional choices—is not possible, for there are no moral principles or constitutional theories that are beyond question.[5]

Perry believes that the liberal vision of morality and politics is too mechanistic and suspicious of individuals, moral communities, and constitutional adjudication as a forum for debate about moral values. He attacks liberal theory for its failure to be neutral and impartial with respect to the basic differences that constitute moral dissensus and for its attempt to avoid dissensus rather than nurturing it. Perry rejects the possibility of finding a master principle that can resolve major political, moral disputes because such a principle denies reliance on particular moral beliefs that have withstood the test of experience of moral communities. "It not merely ignores the priority of the particular; it goes so far as to assert or imply the priority of the general—the general understood not as a memorandum of particulars, but as somehow independent of them." Perry wants to increase moral discourse, and the point of departure for moral discourse is to be the particular shared beliefs among the interlocutors.[6] Though there can be moral knowledge and knowledge of the conditions under which human beings flourish, there is no way to know the truth. All we can do is create a deliberative, transformative politics to seek the truth, which changes as we grow.

In moral foundationalism, then, acceptance of any specific moral theory or principle prior to the process of deliberative, transformative politics cuts off the possibilities of the moral-political deliberation process by definition. Just as no theory or principle can be neutral, no list of when government coercion should be permitted, and no moral foundational argument supporting originalism or nonoriginalism can be neutral. Perry writes that "liberalism-as-tolerance is an admirable ideal. Liberalism-as-neutrality is a phantom, a will o' the wisp."[7] Therefore, trust in process can be the only basis for arguing for constitutional faith.

Perry's faith in pluralist politics is evident in his argument that one form of contractualism—"Good prior to Right" contractualism—offers a promising basis for a theoretical justification of deliberative, transformative politics. This contractualism constitutes a system of rules, a modus vivendi among people with different ultimate commitments, a system of mutual advantage to which people adhere not because it expresses their deepest self-understandings, but for more prudent reasons that serve their other values. In this form of contractualism, different ideals of good are not excluded from arguments of justice. Rules build on a justice notion and are useful for moral communities.

Rawls's concept of an overlapping consensus is such a theory, for it suggests that constitutional principles might be legitimated through achieving a consensus of opposing philosophical and religious doctrines that are likely to exist and gain adherents in a more or less just constitutional, democratic society. In this consensus theory, citizens' conceptions of human good determine their acceptance of principles of justice. The rules, created to further moral thought, are open-ended and a product of deliberation, not imposed from above by institutions or scholars.[8] Overlapping consensus theory also supports the place of moral communities as actors in Perry's pluralist system.

In language reminiscent of the relativism in social, legal, and political theory of the 1950s, Perry argues that the diversity within American culture explains our ability to settle sensitive and complex moral issues through a stable process of deliberation. The various philosophical, religious, and moral doctrines that constitute Rawls's "overlapping consensus . . . suppl[y] the only available justificatory basis for principles of justice. Happily, in America the overlapping consensus happens to support and nourish, rather than subvert, democratic politics."[9]

Perry's arguments against legislative coercion similarly reflect his faith in moral community interactions for a moral growth. We should not frustrate the basic capacity of social and political conditions for self-critical evaluation of moral questions, Perry argues. A tradition of tolerance of individuals and moral communities and a presumption against coercion will protect general moral interests. Fellowship and friendship, which are necessary to nourish community, are aided by reduced government coercion, for compassionate government creates less resentment. Thus Perry contends that law should seek to establish and maintain only the minimum level of actualized morality that is necessary for a healthy social order.

Perry's discussion of the utility of coercive legislation also reveals that faith in pluralistic society lies at the core of his argument for a deliberative, transformative politics. He favors coercive legislation primarily to enhance the well-being of those who cannot protect themselves and to protect basic social institutions such as the courts, which he views as "institutions whose effective functioning is itself crucial to the satisfaction of fundamental interests."[10] He argues that our highly pluralistic society protects us from the dominance of a single moral community or an idiosyncratic viewpoint and encourages self-critical deliberations on morals and matters of principle.

Because in politics and law moral discourse often ends before agreement or consensus is reached, the presence of a constitutional community is another important condition that promotes self-critical rationality and moral-political deliberation. This community he defines as "comprising those persons and groups in the morally pluralistic society who share a commitment to the aspirations signified by the constitutional text." Constitutional adjudication sorts out our criteria for the settlement of differences. Perry praises moral communities for agreeing to settle conflicts using constitutional adjudication and the constitutional community and reports that the constitutional community is seen by most as "a splendid achievement" and as "deeply satisfying, even ennobling," thus allowing all of us to realize our true lives and well-being.[11]

Deliberation, not merely politics, is central for Perry if individuals are to flourish and the dialectic among citizens, moral communities, and the moral interests of our society as a whole is to be fostered. Manipulative politics presupposes the authority of existing preferences and is simply an instrument a citizen or group uses to get what it wants. In deliberative, transformative politics, in contrast, "questions of what ought we to want and, therefore, who ought we to be are open, not closed." "Deliberation as to what our real interests are, as opposed to preferences, is what is sought. Deliberative politics is essential to self-knowledge . . . We come to know our authentic selves, in the sense of what sort of persons we should be, and thus what we should want—not monologically, but dialogically."[12]

Though Perry is concerned about individuals finding out who they are and how they can flourish, his unit of analysis is not primarily the individual. He views the individual as "inevitably a partisan in the subjective circumstances—as inevitably a member of some particular moral (perhaps religious) community within a larger pluralistic society." The diverse moral communities of American society rather than the multiplicity of individual moral perspectives, is the central focus of his analysis. "Basic moral beliefs . . . are less the property of human beings *qua* particular individuals than of human beings *qua* members of particular communities." The interdependence of the particular and the general, neither of which has priority, is the basis of rights protection.[13] The dialectic process between individuals, moral communities, and constitutional adjudication energizes a deliberative, transformative politics.

Thus, an aspect of flourishing is locating mutually acceptable bases of accommodation with those with whom we find ourselves in fundamental moral disagreement. Individuals have an interest in both personal capacities and social and political conditions that are prerequisites to flourishing, including capacities and conditions we may not presently understand as prerequisites.[14] Perry seeks to discuss the social and political conditions that facilitate the exercise and growth of self-critical rationality. Thus, Perry's book is about both process and rights values, but rights are only prerequisites for the process, not ends in themselves.

Tushnet: Liberal Constitutional Theory as Incapable of Constraining Politics

Mark Tushnet believes that neither constitutional adjudication as a process nor liberal constitutional thought allows the openness by which the interests of all in society can be mediated. Tushnet's central argument is that conflicts between liberal and republican principles in modern constitutional theory undermine the restraining force of liberal constitutional theory. Also, theorists have failed to refit liberal theory to modern economic, social, and political realities. For example, Ely's representation-reinforcing constitutional theory fails as a neutral liberal theory constraining jurists because of the following attributes: its view of democracy is too constricted; it does not view basic individual rights, which are directly related to considerations of political malfunction, as part of the process-based constitutional theory; judges can pick and choose what constitutes a malfunction in the political system; the view of political process does not deal with issues of citizen inertia; it is a purely formal theory that seeks static pluralist polity principles and fails to take into account complex differences in power; it is not more neutral than non-process-based theory because choices must be made about political reality, which cannot be neutral; it is hard to determine, under this theory, whether outcomes are the result of community choice or discrimination; the complexity of coalition formation undercuts Ely's attempt to see this theory as principled; and when informal constraints are built into representation-reinforcing theory, the theory loses any supposed neutrality. In this light, the choice of pluralism rather than socialism as a central value of political process becomes a question of the ideology of the judge, a choice that cannot be neutral.[15]

The jurisprudence of political philosophers such as Dworkin and Rawls also fails to be neutral because doing justice, that is, producing morally acceptable decisions, consists of making ad hoc choices that connect general truths and particular results. Systematic moral theory cannot explain why a specific instance of real behavior should be classified as cruel or bad. But constitutional theories that reject a search for constraints by courts do not work either, because they do not have dialogue at their core. Unelaborated majoritarianism is anticonstitutional, noncomparative, and inconsistent. For Tushnet, it is the conflict between liberal principles of rules above politics and the Constitution as a constraint on citizens on the one hand and republican values of trusting political discourse on the other that makes modern constitutional theory and practice so consequentialist, manipulative, and contextual.

Constitutional theories that take from different liberal theories and allow a balancing of interests, such as those of Gerald Gunther and Douglas Laycock, are also inadequate, for they give judges the power to exercise unreviewable discretion. Because judges are largely white, male, heterosexual, aged, and wealthy, they should not be trusted by those unlike themselves. The sociological defense of balancing falsely assumes that judges agree on fundamental values and that no differences exist between outsiders and insiders, an assumption that violates the liberal tradition's premise that we are all outsiders at some time when the state seeks to exploit us. Constitutional theory is indefensible when it allows judges to uphold the worst and invalidate the best programs that the legislature devises.

Structuralist constitutional theory, such as Tribe's structural due process notion, which says courts should look only at the decision process and not at the substance of the choice, also fails as a constraining theory of neutral principles. A simple abstract rule cannot control the multiple forms of social reality, nor can it act as a description of what courts do. Abstractions can be manipulated at many levels. An imaginary democratic process seeking accountability overstates the degree to which accountability happens. Judges are unconstrained as to what the appropriate agency is for making a decision. This would suggest that Theodore Lowi's juridical democracy will not work either.

Efforts to impose procedural requirements on bureaucracies based on entitlements in positive law and natural law principles, such as in "new property" rights of welfare recipients, also are arbitrary choices by judges. They show too much deference to a view of rationalized bureaucracy as good, while the reality is that street-level bureaucracies operate without regard to professional norms. The constraining nature of the "new property" rights is minimal. A more political notion of bureaucratic power, with the objective of citizen participation rights, might help.

Tushnet thus demonstrates distrust of any form of constitutive theory or moral theory to constrain politics. He seeks a constitutional theory that is more explicitly political and naturalistic, one that centers on economic, social, and political power. Tushnet's view of the fairness of American politics is in some respects more critical than that of Dahl, Truman, and pluralist scholars of the 1950s and of post-1965 critical pluralist scholars, such as McConnell and Lowi. However, his theory does reveal trust of some polity principles, such as the decentralization of political power and the authority to make constitutional choices, that are counter to many of the concerns of critical pluralist interpreters of American politics and legal theory.

Levinson: The Impossibility of Neutral Principles
For Sanford Levinson, neutral principles are not possible, for truth is culturally shared conventions. Instead of truth we have social and moral visions that tell us what is best. Therefore, neither one social theory nor faith in legal craft can replace the application of good moral values to choices by judges and lawyers. Given these premises, Perry's heroic objective of creating a deliberative, transformative politics based on the development of aspirations through the development of due process of law, equal protection, and First Amendment principles fails; most jurists and lawyers do not view the Constitution as a heroic set of aspirations.[16]

The Constitution and Originalism
Perry, Tushnet, and Levinson agree that originalism cannot be sustained as a neutral constitutional theory. They also agree that there are built-in assumptions and choices about polity and rights values that are not discussed by many originalist scholars. Their different approaches to originalism and nonoriginalism offer further insight into their view of polity and rights principles, civic republicanism as a transformative constitutional theory, and the role of the Supreme Court as a forum for change.

For Perry, unlike Tushnet and Levinson, originalism is a viable approach, different from nonoriginalism in that there are fewer choices about rights to be

220 made by jurists taking an originalist position. Choices about whether to accept originalism or nonoriginalism of judicial role for Perry are always speculative, contingent, provisional, and, therefore, revisable. However, he finds the choice of originalism more questionable in the area of human rights than in the areas of federalism or separation of powers, where more trust can be placed in the political system to produce morally just and popularly supported constitutional choices.[17] For Tushnet, the social and economic differences between the Founding Period and today make originalism an unacceptable basis for constitutional adjudication.[18] For Levinson, the fact that the Framers violated written process values in the Articles of Confederation when they sought ratification of the Constitution, drawing on higher values of polity, the good of society, and rights protection, is an important argument for not following originalist proceduralism and narrow textualism.[19]

Perry: Originalism and Aspirational Rights
Michael Perry argues that originalism preempts deliberative, transformative politics. He argues that the Supreme Court's lack of electoral accountability is not a cogent argument for originalist review, because electoral accountability does not have an axiomatic or canonical status in the American political culture. All conceptions of judicial roles embody the tension between electoral accountability and individual rights. Therefore, to decide whether nonoriginalist or originalist moral values and views of democracy are better at achieving justice, one must compare the success of courts as rights protectors with that of politically accountable institutions.[20]

Perry argues that originalism is not more neutral or authoritative than nonoriginalism, because judges can manipulate levels of generality of polity and rights values in our Constitution, which is filled with multiple meanings.[21] Sophisticated originalism admits that judges cannot retrieve actual original understanding; a judge simply constructs an imagined original understanding that is sensitive to available historical materials. But a more important problem with originalism is that it does not nurture the process of constitutional adjudication and deliberative, transformative politics that Perry envisions.

Perry argues that in the American community, the Constitution may be viewed as a sacred text, which recalls fundamental aspirations, disturbs, and is prophetic and comprehensive but indeterminate. It looks ahead, not behind, and is in a dialogic relationship with past and present. The community must critically interpret and deliberate about rights aspirations and polity principles in the Constitution, not merely assume that the words of the Constitution speak for themselves. It contains aspirations of social justice, brotherhood, and human dignity. Moral communities in our pluralist society share these aspirations for living a life in common. For the nonoriginalist, these aspirations are indeterminate and acquire meaning as judges decide particular cases and the wider society debates constitutional questions.[22] The Constitution's comprehensiveness, rightness, and semantic autonomy allow it to grow in meaning. The indeterminacy of its aspirations are the means through which the diverse American political-constitutional community compromises differences, deliberates, and transforms society.

Perry argues that there are three types of originalism: (1) democratic originalism which emphasizes the proper role of courts in a democratic society; (2) structural originalism, which is based on separation of powers doctrine; and (3) constitutional originalism, whose basic premise is that only the originalist judicial role is legitimate because it is the only one authorized by the Founders. Perry sees constitutional originalism as "question begging" because it presupposes an affirmative argument for originalism; democratic and structural originalism alone are legitimate bases of constitutional choices.[23]

In a fascinating discussion of why neither originalism nor nonoriginalism necessarily produces more authoritative constitutional choices he launches a devastating attack on originalism that holds the clue to the judicial role he favors. He argues that because the American constitutional tradition is never settled, the debate must focus on who should have the authority to define judicial role: present majorities, past majorities, present popular majorities, past popular majorities, or the Framers. Because constitutional aspirations include moral content about human dignity and rights and a set of problematics about political process, constitutional decisionmaking turns on how justices view and apply these process and rights aspirations.

Perry argues that in the American political tradition there are two major values in tension with each other: popular sovereignty or political will and fundamental rights, such as human dignity and individual liberty as limits on politics. Any conception of judicial role represents a way of embodying the tension between popular sovereignty and fundamental law as a limit on politics. No plausible conception of judicial role, including originalism, eradicates this tension, because judicial review of any sort compromises popular sovereignty. Which value should prevail is an impossible question to answer. Neither originalist nor nonoriginalist responses to the tension between these values is more authoritative by definition. An individual's acceptance of originalist or nonoriginalist arguments about judicial role is always *"contingent, speculative,* and *provisional* and therefore *revisable."* It is contingent because it is rooted in one's sense of justice. It is speculative because it is based on counterfactual views of tradition, history, and institutional behavior. Thus, Perry argues against scholars who denounce nonoriginalism because its wider-ranging constitutional decisionmaking undermines the ideal of electorally accountable policymaking. He no longer assumes that electorally accountable policymaking has such axiomatic status in American political and legal culture that any judicial role that compromises it is illegitimate.[24]

Given Perry's rejection of moral foundationalism of either polity or rights values, the principles in the text of the Constitution cannot be a basis for his choosing nonoriginalist jurisprudence. Like instrumental interpretations of Supreme Court decisionmaking and doctrinal change, Perry must argue for nonoriginalism in terms of a comparison of the *outcomes* derived from the two interpretations: whether originalism allows deliberative, transformative politics and therefore is respectful of the self-constitutive person and of the plurality of moral communities. He argues that originalism keeps better faith with our tradition's aspiration for electorally accountable government. However, it does not keep faith with the other major component of our constitutional tradition: justice and fundamental rights.[25]

Tushnet: Originalism, the Founders, and Economic Change

Tushnet believes that since the Framers did not understand the extent to which private property would transform society and its governing coalition, originalists and those who wish to reintroduce civic republicanism must consider whether republican deliberative politics is possible in the present age of bureaucracy, unequal wealth, and decline of civic virtue. To make originalism and its hope for neutral principles work, Tushnet points out, requires an understanding of social institutions. If sociological understanding is to have normative force rather than just descriptive validity we must move into the republican tradition in which individual conceptions are seen as derived from and subsidiary to an underlying societal perspective. The problem in viewing the judge and consitutional principles as constraints on politics is to find and construct the requisite shared conceptions at a time when people have different views on the nature of polity and rights. Yet Tushnet does not accomplish this in his own views about decentralization of judicial review.[26]

Likewise, Tushnet argues that Perry's community values approach, which emphasizes adjudication based on deliberation among plural communities and agreement on aspirations and civic virtue, will not work because economic growth has destroyed communities where each person knows and accepts his or her place. Because scholars assume we know what the community is and that a community now exists, when in fact judicial choices are made by judges who are not representative of the communities, community value approaches are pernicious.[27] Tushnet argues that the inequality of power between judges and citizens makes true deliberation impossible. Republicanism can work, he maintains, only if there is a mix of economy and politics that is closer to that of the Founding Period.

This rejection of Perry's communitarianism is ironic given Tushnet's faith in consensual groups with similar moral values as units of constitutional deliberation and his rejection of the idea of a limiting role for the Supreme Court over community values. Perry accepts this role, even though his call for judicial self-restraint seriously undermines this concept.[28]

Levinson: The Founders' Pragmatism and Originalist Interpretation

Levinson's pointed opposition to originalism is built on whether the Founders followed the law when they established the Constitution.[29] He argues that the Framers revealed their lack of support for originalism by changing the ratification process required by the Articles of Confederation in the approval of the Constitution. The Founders were willing to take risks on behalf of the values in the Constitution and did not follow written law. Political sagacity is a product of a complex dialectic between leader and populace, not adherence to written text or preexisting intentions.

Levinson argues that all we have are shared general visions of individualism and community. The moral content of law must be interpreted, and to idolize the Constitution or deify the Founders discourages revelations by future generations of what the text means. Only by bringing in moral choices, not necessarily using values that have been constitutionalized by the Framers or the interpretive community, will justices enable the Constitution to serve its role in the American civil religion.

Constitutional Faith, the Supreme Court, and Civic Republicanism

Reduced Supreme Court Role under Perry's Civic Republicanism

A major question for Perry is, "How can I . . . hope to engage in productive moral discourse with persons outside my moral community, given our moral differences and the absence of transcendent principles of justice?" The answer lies in constitutional adjudication, which, at its idealized best, is both a species of moral discourse and a model of deliberative, transformative politics.[30] He claims that constitutional adjudication can make available to us a deliberative, transformative politics, as distinct from a politics that is merely manipulative and self-serving even in, and perhaps because of, our morally pluralistic society.

Nonoriginalism is essential if the community is to succeed in its struggle to remain faithful to constitutional aspirations. The Court's insularity from politics allows it the latitude to engage in the pursuit of political and moral knowledge in a relatively disinterested manner. Procedures, such as the hierarchical appeals process and use of en banc proceedings for important constitutional issues, offer additional reasons not to fear judges' selections of aspirations to apply. Only beliefs widely shared by judges can be determinative. Because judges are strongly identified with the living constitutional tradition, they are

224   likely to be concerned that the institutional authority be allocated so the tradition stands a better chance of achieving justice.[31]

Compared to Tushnet and Levinson, Perry has the deepest faith in constitutional adjudication and courts as forums for transformative, deliberative politics about the aspirations of individuals and moral subcommunities in our pluralistic nation. The indeterminate quality of these aspirations, which include freedom of speech, equal protection of the law, and due process of law, makes it possible for them to be shared by groups with different viewpoints. The sharing of these indeterminate norms in the American political-constitutional community helps foster a societal consensus in which different moral choices are respected. Perry views the Court's record on individual rights in the modern period (after *Brown v. Board of Education* [1954]) as admirable. He concludes that the Court's decisions are in line with public opinion, and, if not, appointment processes bring it in line.[32] Here we see Perry's view of normal pluralist politics. Courts must be the central actors; normal politics cannot decide aspirations because it is manipulative and self-serving and citizens and elected officials tend to act on mere preference. Getting others to do what you want, including bargaining, is not deliberative and transformative, because others become instruments of personal satisfaction, producers and consumers rather than citizens whose self-constitution involves deep moral considerations of what it means to flourish as human beings. If politics is the instrument of individual or group maximization of preference, we also need a deliberative, transformative politics that will consider issues not merely in terms of preference, but also in terms of what it means to flourish.

This judicial role is crucial in our society because of the value legislators place on incumbency. The sheer volume and complexity of issues considered by legislatures and skepticism about the possibility of productive moral discourse inhibits careful deliberation. Therefore, in order for deliberative, transformative politics to happen, courts are to encourage citizens and elected officials to talk seriously about the possibility of deliberative politics. Courts do this by exemplifying deliberative, transformative politics in their discursive practice and by engaging other branches and agencies of the government in deliberative discourse. Thus, the nonoriginalist judicial role is a way to institutionalize the ideal of self-critical rationality. Perry also makes a strong argument for judicial self-restraint as a component of nonoriginalism. He calls on judges to be cautious in engaging in nonoriginalism, especially if other public officials have truly deliberated a policy issue and concluded that it is not ruled out by the relevant constitutional aspiration, if it is a complex issue, or if the consequences of resolving the issue are difficult to foresee.[33]

Judges should overturn governmental policy only when they think it violates aspirations in the Constitution, not when they simply disagree with the policy choice. The Supreme Court is not the supreme actor in American politics, but only one among many seeking to persuade the others within the on-going political process. The Court should not preempt discourse between the judiciary and the political community, not because it is undemocratic for the Court to act, but because the Court might learn from the discourse. Most importantly, Perry differentiates between constitutional interpretation and amendment as two quite different types of dialogue between past and present. Constitutional interpretation is understood as mediation of past and present and is to have a dialogic and critical stance toward the present in regard to past and future. Constitutional adjudication is to be confined to changes or innovations that are "molecular" in scope. Amendment is the way to decisively reject an aspect of tradition and establish a new aspiration in its stead.[34]

Thus, even though Perry argues that a judge's view of popular will and fundamental rights are in tension and that the value of following popular sovereignty and electorally accountable policymaking does not have axiomatic or canonical status in the American political-legal culture, his support of judicial self-restraint when aspirations in the Constitution are not clear gives more deference to electorally accountable policymaking as a value than he allows to originalists and thus becomes a strong counter to fundamental rights.

There are major inconsistencies between Perry's admonition that the judicial role is problematic in both contemporary constitutional adjudication and the more deliberative politics that he seeks and his claim that his vision of the Court role harbors no latent moral foundationalism. Perry views the judicial role as always problematic, as "deliberately counter-majoritarian. . . . By hypothesis, the judge thinks [majoritarian beliefs] incorrect."[35]

If concepts of judicial role are flexible, and no specific view can be considered as authoritative, how is it possible for any one view of judicial role to be considered a given? Perry seems to be arguing that the important reasons why constitutional adjudication and civic republicanism will maintain the critical element necessary for self-critical rationality are the constraining force of the Supreme Court, an inherent quality of judging in its dialogue with legislatures, moral communities, and citizens. Therefore, a major question to be considered is whether judicial review retains its countermajoritarian basis, its inherent critical element as rights protector, under the reforms that Perry advocates.

Tushnet's Distrust of the Supreme Court and Constitutional Adjudication

Of the three scholars Tushnet has the least faith in constitutional adjudication because of the failure of constitutional principles and courts as arbiters of the Constitution. He views constitutional theory and constitutional adjudication as efforts to fill the gap created by the decline of the republican tradition in the Framers' approach to institutional design, to overcome the success of liberal

226 values in American thought, and to specify how judicial review can exist without becoming judicial tyranny.

Constitutional theory fails because its objective of dialogue between the republican and liberal traditions is not possible; the liberal tradition has become too powerful and the republican tradition is too weak. Scholars and jurists who seek republicanism seem to forget that reasonably equal wealth is a prerequisite for its success. Also, for Tushnet neither the liberal tradition of autonomy, intolerance, hate, and anger, nor the republican tradition of connectedness, love, and toleration accommodates all parts of human existence. The presence of both traditions and the inability to reconcile them without creating a weak, undisciplined theory allows a wide judicial discretion that undermines the autonomy and legitimacy of courts in the liberal tradition.[36]

Another reason we cannot place our faith in constitutional adjudication is that we cannot place our faith in judges. Tushnet argues that the success of private property has produced judges who are wealthy, white, and unrepresentative of the nation and thus not autonomous enough from the governing coalition to act as a limit on politics. Constitutional theory, principles, and practice are so open-ended as far as values are concerned that all we have is discretion by judges. The community has no shared conceptions of judge and community.

The Framers hoped to encourage judges to be independent of politics and not merely self-interested through life tenure and national selection. However, because of the way the Founders' commitment to private property has played out over the years—with judges being committed to private property over all other values—judges cannot consult community moral values, according to Tushnet, because they come from a narrow stratum of society. Their values are not common values, but their own values. The interpretive community is shattered. It is both too closed to wider community values and too open to complex principles to give discipline to the force of law. Thus, judges are not representative enough to generate a normatively compelling understanding of plain meaning, history, and consensus of shared understandings or values.[37] Therefore, we cannot explain why either legislators or judges should have a final say on constitutional questions. This undermines judicial review as a process of constraint.

Levinson: Constitutional Adjudication
Levinson offers a subtle analysis of the implications of the hermeneutical approach for the possibility of liberal theory and civic republicanism. His argument about the open-ended nature of the words and phrases in the Constitution and of constitutional values and the resulting contingent nature of constitutional choices is the basis for a devastating attack on originalism as more principled than nonoriginalism, leaving him with only a guarded faith in

constitutionalism, which he argues for because there is no basis other than the Constitution for uniting the nation. However, unlike Perry and Tushnet, Levinson sees identities as individual, not part of moral subcommunities or social and economic classes. Therefore, he answers the question whether he should have faith in the Constitution in the affirmative.[38]

Like Perry, Levinson argues that one should not place blind faith in the Constitution, in positive law, or in courts as final arbiters of the Constitution when moral values external to the Constitution have been violated. Faith in the proceduralism that dominates modern legal decisions and practice is even less justified. Levinson has less faith than Perry that the process of adjudication will result in morally good choices and thus make up for specific bad choices. Thus, Levinson allows a wider role for moral choice than do scholars and practitioners who have faith in procedures and proceduralism. Levinson rejects courts as final arbiters of the Constitution.

Is Deliberative, Transformative Politics Possible under Civic Republicanism?
Perry's Judicial Restraint, States, and the Interpretive Community

Perry rejects the possibility of neutral and constraining law or constitutional theory because of the contingent nature of moral choices, moral skepticism, and the rejection of moral foundationalism. Therefore his view of political and legal process against an assumption of rights values in the Constitution must bear the full weight of his argument for deliberative, transformative politics and the renewal of civic republicanism. Perry's call for judicial self-restraint and dialogue between the Supreme Court, legislatures, and moral communities demonstrates his trust that pluralist politics can produce deliberation and political transformation that would allow individuals, moral communities, and society as a whole to flourish. Yet we must question whether his trust in the pluralist political system is warranted and whether the reforms in judicial review that he seeks—judicial self-restraint and a decentralization of constitutional decisionmaking through dialogue between the Supreme Court, state legislatures, and moral communities—will foster the politics he desires.

Perry's call for Supreme Court self-restraint, with its resulting increase in legislatures' and moral communities' influence over constitutional development, is mistaken because it undermines his goal of deliberative and transformative politics. His view of polity and Court role and how they are linked to rights values also undermines this goal. Furthermore, his faith in pluralist politics and his rejection of moral foundationalism strikes at his assumption that constitutional theory and courts should, by definition, be critical of politics, thus undermining the possibility of political transformation. Finally, his rejection of moral foundationalism and faith in pluralist politics would lead to relativism in political and legal theory similar to that which predominated legal and democratic theory in the 1950s.

Perry's approach to *Roe v. Wade* (1973) is emblematic of the conflict between achieving the kind of politics he desires through Supreme Court self-restraint and the decentralizing of judicial decisionmaking. Perry argues that states should be the primary forum for deciding constitutional issues when constitutional aspirations are unclear, such as on the question of abortion rights. There is disagreement on what liberty interests are at issue since people disagree on when life begins, so the Supreme Court should defer to state legislatures as to how robust the right to abortions should be. The Supreme Court should grant the right to abortion choice only in cases of incest, rape, danger to maternal health, and gross deformity of the fetus—situations in which liberty interests are relatively easy to determine.[39]

On what grounds can this decentralization of constitutional decisionmaking be justified? It cannot be that we want to nurture morally self-constituted women who will make difficult, morally informed choices and thus flourish, for under Perry's theory, state legislatures and dominant moral communities in particular states will make the choices and thus proscribe individual self-constitution. Perry must feel that state legislatures are better at deciding questions of fundamental rights than either the Supreme Court or the individual.

That assumption, which appears to underpin his constitutional theory, is deeply bothersome for several reasons. First, the assumption that decentralizing the process of judicial review when constitutional aspirations are not clear sidesteps a central question in constitutional and democratic theory: Should political institutions be trusted to protect rights? The problem is especially troubling when the level of government to be trusted is the states. According to Perry, states are to make such choices no matter what right is involved if constitutional aspirations are unclear, and especially if they are controversial. By practicing judicial self-restraint, the Court ends up supporting the moral community that is most powerful in a particular state. Thus it is not more respectful of the morally self-constituted individual to allow states to decide the issue of abortion choice but of those whose organizational resources and numbers can win in legislative politics. Thus, for Perry, the moral community, not the individual, is the central operative unit. Ironically, moral communities' values are usually better protected by higher levels of government or by the Supreme Court than by state and local political institutions, as Grant McConnell has argued.[40] Although Perry's objective is to reduce self-interested, nondeliberative politics, the "improvements" he advocates in the role of the Supreme Court would have the opposite effect.

Perry's call for judicial self-restraint and dialogue also contradicts the forceful argument he makes about the differences between deliberation and politics and why electorally accountable political institutions are not good at deliberation. Why do Perry's views about polity apply only when constitutional aspirations are unclear? If anything, the admonitions against trusting politics to decide complex moral questions are even more valid when constitutional aspirations and moral issues are unclear or in a formative stage, especially if transformation, not only deliberation, is an objective.

At issue is what Perry calls the central question in constitutional theory: Which value is most important—popular will as expressed through electorally accountable decisionmaking or fundamental rights? As he argues in his discussion of originalism, in selecting any constitutional theory a choice must be made between popular sovereignty and fundamental rights. For Perry, popular sovereignty seems to have won out. He does not define the differences between a clear and unclear constitutional aspiration—differences that might justify a radically different role for the Supreme Court. Nor does he provide guidelines as to what to do when specific constitutional aspirations and the process value of deference to politics come into conflict.

Like the instrumental approaches of Dahl, Shapiro, Lewis, and White, Perry's approach lacks a systematic analysis of polity that explores the question of which levels and branches of government can be expected to protect rights and moral deliberation on matters of principle and under what circumstances. Such analysis would test whether Perry's faith in decentralized constitutional decisionmaking is warranted and offer specifics on how constitutional aspirations such as First Amendment expression, due process of law, or equal protection of law would fare if constitutional decisionmaking were decentralized. But such study is possible only when one does not assume faith in pluralist, decentralized politics but starts with premises traditional to critical democratic theory—asking whether pluralist politics have protected rights and fostered deliberation and transformation in the past. It is the analysis and questioning of the polity and rights visions within constitutional theory and practice, and the introduction of new visions of polity based on that questioning, that will lead to renewal of civic republicanism.

Many studies have considered the relationship between political structures, pluralist politics, legal change, and rights protection. Scholars such as Grant McConnell, Theodore Lowi, Martin Shapiro, and Michael McCann argue that structural forms have an effect on individual rights, the quality of deliberation about principles and influence of private interests, and the possibilities of transformation of moral, political, and legal values that cannot be explained by merely reporting on the values and interests of specific participants in legal and policy processes.[41] McConnell and Lowi have shown that pluralist, small-constituency politics undermines rights protection and deliberation on moral values and makes it less likely that issues will be seen as matters of principle. It favors the social and economic elite and discourages moral definitions of problems.

These scholars have demonstrated that there is an inverse relationship between nation, state, and local moral communities and rights protection and fairness in public policy. Paul Peterson and Theodore Lowi show that when decisions are left to states and localities there is a greater chance of race and class discrimination than if the national government allocates goods and values.[42] They view the Court as a major protector of rights and political process values in the Constitution and argue for a heightened Court role because pluralist politics, particularly the politics of small constituencies, denies important constitutional protections and equal access to political process.

Perry's response to *Roe v. Wade* is not the only indicator of the need for more formal analysis of the relationship between level and branch of government and rights protection. Perry and most nonoriginalists accept Jesse Choper's view that federalism and separation of powers issues should be left to the national government to decide so courts can concentrate on human rights questions.[43] If states localities, and national institutions such as Congress are likely to deny rights because of pluralist politics, logrolling, and small-constituency power, then the Supreme Court must look at federalism and separation of powers issues in terms of whether rights are being denied and whether institutions can be trusted to protect rights in the future. Justice Powell's argument in *INS v. Chadha* (1983) is a good example: On rights questions, such as whether an immigrant alien can get a fair hearing from a subcommittee in Congress, the Court should be especially careful to ascertain whether separation of powers principles are being adhered to.[44] A theory of the relationship of courts to the political process would help us understand the consequences of leaving constitutional choices to different institutions.

By contrast, the way Perry views the question of whether government should coerce individuals suggests that he eschews a complex, critical pluralist view of polity and Court role. He makes the argument against legislative coercion in terms of the individual versus government, but his analysis is not expressed in terms of interest groups or secondary institutions versus individual rights.[45] To use the individual as the unit of analysis tips the normative scales against government. Perry does not discuss the role of interest groups, economic institutions, and social stratification or the question of whether government or courts should be trusted to protect the self-constituted individual. The lack of a structural explanation of power in the American polity undermines faith in judicial self-restraint and dialogue as a central part of the process of constitutional adjudication. Will legislatures or courts be better at limiting private interest group power? The presumption against government coercion and in favor of government inaction will allow conventional values to flourish. Perry also assumes that economic inequality is not a structural barrier to moral communities' deliberations.

Finally, calling for conditions to support individual self-critical capacity does not necessarily mean that the political system overall will have the self-critical potential that Perry seeks.[46] Perry assumes that moral communities, as the central unit of his vision for a renewal of civic republicanism, will perform in the moral interests of their members and for the overall good of society. That assumption needs careful study. Even David Truman, the father of modern group politics, had more questions than Perry about whether pluralist politics will allow political change or result in a stasis in the political system because of class, race, or social stratification.[47]

Both Perry and Tushnet use Dahl to justify their different statements about whether we should have faith in judicial review and constitutional adjudication.[48] While they both accept Dahl's formulation that Supreme Court decisions are in line with public opinion, each uses it differently. Tushnet uses it to show that courts are part of the governing coalition and power structure and that constitutional law is therefore not a significant counterbalance to social, economic, and political inequality. Perry uses Dahl to justify a pluralist group analysis, with the moral community's politics viewed like Madisonian interest group politics. Tushnet uses Dahl's formulation to argue for defining the boundaries of decisionmaking so the political system can be more deliberative and egalitarian in its decisions about rights. If both scholars use a similar polity argument to justify their theories they must be viewing the polity in nonspecific, nonanalytic terms.

As with instrumental interpretations of Supreme Court decisionmaking and doctrinal change, if polity values are a given, then they cannot constitute a problematic in constitutional theory. However, it is ironic that Perry views process rules as foundational because, as a nonoriginalist, he tells us that process norms are not neutral or constraining because of their rejection of moral foundationalism. If neither process nor rights values can be neutral, then there must be a discussion about them in relationship to moral, substantive choices about human flourishing. Perry's discussion of process values in interest terms and rights values in aspirational terms undermines his constitutional theory.

While Perry praises the overall system of constitutional adjudication, he must view the most accomplished practitioners of liberal theory as violating both the objective of neutral law and the idea of allowing individual self-constitutive political and legal actors to make their choices. His faith in the marketplace of politics when value conflict exists understates the role of the interpretive community in the development of constitutional principles respective of rights. A too relational view of constitutional principles with the unit of analysis at the individual or moral community level overstates the individual nature of choices and the role of general politics in making those choices. This orderly debate and growth may be more contingent on the interpretive community pushing and pulling than on the openly contingent quality of choice.

232   At one level, viewing the interpretive community as justification for choices violates the self-constituted person. Yet there are severe drawbacks, in terms of the complexity and legitimacy of constitutional adjudication, to viewing the primary unit of analysis and choice as either individual actors or representatives of moral communities.

The lack of clarity about the relative places of the individual, the moral community, and the overall process of constitutional adjudication is also evident in Perry's discussion of government coercion. The argument against legislative coercion is viewed in terms of individual versus government, not individual versus groups or individual versus private institutions. Perry's arguments against legislative coercion are that citizens can be hurt by legislators' human fallibility, self-critical rationality, and conventional thought and lifestyles. Coercion also undermines fellowship and community. While these concerns are real, they are at a very general level of analysis.

Perry suggests that our society expects some government coercion. Coercion may be accepted to protect fundamental interests that enhance one's level of well-being, to help weak individuals who cannot help themselves, and to protect the ability of courts and social institutions to perform their societal roles. Perry's concerns about government coercion of the individual must be considered in the light of whether individuals would be aided by government coercion that could counterbalance the power of corporations, private groups, and other powerful entities in our political and economic system. His failure to present a structural explanation of power undercuts our ability to accept the argument against government coercion as a principle.

Perry needs to offer a more subtle theory of polity and the relationship of political institutions. Will the legislature be better than the courts at limiting powerful private interests against the weak? Will the needs of individuals be better protected by courts or political institutions? Will inaction by the legislature or coercion of some groups add or detract from the self-constituted individual performing in our society as Perry desires? The presumption for inaction by Courts under judicial self-restraint may unleash private forces in liberal, self-interested society. Thus, arguments about government coercion must be rooted not only in moral principles of human good but also in views about power in society.

Although Perry validly argues that the use of coercive power is rooted in a system of normative commitments, he neglects to say that it is also rooted in views about power in society as it relates to human good. He admits that his view is not neutral regarding competing conceptions of human good, but he, like all constitutional theorists and jurists, cannot be neutral regarding competing notions of polity either. Competing values of polity, which are not merely sets of moral commitments of human good but are based on clearly defined linkages between social, racial, and economic inequalities and political system malfunctions today, could be the basis for newly defined polity principles. Constitutional scholars in the 1970s and the 1980s have been more concerned with differences of moral good than they have with polity principles.

In order to define legislative fallibility, self-critical rationality, self-interest, compassion, and conscience, we need to have a theory of polity and to ask under what conditions legislative coercion will be justified.[49] The issue is different from deciding to trust legislatures or courts, for legislatures must deal with economic and social power and structures. Here we must decide whether we trust regulation or market forces.

Thus, the question of institutional coercion involves views of both moral aspirations and polity expectations. Perry validly argues that the legislature cannot coerce if it is outside the limits of tolerance of the politically dominant. Yet if we ask what criteria for coercion ought to be tolerated, where do we find the answer? Such criteria are rooted in moral visions, but how do we select which vision to use? Perry's rejection of moral foundationalism and faith in a system of constitutional adjudication in which judicial self-restraint is a central value forces him to trust the political market forces present at any given time. Also, while Perry uses general process arguments in support of coercion, there is no systematic discussion of examples of the conditions under which institutions should be trusted. Rather than making trust a problematic, Perry offers a trust of pluralist politics that undermines the concerns for the self-constituted individual as well as discrete and insular minorities.

Tushnet's Decentralized Constitutionalism and Economic Redistribution

For Tushnet, it is necessary to construct constitutional theory that makes accurate assumptions about social and economic realities. Such a theory would result in a civic republicanism that recognizes the unrepresentativeness of judges. It would also mean that originalists would have to build their theory on differences between the contemporary social and economic systems and those that existed at the Founding. It would then be necessary to take a critical pluralist approach that reinterprets constitutional principles in light of inequalities within the polity.

Such a theoretical approach is difficult to accomplish because it means rejecting liberal values regarding the autonomy of law and courts while creating a new definition of political institutions in society. It requires judges to look not just at procedure but also at outcomes as indicators of process and to rethink process values, thus reducing the constraining power of accepted principles. It also requires a great reduction in respect for present judges as representative and principled and a reconsideration of how we pick judges. If Tushnet takes the sociological view that all is political, then it may be impossible ever to sustain the notion that law and constitutional adjudication are based on a set of principles that are different from a reading of "what is." This is especially so if "what is" is defined by groups of citizens who are viewed in subjective interest terms as having specific preferences.

Tushnet offers a critical pluralist interpretation of the American political system in which he finds enough social and economic inequality to undermine civic republicanism. He argues that civic republicanism is not possible without substantial equality of wealth and that it can be promoted by decentralization and broadly distributed property holdings. Decentralization requires that the forums for decisionmaking on important constitutional questions be changed from states. More decentralization under the present system would end with political decentralization but economic power too tightly controlled, which would make things even worse.

Tushnet offers an alternative synthesis to present constitutional theory and doctrine that he calls an "implicit inchoate vision of a society as commonwealth, inhabited by citizens who seek to promote the common good rather than individual interests."[50] To put such a vision into effect will permit a review of a definition of citizenship consistent with the idea of commonwealth.

Tushnet is enamored of a discussion of federalism and changes in decisionmaking units in this new commonwealth.[51] He will need to consider how to revitalize those aspects of the federal system that are, in part, the embodiment of the republican tradition. Revitalizing federalism as designed by the Framers will require a rethinking of the concept of property as the foundation of citizens' independence and will probably lead us to conclude that revitalized federalism demands the expansion of "new property" entitlements, development of the idea of government as the employer of last resort, creation of tenure in private employment, and the like.

A revitalized federalism must insist on, and indeed expand on, the Framers' commitment to decentralization with different boundaries. We could take our model from what Tushnet calls intentional communities that operate on the principle of consensus in decisionmaking rather than the majority rule that characterizes the present system. That will require mutual forbearance and a proposal to convince others to go along. This revitalization will eventually be more possible than it is today because people in small intentional communities will have a greater interest in keeping the community together.

Drawing on the Framers, Tushnet argues that community members having face-to-face interactions in a small community learn to tolerate the foibles of others and appreciate their contributions, making consensus more likely than in a large group or in bureaucratic, technical government. Face-to-face interaction may reduce the importance of means arguments and bottom-line outcomes viewed in self-interested terms. Tushnet has enough faith in present constitutionalism to argue that the republican ideal is not external to our Constitution and its traditions. However, unlike present liberalism, the constitutional thought of the commonwealth builds on our real experience with friends, families, churches, and neighborhoods. It will build on the warmth, love, and connectedness of our complex real experiences, not on moments of fear, anger, and alienation.

Tushnet would use any methods to attain this, either political action or court power, depending on which is most conductive to success. The commonwealth will probably not have a constitution or liberal constitutional theory. A republican constitutional theory will come from a dialogue and be part of the dialogue of change. It will not be directed at judges and will not be a set of legal rules that determine anything, but rather will contain rules of thumb that experience has proven useful. So it appears less a top-down theory of constraints than a bottom-up set of expectations to help intentional communities function. This decisionmaking process is good in itself and should not be evaluated in terms of individual rights or foundational notions of justice. Thus, there is no foundationalism for Tushnet. "Neither the liberal tradition nor the republican one can accommodate the aspects of experience that the other takes as central. Critique is all there is."

While Tushnet emphasizes a critique of present constitutional theory and practice, it is not clear that either his proposed remedy or his ideas on how to study these phenomena will work, because small-constituency politics may produce even more inequality than we have today. McConnell, Lowi, and many other scholars of small group politics have emphasized that informal power relationships in small groups produce antiminority policy and political forms and policies in opposition to the needs of those outside the group. The formality and bureaucratization in our liberal society that Tushnet now loathes actually protect the weak and those without access.

It is difficult to set up intentional groups because there must be choices about whether they are based on religious, class, work, or ethnic characteristics or any other foundation. Also, the problem of mobility among the groups must be considered. Once set up, these communities will need foundational principles to ensure that they do not violate the rights of those within them or harm those outside.

Tushnet hopes that through greater economic equality the effects of self-interest politics will decline. However, producing economic near-equality alone does not settle the problem. It is possible to have conflict on many different dimensions, and it is simply wrong to argue that if all have somewhat equal economic resources and property there will be an equalization of power in a decentralized republican commonwealth. Also, Tushnet's view that we cannot have both liberal and republican approaches to the place of the individual in the political process is questionable. Liberalism has helped limit the worst aspects of small-constituency inequalities of power. It asks questions about whether elected officials abuse their power, whether minorities are getting their due, and what policy must be made at the center to protect the rights of individuals. These questions will remain even in a decentralized commonwealth. The liberal Framers were correct when they told us to fear small-constituency politics. The problem arises in liberal, modern constitutionalism, with changes at the top of government that make the Madisonian solution unworkable because it is not subtle enough to deal with real power and inequality.

Tushnet demonstrates the inability of modern constitutional thought to deal with real power. However, Tushnet's approach retards the development of a full and complex picture of what courts actually do when they apply polity and rights principles. It would be better for Tushnet to argue first why constitutional choices based on contemporary polity and rights principles do not fit reality or to argue for a revised theory of polity and rights that fits with "what is."

Like Perry and Levinson, Tushnet has no faith in our present constitutional polity and rights principles. Nor does he offer refinements of those principles to meet the problems he has identified. Tushnet's critique of modern constitutional theory is masterly as an analysis of the conflicting polity and rights principles in our present liberal and civic republican polity. However, he does not offer the kind of systematic discussion of the relationship of polity and rights values that would suggest how present constitutional aspirations, individual rights, and polity principles can overcome the problems he has identified in contemporary constitutional theory and practice.

Levinson: Training Lawyers in Moral Visions

Given the prominence of liberal, self-interested values and unwarranted respect for proceduralism today, the question for Levinson becomes how to reproduce some aspects of civic republicanism. For lawyers the way to do this is to buck proceduralism and introduce moral concerns into their work, thereby offering the deliberation that does not adequately take place in the wider political system.[52] Levinson argues that if we can train lawyers to play the role the citizen would play in civic republicanism, then society will benefit. Citizens, especially lawyers, have an obligation to evaluate judicial choices on moral grounds other than those stated by judges or those implicit in positive law. They may even be obligated to break the law because the law, even if established by a constitutionally correct process, can produce morally suspect and unjust outcomes.

Levinson believes that we need to talk about the kind of people we select as lawyers and the education we want to give them. Levinson hopes that the properly trained lawyer will consider moral values in making choices. Part of the reason for intervention into the legal system at the level of legal training is that constitutional choices are so specific that we can only know what the

Constitution is as judges and lawyers interact and make choices. Thus, the interpretive community cannot be trusted to protect us to the degree that Perry believes it will. Levinson fears that the interpretive community, especially lawyers, will be bogged down in proceduralism rather than discussing moral issues in the law. Given the postmodernist sense of the contingency of culture and what binds us as a political community along with the failure of achieving a "one best way" moral theory, the best we can hope for are lawyers trained to understand the moral dimension of law and law schools that are diverse in their moral values and approaches to law.

In contrast to Perry, Levinson does not view lawyers and constitutional adjudication as surrogate forums for dealing with dissensus among moral subcommunities. He has less concern about the overall polity. Although morally knowledgeable citizens would be good, Levinson focuses on lawyers' participation in the process of constitutional adjudication rather than citizen participation in a structured, self-interested liberal politics.

Levinson questions whether proceduralism and mere craft are equal to goodness. Proceduralism becomes a blanket term for procedure used in relationship to a client's narrow interests, or perhaps faith in overall procedure and ability of all to participate. He uses the term "proceduralism" too generally, though, seeming to encompass all that is not open-ended moral values. We need to know what procedures will allow or impede dialogue. Nor does Levinson consider the possibility that proceduralism might aid moral choices by providing a forum for wider values.

Levinson offers no sustained analysis of the place of law in society, only of lawyers who are too narrow. This insight undercuts our faith in legal training as a response to liberal self-interested politics. Saying that all choice is contingent and relational does not offer a vision of a polity in which the citizen-lawyer can exist. We need to know what principles about the nature of polity should be followed. If the problem is modern interest group liberalism and self-interested politics, then merely saying all is contingent does not remove us from the bind of self-interest. Will we expect lawyers to be citizens with moral values merely because law schools teach them values? Doesn't law school come fairly late in one's training for the inculcation of moral values? Perhaps we need liberal arts undergraduate or secondary school education in moral values and polity. Levinson, unfortunately, fails to offer a structural analysis of why morally trained lawyers can produce legitimate constitutional choices for society.

Rejecting Moral Foundationalism and the Possibility of Transformative Politics

Perry, Tushnet, and Levinson seek a remedy for the decline of faith in constitutionalism, not by seeking concepts of rights or legal principles, but through better process. For Perry, constitutional adjudication with a strong dose of judicial self-restraint, the dialogic relationships between Court and Congress and between Court and state legislature, with the influence of moral subcommunities on individuals and on the deliberative, transformative politics, limits raw self-interest. The constitutional adjudication process represents moral subcommunities' values as well as overarching aspirational values, such as due process, equal protection, and First Amendment rights. Perry seeks more judicial restraint by the Supreme Court under a nonoriginalist regime.

Tushnet seeks decentralization of the political system and reduction in top-down judicial principles, for they can be manipulated by courts from above. The sociological and economic basis of the court system, the conflict between dominant liberal and subordinate civic republican values in American thought, and the failure of that thought to incorporate the greater economic inequality of today undermine the possibility of a transformative, deliberative politics that is fair to all. Only a major restructuring of politics through decentralization of political and perhaps economic power, and a new bottom-up "Constitution" of guidelines, not law, will produce a deliberative, transformative politics fair to all.

Levinson seeks changes in the training of lawyers within the constitutional adjudication process. He hopes that training lawyers in moral values and their application will lead to more just decisions than trusting the constitutional adjudication and political processes.

The problem with each of these reforms, *which are based on foundational polity principles*, is twofold. First, the views of polity presented by these scholars do not adequately consider the ineffectiveness of small constituencies in protecting individual rights and the interests of minorities and poorly represented groups. Thus, there is little possibility that the reforms these scholars seek can produce the civic republicanism they desire. Second, there is little left of the Constitution when they get through with their analyses. All accept the legal realist notion that the law is what judges say it is, yet they differ as to whether judges should be trusted as final arbiters of the law. They seek a wider role for lawyers, citizens, and legislatures in a civic republicanism that suggests a distrust of judges. All seek a justification for constitutional adjudication in the age of legal realism. They differ as to how much non-self-interested behavior is possible now and through reform. They lack faith in foundational polity and rights principles, yet hold foundational assumptions trusting constitutional adjudication to smooth the rough edges of individual, subgroup morality. Blind faith in process without faith in foundational ideas denudes constitutional theory of a standard of evaluation other than faith in process.

Rejecting the Possibility of a Neutral, Constraining Constitutional Theory

Perry and scholars of the hermeneutical school argue that since neutral principles are not possible in this age of moral skepticism and legal realism, the justification for judicial review and the renewal of civic republicanism must rely on process arguments and procedural reforms. His argument about the failure of the liberal political-philosophical project is overstated. While legal realists offer a valid argument that law as neutral principles cannot be "found" through the process of analogy, constitutional adjudication may be defined as a bounded search for principles, even if completely neutral law and decision-making is not possible. The notion of seeking neutrality, knowing that the objective is not fully attainable, better fits the reality of constitutional decisionmaking and places constitutional theory and principles in their proper central place within it.

Though one coherent, neutral constitutional theory may be impossible to achieve, a number of middle-range theories under liberalism are possible. These limit the range of constitutional choices and are more constraining than Perry (as well as Levinson, and particularly Tushet) is willing to admit. He makes a cogent argument that originalists limit the range of polity values too narrowly and refuse to see fundamental rights and moral values in the Constitution. However, Perry himself makes constitutional choices too contingent on "what is" in the political process through his trust of dialogue and state legislatures. Constitutional theory must be perceived as founded on a set of rights and process theories that offers discipline to judges or it becomes too process-oriented to be considered legitimate. It is the acceptance of a range of foundational principles that offers discipline and legitimacy to lawmaking.

To say that there cannot be neutral principles does not mean that there cannot be better, or bounded, principles. If the argument was not expressed in terms of a general attack on the liberal political-philosophical project, but rather was made at the level of which polity and rights principles are best, for what reasons, and what their relationship should be, then we could get into a useful debate relating theory to practice. This emptiness of much liberal and civic republican constitutional theory—its failure to provide guides for courts making constitutional choices—leaves courts too free to apply will.

Perry argues that truth is contingent on acceptance of webs of belief; there is no perspective that transcends all webs of belief.[53] Yet there seem to be some truths, such as equal protection of the law, the right of free speech, the right of privacy, the principle that no man should be a judge in his own case, a fear of raw majoritarianism, and separation of powers that are contained in and inspired by the Constitution and are more than mere aspirations. These truths have a moral force, in part because of their acceptance over time. To say that these ideas are so open-ended, so contingent, and so open to debate that they mean only what courts say they mean undermines their moral authority and that of the Constitution.

Perry's and Tushnet's requirement of completely neutral principles in order to demonstrate that the liberal philosophical project is not spent, and their move to a naturalist approach, must be analyzed in relation to a view of open-ended rights values in the Constitution and a rejection of moral foundationalism. However, to move to a naturalist perspective leaves constitutional adjudication too open-ended for the possibility of a disciplined constitutional law process. Viewing the Constitution as *the* principles or as a set of moral values, all of which may be seen as equally valid, to be tested through debate, presents an ideal-typical and distorted view of constitutional thought as having two extremes, neither of which is consistent with what happens in the process of constitutional adjudication.

Perry has not shown that the search for neutral principles is misguided. Nor has he demonstrated that this objective undermines the idea of the self-constituted citizen or the participation of moral communities in constitutional adjudication. He has demonstrated, quite convincingly, only that completely neutral principles are not possible and that originalism is not more neutral than nonoriginalism.

Tushnet has done a better job than Perry or Levinson of showing the discontinuities in liberal thought that make civic republicanism and deliberation along clear foundational principles less possible. He seems to accept the view that liberal constitutionalism relies on ideas and that ideas limit human action. For Tushnet the most important limiting idea is that economic equality violates individual rights notions that are central to liberalism and capitalism. However, if constitutional theory is viewed as a middle-range theory of polity and rights values that constitute a set of questions in a bounded or disciplined conflict, then our faith in liberalism would be on a higher ground than when we argue that we should trust nonoriginalist constitutionalism because the process is open and good.

For Levinson, moral theories are important. However, since no one moral theory can be viewed as necessarily better than another, all we can hope for is that law schools have diverse, at times unconventional, faculties that allow discussion of the nature of moral choices behind the law rather than the possibility of a neutral, constraining moral theory behind the law. Moreover, Levinson's failure to delve deeply into the contemporary polity and rights principles used by lawyers to make constitutional arguments may be the result of his views about the open-ended, unbounded nature of constitutional principles. While polity and rights values may not constitute the truth, they have a bounded quality and a legitimacy that are separate from the individual choices of participants in each case. Also, while at first glance Levinson, unlike Tushnet, appears positively disposed toward the transformative potential of constitutional theory because it can include almost anything, he offers only a statement of hope. He overstates the degree to which the interpretive community is split on what constitutes important polity and rights principles and understates the degree to which arguments about specific polity and rights principles are viewed as knowledge by law students and the degree to which they discipline choices by jurists. Looked at more closely, Levinson's view of constitutional theory as unbounded undermines the possibility of its transformative potential, leaving him to rest the possibility of a transformative society on populating the adjudication process with lawyers who are moral and just.

Also, while Levinson says constitutional choices should be based on written and unwritten text and tradition, he offers no rules about the nature of those choices. Without such rules and examples it is hard to be even guardedly optimistic about his theory. We still need to know which polity and rights values are best, and what to do when process and rights values are in conflict. A constitutional theory must analyze degrees of contingency and ranges of polity and rights choices. It must specify, for example, whether there are more contingent choices in First Amendment cases than in substantive due process cases. Such a theory will provide more discipline and structure in both constitutional theory and practice than these scholars suggest. It is the analysis and questioning of the polity and rights visions within constitutional theory and practice, the introduction of new visions of polity to replace interest group liberalism, and the introduction of new concepts of individual rights that will further the development of constitutional theory and legitimate the legal process.

The work of these three scholars differs in whether they rest their argument on polity, rights, or polity and rights arguments, and their relationship. It is the assumptions in a work that determine its quality. While each of these scholars attempts to justify noninterpretive constitutional adjudication in an age of hermeneutical analysis, justification at the general level of contingency undercuts the legitimacy of constitutional adjudication and fosters instrumental rather than constitutive interpretation of constitutional decisionmaking and doctrinal change.

To understand why the new civic republicanism undermines the transformative, deliberative politics that Perry, Tushnet, and Levinson seek, we need to explore the relationship of rights principles and polity/institutional forms that each favors. All three argue against mere proceduralism and for moral choices in the law. However, their attacks on proceduralism, while justified, become not arguments for articulating the relationship of procedure and rights or the possibilities of procedure. They become instead arguments for open-ended rights and for new institutional forms. Taken too far, these arguments undercut the legitimacy of constitutional theory, constitutional adjudication, and the courts because it is proceduralism, not by itself but in combination with rights concerns, that gives constitutional theory and practice its principled nature. Perry, Tushnet, and Levinson are correct in their opposition to proceduralism, because a constitutional theory based on narrow proceduralism becomes out of touch with the economic and social realities of our day. As these scholars eloquently argue, we need development of rights and polity values that fit with changes in our society.

Instrumentalism and Self-Constituted Persons

Perry views moral and rights values as central to the self-constituted individual. He does not see polity values, rules about process, and interest in process rules as aspirational in the same way as rights. Polity values are not in a tension with moral values but are instrumental in making moral choices. It is not clear whether Perry sees substantive choices behind constitutional adjudication process accommodations. He seems to view them merely in terms of their utility in the process of moral deliberation of the individual and moral community. He does not treat the self-constitutive person as if process and rights values together constitute the thought processes employed in deciding constitutional issues. Perry must then be postulating a distinction between process and rights norms in citizens. What is the justification for this distinction? Why are people utilitarian when they think about processes by which moral communities decide norms but highly open to consideration of moral values and rights?

Thus, process values are less aspirational and open-ended to the individual than are rights. If many moral communities agree on process values, they do so either because they are foundational or because they are utilitarian.[54] However, Perry argues that preference utilitarianism and experience utilitarianism do not allow deliberation and transformative politics. Why does the same not apply to polity values? Deliberative, transformative politics requires open-ended polity values, for changes in polity are central to allowing moral values consideration. Moral choices cannot be merely self-constitutive because they are meaningful only as part of economic and political frameworks. One cannot talk about aspirations in a vacuum.

Why isn't the self-constituted person asked to balance polity and rights values as a way to decide norms? Are process norms viewed as questions of prudence rather than assumptions that are critical of political institutions as rights protectors? If there is substance behind process, why is it any less critical to self-constitution than is the substance behind rights? The problem may lie in viewing popular sovereignty as a matter of polity principles rather than questioning the capability of elected bodies to protect rights.

Perry sees moral ideas as constitutive and polity ideas as part of the system of justification for Court power. This approach reduces the constitutional problematic in an effort to support rights and no longer calls for a deliberative, transformative politics about polity. However, permitting individual self-critical capacity and condition does not necessarily mean that the overall political system has a self-critical potential. Individuals may be able to flourish while groups of individuals may still be denied political power. Perry respects moral pluralism and diversity and assumes that pluralism will flourish. The unit of analysis in the first two parts of Perry's *Morality, Politics, and Law* is the individual seeking to flourish. If the individual is to flourish, belief in moral pluralism must be respected. Although Perry makes a strong statement about the self-constitutive nature of the individual, he does not discuss the group constitutive nature. He makes a strong argument against society's accepting a single moral theory because it denies the self-constitutive statement of the individual and ignores the marketplace of many moral theories that could inform aspirations. Yet the book's argument is not very good at moving from the individual, to group, to courts and political institutions.

The Constitution contains both rights and process elements and more orderliness than Perry suggests. Interpretive activity creates tradition, as Perry argues, by the dialogic relationship between text and community, past and present. While the liberal political-philosophical project is not neutral, it is part of a tradition of polity and rights values that is orderly and bounded. If the Constitution has prophetic, disturbing qualities, as Perry argues, they should be viewed as the product of polity as well as rights.

Polity Principles in Perry's View of Judging

We can also see the relationship of polity and rights values in Perry's view of judging. Perry argues that the first step in constitutional decisionmaking is choosing the norms to be applied in a particular case; the second step is to apply those norms to the case at hand.[55] Conceiving the first step as including the consideration of polity and rights values fosters a deliberative and transformative politics. Then aspirational values in the Constitution can be considered in relation to political structural realities.

For Perry, there is no critical polity moment to consider the structural conditions of First Amendment, due process, and equal protection rights for groups and individuals in the pluralist political system. This lack is evident in his discussion of *Roe v. Wade*.[56] He does not discuss what to do when rights and process values conflict. Nor does he offer guidelines about what to do when a constitutional right and the process value of deference to politics come in conflict when no clear aspirations are present.

Judges are concerned with which polity is best at rights protection. Should they trust political institutions? Justices have constitutional theories of process. We saw this in *Roe v. Wade*, when Justice Blackmun decided to create a right to abortion choice during the first two trimesters of pregnancy and let state legislatures decide what to do about the third trimester. The problem of the *Roe* decision is similar to the problem with Perry's argument. Blackmun's opinion changes from a rights basis of choice in the first two trimesters to a process basis in the third, which undermined the moral strength of the right to abortion choice. Rather then viewing the choice as inherently constitutive of the person, the Court put the decision in highly relational terms, allowing the moral interest group structure of the states to determine whether to protect fetal life. This choice undercuts the constitutive nature of the initial right acknowledged for the first two trimesters.

Pure human good is not the only issue in constitutional decisionmaking. Nonneutral but disciplined choices about polity must also be considered along with alternative process possibilities. Justices have views about whether states, courts, groups, individuals, or any particular institution should be trusted to protect moral rights values such as human dignity. Landmark cases such as *San Antonio Independent School Board v. Rodriguez* (1973), *Plyler v. Doe* (1982), *Milliken v. Bradley* (1974), *Warth v. Seldin* (1975), and Powell's concurrence in *INS v. Chadha* (1983) provide evidence that judges' views about polity and judicial review, not only moral aspirations, are central to their opinions (see Chapter 5). Whether the Court acts to create an individual right is decided in relationship not just to justices' views of fundamental rights, but also to premises they hold about the likelihood that political institutions will protect that right. For example, such concerns are built into the tension between free exercise of religion and the need for institutional separation of church and state in the religion cases. The choice by the Court in religion cases is whether to concentrate on the process or free exercise grounds for decisionmaking. The Court must consider ranges of expectations about institutional performances in favoring or being neutral to religion along with free exercise concerns (see Chapter 4).

Whether a constitutional theory incorporates critical pluralist or pluralist polity values about what can be expected of branches and levels of government in protecting fundamental rights and whether those polity values are part of the critical component of Court choice are central to whether a deliberative and transformative politics regarding human rights is possible. Thus, there is far less agreement on process or polity values among moral communities than is suggested by Perry, though there is enough agreement at times to allow a resolution of a set of issues. However, to allow the presence of controversy to determine the decisionmaking arena denies that there is a more important problem: the choices must confront fundamental rights in the Constitution even when aspirations are not clear and when the majority, or a vocal minority, opposes support of the unclear aspirations.

Perry validly argues that discussion and evaluation of breaking the law cannot be neutral as to principles and that there is no obligation to obey the law in all instances simply because it has been democratically passed.[57] There is no absolute, unconditional rule of conduct in all situations. However, the argument that general moral values alone should determine one's response to law also has serious drawbacks. If one could devise a theory of structural inequality—a way to judge whether democracy has taken in all views or not—then the notion of whether disobedience is just is more supportable. Perry seems to admit this when his trust of dialogue undercuts the right of an individual to have an abortion. When courts have made decisions about justification for civil disobedience, they have asked about polity, not just rights, and have balanced the two.

Thus, the example of the Holocaust, which both Perry and Levinson use in arguing against process-based constitutional adjudication and for nonoriginalist thought with a central focus on moral values, does not justify a constitutional theory that centers only on moral choices. This example rightly suggests that process by itself should not be the basis for the legality of government acts, because a Holocaust could be legitimated with constitutionally correct procedures and still be morally wrong; but it does not explain why only moral values should be the focus of constitutional theory.

Polity Justifications Alone Deny a Prescriptive Base to Theory and Practice

Blind faith in process without foundationalism—the idea that some ideas are better than others because they are contained in the Constitution or in our constitutional tradition—will not produce a transformative constitutional theory. Process justifications of constitutional adjudication and civic republicanism are not forceful enough to sustain the individual rights that Perry seeks. For aspirations to have staying power, polity and rights values must be more than weak guides to individual or group decisionmaking; they must have authority. Legal philosophy can play this role in a way polity arguments cannot. For aspirations to stay alive there must be reference points to determine what a right is. Ideas must become accepted as good moral choices, which Perry admits is possible. For this to happen there must be acceptance above the individual level that certain rights and polity principles are clearly more trustworthy than others.

Choosing among the theories of Ronald Dworkin, John Rawls, Bruce Ackerman, Richard Posner, Robert Nozick, and Charles Fried does make a difference as to whether moral values and polity principles in the Constitution are sustained. The fact that no theory is neutral does not mean that each is equally consistent with human rights and polity values in the Constitution. At issue is whether critical theory is possible in an age of moral skepticism. There is a point between the mechanistic foundationalism that dominated legal thought prior to the legal realist movement and moral skepticism, or moral choice as merely individual or group constitutive, that must be defined. Failure to do so will strip constitutional theory and practice of its critical element. Justification based only on a general notion of aspirations in the Constitution and trust or constitutional adjudication as process undercuts the moral force of rights values and, more importantly, makes unwarranted assumptions about the segmentation of rights and process values in the Constitution.

A constitutional theory that relies on a view of process rather than specific rights principles must be regarded skeptically, for it raises the question whether there are any standards of evaluation other than faith in the process. One way to approach this problem is to ask whether there is a concept of public interest in Perry's work outside the choices made by the system of dialogue and judicial self-restraint. Because the constitutional adjudication process is to be trusted, the views of participants in the process become the benchmark of justice, except when there is a clear violation of rights. Though no one person, group, or theory can be good, the system can do justice. Such a setting undercuts any concept of the public interest.

Process, and the views of participants in the process, form the benchmark of justice for Perry, except when there is a clear violation of rights. This is a deeply legal realist approach—not in the sense that moral arguments are not to be prized, but in the sense that moral ideas, and their validity, are merely products of constitutional adjudication. They receive validity from an assumption that the process is open enough to produce many moral viewpoints and reach moral-constitutional choices that are to be prized. The benchmark cannot be one concept of moral-legal good, but that morally thinking persons, in interaction with a moral community, in interaction with other moral communities, in contact with moral aspirations in the Constitution, in contact with judges who play a role only to support dialogue in legislatures and among moral communities, will produce just decisions.

If standards of evaluation are to perform a critical function in society, which Perry says is the function of constitutional law and adjudication, then all standards of evaluation and constitutional theories cannot be viewed as equal before the constitutional adjudication process. The fact that Perry argues that when aspirations in the Constitution are clear, courts should take on political institutions, irrespective of a concern for judicial self-restraint and dialogue, does not sufficiently ameliorate the problem of the lack of standards of evaluation other than faith in the process itself. Perry is arguing for faith that judges will stop clearly agreed-upon violations of constitutional values.

However, since there is no discussion of where the line is drawn between aspirations that are clearly defined and those that are not, Perry's level of trust in pluralist politics is even more pronounced. But such a line cannot be drawn, because all principles are the product of an individual judge's choices. His faith thus rests on collective decisionmaking, on the Supreme Court and appeals courts, and on the hierarchical structure of all constitutional courts in the nation.

To make the argument that we should trust process hold, we would need benchmarks for determining what constitutional principles are necessary to support self-constituted persons and the process that Perry favors. However, he cannot provide these benchmarks because he rejects moral foundationalism. If one agrees that there is enough discipline in liberal thought and legal theory to say that some views of political process and individual rights are not accepted, then Perry would be able to sustain the legitimacy of the constitutional process he now accepts on faith. To do this he would have to argue that liberal legal-political thought does not fail merely because it is not neutral in the ultimate foundational sense of a coherent theory or because it is not always originalist. He would have to look at standards of evaluation in rights and process terms and decide what is morally within the framework of values, just as judges do.

At issue is whether constitutional adjudication will continue to be seen by the American public as legitimate. It will retain its legitimacy if courts engage in judicial self-restraint when moral subcommunities conflict and no clear aspirational values are threatened. However, to gain additional legitimacy for constitutional adjudication one needs to argue that foundational polity and rights principles do exist and that justices make choices of principles from a range established by the interpretive community. For the judge is different from the citizen who seeks to flourish, and the citizen has to know that there is a difference. Perry says that though there can be moral knowledge, there are no first principles. Yet he seems to admit there are first principles in the Constitution when he lists the aspirations. However, we cannot know the status of these first principles other than to say "Participate in the dialogue."

A Return to 1950s Relativist Democratic and Social Theory

There are significant similarities between the view of polity in Perry's constitutional vision and those of Robert Dahl and David Truman, the most articulate proponents of interpretations of American politics based on the relativist democratic theory of the 1950s. The overlapping consensus notion as a justification for the marketplace of ideas also has ramifications for the legitimacy of strong polity and rights-based foundational constitutional principles and the importance of viewing these principles as in conflict in the process of constitutional adjudication. If everything is decided by debate and the force of ideas about protecting rights, whoever has the power to dictate that debate wins, as long as no clear-cut rights violations exist. A critical pluralist mistrust of raw politics is lost in such an argument.[58]

The justification for constitutional adjudication as deliberative, transformative politics is not based on a contract theory, Founding principles, or moral theory. It is based on a faith that the process of individual development in and commitment to moral communities—religious, intellectual, and philosophical—will produce a transformative, deliberative politics. The aspirations in the

248   Constitution and the process values and forms are the means for that value development within moral communities to be less insular and more transformative than it would be without constitutional adjudication as dialogue or judicial self-restraint.

Perry does not support contract theory as a basis for constitutional adjudication, because democratic politics cannot be given a justificatory priority over religion and philosophy as basic normative commitments of the many moral communities that constitute the pluralistic American political community. A tolerant democratic politics finds its support when the religion and philosophy of the many moral communities together constitute a pluralistic American political community. The overlapping consensus among moral communities has priority over democratic politics per se or a statement of the requirements of democracy and individual rights. Justification of constitutional principles does not arise from social contract, which gives power to democratic politics, but from the areas of overlapping consensus among moral communities about what constitutes human good. That consensus becomes the basic component of justice. It can be the only justification when aspirations are not clear in the Constitution or the words of the Constitution do not clearly reject certain behavior. So Perry's faith is in dialogue and judicial self-restraint because of a faith in cultural diversity, a faith in moral communities accepting the basic aspirations of the Constitution, a faith that the marketplace will consist of more than one group, and a faith that because we have religiously, intellectually, philosophically diverse moral groups, there will be moderation. "Happily in America the overlapping consensus happens to support and nourish, rather than subvert, democratic politics," Perry concludes.[59]

A similar role for interest group elites is found in David Truman's theory (see Chapter 3). However, instead of interest group actors and the wider community taking the lead to protect all of us, Truman's theory suggests that constitutional scholars, lawyers, and jurists will take the lead in the internal constitutional adjudication process. It is not clear what support of aspirations means to Truman, since judges' range of interpretation is wide. Therefore, the notion of rules of the game is more of a critical debate for Perry than for Truman. Perry asks that the wider political system participate. In the end, he trusts the process to sort out what aspirations are and how they are applied. Like Truman, Perry sees no standard of evaluation outside the process, but he does not see political and group leaders' beliefs in the rules of the game of politics or fear that groups will form by leaders' failure to follow such rules.

Rawls's view of overlapping consensus seems similar to Truman's view of potential interest groups. For both men it is a hope, not a reality. The problem with trust of pluralism and process is that there is no problematic built into it that can test whether or not it is so. Perry is so concerned about opposing originalism that he overlooks the larger picture—the need for an inherently critical constitutional jurisprudence. Inherent in the Founders' vision and in our Constitution is the notion that politics does not measure up and should be questioned. Yet reliance on courts and politics as safeguards against violation strips the theory of its critical potential at a time when the Court has pulled back from supporting the rights values it had enunciated.[60]

Chapter Eight
Conclusion: The Rehnquist Court and the Future

After a summation of the major arguments presented in this book I offer additional evidence for a constitutive interpretation of Supreme Court decisionmaking and doctrinal change by examining landmark cases decided in the 1991–1992 term of the Rehnquist Court, which now consists of a substantial majority of Reagan and Bush appointees. These recent decisions provide clear evidence of the dialogue on doctrinal change between the Supreme Court and the interpretive community. The likelihood that new appointees will tend to be more noninterpretive and nonoriginalist in judicial philosophy than the Reagan-Bush appointees is additional evidence to support the major premise of the book—that we must employ constitutive rather than instrumental or originalist interpretations of Supreme Court decisionmaking and doctrinal change to understand the development of constitutional law in the future.

The Warren Court

In arguing for a constitutive rather than instrumental interpretations of the Supreme Court, I have focused on the validity of constitutive compared to instrumental interpretations by looking at either the internal Court decisionmaking process or at external factors, with a particular regard for the relationship between the interpretive community, constitutional theory, and doctrinal change. Careful analysis of the Warren and Burger Courts, and a briefer look at the Rehnquist Court era that follows, shows that they rejected the key assumptions of the instrumental election returns approach: that the interpretive community is epiphenomenal to doctrinal change and that the Court follows elections returns. They also rejected the instrumental policymaking approach as to the role of the interpretive community and doctrinal change: that the Supreme Court follows the New Deal policy wants of the interpretive community. The evidence does not support these instrumental interpretations because they do not view both the internal Court decisionmaking process and the relationship of the Court to the interpretive community as constitutive processes.

The Warren Court could not accept the United States as a normative phenomenon. Chief Justice Warren and a majority of the Warren Court represented the view that the polity was not operating as the pluralist equilibrium model had said it would, and they took this position before its formalization by scholars in the late 1950s and early 1960s. One way to explain the Warren Court and doctrinal change is to look at them in light of the interpretations of the political and legal systems that dominated the interpretive community and society of the day. The Warren Court kept alive a debate over the place of relativist democratic views of polity and intuitive justice notions that were set in place by developments in social and legal theory, which helps explain the Court's decisionmaking.

In the Warren Court era there was a mismatch between the view of polity on the Court and that of the nation and most of the interpretive community. To explain this mismatch between what the Warren Court was doing and scholars' perceptions of the Court, we need to understand that how the Court views the political system—its polity principles—has much to do with the nature of doctrinal change. Polity principles mediate the way rights issues are debated in the Supreme Court, the interpretive community, and the wider society. The genius of the Warren Court was not that it created rights, as most scholars argue, but that it rejected the apologetic pluralism of its age, as represented in the scholarship of Robert Dahl and David Truman, and placed into its jurisprudence a critical pluralist interpretation of politics, as later represented in the scholarship of Grant McConnell and Theodore Lowi.[1]

However, while the critical pluralist view of polity of the Warren Court did significantly counter political and social inequality, it did not trigger radical change because it did not make manifest the effects of deep social, gender, and economic inequality on our nation's citizens. For example, in *Shapiro v. Thompson* (1969), views about the denial of welfare to the poor were debated in terms of the right to travel interstate, not in terms of class position and political power. Moreover, Chief Justice Warren—whom commentators traditionally view as driven by a deep commitment to equality—was a dissenter in that case, upholding the District of Columbia's waiting period requirement based on his polity view of the relationship between states and national governments.

It is important to note that the Warren Court's genius was not of its own making. It can be explained only by looking at the doctrinal change on the Court in light of the wider interpretive community in which it was operating. The conceptions of politics and law in the 1950s and 1960s that grew out of this struggle to define what constitutes democracy and law and why democracy exists explain the nature of the debate about the Warren Court. It is the introduction of a relativist theory of democracy along with a redefined scientific naturalism and scholars' continued support of non-Euclidean and legal realist premises that explains our misperceptions of the Warren Court. The Warren Court's rejection of these premises in its dialogue with the interpretive community helps explain both the constitutive decisionmaking process and doctrinal change in the Warren Court era, not the Court's wish to follow election returns or to secure policy wants.

The Burger Court

Analysis of the internal Burger Court decisionmaking process demonstrates that the dominant no counterrevolution interpretation of the Burger Court era is similarly unpersuasive because it, too, is an outgrowth of faulty instrumental, rather than constitutive, assumptions. A constitutive interpretation of Burger Court establishment of religion cases shows that there was far more coherence and principled yet complex decisionmaking in the Burger Court than suggested by the no counterrevolution view. For the most part, the centrist and extreme justices did not play the role assigned to them by the instrumental, no counterrevolution interpretation of internal Court decisionmaking. A constitutive interpretation of equal protection cases suggests the limitations of Martin Shapiro's instrumental policymaking approach to the Burger Court.[2]

I argued that *San Antonio Independent School District v. Rodriguez* should not be viewed as a watershed case, marking a new direction for the Burger Court in which it stopped cold the fundamental rights and interests strand of equal protection. This analysis misreads what the Warren Court did in the *Shapiro* case and misinterprets the place of *Rodriguez* in constitutional history. Most important, a look at both *Shapiro* and *Rodriguez* in light of *Plyler v. Doe* (1982) demonstrates that traditional instrumental interpretations of both Court eras are misguided. Rather, the Burger Court's fundamental rights and interests cases, the expansion of classifications in the law that are subject to heightened judicial scrutiny, and separation of powers cases signal a different, more complex, and more rights-protective jurisprudence than found in the Warren Court era.

In contrast to the policymaking approach, the Burger Court did not employ "a strange melange of Warren Court substantive equal protection approaches, ritualistic recitals of New Deal deference to the judgment of the legislature, and ambiguous combinations of the two." Nor was the Burger Court less sympathetic to the welfare recipient and the poor than the Warren Court; nor did it demonstrate an incoherent jurisprudence with varying degrees of deference to the legislature and choices shifting from case to case, based on the justices' personal views of policy choices.[3]

I find far more coherence, regularity, and uniqueness in Burger Court decisionmaking than do the instrumentalist scholars, which suggests that they have misperceived and oversimplified Burger Court decisionmaking. This finding cannot constitute an explanation for the oversimplification, however. For that we must place Burger Court decisionmaking in the context of the scholarship of its era, both in terms of the interpretive community of constitutional scholars and jurists commenting on the Court and in terms of political scientists and political theorists. Only in this way can we explain why there is such a simplified analysis of Burger Court jurisprudence. Then we find that instrumental no counterrevolution and policymaking interpretations of doctrinal change are based on faulty assumptions about the influence of the interpretive community on Burger Court doctrine. Far more systematic noninterpretive constitutional theories were created in the Burger Court era than in the Warren Court era. These theories led to more complex definitions of basic polity and rights principles and of how the Court should view the relationship between them as it makes constitutional choices.

After first trying in the 1970s to provide constitutional theories that integrated polity and rights principles,[4] major nonoriginalist constitutional scholars had broken into two camps by the late 1970s and early 1980s, dividing over the issue of whether constitutional choices and theory should be based primarily on polity or on rights principles. One group, led by John Hart Ely, advocated that all constitutional decisionmaking should be based on a view of the Constitution as a set of polity principles; the role of the Court was to stop malfunctions in the polity.[5] Another group of scholars argued that the role of constitutional theory and practice was to discover and protect fundamental rights in the Constitution, with polity principles as secondary to, and flowing from, substantive moral values. In the 1980s, many scholars who eschewed polity-based theory on questions of abortion and other rights issues argued that constitutional choices should be made on the basis of social, economic, and political factors that cause inequalities for women, the poor, and other groups. This new naturalism in constitutional theory could not help guide Court action because the Burger Court continued to employ both polity and rights principles in making its choices.[6]

Unlike constitutional scholars during the Burger Court era, constitutional scholars of the 1950s, such as Paul Freund, Herbert Wechsler, and Alexander Bickel, while much less rigorous and systematic in their theory and too accepting of apologetic pluralist interpretations of American political institutions, tried to juxtapose polity principles with fundamental rights; scholars in the 1970s attempted this and ultimately failed.[7] Scholars of the 1980s have given up trying to link polity and fundamental rights principles in their constitutional theories.

The complexity of polity and rights principles and constitutional theory in the Burger Court era changes the boundaries of constitutional debate and the standards for evaluating its jurisprudence. This means that justices like Powell, Blackmun, Stewart, White, and Burger can no longer take an originalist view of Court power or view the Court's primary objective as allowing equal formal access to the political systems, as the Warren Court and many pluralist scholars did. Supreme Court justices realize that all choices about polity and funda-

254 mental rights and their relationship need justification and specification. The relationship between rights and moral choices in the Constitution and polity principles is now seen by most (but not all) jurists as both open-ended and subject to discussion, choice, and analysis.

This means that unlike on the Warren Court, on the Burger Court justice as a value needed definition in terms of both rights and polity principles and their relationship. Choices about institutions and their autonomy must be made, because after the decline of the view of society as in equilibrium, or the total rejection of pluralism, there must be an affirmative statement about polity principles and fundamental rights. If there is not, mere negativism becomes ideological (as with the pluralist institutional functional arguments). Constitutional theory in the Burger Court years provided the theoretical structure for the choices. The interpretive community, jurists, and scholars in the social sciences and humanities must hone theory to practice and practice to theory, while accepting that there are principles, normative values, that have a solidity and grow over time.

Constitutive Decisionmaking on the Rehnquist Court

Until the 1991–1992 term, it was hard to decipher the direction of the Rehnquist Court because it takes a few years for justices' visions of polity and rights principles, and their relationship, to coalesce. It was not until then that a majority of the Supreme Court consisted of Reagan-Bush appointees: Sandra Day O'Connor (1981); William H. Rehnquist as chief justice (1986); Antonin Scalia (1986); Anthony Kennedy (1988); David Souter (1991); and Clarence Thomas (1991). Before the landmark decisions handed down in the spring of 1992, it was not clear what direction the Rehnquist Court would take in crucial areas such as the right of privacy and abortion choice, equal protection and race, and freedom of religion. Would the Rehnquist Court have a clear vision of polity and rights principles to guide it? Would it reimpose an ideological lull on Court activity, as the Warren Court did in its first six years? Would it support instrumental or constitutive interpretations of Supreme Court decisionmaking, the relationship between courts and politics, and between Courts and the interpretive community?

Like the Burger Court before it, the Rehnquist Court is often misunderstood by commentators focusing exclusively on the political views of the justices or on the influence of political elites on Court decisionmaking. Like all Courts, the Rehnquist Court makes decisions based on polity and rights principles, not on the premises of the election returns or policymaking approaches. The 1991–1992 term is no exception to this rule, showing the Rehnquist Court developing key polity and rights principles to guide future Court decisionmaking.[8]

The Supreme Court's recent landmark abortion decision in *Planned Parent-hood of Southeastern Pennsylvania v. Casey* (1992) rejects key assumptions in the instrumental theories of Robert Dahl and Martin Shapiro and the more recent contribution of Gerald Rosenberg.[9] Moreover, the rare joint plurality opinion in *Casey* by Reagan-Bush appointees O'Connor, Souter, and Kennedy confirms that individual justices, and the Court as a decisionmaking institution, make constitutional choices based on both individual rights values, such as a commitment to a woman's constitutional liberty interest in abortion choice, and key polity principles, such as a commitment to stare decisis, Supreme Court autonomy from the majoritarian political system, and the role of the Court as a countermajoritarian institution in our system of checks and balances. *Casey* is a landmark decision because it both sets out polity principles for the Court to follow in the future and suggests Court commitment to a new right of personhood.

The Joint Opinion by Justices O'Connor, Kennedy, and Souter

The *Casey* plurality could have chosen not to confront head-on the constitutionality of abortion choice. Alternatively, the plurality could have overturned *Roe v. Wade* (1973), following the wishes of Presidents Reagan and Bush, who had appointed all of the justices who wrote the joint opinion. Doing so would have offered strong confirmation to the election returns/policy-wants theories of Robert Dahl, Martin Shapiro, Mark Graber, and Gerald Rosenberg.[10]

Dahl and Graber, for example, argue that the Court is willing to listen to invitations from elected officials, particularly when the justices share the values of the presidential wing of the national coalition. The joint opinion in *Casey* begins, however, with a rebuke of the Bush administration's efforts to overturn the right of abortion choice: "Liberty finds no refuge in a jurisprudence of doubt. Yet 19 years after our holding that the Constitution protects a woman's right to terminate her pregnancy in its early stages, that definition of liberty is still questioned. Joining the respondents as *amicus curiae*, the United States, as it has done in five other cases in the last decade, again asks us to overrule *Roe*."[11] Graber argues that justices rarely disappoint presidents on those issues of immediate concern to them and their followers. Yet O'Connor, Souter, and Kennedy—three Reagan-Bush appointees—refused to overturn *Roe*.

Additionally, *Casey* offers clear evidence to counter Shapiro's view that justices decide cases based on personal policy wants. The joint opinion states, "Some of us as individuals find abortion offensive to our most basic principles of morality, but that cannot control our decision. Our obligation is to define the liberty of all, not to mandate our own moral code." Instead, a commitment to developing polity and rights principles guides all but the most conser-

256   vative originalist justices, leading the plurality in *Casey* to reaffirm the central holding of *Roe* and strengthen the right of abortion choice: "The reservations any of us may have in reaffirming the central holding in *Roe* are outweighed by the explication of individual liberty we have given combined with the force of *stare decisis.*"[12]

Polity Principles in Casey

To understand the landmark decisions of the 1991–1992 term, including *Casey, Lee v. Weisman* (graduation prayers), *R.A.V. v. St. Paul* (hate speech), and *United States v. Fordice* (university desegregation), we must focus on both rights principles and polity principles. Together, they show in *Casey* why the plurality rejects the election returns and policymaking approaches of Dahl, Shapiro, Graber, and Rosenberg.

The first polity reason that the joint opinion gives for reaffirming *Roe* is the Court's continuing commitment to stare decisis: "The obligation to follow precedent begins with necessity, and a contrary necessity marks its outer limit." Moreover, Justices O'Connor, Souter, and Kennedy craft an important new test in *Casey* for when the Court should overturn past decisions. The joint opinion states that decisions will be overruled only if they (1) prove unworkable in practice, (2) cause inequities in effect, (3) damage social stability, (4) are abandoned by society, or (5) rely on key fact assumptions that have changed. Applying this test to *Roe v. Wade*, the plurality finds that it meets none of the conditions.[13]

Most important, the justices in *Casey* emphasize the polity principle that the Court is autonomous of the political branches of government. Justice Blackmun, for example, in a concurring opinion states that since its founding our country "has recognized that there are certain fundamental liberties that are not to be left to the whims of an election."[14] This concern that the Court remain a countermajoritarian institution prevents it from following the lead of the majority coalition or the policy wants of individual justices. Instead the Court seeks to uphold precedent, the rule of law, and its own legitimacy. *Casey* shows three Reagan-Bush appointees, along with Justices Blackmun and Stevens, committed to the polity principle of maintaining the Court's autonomy, even though it means rejecting the Bush administration's policy wants as well as the personal policy wishes of the justices.

Evidence for the Court's commitment to autonomy as an important polity principle abounds in *Casey*. The joint opinion makes frequent mention of the danger to the Court's legitimacy that would come from overturning *Roe*. The joint opinion recognizes the political pressure on the Court to do so but fears "an unjustified repudiation of the principle on which the Court staked its authority in the first instance." The plurality further recognizes that "to overrule under fire in the absence of the most compelling reason to reexamine a watershed decision would subvert the Court's legitimacy beyond any serious question.'' Finally, Blackmun's concurring opinion seems to offer a clear rebuke of both the Bush administration and the election returns theories of Dahl and Rosenberg: ''What has happened today should serve as a model for future Justices and a warning to all who have tried to turn this Court into yet another political branch.''[15]

Thus, O'Connor, Kennedy, Souter, Blackmun, and Stevens each hold polity principles that distrust the ability of the majoritarian political system to protect individual rights. In *Casey*, these key polity principles are a respect for stare decisis, a commitment to Court autonomy from politics, and a concern for the Court's legitimacy and the rule of law. We see alternative polity principles in Justices Rehnquist's, Thomas's, and Scalia's deep trust of the political system to decide questions of individual rights. Therefore, *Casey* and other important cases in the 1991–1992 term suggest that there are two groups of justices. O'Connor, Souter, Kennedy, Blackmun, and Stevens hold polity principles that favor stare decisis, the rule of law, and the Supreme Court as a countermajoritarian institution in our system of separation of powers. These justices have staked out a new path for the Court, rejecting the originalist position of Rehnquist, Scalia, and Thomas and thus maintaining a commitment to the rule of law and developing polity and rights principles. Justices White, Rehnquist, Scalia, and Thomas hold polity principles that are more trusting of majoritarian politics to resolve individual rights questions and would overturn the settled constitutional principles of the past when they personally disagree with them.

Rights Principles: Personhood, Not Privacy

The justices also hold different views of what rights principles are at issue in *Casey* and how much the political system can be trusted to protect these principles. Most important, *Casey* shows that rights principles are not static but continue to evolve as our nation changes. The plurality gives greater voice than ever before to a new right of personhood that complements and even enlarges the right of privacy developed in *Griswold v. Connecticut* (1965), *Eisenstadt v. Baird* (1972), and *Roe*. In important ways, this shift in emphasis to a right of personhood reflects the Supreme Court's continuing commitment to the rule of law and to polity values that are critical of majoritarian politics and demonstrates that the Court can innovate on its own, following the rule of law, without guidance from elites in the political system. The new emphasis on personhood also suggests that the Court is responsive to the wider interpretive community of scholars, journalists, and the public as much as to elites in the political system.

The right of privacy is one of the chief legacies of *Roe*. Whether this right remained as strong after *Bowers v. Hardwick* (1986) was an open question until

258   *Casey*. Some suggested that *Bowers* marked the "death of substantive due process as a principled doctrine of law."[16] In *Casey*, however, the plurality reaffirms the central holding of *Roe* while giving voice to a new right of personhood. This right differs from the right of privacy in *Roe* in the greater emphasis it places on physical autonomy as a rights value, individual freedom to make "the most intimate and personal choices . . . central to personal dignity and autonomy," and gender equality as an element of abortion choice. The joint opinion acknowledges, for the first time, that equality is a component of the right of abortion choice: "The liberty of the woman is at stake in a sense unique to the human condition and so unique to the law. The mother who carries a child to full term is subject to anxieties, to physical constraints, to pain that only she must bear." These three new specifications of the right of privacy combine in a key paragraph in the joint opinion to define what will, perhaps, prove to be *Casey*'s most enduring achievement—an expansion of *Roe*'s right of privacy that, at the same time, clarifies its substance: "At the heart of liberty is the right to define one's own concept of existence, of meaning, of the universe, and of the mystery of human life. Beliefs about these matters could not define the attributes of personhood were they formed under the compulsion of the State."[17]

As this quotation reveals, the rights innovation in *Casey* does not stand alone but is connected to the plurality's polity principles, which show a distrust of the capacity of majoritarian politics to protect women's abortion choice. *Casey*, like earlier landmark cases by other conservative Courts, shows that polity and rights principles work together and that the Court can derive innovative fundamental rights from strong polity principles. For example, the newly recognized equality component of abortion choice stems from the Court's recognition of changing dynamics of political representation and empowerment of women in society: "The ability of women to participate equally in the economic and social life of the Nation has been facilitated by their ability to control their reproductive lives." It is significant also that Justice Rehnquist, in dissent, takes umbrage not at the equality component of abortion per se but rather at its polity relation to the political empowerment of women.[18]

The plurality's turn toward a new emphasis on personhood also suggests that the Court speaks to the interpretive community of scholars, lawyers, and the media as much as to the wider public. The plurality recognizes scholarly criticisms of the right of privacy and the trimester framework in *Roe* without abandoning its central holding. The Court acknowledges that the trimester system is unworkable and gives new emphasis to the state's interests in protecting potential life without abandoning either the right to privacy or precedent. Instead, the plurality attempts to answer scholarly criticisms of the concept of privacy by grounding it in a more tangible framework of physical autonomy, personal choice, and equality.

If this analysis is correct, it casts doubt on the instrumental interpretations of Dahl and Rosenberg, which claim that the Court has little effect on society unless it follows the majority coalition's lead. Rosenberg's analysis of the Court's ability to produce social change focuses on the direct impact from landmark decisions,[19] but he fails to consider ways in which Court decisions affect the interpretive community. He does discuss the media and public opinion, but the Court pays more attention to the rule of law, stare decisis, and the legal interpretive community than it does to the media or public opinion.

It is true that the Court in *Casey* restricts somewhat the ability of women to procure an abortion compared to the near absolute right of privacy in *Roe*, a result of heightened recognition of the state's polity interest in protecting potential life. However, the undue burden test crafted by the plurality shows a clear commitment to protecting a woman's right to abortion up to the point when the fetus becomes viable. Government may place certain limited obstacles in the path of a woman's choice, according to the undue burden test, but may not proscribe first- and second-trimester abortions. The point is not that the Rehnquist Court supports *Roe v. Wade* root and branch, for obviously it does not, but that *Casey* demonstrates that polity and rights principles evolve in such a way that the Court refuses to think of itself as merely a policymaking institution.

Casey is more than a confirmation of the central premise of *Roe v. Wade*. When read in light of the other landmark cases of the extraordinary 1991–1992 Court session, it is a clear statement that Justices Souter, O'Connor, and, most surprisingly, Kennedy have decided to make constitutional choices based on precedents and in light of the new complexities of life in the United States.[20]

The Rehnquist Court and Religion

In a second landmark decision of the 1991–1992 term, *Lee v. Weisman* (1992), the Court refused to uphold a junior high school's use of prayer at graduation ceremonies, despite encouragement from the Bush administration to do so. As in *Casey, Weisman* shows traditionally conservative Justices Kennedy, O'Connor, and Souter staking out polity and rights principles to guide the Court in the future. The *Weisman* majority written by Kennedy emphasizes the Court's autonomy from politics and the need for the Court to follow established precedents rather than resorting to policy wants: "The controlling precedents as they relate to prayer and religious exercises in primary and secondary public schools compel the holding here that the policy of the city of Providence is an unconstitutional one."[21] Far from treating precedent as merely a means for procuring policy objectives, Justice Kennedy reaffirms the

260 Court's commitment to the First Amendment in spite of his clear personal preference for school prayer.

The *Weisman* majority also emphasizes the Supreme Court's autonomy from the majoritarian political system. As in *Casey*, the Court rebuffs the Bush administration's attempt to lead it: "Thus we do not accept the invitation of petitioners and amicus, the United States, to reconsider our decision in *Lemon v. Kurtzman*." In language nearly identical to that in *Casey*, the majority emphasizes the need to maintain Court legitimacy as an important polity principle: "To compromise that principle today would be to deny our own tradition and forfeit our standing to urge others to secure the protection of that tradition for themselves." Justice Souter, in a concurring opinion, emphasizes the value of Court autonomy: "We have not changed much since the days of Madison, and the judiciary should not willingly enter the political arena to battle the centripetal force leading from religious pluralism to official preference for the faith with the most votes."[22] One could hardly ask for a clearer statement of Court autonomy and the importance of countermajoritarian polity principles to protecting individual rights.[23]

Other Cases from the 1991–1992 Term

A number of other cases from the 1991–1992 term show the Court's commitment to polity and rights principles and rejection of election returns and personal policymaking. *United States v. Fordice* (1992) and *R.A.V. v. City of St. Paul* (1992) both show the Court developing polity and rights principles to guide it in the future. In both cases the Court surprised many by reaffirming and even strengthening key equal protection and First Amendment principles. In *Fordice*, the Court unanimously reaffirmed that public universities and colleges must seek to eliminate de facto discriminatory practices if those practices lack clear educational purposes and result from prior de jure discrimination. All nine of the justices took note of the important precedents in the field of school desegregation and the increasing importance of university education to minority empowerment.

In *R.A.V. v. City of St. Paul*, the Court confronted another divisive issue— hate speech. Rather than waiting for leadership from the political branches, all nine justices affirmed the First Amendment. Additionally, the Court emphasized concern about majoritarian laws that restrict free speech. The Court seemed to raise its scrutiny of "fighting words" restrictions in response to recent issues of minority-imposed "politically correct" speech regulations. This is not a case of individual justices simply imposing their policy wants, for there can be little question that each justice is personally opposed to hate- or bias-motivated speech. Justice Scalia's majority opinion makes this clear: "Let there be no mistake about our belief that burning a cross in someone's front

yard is reprehensible. But St. Paul has sufficient means at its disposal to prevent such behavior without adding the First Amendment to the fire.''[24]

Casey, Weisman, Fordice, and *R.A.V.* are the four most significant Supreme
Court decisions of 1992. Together they show that the justices reject the lead
of the dominant political coalition and personal policy wants in favor of reaffirming and strengthening key polity and rights principles. The Rehnquist
Court, like all Courts, bases its decisions on polity and rights principles that
evolve as the nation evolves. No matter what direction the political winds
have blown, the Court has shown a concern for stare decisis, autonomy, and
legitimacy that does not fit the descriptions offered by Dahl, Shapiro, Rosenberg, or Graber. The swing to the right in the Reagan and Bush years has been
reflected in these cases, both through the influence of new members of the
Court and in the type of cases that are brought to the Court. However, the
Court has decided these cases without stripping the decisionmaking process of
discipline or its reliance on polity and rights values.

Why We Misperceive the Warren, Burger, and Rehnquist Courts

To understand our misperceptions of the Warren, Burger, and Rehnquist
Courts, we need to link doctrinal innovations to changes in interpretations of
the American political system and the constitutional theory during each
Court era. This is an especially effective way to explain why simplistic visions
of the Warren and Burger Courts dominate the academy and the broader society. When we analyze these Courts' views of polity, we see that the Burger
Court was more liberal and questioning in its fears of structural inequality for
American citizens than was the Warren Court, which was still working within
the dominant apologetic pluralist view of American politics of its day, even as
it rejected many of those positive views about polity in its interpretation of society. It was not the Warren Court's view of equality alone that was innovative, for the scholars of the day agreed that fundamental rights could be open-
ended, but its view of polity, which differed from those espoused by many
members of the political science, social science, and humanities academy.

During the Warren, Burger, and Rehnquist Court eras, interpretations of
the American political system and standards for evaluating constitutional
questions within the interpretive community changed. The Warren Court rejected the apologetic pluralism of political scientists wedded to relativist democratic theory and accepted less apologetic process and substantive fundamental rights values held by prominent legal scholars of the day. But it did not
range far outside the pluralist vision of polity of the 1950s and early 1960s.
The Burger Court's constitutional choices reflected the complexity of the polity and rights principles of its time, while allowing a juxtaposition of polity
and rights principles in its jurisprudence. Scholars who chose either rights or

polity-oriented constitutional theory failed to analyze the relationship of polity to rights principles.

Part of the reason for this is that political scientists and legal scholars who accepted the election returns and policymaking approaches to doctrinal change and the no counterrevolution interpretation of the Burger Court continued to rely on core values that grew out of non-Euclidean and scientific naturalist assumptions founded on relativist democratic theory and legal realist interpretations of the political and legal systems.[25] These core values led to viewing the Supreme Court as a policymaking institution, concerned primarily with securing policy outcomes rather than employing polity and rights principles and the evaluative standards fostered by the interpretive communities of each Court era.

It is impossible to accept the view that the Supreme Court makes its constitutional choices instrumentally, because in the Warren, Burger, and Rehnquist Court eras the debate about which polity and rights principles to employ and how to apply them was far more textured and sincere than the elections returns or policymaking approaches suggest. Also, the interpretive community is not epiphenomenal to Supreme Court decisionmaking. The case analysis suggests that the Warren, Burger, and Rehnquist Courts were aware of the apologetic pluralist definitions of American history, politics, and legal institutions and refused to accept them.

The Warren Court was aware of general constitutional theory of its day and needed that awareness for its legitimacy and discipline, even as it rejected central tenets held by members of the interpretive community. The Warren Court was aware that the Constitution consists of fundamental rights and polity principles and that there are different views about how to apply them in specific cases. Justices were aware of precedent—past definitions of fundamental rights and polity principles—and looked at precedent in relationship to their own training, views, and actions in real life. Case analysis offers evidence that the justices in the Burger Court era had accepted the more complex polity and rights-based constitutional theory of their day and critical pluralist interpretations of polity. In recent Rehnquist Court decisions the Court viewed abortion and school prayer in terms of polity principles of stare decisis and Court autonomy and revealed a more complex understanding of equality and personhood.

Supreme Court justices may choose to reject or accept polity and rights principles in different degrees. There is a dialogic relationship between the Supreme Court and the interpretive community that creates the political theory, interpretations of the workings of political institutions, and the constitutional theory of each era. The Court is autonomous of the *direct* influence of electoral politics and the interpretive community. However, the Court makes its choices in relationship to the boundaries of the debate within the interpretive

community and the wider, informed society over polity principles such as the   *263*
proper role of the Supreme Court and fundamental rights visions, not as a
result of following the policy wants of the majority coalition.

Evidence from the Warren, Burger, and Rehnquist Court eras confirms the
limitations of instrumental election returns, policymaking, and civic republican approaches to Court decisionmaking, which emphasize the lack of separation of law from politics. Justices rely instead on deeply held rights values *and*
important polity principles when making decisions. Non-Euclidean and scientific naturalist principles, along with the resulting relativist democratic theory,
continue to influence the way many political scientists study and evaluate the
Supreme Court and the American political system as forums for change.

Conclusion: Constitutional Theory and Supreme Court Decisionmaking in the Future

Modern civic republican constitutional theory, as represented by the important early works of Michael Perry, Mark Tushnet, and Sanford Levinson,
brings us full circle to many of the limits, or problems, identified in the instrumental interpretations of Warren and Burger Court decisionmaking and doctrinal change examined in Parts One and Two. Issues explored in our discussion of modern civic republican theory also raise questions about the ability of
nonoriginalist constitutional theory in the Warren and Burger Court eras to
provide adequate guidance to the constitutive Supreme Court decisionmaking
process.

Supreme Court justices do not apply constitutional theories and principles
instrumentally to support their individual policy wants or those of the majority
coalition in power. They do not view the Court's function in narrow safety valve
terms, nor do their biographies predetermine case outcomes. The Court views
individual rights as an important component of our constitutional tradition and
sees a close interrelationship between polity and rights principles, with each
strengthening the other. There are two major problems with this first wave of
civic republican constitutional theory, born of modern hermeneutics: it proceeds
from instrumentalism or wanted outcomes—deliberative, transformative politics
(Perry), economic and sociological naturalism (Tushnet), or antiproceduralism
(Levinson)—to theory without stopping to tie constitutive polity and rights principles together; and polity principles, especially those of Perry and Levinson, are
less critical and complex than those employed by the Warren and Burger Courts,
and perhaps even the Rehnquist Court.

Based on the limitations identified in the constitutional theory of the Warren and Burger Court years and the first wave of civic republican theories, we
need a constitutional theory that will explore the relationship between aspirational rights and polity values. There is a middle ground between acceptance
of neutral foundational liberal theory as a must—originalism—and the value

264   relativism of contemporary, naturalistic constitutional theory. This middle-range polity and rights theory would provide ways to analyze specific doctrinal areas that would maintain the critical potential of polity and rights values.

By viewing the polity in critical pluralist terms and developing a new critical pluralist theory of polity that employs the findings of modern political and social science, rather than viewing the relationship between the Supreme Court and political institutions in reciprocal terms, we can keep alive the inherent critical distance between the Court and political institutions that Perry describes as basic to our constitutional values. For example, this critical distance can be sustained by drawing on social science analyses of the effects of trusting electorally based political institutions, such as states, as protectors of rights to see whether federalism and judicial self-restraint would be an aspirational polity notion.

It also would suggest that while completely neutral constitutional theory is not possible, constitutional decisionmaking is more bounded than is suggested by contemporary constitutional theory influenced by hermeneutics. By emphasizing the contingent nature of all choices, Perry and others fail to see that there is a finite range of constitutional choices that all judges agree on. A constitutional theory should not talk about the contingent nature of choices in general terms. It must analyze degrees of contingency and ranges of polity and rights choices and specify whether, for example, in the First Amendment there are fewer contingent choices than in substantive due process doctrine. When this is done, we will see far more discipline and structure in constitutional theory than is evident in the most recent wave of theory.

Unfortunately for Perry's objectives, the contextualism and trust of politics when constitutional aspirations are clear will support what Lowi has called interest group liberalism or a self-interested politics, a politics short on deliberation about moral issues and long on catering to private interests. By calling for decentralized decisionmaking on issues of constitutional importance and by rejecting moral foundationalism, Perry supports the nature of economic and social power that exists in narrow constituencies. I fear that the constitutional theories of Perry, Tushnet, and Levinson will rekindle the moral relativism and subordination of the Supreme Court to politics that was evident in the 1950s and 1960s. Unfortunately, the success of legal realist values today comes at a time when the idea of fundamental rights is weaker on the Supreme Court, and in the wider society.

Constitutional theory and practice must continue to question polity and rights protection. They cannot accept governmental structures as working well, nor can they accept the sociological conditions of individuals as the sole basis for making choices. To do either undermines the importance of the relationship of political institution and structural forms to the rights values in the

Constitution, with a view of government and rights protection that is inherently critical.

The Burger Court continued that questioning, even though it was expected to be "conservative" in the areas of equal protection and the separation of church and state and added new questions to those of the Warren Court. The Rehnquist Court and future Courts will require for their constitutive decisionmaking process even more complex polity and rights principles than the Warren and Burger Courts. They will need more subtle constitutional theories about the relationship between polity and rights principles in order to help our nation meet its problems, especially as it becomes more diverse. The dialogue between the Court and the interpretive community will become more important in the future because of the need to reconsider the nature of constitutional principles in a more complex society. Constitutional theory must be up to this task. It must not simply mirror polity and rights principles from the past.

In Chapter 7 we argued that the first wave of civic republican approaches to constitutional theory, in employing arguments against foundational principles while also encouraging judicial self-restraint and a decentralized process for making constitutional choices, reject the notion of the Supreme Court and constitutional law as countermajoritarian yet still respect fundamental rights in the Constitution. This may well bring us back to a period like the "end of ideology" era, dominant in the 1950s. Only the rejection of the nominalism of this era by the Warren Court and by many prominent constitutional scholars saved our nation from the worst ravages of such a constitutional vision.[26]

It will be interesting to see whether the Rehnquist Court will accept or reject the shift in direction to civic republicanism and naturalism in rights-based constitutional theory or any of the other new formulations of polity and rights principles and their relationship. I suspect that it will reject the new civic republicanism and the new naturalism in individual rights for reasons similar to those that motivated the Warren Court to reject the static institutionalism of its age and the Burger Court to reject constitutional theory built only on polity or rights principles. Neither met the requirement of a critical constitutional theory. Like the Courts before it, the Rehnquist Court and future Courts will have a choice as to whether and how to embrace the constitutional theory of the day in their constitutive decisionmaking process. Recent landmark decisions by the Rehnquist Court offer evidence that it has decided to view Supreme Court decisionmaking in constitutive terms.

In each age of the Supreme Court the conceptualization of cases and expectations of Court process changes. This influences the degree to which we see what justices do as principled. Through time, what it means to be "con-

266 servative'' changes and the bounds of the debate are different. Problematics about institutions and the faith that we hold in them also changes, as do the individual rights we believe are needed to protect fundamental constitutional values. With these changes come changes in the thinking of all but the most originalist of justices about what issues are raised in each case.

Notes

Chapter 1. Introduction: Supreme Court Decisionmaking and Doctrinal Change

1. For important statements of the "no counterrevolution" approach to the Burger Court, see Vincent Blasi, ed., *The Burger Court: The Counter-Revolution That Wasn't* (New Haven, Conn.: Yale University Press, 1983); Bernard Schwartz, *The Ascent of Pragmatism: The Burger Court in Action* (New York: Addison-Wesley Publishing Co., 1990); Richard Y. Funston, *Constitutional Counter-Revolution? The Warren Court and the Burger Court: Judicial Policy-making in Modern America* (Cambridge, Mass.: Schenkman Publishing Company, 1977); Francis Graham Lee, *Neither Conservative nor Liberal: The Burger Court on Civil Rights and Liberties* (Malabar, Fla.: Robert E. Krieger Publishing Co., 1983); and Charles M. Lamb and Stephen C. Halpern, eds., *The Burger Court: Political and Judicial Profiles* (Chicago: University of Illinois Press, 1991).

2. See Owen Fiss, "Objectivity and Interpretation," *Stanford Law Review* 34 (1982): 746–747; "In law the interpretive community is a reality. It has authority to confer because membership does not depend on agreement. Judges do not belong to an interpretive community as a result of shared views about particular issues or interpretations, but belong by virtue of a commitment to uphold and advance the rule of law itself. . . . Judges know that if they relinquish their membership in the interpretive community, or deny its authority, they lose their right to speak with the authority of the law." For Fiss, the interpretive community, consisting of scholars, legalists, and jurists who build bridges between law and the humanities, establishes sets of evaluative standards in procedural and substantive norms and creates a strong critical environment through which to criticize or defend constitutional choices (pp. 754–757). Finally, for Fiss, a great judge (and he names Earl Warren as one) is both disciplined and liberated by conflicts within the interpretive community (p. 758).

3. See Robert Dahl, "Decision Making in a Democracy: The Supreme Court as a National Policy-Maker," *Journal of Public Law* 6 (Fall 1957): 279–295; and *Democracy in the United States: Promise and Performance*, 4th ed. (Boston: Houghton Mifflin, 1981), pp. 143–163. See also Richard Y. Funston, "The Supreme Court and Critical Elections," *American Political Science Review* 69 (1975): 795–811; Chapter 8, "The Warren Court in Retrospect," pp. 297–325, and Chapter 9, "The Burger Court in Perspective," pp. 327–367, in *Constitutional Counter-Revolution?* For a critical view of the election returns approach, see David Adamany, "Legitimacy, Realigning Elections, and the Supreme Court," *Wisconsin Law Review* (1973): 790–846; and Jonathan Casper, "The Supreme Court and National Policy Making," *American Political Science Review* 70 (1976): 50–63.

4. See Martin Shapiro, "Fathers and Sons: The Court, the Commentators, and the Search for Values," in Blasi, *The Burger Court: The Counter-Revolution That Wasn't*, pp. 218–238; "The Supreme Court: From Warren to Burger," in Anthony King, ed., *The New American Political System* (Washington, D.C.: American Enterprise Institute, 1978), pp. 179–211; "The Supreme Court from Early Burger to Early Rehnquist," in Anthony King, ed., *The New American Political System*, 2d version (Washington, D.C.:

268 American Enterprise Institute, 1990), pp. 47–85; and "The Constitution and Economic Rights," in M. Judd Harmon, ed., *Essays on the Constitution of the United States* (Port Washington, N.Y.: Kennikat Press, 1978). Also, see Chapter 1, "The Supreme Court as Political Agency," and all of Martin Shapiro, *Law and Politics in the Supreme Court: New Approaches to Political Jurisprudence* (Glencoe, Ill: Free Press of Glencoe, 1964), for the first major statement of Shapiro's policymaking approach to the Supreme Court. Lief Carter, who also views Supreme Court decisionmaking as policymaking, sees the process in much less instrumental terms. See Lief H. Carter, "When Courts Should Make Policy: An Institutional Approach," in John Gardiner, ed., *Public Law and Public Policy* (New York: Praeger Publishers, 1977), pp. 141–157; and Carter, *Contemporary Constitutional Lawmaking: The Supreme Court and the Art of Politics* (New York: Pergamon Press, 1985).

 5. See Shapiro, "The Supreme Court: From Warren to Burger," p. 199.

 6. See Anthony Lewis, "Historic Change in the Supreme Court," in Leonard Levy, ed., *The Supreme Court under Earl Warren* (New York: Quadrangle Books, 1972) pp. 73–80; and "Earl Warren," in Richard H. Sayler, Barry B. Boyer, and Richard E. Gooding, Jr., eds., *The Warren Court: A Critical Analysis* (New York: Chelsea House, 1969), pp. 1–31. See also Archibald Cox, *The Role of the Supreme Court in American Government* (New York: Oxford University Press, 1976) and *The Warren Court: Constitutional Decision as an Instrument of Reform* (Cambridge, Mass.: Harvard University Press, 1968).

 7. See Chapter 14, "The Mosaic of the Warren Court: Frankfurter, Black, Warren, and Harlan," in G. Edward White, *The American Judicial Tradition* (New York: Oxford University Press, 1976), pp. 317–368; and Chapter 16, "The Burger Court and the Idea of 'Transition'," in G. Edward White, *The American Judicial Tradition*, expanded ed. (New York: Oxford University Press, 1988), pp. 421–459. Also see G. Edward White, "Earl Warren as Jurist," *Virginia Law Review* 67 (April 1981): 461–551, and *Earl Warren: A Public Life* (New York: Oxford University Press, 1982.)

 8. Major statements of this view of the Warren Court include the following works: Alexander M. Bickel, *Politics and the Warren Court* (New York: Harper and Row, 1965); Cox, *The Warren Court*; Levy, *The Supreme Court under Earl Warren*; Philip Kurland, *Politics, the Constitution, and the Warren Court* (Chicago: University of Chicago Press, 1970); Clifford M. Lytle, *The Warren Court and Its Critics* (Tucson: University of Arizona Press, 1968); Bernard Schwartz, *Super Chief: Earl Warren and His Supreme Court—A Judicial Biography* (New York: New York University Press, 1983); White, "The Mosaic of the Warren Court: Frankfurter, Black, Warren, and Harlan."

 9. See White, *The American Judicial Tradition*, pp. 420–466, for an excellent argument as to why, if we proceed carefully, we can explore differences among Supreme Court eras in general and the Warren and Burger Court eras in particular. Though I will take issue with the "no counterrevolution" interpretation of the Burger Court era (which White supports) and with White's interpretation of the Warren Court era (because it employs instrumental rather than constitutive assumptions of Supreme Court decisionmaking and doctrinal change), I will compare the Court eras to test the validity of how they have been interpreted in the past.

 10. No. 91-744, the decision in which the Rehnquist Court, consisting of a majority of Reagan-Bush appointees, reaffirmed the right to abortion choice.

 11. See Dahl, "The Supreme Court as a National Policy-Maker."

 12. See Funston, "The Supreme Court and Critical Elections" and *Constitutional Counter-Revolution?*; and Gerald Rosenberg, *The Hollow Hope: Can Courts Bring about Social Change?* (Chicago: University of Chicago Press, 1991), which seek to prove empiri-

cally that the Supreme Court follows politics and elections in making constitutional choices.

13. Dahl, "The Supreme Court as a National Policy Maker," pp. 279–281.

14. See Laura Kalman, *Legal Realism at Yale, 1927–1960* (Chapel Hill: University of North Carolina Press, 1986), p. 5, for a discussion of "legal realists" as scholars who "focused on the interrelationship between law and society and refused to believe that legal concepts and rules were the sole determinants of judicial decisions."

While legal realists differed in the degree to which they dismissed the role of foundational polity and rights and rule-making principles in judicial decisionmaking, in contrast to the place of personal policy wants of judges, the most radical legal realists argued that "the law" and the Constitution were what judges said they were. They argued that the personal policy wants of judges, born of their own past lives and not their adherence to neutral legal principles, were the primary determinants of judicial outcomes.

15. This and the following paragraphs are based on Dahl, "The Supreme Court as a National Policy Maker," pp. 286–294 (quotations from pp. 293 and 285).

16. Ibid., p. 292. Dahl apparently believes that Congress has been as concerned as the Supreme Court about securing individual rights; this belief is both a general institutional comparison and a probabilistic statement about the Supreme Court and electorally based bodies.

17. Ibid., pp. 283 and 291.

18. Shapiro, "The Supreme Court: From Warren to Burger," pp. 179–210.

19. Ibid., pp. 199–200. For a similar view of the role of clerks and internal Court decisionmaking, see David O'Brien, *Storm Center: The Supreme Court in American Politics*, 2d ed. (New York: W. W. Norton, 1990), pp. 159–171. See also Schwartz, *The Ascent of Pragmatism*, pp. 35–39. As I shall explore in later chapters, the internal process view of explaining doctrinal change understates dramatically the place of forces outside the Court, such as the interpretive community and the influence of justices' polity and rights principles on their constitutional choices.

20. Shapiro, "The Constitution and Economic Rights," pp. 84–96 (quotation on p. 85). The preferred position (or preferred freedoms) doctrine holds that some constitutional rights particularly those guaranteed by the Bill of Rights (especially the First Amendment), are fundamental to a free society and thus deserve more judicial protection than other constitutional values. The *Carolene Products* footnote was the first major articulation of this doctrine by a Supreme Court justice.

21. Shapiro, "The Supreme Court: From Warren to Burger," p. 189. Shapiro continues, "The word 'myth' here is not meant to suggest a falsehood as such, but rather a selective version of reality made larger than life and employed as a guide to the interpretation of all subsequent reality."

22. The remainder of this section is based on Shapiro, "The Supreme Court: From Warren to Burger," quotations on pp. 89, 86, 93, 200–201, 193, 180, 182, 181, 181–182, and 181.

23. Lewis, "Historic Change in the Supreme Court," pp. 79 (quotation), 79–80.

24. The remainder of this section is based on White, "The Mosaic of the Warren Court"; quotations on pp. 339–340, 325, 340, and 341.

25. White, "The Burger Court and the Idea of 'Transition,' " in *The American Judicial Tradition*, pp. 420–459.

26. Robert McCloskey, *The American Supreme Court* (Chicago: University of Chicago Press, 1960); Walter F. Murphy, *Elements of Judicial Strategy* (Chicago: University

of Chicago Press, 1964), especially Chapter 7, "Ethics and Strategy," pp. 176–197. See also Walter F. Murphy and Joseph Tanenhaus, *The Study of Public Law* (New York: Random House, 1972), for a call for a behavioral analysis of Supreme Court decision-making, but one that understands that polity and rights principles, not merely the influence of elections or policy wants, inform Supreme Court decisionmaking.

27. See Michael Perry, *Morality, Politics and Law* (New York: Oxford University Press, 1988), p. 163, which draws on McCloskey's analysis.

28. The following is based on McCloskey, *The American Supreme Court*; quotations on pp. 13, 225, and 22.

29. Although my analysis of constitutive decisionmaking in the Warren and Burger Court eras is in the tradition of McCloskey's interpretation of the Supreme Court and constitutional change, I consider that McCloskey, like other legal scholars of the 1950s and 1960s, was too willing to accept instrumental assumptions about Supreme Court decisionmaking and overstates the degree to which the Court looks over its shoulder at popular will and political reality in making constitutional choices.

30. See Walter F. Murphy, "The Art of Constitutional Interpretation," in Harmon, ed., *Essays on the Constitution of the United States*, pp. 130–159, and "Constitutional Interpretations: The Art of the Historian, Magician, or Statesman?" 87 *Yale Law Journal* 1752 (1978). Also see Walter F. Murphy, James E. Fleming, and William F. Harris, *American Constitutional Interpretation* (Mineola, N.Y.: Foundation Press, 1986).

31. For a discussion of the terms "polity" and "rights" principles as applied to the Burger Court's aid to parochial education cases see Chapter 4. Also see Ronald C. Kahn, "Polity and Rights Values in Conflict: The Burger Court, Ideological Interests, and the Separation of Church and State," *Studies in American Political Development* 3 (1989):279–293; and Ronald Kahn, "Ideology, Religion and the First Amendment," in Gerald Houseman and Michael McCann, eds., *Judging the Constitution: Critical Essays in Judicial Lawmaking* (Glenview, Ill.: Scott, Foresman, 1989), pp. 409–441.

32. See Ronald Kahn, "The Burger Court, Equal Protection of the Law and the Ascent of Pragmatism: A Critique" (paper delivered to 1990 Annual Meeting, American Political Science Association, San Francisco, August 30–September 2, 1990.)

33. The Constitution was ratified by "conventions" in the states—not by the states per se but by "the people" in convention. This point is central to constitutional theory and practice and why the laws enacted by the national government are "supreme" over laws of the states and why fundamental rights of the people may limit laws of the states and of the national government. The Federalists believed that national government supremacy, separation of powers, and complex procedures for the selection of public officials and law-making would best protect the rights of citizens against the national government and that there was thus no need for a bill of rights. The Anti-Federalists believed that basic individual rights should be listed, as should the notion that the Bill of Rights does not exhaust the rights of the people (the Ninth Amendment).

34. See Herbert Storing, *What the Anti-Federalists Were For: The Political Thought of the Opponents of the Constitution* (Chicago: University of Chicago Press, 1981), pp. 15–23.

35. See Gerald Garvey, *Constitutional Bricolage* (Princeton, N.J.: Princeton University Press, 1971), pp. 9–25, for a discussion of a syntactical approach to the study of constitutional law and politics, one that explores the fit between law and changes in political culture.

36. See Storing, *What the Anti-Federalists Were For*, Chapter 3; Gordon S. Wood,

The Creation of the American Republic, 1776–1787 (New York: W. W. Norton, 1969), pp. 471–518; and Rufus S. Davis, *The Federal Principle* (Berkeley: University of California Press, 1978), pp. 74–120.

37. See Garvey, *Constitutional Bricolage*, pp. 85–100.

38. See Edward S. Corwin, *The Commerce Clause versus States Rights* (Princeton, N.J.: Princeton University Press, 1936), and "The Passing of Dual Federalism," *Virginia Law Review* 36 (1950): 1–23. Davis, in *The Federal Principle*, pp. 74–120, argues that both rights and polity principles, concepts of the proper distribution of power among different institutions in society, guided the thinking of the Supreme Court in both the Marshall and Taney eras.

39. See Garvey, *Constitutional Bricolage*, Chapter 6, pp. 101–122.

40. Corwin, "The Passing of Dual Federalism," p. 22.

41. See Garvey, *Constitutional Bricolage*, pp. 101–122.

42. See Howard Gillman, *The Constitution Besieged: The Rise and Demise of Lochner Era Police Powers Jurisdiction* (Durham, N.C.: Duke University Press, 1993), pp. 10–11, for the argument that the judicial standards used by the *Lochner* Court to evaluate the power of legislatures "were not illegitimate creations of unrestrained free-market ideologues, but rather had their roots in principles of political legitimacy that were forged at the time of the creation of the Constitution and were later elaborated by state court judges as they first addressed the nature and scope of legislative power in the era of Jacksonian democracy." Gillman argues that the crisis in American constitutional law at the turn of the century is not a story of "the sudden corruption of law and the judicial function, but rather of how the judiciary's struggle to maintain the coherence and integrity of a constitutional ideology averse to class politics was complicated and ultimately derailed by the maturation of capitalist forms of production and the unprecedented efforts of legislatures to extend special protections to groups that considered themselves vulnerable to increasingly coercive market mechanisms."

Like Gillman, I seek to "encourage a renewed appreciation of the extent to which judicial behavior . . . may be motivated by a set of interests and concerns that are relatively distinct from the preferences of particular social groups, the policies prescribed by particular economic theories, or the personal social and political loyalties and sympathies of individual judges. It was the mischaracterization of turn-of-the-century constitutional jurisprudence that led political scientists to view judicial opinions as empty rhetoric designed to mask policy preferences rather than as principled explanations for legal decisions." Most importantly, Gillman's methodology and organizing assumptions oppose the ahistoricism of legal realist and behavioral political science theories of judicial decisionmaking that "led political scientists to view judicial opinions as empty rhetoric designed to mask policy preferences rather than as principled explanations for legal decisions."

43. Garvey, *Constitutional Bricolage*, pp. 129–139.

44. These ideological interests, in both polity and rights principles, are born of justices' political philosophies and activities in politics. Like mayors, they operate against their electoral and organizational interests in the name of "ideological interests," but they are even more prone than mayors to make constitutional choices against their short-term policy wants because of the need for a rule of law and principled jurisprudence. J. David Greenstone and Paul E. Peterson, *Race and Authority in Urban Politics* (New York: Russell Sage Foundation, 1973), pp. 125–133.

45. See John Sprague, *Voting Patterns on the United States Supreme Court* (Indianapolis: Bobbs-Merrill, 1968), pp. 151 and 64. Sprague looked at all cases in the appellate

jurisdiction of the Supreme Court in which the constitutionality of state and local statutes and the validity of acts done under state authority were at issue. He also studied all cases in which it was alleged that a right, title, privilege, or immunity specially set up and claimed under the Constitution, treaties, or statutes of, or commissions held or authority exercised under the United States, had been denied. Finally he studied all cases in which the Supreme Court made a decision on the merits of the federal constitutional question presented.

46. Pritchett, *The Roosevelt Court—A Study in Judicial Politics and Values, 1937–1947* (New York: Macmillan, 1949), pp. 253–263 (quotation on p. 256).

47. Doris Provine, *Case Selection in the United States Supreme Court* (Chicago: University of Chicago Press, 1980), p. 100.

48. Pritchett, *Civil Liberties and the Vinson Court* (University of Chicago Press, 1954), p. 198; Provine, *Case Selection*, p. 123.

49. Pritchett, *Civil Liberties and the Vinson Court*, pp. 198–200.

50. Provine, *Case Selection*, p. 123.

51. Ibid., pp. 172 and 130.

52. This and the following paragraph are based on Harold Spaeth and Stuart H. Teger, "Activism and Restraint," in Stephen C. Halpern and Charles M. Lamb, eds., *Supreme Court Activism and Restraint* (Lexington, Mass.: D. C. Heath, 1982), pp. 277–301 (quotation on p. 295). See Jeffrey A. Segal and Harold J. Spaeth, *The Supreme Court and the Attitudinal Model* (New York: Cambridge University Press, 1993), for the most recent statement of the view that Supreme Court justices vote their policy choices. For a study that challenges the premise that Supreme Court justices should be viewed primarily as political, not legal, actors, see Lee Epstein and Joseph F. Kobylka, *The Supreme Court and Legal Change: Abortion and the Death Penalty* (Chapel Hill: University of North Carolina Press, 1992), pp. 301–310. For a study that assumes that the Supreme Court is constitutive, not instrumental, in its decisionmaking, see H. N. Hirsch, *A Theory of Liberty: The Constitution and Minorities* (New York: Routledge, 1992), which argues that at the core of Supreme Court decisionmaking and social change is the way the Supreme Court analyzes social reality in the light of precedent, that is, the way it interprets "social facts." Also William F. Harris II, *The Interpretable Constitution* (Baltimore: Johns Hopkins University Press, 1993), pp. xiii and 46–83, for the view that the Constitution consists of two texts, the Constitution itself and what he calls the text as "the working polity which it signifies." Harris, as with Hirsch's use of the concept of "social facts," is trying to link up Supreme Court decisionmaking to on-the-street behavior through the introduction of important new constitutional theories. Again, both view Supreme Court decisionmaking as what I have called a constitutive process.

53. Chapter 11, "Libertarian Restraint: Justice Frankfurter," pp. 210–226 in Pritchett, *Civil Liberties*.

Chapter 2. Equal Protection on the Warren Court

1. Richard Funston, *Constitutional Counter-Revolution? The Warren Court and the Burger Court: Judicial Policy Making in Modern America* (Cambridge, Mass.: Schenckman, 1977), p. 302.

2. Martin Shapiro, "Father and Sons: The Court, The Commentators, and the Search for Values," in Vincent Blasi, ed., *The Burger Court: The Counter-Revolution That Wasn't* (New Haven, Conn.: Yale University Press, 1983), pp. 225, 219, 237, and 220.

3. Vincent Blasi, "The Rootless Activism of the Burger Court," in Blasi, *The Burger Court*, pp. 214, 216, and 212.

4. Anthony Lewis, "Historic Change in the Supreme Court," in Leonard Levy, ed., *The Supreme Court under Earl Warren* (New York: Quadrangle Books, 1972), p. 78.

5. G. Edward White, "Earl Warren as Jurist," *Virginia Law Review* 67 (April 1981): 461, 462, 541, and 537.

6. See Chapter 4, "Egalitarianism and the Warren Court," pp. 98–169, in Philip B. Kurland, *Politics, the Constitution, and the Warren Court* (Chicago: University of Chicago Press, 1970).

7. *The Warren Court: Constitutional Decision as an Instrument of Reform* (Cambridge, Mass.: Harvard University Press, 1968), p. 6.

8. "Introduction," in Levy, *The Supreme Court under Earl Warren*, p. 16.

9. Blasi, "The Rootless Activism," p. 216.

10. Funston, *Constitutional Counter-Revolution?* p. 305.

11. White, "Earl Warren as Jurist," pp. 540–542.

12. Thus, visions of polity in the Constitution, not only individual rights principles, may be viewed as open-ended and not necessarily based on beliefs of the Founders. Polity principles are subject to nonoriginalist interpretations.

13. Levy, "Introduction," p. 5.

14. Funston, *Constitutional Counter-Revolution?* p. 300.

15. Cox, *The Warren Court*, pp. 7, 8, and 10.

16. Funston, *Constitutional Counter-Revolution?* p. 310.

17. Philip Kurland, "The Court Should Decide Less and Explain More," in Levy, *The Supreme Court under Earl Warren*, pp. 228–238.

18. Funston, *Constitutional Counter-Revolution?* pp. 301–305.

19. Robert G. McCloskey, "Deeds without Doctrine: Civil Rights in the 1960 Term of the Supreme Court," *American Political Science Review* 61 (1962): 71, as quoted in Clifford M. Lytle, *The Warren Court and Its Critics* (Tucson: University of Arizona Press, 1968), p. 101.

20. "Towards Neutral Principles in Constitutional Law," *Harvard Law Review* 73 (1959): 15.

21. See Lytle, *The Warren Court and Its Critics*, pp. 105 and 107.

22. Anthony Lewis, "Earl Warren," in Richard Sayler, Barry B. Boyer, and Robert Gooding, Jr., eds., *The Warren Court: A Critical Analysis* (New York: Chelsea House, 1969), pp. 3–4.

23. Cox, *The Warren Court*, pp. 21–23.

24. White, "Earl Warren as Jurist," p. 543.

25. Funston, *Constitutional Counter-Revolution?* p. 306.

26. Kurland, *Politics, the Constitution, and the Warren Court*, p. xxiii.

27. Funston, *Constitutional Counter-Revolution?* pp. 313–314. As I contend in Chapter 3, Funston places the cart before the horse. By focusing on the Supreme Court in explaining the decline in the legitimacy of American politics, Funston fails to base the problem of the decline in our trust of government, as Lowi does, on the growth of relativist democratic theory and the resulting faith in interest group politics and institutional practices viewed as good in themselves, thus undermining the public-private distinction in Federalist 10.

28. Ibid., p. 322.

29. Robert Bennett, "The Burger Court and the Poor," in Blasi, *The Burger Court*, pp. 47–56. See Funston, *Constitutional Counter-Revolution?* pp. 66–73; Shapiro, "Fathers and Sons," p. 219; Bernard Schwartz, *The Ascent of Pragmatism: The Burger*

274   *Court in Action* (New York: Addison-Wesley, 1990), pp. 288–292; Jacob W. Landynski, "Justice Lewis F. Powell, Jr.: Balance Wheel of the Court;" and Charles M. Lamb and Stephen C. Halpern, "The Burger Court and Beyond," in Charles M. Lamb and Stephen C. Halpern, eds., *The Burger Court: Political and Judicial Profiles* (Urbana: University of Illinois Press, 1991), pp. 292–294 and 437.

30. 304 U.S. 144 (1938), pp. 152–153, n. 4.
31. 314 U.S. 160 (1941), pp. 174–175.
32. Ibid., p. 178.
33. 316 U.S. 535 (1942), p. 541.
34. 351 U.S. 12 (1956), pp. 15–19 (quote on p. 19).
35. Ibid., pp. 20–23.
36. 380 U.S. 89 (1965), p. 99.
37. 383 U.S. 663 (1966), pp. 663–668.
38. Ibid., p. 678.
39. Ibid., pp. 680–686.
40. 395 U.S. 621 (1969), pp. 627–628.
41. 357 U.S. 116 (1958), pp. 126 and 129.
42. Laurence Tribe, "Structural Due Process," *Harvard Civil Rights–Civil Liberties Law Review* 10 (1975): 269–321.
43. 381 U.S. 1 (1965), pp. 14 and 16–17.
44. Ibid., pp. 20–23.
45. Ibid., pp. 23–26.
46. 388 U.S. 1 (1967), p. 2.
47. Ibid., pp. 10–11.
48. Ibid., pp. 8–10 and 12.
49. See Shapiro, "Fathers and Sons," p. 219.
50. *Shapiro v. Thompson*, 394 U.S. 618 (1969), note 8; see also *U.S. v. Guest* (1966); *Corfield v. Coryell* (1823); *Edwards v. California* (1941); *Passenger Cases* (1949); *Kent v. Dulles* (1958); *Aptheker v. Secretary of State* (1964); *Zemel v. Rusk* (1965).
51. *Shapiro v. Thompson*, 394 U.S. 618 (1969), pp. 631–632.
52. Ibid., pp. 637–638.
53. Ibid., p. 648.
54. Ibid., p. 649.
55. Ibid., pp. 655–676.
56. Ibid., p. 662.
57. See Mark Tushnet, *Red, White, and Blue* (Cambridge, Mass.: Harvard University Press, 1988), p. 197; and Jonathan Casper, "The Supreme Court and National Policy Making," *American Political Science Review* 70 (1976): 50.
58. Henry Abraham, *The Judicial Process*, 5th ed. (New York: Oxford University Press, 1986), p. 293. This number is quite small when compared to the overall workload of the Court, which "decides" in some degree each year over 5,000 cases but hears fully with oral arguments and written opinions between 150 and 200 cases. The Warren Court declared only 25 acts of Congress unconstitutional in sixteen years (1.56 per year), and the Burger Court only 34 in its seventeen years (2 per year). Thus declaring acts of Congress unconstitutional is a poor determinant of the relationship of law and politics and of the impact of the Supreme Court on our political system and society. Cases that involve directly the constitutionality of national laws do not offer a picture of the Supreme Court as a monitor of national government action. See David M. O'Brien, *The Storm Center*, 3d ed. (New York: W. W. Norton, 1993), p. 63, for a list-

ing of Supreme Court cases overruled, acts of Congress declared unconstitutional, and state laws and municipal ordinances overturned by the Supreme Court.

59. Casper, "The Supreme Court and National Policy Making," pp. 50–63.

60. This discussion is based on Richard Funston, "The Supreme Court and Critical Elections," *American Political Science Review* 69 (1975): 795–811 (quotation on p. 810).

61. Dahl, "Decision-Making in a Democracy: The Supreme Court as a National Policy-maker," *Journal of Public Law* 6 (1957): 285 and 294.

62. An alternative explanation might be that segregation was not ended because of deep and irremediable structural inequalities in the pluralist political system itself (such as the congressional committee system and states' right principles) that retard the process of incremental and orderly change.

63. See Tushnet, *Red, White, and Blue*, pp. 196–201, for a view of Dahl as a legal realist whose political science approach has been appropriated by lawyers. While accepting some of Dahl's views, Tushnet still fears judicial tyranny because politics—that is, the amending process, control of court jurisdiction, and appointment of new justices—is limited in its ability to constrain the Supreme Court. Thus, two legal realists, a moderate from the 1950s and a radical from the 1980s, are united in their opposition to constitutional principles and theory as a limit on politics.

64. Dahl, "Decision-making in a Democracy," p. 294.

65. Laurence Tribe, *God Save This Honorable Court* (New York: Random House, 1985), pp. 74–76 and 140–141.

66. Vincent Blasi, "The Rootless Activism of the Burger Court," in Blasi, *The Burger Court*, p. 216.

67. *Shapiro v. Thompson*, 394 U.S. 618 (1969), pp. 639–641.

68. Adamany, "Legitimacy, Realigning Elections, and the Supreme Court," *Wisconsin Law Review* (1973): 808–811.

69. See, for example, Kennedy and Scalia's position in *Texas v. Johnson* (1989), the flag burning case, or the recent abortion rights opinion in *Planned Parenthood of Southeastern Pennsylvania v. Casey* (1992). We also see this phenomenon in race discrimination cases, such as *Palmer v. Thompson* (1971) and *Crawford v. Board of Education* (1982), and in Communist subversion cases; *U.S. v. O'Brien* (1968), the draft card burning case; *Roth v. United States* (1957), the obscenity case; *Brandenburg v. Ohio* (1969), the Ku Klux Klan subversive advocacy case; and the passport cases. In all these cases justices supported polity and rights principles counter to their policy concerns.

70. Shapiro, "The Constitution and Economic Rights," in M. Judd Harmon, ed., *Essays on the Constitution of the United States* (Port Washington, N.Y.: Kennikat Press, 1978), p. 86.

71. Shapiro, "The Supreme Court: From Warren to Burger," in Anthony King, ed., *The New American Political System*, 2d version (Washington, D.C.: American Enterprise Institute, 1990), pp. 181 and 191.

72. Ibid., p. 201.

73. As I shall explore in the next chapter, Shapiro also trivializes the role of constitutional theory, theories of polity, and the influence of justices' previously formed polity rights principles on judicial decisionmaking and on doctrinal change.

74. See Martin Shapiro, "Political Jurisprudence, Public Law, and Post-Consequentialist Ethics: Comment on Professors Barber and Smith," *Studies in American Political Development* 3 (1989): 88–102.

75. White, "Earl Warren as Jurist," p. 462.

76. Ibid., pp. 477–478 and 481–486.

77. Ibid., pp. 550–551.

78. See Bernard Schwartz, *Superchief: Earl Warren and His Supreme Court—A Judicial Biography* (New York: New York University Press, 1983), for a Warren-centric interpretation of the Warren Court era.

Chapter 3. Misperceiving the Warren Court: The Limits of Instrumentalism

1. (New Haven, Conn.: Yale University Press, 1982), pp. 2 and 10.

2. Michael Perry, *Morality, Politics, and Law* (New York: Oxford University Press, 1988), pp. 164 and 165.

3. See Edward A. Purcell, Jr., *The Crisis of Democratic Theory: Scientific Naturalism and the Problem of Value* (Lexington: University Press of Kentucky, 1973) (quotation on p. 49).

4. This section is based on ibid. (quotations on pp. 201, 202, 204–205, and 210–211).

5. See ibid., Chapter 13, "Relativist Democratic Theory and Postwar America," pp. 235–266, for this argument (quotations from pp. 253–254).

6. David Truman, *The Governmental Process: Political Interests and Public Opinion* (New York: Alfred A. Knopf, [1951] 1964), p. 261. The remainder of this section is based on Chapter 6, "Internal Politics: The Problem of Cohesion," pp. 156–187; Chapter 7, "Internal Politics: The Tasks of Leadership," pp. 188–210; Chapter 16, "Group Politics and Representative Democracy," pp. 501–535; and pp. 3–5 and 333–336.

7. Purcell, *The Crisis of Democratic Theory*, p. 260.

8. Robert A. Dahl, *A Preface to Democratic Theory* (Chicago: University of Chicago Press, 1956), p. 143.

9. Purcell, *The Crisis of Democratic Theory*, p. 260. See also Dahl, *A Preface to Democratic Theory*, Chapter 1, "Madisonian Democracy," pp. 4–34; Chapter 3, "Polyarchal Democracy," pp. 63–84; and Chapter 5, "American Hybrid," pp. 124–152, for his radical transformation of Federalist no. 10 principles and normative, evaluative principles of American political theory.

10. See Ronald C. Kahn, "The Burger Court, Boundary Setting, and Local and State Government Power," *Proteus* 4 (Fall 1987): 37–46, for a more extended argument about differences between Dahl's (and pluralists') interpretation of polity and those of critical pluralist scholars, such as Grant McConnell and Theodore Lowi.

11. Dahl, *Democracy in the United States*, 4th ed. (Boston: Houghton Mifflin, 1981) p. 173.

12. See Purcell, *The Crisis of Democratic Theory*, pp. 260–261.

13. See Dahl, *Democracy in the United States*, pp. 160–163, and "Decision Making in a Democracy: The Supreme Court as a National Policy-Maker," *Journal of Public Law* 6 (1957): 279–295.

14. Purcell, *The Crisis of Democratic Theory*, p. 262.

15. See references to these works in ibid., p. 314 (n. 61).

16. G. Edward White, "Earl Warren as Jurist," *Virginia Law Review* 67 (1981): 550–551.

17. See Purcell, *The Crisis of Democratic Theory*, Chapter 5, "The Rise of Legal Realism," pp. 74–95; Chapter 8, "Counterattack," pp. 140–141; Chapter 9, "Crisis in Jurisprudence," pp. 159–179; and Chapter 13, "Relativist Democratic Theory and Postwar America," pp. 247–249, for Purcell's analysis of the influence of non-Euclid-

eanism and scientific naturalism on the legal realist movement and his view of law and legal theory as well as the interpretive community's response to legal realism. Purcell stops the analysis in the 1950s and does not show the effects of non-Euclideanism and scientific naturalism on law and social science beyond the heyday of pluralist political analysis and of law as part of judicial process in a pluralist regime in the 1950s.

18. This section is based on ibid., Chapter 5, "The Rise of Legal Realism," pp. 75–94 (quotations on pp. 89, 91, and 94).

19. Nominalism is the doctrine that abstract concepts, general terms, or universals have no objective reference but exist only as names. Like particularism, it rejects the use of a priori conceptual tools or foundational principles and assumes that only objective behavior and facts and statistics constitute knowledge. Purcell writes, "Even more clearly did ethical relativism and, in a sense, ethical nihilism flow from the new objectivism. Particularism held that for a concept to be valid and meaningful it had to refer directly to an individual concrete thing. Thus, nominalistic particularism denied even the possibility of a criterion or norm, since by its definition a norm implies something above or beyond any particular object. Functionalism held that knowledge was based on and confined to practical operations, which denied the possibility of a further standard for the worth of the function itself." Ibid., p. 42.

20. Bruce Ackerman, *Reconstructing American Law* (Cambridge, Mass.: Harvard University Press, 1984), pp. 23–28.

21. Ibid., pp. 38–39 (quotation on p. 38, n. 9).

22. Ibid., p. 39–40. In the preface to the photoduplicated Hart and Sacks manuscript, "The Legal Process: Basic Problems in the Making and Application of Law" pp. iii–iv, the authors write, "A legal system *is* a system—a coordinated functioning whole made up of a set of interrelated, interacting parts. The solution of specific legal problems constantly requires an understanding of the functions and relationships of more than one institutional process and frequently of several. . . . Many of the most frequently recurring difficulties in the law [are not the law itself but rather] difficulties which are intrinsic in the whole enterprise of organizing and maintaining a society which will effectively serve the purposes which societies exist to serve." The authors then emphasize that lawyers must debate the nature of discretion for courts and other institutions while realizing the limits of judicial action in a complex regulatory state.

23. Hart and Sacks, "The Legal Process," pp. 6–9.

24. Sanford Levinson, *Constitutional Faith* (Princeton, N.J.: Princeton University Press, 1988), pp. 163–179.

25. Major works of Alexander Bickel include *Politics and the Warren Court* (New York: Harper and Row, 1965); *The Least Dangerous Branch: The Supreme Court at the Bar of Politics* (Indianapolis, Ind.: Bobbs-Merrill, 1962); *The Supreme Court and the Idea of Progress* (New Haven, Conn.: Yale University Press, 1978, first printed, 1970); and *The Morality of Consent* (New Haven, Conn.: Yale University Press, 1975). Several of Bickel's more important articles are "The Supreme Court, 1960 Term–Forward: The Passive Virtues," *Harvard Law Review* 75 (1961): 40, and "The Original Understanding of the Segregation Decision," *Harvard Law Review* 69 (1955): 1. See also Edward A. Purcell, Jr., "Alexander M. Bickel and the Post-Realist Constitution," *Harvard Civil Rights–Civil Liberties Law Review* 11 (1976): 521–564, and Anthony Kronman, "Alexander Bickel's Philosophy of Prudence," *Yale Law Journal* 94 (June 1985): 1567.

26. See Bickel, *The Least Dangerous Branch*, pp. 250–272.

27. See Bickel, *Politics and the Warren Court*, pp. 185–186; see also *The Supreme Court and the Idea of Progress*, pp. 112–116.

28. See *The Supreme Court and the Idea of Progress*, Chapter 3, "The Web of Subjectivity," pp. 44–100 and 114 (quotation).

29. Bickel, *The Morality of Consent*, p. 20.

30. See Purcell, "Alexander M. Bickel," pp. 521–564.

31. The following is based on Kronman, "Alexander Bickel's Philosophy of Prudence," pp. 1567–1597 (quotations on pp. 1569, 1570, 1573, 1587–1589, and 1597).

32. This ambiguity is caused by the fact that scholars such as Dahl and Truman say that their studies, and theories of politics, are descriptive and empirical, using value-free methods of social science. Yet their works are based on the (non-value-free) implicit prescriptive assumption that the American political system is unique among political systems because it runs very well indeed, when compared with not only totalitarian but also nontotalitarian political systems, such as those in Europe, where compromise is not supported as a basic value and there is greater interest in ideological conflicts between right and left than in being pragmatic.

33. See Paul Freund, *The Supreme Court of the United States: Its Business, Purposes, and Performance* (Cleveland, Ohio: World, 1961).

34. Ibid., pp. 189–190.

35. Ibid., pp. 114–115.

36. Wechsler's two most important contributions are "Towards Neutral Principles of Constitutional Law," in Herbert Wechsler, ed., *Principles, Politics, and Fundamental Law: Selected Essays* (Cambridge, Mass.: Harvard University Press, 1961), pp. 3–48, and "The Political Safeguards of Federalism," *Columbia Law Review* 54 (1954): 542–550.

37. Wechsler, "Towards Neutral Principles," pp. 17–29.

38. Purcell, *The Crisis of Democratic Theory*, pp. 255–256.

39. Ibid., p. 255

40. Kronman, like most legalists, points his discussion to rights values today and not to differences in polity values by scholars today or in the Bickel period. He does show how rights values, moral values, were a muted, unclear category of thought. In Bickel's theory, it was just there, only to come out from internal decision-making, the outcome of which is balanced with pluralist polity principles or prudence. In addition, Kronman assumes that it was the difference between outcomes wanted by scholars today and Bickel's prudence that motivated opposition or disregard for his constitutional theory. Again this view does not pay homage to important differences in pluralist and critical pluralist structural analyses about politics among Bickel, and Bickel supporters today, and those who oppose his prudence.

41. Purcell, *The Crisis of Democratic Theory*, p. 257.

42. Dahl, "Decision-Making in a Democracy," 291 and 293–294.

43. Ibid., pp. 278–281.

44. Owen Fiss, "Objectivity and Interpretation," *Stanford Law Review* 34 (1982): 755–762.

45. Richard Funston, "The Supreme Court and Critical Elections," *American Political Science Review* 69 (1975): 808–811.

46. See Fiss, "Objectivity and Interpretation," pp. 746–750, for why the interpretive community is important to judicial decisionmaking, to the boundedness of constitutional choices, and to the legitimacy of the rule of law. These arguments have particular resonance with regard to Supreme Court justices, given their responsibilities to consider constitutional questions concerning conflict in society.

47. Martin Shapiro, Chapter 10, "The Supreme Court: From Warren to Burger,"

in Anthony King, ed., *The New American Political System* (Washington, D.C.: American Enterprise Institute, 1978), pp. 209–210 and 201.

48. Martin Shapiro, "Fathers and Sons: The Court, the Commentators, and the Search for Values," in Vincent Blasi, *The Burger Court: The Counter-Revolution That Wasn't* (New Haven, Conn.: Yale University Press, 1983), pp. 236–238.

49. Shapiro, "The Supreme Court," pp. 188–194 and 206, and "Fathers and Sons," pp. 218–225, 226–228, and 236–238.

50. Ibid., p. 238.

51. G. Edward White, "Earl Warren as Jurist," *Virginia Law Review* 67 (1981): 541.

52. Ibid., pp. 539–542.

53. Ibid., pp. 461–551 and 548–549.

54. Ibid., p. 464. For the Hart and Sacks argument see "The Legal Process."

55. Ibid., p. 465.

56. Ibid.

57. Theodore Lowi, *The End of Liberalism: The Second Republic of the United States*, 2d ed. (New York: Norton, 1969), pp. 50–63 and 271–298. See Chapter 6, pp. 184–185, for a discussion of the relationship of Lowi's critical pluralist interpretation of American politics to developments in constitutional theory in the 1970s and 1980s.

58. Grant McConnell, *Private Power and American Politics* (New York: Alfred A. Knopf, 1966), and Lowi, *The End of Liberalism*, for the two major critical pluralist interpretations of American politics, which criticize the apologetic pluralist interpretations of American politics of Robert Dahl and David Truman.

Chapter 4. Constituting the Separation of Church and State

Chapter 4 is a substantially revised version of "Polity and Rights Values in Conflict: The Burger Court, Ideological Interests, and the Separation of Church and State," *Studies in American Political Development* 3 (1989): 279–293, and "Ideology, Religion, and the First Amendment," in Michael McCann and Gerald Houseman, eds., *Judging the Constitution: Critical Essays on Judicial Lawmaking*, (Boston: Scott Foresman, Little, Brown, 1989), pp. 409–441.

1. See Vincent Blasi, "The Rootless Activism of the Burger Court," Chapter 10 in Vincent Blasi, ed., *The Burger Court: The Counter-Revolution That Wasn't* (New Haven, Conn.: Yale University Press, 1983), pp. 198–217, and Bernard Schwartz, *The Ascent of Pragmatism: The Burger Court in Action* (New York: Addison-Wesley, 1990) and additional works on the Burger Court cited in note 1 of Chapter 1.

2. Blasi, "The Rootless Activism of the Burger Court," p. 212.

3. Martin Shapiro, "Fathers and Sons: The Court, the Commentators, and the Search for Values," Chapter 10 in Blasi, *The Burger Court*, p. 230.

4. See Blasi, *The Burger Court*; Richard Y. Funston, *Constitutional Counter Revolution? The Warren Court and Burger Court: Judicial Policy Making in Modern America* (New York: John Wiley and Sons, 1977); Francis Lee, ed., *Neither Conservative nor Liberal: The Burger Court on Civil Rights and Liberties* (Malabar, Fla.: Robert E. Krieger, 1983); William R. Thomas, *The Burger Court and Civil Liberties*, rev. ed. (Brunswick, Ohio: King's Court Communications, 1979); Herman Schwartz, ed., *The Burger Years: Rights and Wrongs in the Supreme Court, 1969–1986* (New York: Penguin Books, 1987); and Charles M. Lamb and Stephen C. Halpern, eds., *The Burger Court: Political and Judicial Profiles* (Chicago: University of Illinois Press, 1991).

5. Blasi, "The Rootless Activism" (quotations from pp. 216, 211, and 200).

6. Ibid., pp. 210–211.

7. Schwartz, *The Ascent of Pragmatism*, p. 401.

8. Blasi, "The Rootless Activism," p. 211.

9. Schwartz, *The Ascent of Pragmatism*, p. 400.

10. Ibid., p. 408. Schwartz writes of the Burger Court, "We are all activists now," and of *U.S. v. Nixon* (1974), the case that required the president to surrender the White House tapes in the Watergate case, "The *Nixon* decision process demonstrates the willingness of the Justices to mold the crucial constitutional principles to accord with their individual policy perceptions."

11. Ibid., pp. 411–412.

12. Blasi, *The Burger Court*, p. 211.

13. In this chapter I have used the term "process" in place of the term "polity" to refer to the principles in the religion clauses that inform the relationship between public bodies and private, religious institutions. I did this because many polity principles in the establishment clause, such as a limitation on the entanglement between government and religion, speak to the government's relationship to the learning process *within* parochial schools or the ability of religious institutions to be free of government direction, support, or opposition.

14. The dilemma is, given a clear separation of public and private space in liberal legal thought, how can constitutional law protect individuals, such as with regard to freedom of religion or in spheres of privacy in matters of sexual relations, against negative actions in private space caused by individuals and such factors as gender roles or the effects of the economic system? Or should we consider, as Cass Sunstein does in *The Partial Constitution* (Cambridge, Mass.: Harvard University, 1993), pp. 25–37, that much of private space is a product of public choices. See Karl Marx, "On the Jewish Question," in Robert Tucker, *The Marx-Engels Reader*, 2d ed. (New York: W. W. Norton, 1978), pp. 26–52, for an analysis of how under liberalism religious liberty and separation of church and state, like property, are part of the broader separation of thought and reality into public/political and private/civil spheres, thus allowing self-interest rather than collective equalitarian values to dominate.

15. As defined in Chapter 1, polity and rights principles are analytically distinct and serve as heuristic tools for understanding the nature of doctrinal change and judicial decisionmaking. Constitutional theories and interpretations of the Warren and Burger Courts that emphasize either polity or rights principles, but not both, and undervalue the connectedness of polity and rights principles are unable to interpret the Supreme Court's actions when it makes constitutional choices and therefore fail as guides to future Court action.

16. See Harold J. Spaeth and Stuart H. Teger, "Activism and Restraint: A Cloak for the Justices' Policy Preferences," in Stephen C. Halpern and Charles M. Lamb, eds., *Supreme Court Activism and Restraint* (Lexington, Mass.: D.C. Heath, 1982), for a view of Supreme Court decisionmaking different from the one argued here.

Ideological interests can be discerned when justices attempt to pattern case merits along systematic, nonrandom outlines and make them conform to particular philosophies. For example, the fact that individual justices have advocated widely varying interpretations of the standard established in *Lemon v. Kurtzman* (1971) for deciding whether a government action violates the separation of church and state results in differing prohibitions on state intervention in religious affairs. This patterning of cases to principles is a more flexible positivism for Justices Harry Blackmun, Lewis Powell, Sandra Day O'Connor, William Brennan, and Thurgood Marshall, as distinguished from former Chief Justice Warren Burger and Justices Byron White and William Rehnquist, who are ideological in the strictest, most rigid sense. A flexible ideology consists of process and rights principles serving to inform the structural logic of judicial *choices*, not just guaranteed or expected outcomes. For example, Justice Stevens has a striking fixation with rule of law ideals—notions of impartiality and equality—whereas Justices Brennan and Marshall are more concerned with questions of moral right or wrong and come to each case with specific questions to ask. In this area of Burger Court jurisprudence at least, these justices can vote for the "wall of separation" between church and state, their personal perspectives congruent with the issues at hand. Ideological commitments involve case-by-case issue *definition* rather than just *determination*.

17. See, for example, the individual autonomy notions of Justice O'Connor in *Wallace v. Jaffree* (1985) and *Grand Rapids School District v. Ball* (1985).

18. My proposed approach differs from that of modern constitutional scholars who see their role as *advocacy* of a rights- or process-based interpretation. John Hart Ely, for example, views the Constitution as consisting of process values to allow groups equitable participation in political structures. He advocates judicial review to allow equal respect for all discrete and insular minorities and analyzes Supreme Court choices with this main goal in mind. Laurence Tribe and Michael Perry, by contrast, support a wider non-process-based rights creation by the Court. This methodology asks the scholar to explore empirically the actual reliance on and relationship among constitutive process and rights norms used by justices in deciding cases before considering the normative and policy implications of basing constitutional choices on these norms. See John Hart Ely, *Democracy and Distrust: A Theory of Judicial Review* (Cambridge, Mass.: Harvard University Press, 1980); Laurence Tribe, *American Constitutional Law*, 1st ed. (Mineola, N.Y.: Foundation Press, 1978); Jesse Choper, *Judicial Review and the National Political Process: A Functional Reconsideration of the Role of the Supreme Court* (Chicago: University of Chicago Press, 1980); and Michael Perry, *The Constitution, the Courts, and Human Rights* (New Haven, Conn.: Yale University Press, 1982) and *Morality, Politics and Law* (New York: Oxford University Press, 1988).

19. See note 1 of Chapter 1 for a full listing of scholars who view the Burger Court as primarily a pragmatic Court that is unique only because it did not engage in a counterrevolution to the Warren Court.

20. See David M. O'Brien, *Storm Center: The Supreme Court in American Politics*, 2d ed. (New York: W. W. Norton, 1990), pp. 309–323, for the view that the increasing number of plurality, concurring, and dissenting opinions are due to less obeisance by the justices to collective or institutional concerns. This change is driven, in part, by the Court's becoming in effect nine law firms, not by ideological differences among the justices. I argue that one must look to a complexity of polity and rights principles and their relationship, driven by developments in the interpretive community, to explain the increase in the number of plurality, concurring, and dissenting opinions.

21. See David O'Brien, "The Supreme Court: From Warren to Burger to Rehnquist," *Political Science* 20 (Winter 1987): 16, for data that show that Justice Powell voted against the prevailing opinion in case selection least often—seventy times.

22. Blasi, "Rootless Activism," p. 211.

23. He also resurrected in *Aguilar v. Felton* the "political divisiveness" prong he had declared obsolete in *Wolman v. Walter*.

24. *Wolman v. Walter*, 433 U.S. 229 [1977], pp. 264–266.

25. 403 U.S. 602 (1971), pp. 623–624.

26. See Ronald Kahn, "The Burger Court, Boundary Setting, and Local and State Government Power," *Proteus* 4 (1987): pp. 37–46, for a review of the pluralist–critical

pluralist debate in modern political science and constitutional theory and for evidence that process-based norms supporting state and local authority are central to the jurisprudence of Justices Burger, White, Rehnquist, Powell, and O'Connor.

27. Burger writes, "The potential for political divisiveness related to religious belief and practice is aggravated in these two statutory programs by the need for continuing annual appropriations and the likelihood of larger and larger demands as costs and populations grow." In comparing how this aid program is different from the practice since the establishment of exemption from taxes for religious institutions, he writes, "We have no long history of state aid to church related educational institutions comparable to 200 years of tax exemption for churches. Indeed, the state programs before us today represent something of an innovation. We have already noted that modern governmental programs have self-perpetuating and self-expanding propensities." *Lemon v. Kurtzman*, 403 U.S. 602 (1971), pp. 623–624.

28. *Meek v. Pittenger*, 421 U.S. 349 (1975), p. 365.

29. *Wolman v. Walter*, 433 U.S. 229 (1977), p. 259.

30. *Lemon v. Kurtzman*, 403 U.S. 602 (1971), p. 668.

31. *Lynch v. Donnelly*, 465 U.S. 668 (1984), p. 689.

32. *Committee for Public Education and Religious Liberty v. Nyquist*, 413 U.S. 756 (1973), p. 797.

33. *Wolman v. Walter*, 433 U.S. 229 (1977), p. 263.

34. *Aguilar v. Felton*, 473 U.S. 402 (1985), pp. 416–417.

35. *Lynch v. Donnelly*, 465 U.S. 668 (1984), pp. 686 and 701.

36. See Ronald Kahn, "God Save Us from the Coercion Test: Constitutive Decision-making, Polity Principles, and Religious Freedom," *Case Western Reserve Law Review* 43 (1993): 983–1020, for an analysis of recent Rehnquist Court establishment clause cases. I demonstrate that in the present Supreme Court, consisting of a majority of Reagan and Bush appointees including Justices O'Connor, Kennedy, and Souter, the process prong of the *Lemon* test—that the state not entangle itself in religion or cause political divisiveness by supporting religion—is by no means dead. Most importantly, I argue that the importance of this prong of the *Lemon* test in protecting the individual rights of believers and nonbelievers is demonstrated by the current advocacy by scholars who favor increased aid to religious schools of a test based on rights only—the "no coercion" test—in establishment clause cases: the state must not coerce individuals in their free exercise of religion, and this alone, not polity principles, should inform establishment clause cases.

37. *Wolman v. Walter*, 433 U.S. 229 (1977), p. 262.

38. See Grant McConnell, *Private Power and American Democracy* (New York: Alfred A. Knopf, 1966), and Theodore Lowi, *The End of Liberalism*, 2d ed. (New York: W. W. Norton, 1979), pp. 295–313, for critical pluralist visions of the American political system that counter the pluralist visions of Robert Dahl and David Truman.

39. *Aguilar v. Felton*, 473 U.S. 402 (1985), pp. 424–425.

40. *Lemon v. Kurtzman*, 403 U.S. 602 (1971), p. 664.

41. *Roemer v. Board of Public Works of Maryland*, 426 U.S. 736 (1976), p. 768.

42. *Lemon v. Kurtzman*, 403 U.S. 602 (1971), p. 670.

43. *Roemer v. Board of Public Works of Maryland*, 426 U.S. 736 (1976), p. 761.

44. Ibid., p. 769.

45. *Walz v. Tax Commission of New York*, 397 U.S. 664 (1970), p. 714.

46. *Lemon v. Kurtzman*, 403 U.S. 602 (1971), p. 634.

47. See *Roemer v. Board of Public Works of Maryland*, 426 U.S. 736 (1976), p. 769, in which Justices White and Rehnquist take, by and large, a more principled stance to-

ward reliance upon statistical data for determination of case outcomes than their pro-cess-deferential colleagues on the Court (particularly O'Connor and Powell).

48. *Committee for Public Education and Religious Liberty v. Nyquist*, 413 U.S. 756 (1973), p. 802.

49. *Lynch v. Donnelly*, 465 U.S. 668 (1984), p. 701.

50. *Committee for Public Education and Religious Liberty v. Nyquist*, 413 U.S. 756 (1973), pp. 662–671.

51. *Lemon v. Kurtzman*, 403 U.S. 602 (1971), p. 664.

52. *Lynch v. Donnelly*, 465 U.S. 668 (1984), pp. 689–690.

53. *Aguilar v. Felton*, 473 U.S. 402 (1985), pp. 424–425.

54. *Lynch v. Donnelly*, 465 U.S. 668 (1984), pp. 689–690.

55. *Wolman v. Walter*, 433 U.S. 229 (1977), p. 263.

56. *Aguilar v. Felton*, 473 U.S. 402 (1985), pp. 409–410.

57. *Grand Rapids School District v. Ball*, 473 U.S. 373 (1985), p. 389.

58. *Walz v. Tax Commission of New York*, 397 U.S. 664 (1970), pp. 700 and 716.

59. *Grand Rapids School District v. Ball*, 473 U.S. 373 (1985), pp. 398–401.

60. *Wallace v. Jaffree*, 472 U.S. 38 (1985), p. 80.

61. *Lynch v. Donnelly*, 465 U.S. 668 (1984), pp. 687–694. See Paul W. Kahn, "The Court, the Community, and the Judicial Balance: The Jurisprudence of Justice Powell," *Yale Law Journal* 97 (1987): 1–60, for the argument that Powell was too def-erential to community values.

62. See *Epperson v. Arkansas* (1968), invalidating Arkansas' law that forbade the teaching of evolution, and *Edwards v. Aguillard* (1987), which found unconstitutional a Louisiana law requiring the teaching of creationism to balance the teaching of evolu-tion.

63. Anthony Lewis, "Foreword," in Blasi, *The Burger Court*, p. ix.

64. See Chapter 6 for a detailed analysis of these changes in constitutional theory. Also see Laurence H. Tribe. "Unraveling National League of Cities: The New Federal-ism and Affirmative Rights to Essential Government Services," *Harvard Law Review* 90 (1977): 1065–1104; Frank I. Michelman, "States' Rights and States' Roles: Permuta-tions of 'Sovereignty' in *National League of Cities v. Usery,*" *Yale Law Journal* 86 (1977): 1165–1195; and Richard Davies Parker, "The Past of Constitutional Theory—And Its Future," *Ohio State Law Journal* 42 (1981): 223–259, for rights-oriented views of con-stitutional issues in areas in which polity principles dominate. See Ely, *Democracy and Distrust*, for a single-minded polity or process view of the Constitution and constitu-tional interpretation. See Ronald Kahn, "Process and Rights Principles in Modern Constitutional Theory," *Stanford Law Review* 36 (1984): 253–269, for a discussion of the consequences of viewing the Constitution exclusively in either polity or rights terms as Ely and Tribe/Michelman do.

See Roberto Unger, *Law in Modern Society* (New York: Free Press, 1976), pp. 203–204, for a discussion of the basic dilemma of modern liberal jurisprudence: how to meet the objectives of formality, equity, and substantive justice. Bright-line distinc-tions between church and state achieve formality and equality to a degree but may un-dermine free exercise values; securing substantive justice for free exercise rights in some cases undermines formality and equity. For example, in *Wisconsin v. Yoder* (1972), the Supreme Court allowed Amish children to leave school prior to the year mandated by state law because the Court viewed the Amish as a traditional religious community, unlike other unnamed sects. Also see Mark Tushnet, *Red, White and Blue: A Critical Analysis of Constitutional Law* (Cambridge, Mass.: Harvard University Press, 1988) for a critique of liberal constitutional law as failing to meet its principles.

65. Shapiro, "Fathers and Sons," p. 238.

66. See Kahn, "The Burger Court, Boundary Setting, and State and Local Power," pp. 37–46.

67. Blasi, "Rootless Activism," pp. 198–199.

68. John Brigham, *The Cult of the Robe* (Philadelphia: Temple University Press, 1987), pp. 21–22.

69. See J. David Greenstone and Paul E. Peterson, *Race and Authority in Urban Politics* (New York: Russell Sage Foundation, 1973), pp. 125–126, for an explanation of how the "ideological interests" of big city mayors for or against citizen participation or universalistic reform values led to choices that were not, in pragmatic terms, in their electoral and organizational interests. With regard to justices, it is even more to the point that they make constitutional choices based on polity and rights principles that differ from their policy wants.

70. See Brigham, *Cult of the Robe*, Chapters 1 and 2, argues that behavioralism as viewed by political scientists is undercut by ideologies of authority upon which the Supreme Court relies within its institutional framework and which impose constitutive characteristics on the values that motivate judicial action.

Chapter 5. Equal Protection on the Burger Court

1. See Martin Shapiro, "Fathers and Sons: The Court, the Commentators, and the Search for Values," in Vincent Blasi, ed., *The Burger Court: The Counter-Revolution That Wasn't* (New Haven, Conn.: Yale University Press, 1983), pp. 218–238, and the works listed in Chapter 1, note 4, for the policymaking approach.

2. Shapiro, "The Supreme Court: From Warren to Burger," in Anthony King, ed., *The New American Political System* (Washington, D.C.: American Enterprise Institute, 1978), pp. 202–203.

3. Ibid., pp. 209–210.

4. Ibid., p. 209.

5. Martin Shapiro, "The Constitution and Economic Rights," in M. Judd Harmon, ed., *Essays on the Constitution of the United States* (Port Washington, N.Y.: Kennikat Press, 1978), p. 90.

6. Shapiro, "The Supreme Court: From Warren to Burger," pp. 208–209.

7. Ibid., pp. 202–203; see pp. 205–209 for the comparison of Warren and Burger Court decisionmaking processes.

8. *San Antonio Independent School District v. Rodriguez*, 411 U.S. 1 (1973), pp. 18–44 (quotation on p. 29).

9. Ibid., p. 39.

10. Ibid., pp. 36–37.

11. Quoting *Dandridge v. Williams*, 397 U.S. 471 (1970), p. 487; and *San Antonio Independent School District v. Rodriguez*, 411 U.S. 1 (1973), pp. 43 and 44.

12. These include *Dandridge v. Williams* (1970), *Lindsey v. Normet* (1972), and *Jefferson v. Hackney* (1972). Following *Rodriguez*, other clear statements of polity principles occurred in such important cases as *Keys v. School District Number 1, Denver* (1973), *Milliken v. Bradley* (1974), *Warth v. Seldin* (1975), and especially *National League of Cities v. Usery* (1976).

13. *San Antonio Independent School District v. Rodriguez*, 411 U.S. 1 (1973), pp. 62–70.

14. Ibid., pp. 62–63.

15. Ibid., pp. 70–133.

16. Ibid., p. 99.

17. *Dunn v. Blumstein*, 405 U.S. 330 (1972), pp. 339–340.

18. *United States Department of Agriculture v. Moreno*, 413 U.S. 528 (1973), p. 534.

19. Ibid., p. 541.

20. *Memorial Hospital v. Maricopa County*, 415 U.S. 250 (1974), pp. 262–269.

21. Ibid., p. 255.

22. Ibid., p. 254.

23. This oft-cited case, which was discussed by Congress when it was deciding on the language of the Fourteenth Amendment, is used as evidence that fundamental rights and privileges, and immunities of citizens, exist beyond those expressly stated in the Constitution and its amendments.

24. In *Harris v. McRae* and *Roe v. Wade*, polity and rights principles are seen in the notion of potential life as a concern for the states and the decision to leave to the states the choice of permitting abortion in the third trimester. However, these principles are seen by a majority of the Court in a unique way because the issue is abortion, in regard to which the Court may feel it is engaging in a level of nonoriginalism beyond which it does not want to extend.

25. *Zobel v. Williams*, 457 U.S. 55 (1982) pp. 61–78 (Brennan quotation on p. 67).

26. *Plyler v. Doe*, 457 U.S. 202 (1982), pp. 210–254 (quotations on pp. 218, 220, 221–222, 230, 234, 242, 243, and 245).

27. It is interesting that in *Skinner v. Oklahoma* (1942), a case decided over ten years before the Warren Court era, the Supreme Court argues that to allow the sterilization of three-time chicken stealers but not three-time embezzlers or persons guilty of white collar crimes is to allow the state in the future to take away the right to procreate from groups of citizens who may not be favored by the majority, thus denying equal protection of the law.

28. The Vinson Court, in its higher education desegregation decisions such as *Sweatt v. Painter* (1950) and *McLaurin v. Oklahoma State Regents* (1950), set the precedents for *Brown*.

29. See Paul Brest, Chapter 6, "Race Discrimination," in Blasi, *The Burger Court*, pp. 120–121, for the view that the Burger Court was more innovative than the Warren Court in finding that civil rights statutes prohibit discriminatory effects, not merely discriminatory intentions.

30. *Warth v. Seldin*, 422 U.S. 490 (1975), pp. 498–523 (quotations on pp. 498, 499, 504, 522, and 523).

31. *INS v. Chadha*, 462 U.S. 919 (1983), pp. 941–942.

32. Justice Rehnquist did not take part in the consideration or decision of the case.

33. *United States v. Nixon*, 418 U.S. 683 (1974), pp. 704 and 706.

34. E.g., *Mobile v. Bolden* (1980), *Rogers v. Lodge* (1982), and *United Jewish Organizations v. Carey* (1977).

35. See Bernard Schwartz, *The Ascent of Pragmatism: The Burger Court in Action* (New York: Addison-Wesley, 1990), pp. 35–39. Schwartz views changes in the internal institutional process of the Supreme Court and the quality of leadership by the chief justice as the primary explanations for the far greater dissensus (concurring and dissenting opinions) among justices on the Burger Court as compared to the Warren Court. This internal process argument is quite similar to that of David O'Brien, *Storm Center: The Supreme Court in American Politics* (New York: W. W. Norton, 1986).

36. See Nancy Maveety, *Representation Rights and the Burger Years* (Ann Arbor:

University of Michigan Press, 1991), pp. 221–230, for an excellent study of the apportionment decisions on the Burger Court. Maveety finds a much more complex view of representation, group rights, and pluralism on the Burger Court compared to the Warren Court.

37. See, for example, *Young v. American Mini-Theaters* (1976) and *Heffron v. International Society for Krishna Consciousness* (1981).

38. Richard B. Stewart, "The Reformation of American Administrative Law," *Harvard Law Review* 88 (1975): 1669.

39. Vincent Blasi, "The Rootless Activism of the Burger Court," in Blasi, *The Burger Court*, p. 200.

40. See David M. O'Brien, *Storm Center: The Supreme Court in American Politics*, 2d ed. (New York: W. W. Norton, 1990), p. 182.

41. Ibid., p. 203.

42. Ibid., pp. 245 and 246.

43. Ibid., pp. 309–317.

44. Ibid., p. 319.

45. Schwartz, *The Ascent of Pragmatism*, pp. 1–11, 405–407, 411–412. See H. W. Perry, *Deciding to Decide: Agenda Setting in the United States Supreme Court* (Cambridge, Mass.: Harvard University Press, 1991), pp. 90–91, for a rejection of this view of Warren's significance compared to Burger's in these two Court eras.

46. Shapiro, "The Supreme Court: From Warren to Burger," p. 203.

Chapter 6. The Burger Court and Constitutional Theory

1. See Grant McConnell, *Private Power and American Democracy* (New York: Alfred A. Knopf, 1966); Theodore Lowi, *The End of Liberalism*, 2d ed. (New York: W. W. Norton, 1979); and William E. Connolly, ed., *The Bias of Pluralism* (New York: Atherton, 1969).

2. See Frank Michelman: "Welfare Rights in a Constitutional Democracy," *Washington University Law Quarterly* (1979): 577–593; "Political Markets and Community Self-Determination: Competing Judicial Models of Local Government Legitimacy," *Indiana Law Journal* 53 (1977–1978): 145–206. Laurence Tribe mirrors Michelman's *Usery* argument in "Unraveling National League of Cities: The New Federalism and Affirmative Rights to Essential Government Services," *Harvard Law Review* 90 (1977): 1065–1104; "Structural Due Process," *Harvard Civil Rights–Civil Liberties Law Review* 10 (1975): 269–321; and "The Emerging Reconstruction of Individual Rights and Institutional Design: Federalism, Bureaucracy and Due Process of Law Making" *Creighton Law Review* 10 (1977): 422–439. For other important works by constitutional scholars of the 1970s, see John Hart Ely, *Democracy and Distrust: A Theory of Judicial Review* (Cambridge, Mass.: Harvard University Press, 1980); Laurence Tribe, *American Constitutional Law*, 1st ed. (Mineola, N.Y.: Foundation Press, 1978); and Jesse Choper, *Judicial Review and the National Political Process: A Functional Reconsideration of the Role of the Supreme Court* (Chicago: University of Chicago Press, 1980).

3. See Stephen G. Breyer and Richard B. Stewart, *Administrative Law and Regulatory Policy* (Boston: Little, Brown, 1985), for an innovative text that uses structural inequality theory within the concept of the "reformation of administrative law." See also Michael W. McCann, *Taking Reform Seriously: Perspectives on Public Interest Liberalism* (Ithaca, N.Y.: Cornell University Press, 1986), for an important argument about how critical pluralist values have been placed within the public interest group move-

ment along with structural changes within government agencies that have widened access to government.

4. E. E. Schattschneider, *The Semi-Sovereign People* (New York: Holt, Rinehart & Winston, 1960).

5. See Ronald Kahn, "The Burger Court, Boundary Setting, and Local and State Government Power," *Proteus* 4 (Fall 1987): 37–46, for a discussion of pluralist and critical pluralist interpretations of polity in political science and constitutional theory.

6. See McConnell, *Private Power*, Chapter 4, "The Constituency," pp. 91–118.

7. See ibid., Chapter 5, "Private Government," pp. 119–152, for an argument about private interest groups that counters the views of David Truman, *The Government Process* (New York: Alfred A. Knopf, 1951).

8. See McConnell, *Private Power*, Chapter 10, "The Quest of the Public Interest," pp. 336–368.

9. Ibid., p. 68.

10. Grant McConnell, *The Modern Presidency* (New York: St. Martin's Press, 1976), and *Private Power*, pp. 88–118.

11. See Lowi, *The End of Liberalism*, pp. 50–61, for a definition of this concept.

12. Ibid., Chapter 11, "Towards Juridical Democracy," pp. 295–313.

13. See Chapter 4 for an analysis of the Warren Court–era constitutional theory of Herbert Wechsler, Alexander Bickel, and Paul Freund.

14. In addition to the works cited in note 2 see the following symposia issues on process reinforcement theory and judicial review: *New York University Law Review* 56 (1981): 259–582; *Ohio State Law Journal* 42 (1981): 1–434; and *University of Dayton Law Review* 8 (1983): 443–831.

15. See Ely, *Democracy and Distrust*, pp. 88–101 and 43–72.

16. See Richard D. Parker, "The Past of Constitutional Theory—and Its Future," *Ohio State Law Review* 42 (1981): 223–259, for the argument that Ely's process theory is based on simplistic notions of how political institutions operate.

17. See Chapter 3, "The Small Republic," pp. 15–24, Herbert Storing, *What The Anti-Federalists Were For* (Chicago: University of Chicago Press, 1981), and Chapter 1 of this book.

18. Ely, *Democracy and Distrust*, pp. 160–170.

19. See the following 1970s scholarship of Laurence Tribe: "The Supreme Court 1972 Term: Towards a Model of Roles in Due Process of Life and Law," *Harvard Law Review* 87 (1973): 1–53; "Structural Due Process," *Harvard Civil Rights–Civil Liberties Law Review* 10 (1975): 269–321; "Seven Pluralist Fallacies: In Defense of the Adversary Process—A Reply to Justice Rehnquist," *University of Miami Law Review* 22 (1976): 43–57; "Unraveling National League of Cities"; "The Emerging Reconnection of Individual Rights and Institutional Design: Federalism, Bureaucracy, and Due Process of Lawmaking," *Creighton Law Review* 10 (1977): 433–449; and "Perspectives on *Bakke*: Equal Protection, Procedural Fairness, or Structural Justice?" *Harvard Law Review* 92 (1979): 873–877. See also Parker, "The Past of Constitutional Theory."

20. Parker, "The Past of Constitutional Theory," p. 253.

21. See Laurence Tribe, "The Puzzling Persistence of Process-Based Consitutional Theories," *Yale Law Journal* 89 (1980): 1063–1080, for a critique of Ely's *Democracy and Distrust*. In the 1980s Tribe moved away from trying to incorporate polity principles into his jurisprudence, as seen in *Constitutional Choices* (Cambridge, Mass.: Harvard University Press, 1985), especially Part 3, "The Structure of Substantive Rights," pp. 165–246.

22. Tribe, "Seven Pluralist Fallacies," pp. 43–57.

23. Ibid., p. 53.

24. See Tribe, "Unraveling National League of Cities," and Frank Michelman, "States Rights and States Roles: Permutations of 'Sovereignty' in *National League of Cities v. Usery,*" *Yale Law Journal* 86 (1977): 1165–1195.

25. Tribe, "Unraveling National League of Cities," p. 1066.

26. Tribe, "Perspectives on *Bakke*," pp. 873–877.

27. Tribe, "The Supreme Court 1972 Term." In role-allocation theory it is argued that some types of choices are best not left to electoral politics. With regard to *Roe* Tribe argues that the decision whether to continue a pregnancy is so close to a religious choice that it should be made by the individual, not by elected officials.

28. See Parker, "The Past of Constitutional Theory," pp. 238–239, for the argument that Tribe seeks to protect the security of persons via-à-vis government as a basic value rather than advocating the principle of participation in the polity as a value that will bring citizens substantive rights.

29. Tribe, "The Puzzling Persistence of Process-Based Constitutional Theories," p. 1064.

30. See Tribe, *Constitutional Choices*, Part 3, pp. 165–267.

31. See "Speech as Power: Of Swastikas, Spending, and the Mask of 'Neutral Principles,' " in ibid., pp. 188–221.

32. See "Reorienting the Mirror of Justice: Gender, Economics, and the Illusion of the 'Natural,' " in ibid., pp. 238–246. See also Ronald Kahn, "Review Essay," *American Political Science Review* 80 (1986): 1315–1318, for a critique of this new direction in Tribe's scholarship.

33. See Tribe, "The Abortion Funding Conundrum: Inalienable Rights, Affirmative Duties, and the Dilemma of Dependence," *Harvard Law Review* 99 (1985): 330–343. See also Tribe, *Abortion: The Clash of Absolutes* (New York: W. W. Norton, 1990), especially, Chapter 6, "The Equation's Other Side: Does It Matter Whether the Fetus Is a Person?" pp. 113–138.

34. Chapter 4, "The Scope of National Power vis-à-vis the States," pp. 171–259 in Choper, *Judicial Review and the National Political Process.*

35. Chapter 2, "Non-interpretive Review, Federalism, and the Separation of Powers," pp. 37–60 in Michael Perry, *The Constitution, the Courts, and Human Rights* (New Haven, Conn.: Yale University Press, 1982).

36. Perry, *The Constitution, the Courts, and Human Rights*, p. 5.

37. Martin Shapiro, "Fathers and Sons: The Court, the Commentators, and the Search for Values," in Vincent Blasi, ed., *The Burger Court: The Counter-Revolution That Wasn't* (New Haven, Conn.: Yale University Press, 1983), p. 218.

38. Ibid., p. 220.

39. Ibid., p. 238.

40. We saw this legal realist bent in the last chapter in Shapiro's overemphasis on the place of institutional autonomy as a principle in Burger Court jurisprudence.

41. Shapiro, "The Constitution and Economic Rights," in M. Judd Harmon, *Essays on the Constitution of the United States* (Port Washington, N.Y.: Kennikat Press, 1978), p. 96.

42. Shapiro, "Fathers and Sons," p. 220.

43. See Michael Perry, *Morality, Politics, and Law* (New York: Oxford University Press, 1988), pp. 169–172; and Mark Tushnet, *Red, White, and Blue: A Critical Analysis of Constitutional Law* (Cambridge, Mass.: Harvard University Press, 1988), pp. 311–318. Perry's, Tushnet's, and Sanford Levinson's calls for a new civic republicanism and serious questions about continuing intervention by the Court are not based merely on

a desire to place into law the provisions of the welfare state and to develop a constitutional theory to justify it.

Shapiro is correct in emphasizing that the new commentators reject the view that values are simply a matter of individual preference and cannot be examined by logical discourse and that they reject the scientific naturalism and moral relativism of the 1950s. However, a closer look finds that these scholars do not suggest that a single cohesive set of moral values can sustain constitutional choices. Their opposition to moral skepticism is not transformed into a simplistic view of equality or any one theory as a guiding principle. (See Chapter 7.)

44. See Tribe, "The Puzzling Persistence of Process-Based Constitutional Theories," pp. 1063–1080.

45. Shapiro, "Fathers and Sons," pp. 220–225 and 236–238.

46. Ibid., pp. 225–226.

47. Ibid., 226.

48. This and the following paragraph are based on ibid., pp. 228–229.

49. Ibid., pp. 228–233.

50. Edward A. Purcell, Jr., *The Crisis of Democratic Theory* (Lexington: University Press of Kentucky, 1973), pp. 254–256.

51. I do not support the view that external interest group politics is the prime determinant of doctrinal change. For the most recent and filigreed statement of this argument, see Lee Epstein and Joseph F. Kobylka, *The Supreme Court and Legal Change: Abortion and the Death Penalty* (Chapel Hill: University of North Carolina Press, 1992).

52. See works by Alexander Bickel, Paul Freund, and Herbert Wechsler cited in notes 25, 33, and 36 of Chapter 3; by Jesse Choper, John Hart Ely, Michael Perry, and Laurence Tribe in note 18 of Chapter 4; and by Mark Tushnet and Sanford Levinson in the bibliography.

53. In addition to the works referred to in note 52, see works by Frank Michelman cited in note 2 of Chapter 6.

54. See Laurence Tribe, *Constitutional Choices* (Cambridge, Mass.: Harvard University Press, 1985); and Frank Michelman, "Forward: Traces of Self-Government," *Harvard Law Review* 4 (1986): 4–77.

Chapter 7. The Limits of Civic Republicanism

1. See Michael J. Perry, *Morality, Politics, and Law* (New York: Oxford University Press, 1988); Mark Tushnet, *Red, White, and Blue: A Critical Analysis of Constitutional Law* (Cambridge, Mass.: Harvard University Press, 1988); and Sanford Levinson, *Constitutional Faith* (Princeton, N.J.: Princeton University Press, 1988).

2. See Ronald Kahn, "Pluralism, Civic Republicanism, and Critical Theory," *Tulane Law Review* 63 (1989): 1475–1500, and "Review Essay: Hermeneutics and Constitutional Faith," *Polity* 32 (1989): 165–179, for a first critique of these civic republican constitutional visions.

3. See Perry, *Morality, Politics, and Law*, pp. 131–145, for a detailed, cogent analysis employing modern hermeneutics of the meaning of texts and the Constitution.

4. See ibid., pp. 62–63, 84–87 for Perry's view of what constitutes a person.

5. Ibid., p. 25.

6. Ibid., pp. 55 and 35–36.

7. Ibid., p. 102.

8. Ibid., pp. 85–86.

9. Ibid., p. 87.

10. Ibid., p. 98.

11. Ibid., pp. 157–158.

12. Ibid., pp. 182 and 153.

13. Ibid., pp. 72, 29, 32, and 34.

14. Ibid., pp. 89 and 20.

15. Chapter 2, "The Jurisprudence of Democracy," pp. 70–107, in Tushnet, *Red, White, and Blue*. The remainder of this section is based on ibid., Chapter 3, "Jurisprudence of Philosophy," pp. 108–146; Chapter 4, "Anti-formalism in Constitutional Theory," pp. 147–178; Chapter 5, "Intuitionism and Little Theory," pp. 179–187; and pp. 201–215.

16. Levinson, *Constitutional Faith*, pp. 63–65 and 79.

17. Ibid., pp. 165–169.

18. See Tushnet, *Red, White, and Blue*, pp. 58–59, and all of Chapter 1, "The Jurisprudence of History," pp. 21–69.

19. Levinson, *Constitutional Faith*, pp. 130–135.

20. Perry, *Morality, Politics, and Law*, pp. 156–172.

21. Ibid., pp. 136–145.

22. Ibid., pp. 138, 154, and 140.

23. Ibid., pp. 128–131.

24. Ibid., pp. 160–169, 116, and 164 (quotation on p. 169).

25. Ibid., p. 166.

26. Tushnet, *Red, White, and Blue*, pp. 8–17 and 312–318.

27. Ibid., pp. 143–146 and 176–177.

28. Ibid., pp. 314–318.

29. This section is based on Levinson, *Constitutional Faith*, pp. 129–135 and Chapter 2, "The Moral Dimension of Constitutional Faith," pp. 54–89.

30. Perry, *Morality, Politics, and Law*, p. 72 and Chapter 6, "Interpreting Law: The Problem of Constitutional Adjudication," pp. 121–179.

31. Ibid., pp. 147–169.

32. Ibid., pp. 149, 167, 295 (n. 110), and 300 (n. 168).

33. Ibid., pp. 159–160 and 169–172.

34. Ibid., pp. 170–172 and 142.

35. Ibid., p. 149.

36. Tushnet, *Red, White, and Blue*, pp. 1–17, 313–318.

37. Ibid., p. 313.

38. Levinson, *Constitutional Faith*, pp. 184–195.

39. See Perry, *Morality, Politics, and Law*, pp. 172–179, for his analysis of how *Roe v. Wade* should be decided, based on his theory of judicial review.

40. Chapter 4, "The Constituency," pp. 92–118, in Grant McConnell, *Private Power and American Democracy* (New York: Alfred A. Knopf, 1966).

41. In addition to McConnell, *Private Power*, see Theodore Lowi, *The End of Liberalism*, 2d ed. (New York: W. W. Norton, 1979); Martin Shapiro, *Who Guards the Guardians?* (Athens: University of Georgia Press, 1988); and Michael McCann, *Taking Reform Seriously* (Ithaca, N.Y.: Cornell University Press, 1986).

42. See Paul Peterson, "Federalism, Economic Development, and Redistribution," pp. 246–275 in J. David Greenstone, ed., *Public Values and Private Power in American Politics* (Chicago: University of Chicago Press, 1982); and Lowi, *The End of Liberalism*, Chapter 9, "Federal Urban Policy: What Not to Do and What to Do about Apartheid," pp. 237–268.

43. Chapter 4, "The Scope of National Power vis-à-vis the States: The Dispensability of Judicial Review," pp. 171–259, in Jesse Choper, *Judicial Review and the National Political Process* (Chicago: University of Chicago Press, 1980).

44. *INS v. Chadha*, 462 U.S. 919 (1983), pp. 959–967.

45. Perry, *Morality, Politics, and Law*, pp. 90–104.

46. Ibid., p. 99.

47. David Truman, *The Governmental Process* (New York: Alfred A. Knopf, [1950] 1964), pp. 516–524.

48. See Perry, *Morality, Politics, and Law*, pp. 149 (n. 110) and 168 (n. 168). See also Tushnet, *Red, White, and Blue*, pp. 197–198: "Still, the central thrust of Dahl's analysis is clear and remains compelling: in the medium-to-long-run judicial review doesn't matter very much."

49. Perry, *Morality, Politics, and Law*, p. 101.

50. Tushnet, *Red, White, and Blue*, p. 314.

51. See ibid., pp. 314–318, for this analysis (quotation from p. 318).

52. Chapter 5, "The Law School, the Faith Community, and the Professing of Law," pp. 155–180, in Levinson, *Constitutional Faith*.

53. Perry, *Morality, Politics, and Law*, p. 40.

54. Ibid., p. 87.

55. Ibid., p. 136.

56. Ibid., pp. 172–179.

57. Ibid., pp. 118–119.

58. See Lowi, *The End of Liberalism*, Chapter 11. The problem of trusting pluralist politics is quite similar to that Lowi identifies. He criticizes pluralist scholars for their great faith in the American political system and in bargaining and compromise and for not evaluating government and specific policies on the basis of fundamental polity principles in the Constitution. He argues that this discredits the legitimacy of the Constitution as a standard of evaluation and of American government itself. Unfortunately, as we saw in Chapter 6, critical pluralist interpreters of American politics such as Lowi and McConnell employ foundational polity principles in their analysis of American politics but refuse to use aspirational rights principles as a standard for evaluating American politics.

59. Perry, *Morality, Politics, and Law*, p. 87.

60. See Cass R. Sunstein, *The Partial Constitution* (Cambridge, Mass.: Harvard University Press, 1993). Sunstein, one of the most important of the second wave of civic republican scholars, attempts to link civic republican constitutional values with a quite searching critical pluralist interpretation of American politics.

Chapter 8. Conclusion: The Rehnquist Court and the Future

1. See Grant McConnell, *Private Power and American Democracy* (New York: Alfred A. Knopf, 1966), and Theodore Lowi, *The End of Liberalism*, 2d ed. (New York: W. W. Norton, 1979), for classic statements of the critical pluralist interpretation of American politics. See the works of Robert Dahl and David Truman, *The Governmental Process* (New York: Alfred A. Knopf, [1951] 1964) for classic statements of the pluralist interpretation of American politics.

2. See Martin Shapiro, Chapter 10, "The Supreme Court from Warren to Burger," pp. 179–211, in Anthony King, ed., *The New American Political System* (Washington, D.C.: American Enterprise Institute, 1980). See also Shapiro, "Fathers and Sons: The Court, the Commentators, and the Search for Values," in Vincent

292   Blasi, ed., *The Burger Court: The Counter-Revolution That Wasn't* (New Haven, Conn.: Yale University Press, 1983), pp. 218–238.

3. Martin Shapiro, "The Constitution and Economic Rights," in M. Judd Harmon, ed., *Essays on the Constitution of the United States* (Port Washington, N.Y.: Kennikat Press, 1978), pp. 92–93.

4. See the following articles by Frank Michelman: "Welfare Rights in a Constitutional Democracy," *Washington University Law Quarterly* (1979): 577–593; "Political Markets and Community Self-Determination: Competing Judicial Models of Local Government Legitimacy," *Indiana Law Journal* 53 (1977–1978): 145–206; and Laurence Tribe: "Unraveling National League of Cities: The New Federalism and Affirmative Rights to Essential Government Services," *Harvard Law Review* 90 (1977): 1065–1104; "Structural Due Process," *Harvard Civil Rights–Civil Liberties Law Review* 10 (1975): 269–321; and "The Emerging Reconstruction of Individual Rights and Institutional Design: Federalism, Bureaucracy and Due Process of Law Making" *Creighton Law Review* 10 (1977): 422–439.

5. John Hart Ely, *Democracy and Distrust: A Theory of Judicial Review* (Cambridge, Mass.: Harvard University Press, 1980).

6. See Laurence Tribe, *Constitutional Choices* (Cambridge, Mass.: Harvard University Press, 1985).

7. See Alexander Bickel, *The Least Dangerous Branch: The Supreme Court at the Bar of Politics* (Indianapolis: Bobbs-Merrill, 1962), *Politics and the Warren Court* (New York: Harper and Row, 1965), *The Supreme Court and the Idea of Progress* (New York: Harper and Row, 1970), and *The Morality of Consent* (New Haven, Conn.: Yale University Press, 1975); and Herbert Wechsler, "Towards Neutral Principles of Constitutional Law," in Herbert Wechsler, ed., *Principles, Politics, and Fundamental Law: Selected Essays* (Cambridge, Mass.: Harvard University Press, 1954), and "The Political Safeguards of Federalism: The Role of the States in the Composition and Selection of the National Government," *Columbia Law Review* 54 (1954); and Paul Freund, *The Supreme Court of the United States: Its Business, Purposes and Performance* (Cleveland, Ohio: World, 1961), works by the most prominent scholars of the Warren Court era.

8. We see the problem of trying to characterize a Court era before it solidifies as well as the problem of not viewing Supreme Court decisionmaking as a complex and coherent constitutive process in David G. Savage, *Turning Right: The Making of the Rehnquist Supreme Court* (New York: John Wiley & Sons, 1992).

9. Gerald Rosenberg, *The Hollow Hope: Can Courts Bring About Social Change?* (Chicago: University of Chicago Press, 1991).

10. For the election returns approach see sources cited in note 3 of Chapter 1. For the first major statements of Shapiro's policymaking approach see sources cited in note 4 of Chapter 1; for his most recent call to political scientists to continue to use instrumental assumptions in this approach see "Political Jurisprudence, Public Law, and Post-Consequentialist Ethics: Comments on Professors Barber and Smith," *Studies in American Political Development* 3 (1989): 88–102. See Mark A. Graber, "The Non-Majoritarian Difficulty: Legislative Deference to the Judiciary," *Studies in American Political Development* 7 (1993): 35–73, and Rosenberg, *The Hollow Hope*.

11. *Planned Parenthood of Southeastern Pennsylvania v. Casey*, No. 91–744 (1992), joint opinion 1–2.

12. Ibid., joint opinions 8 and 11.

13. Ibid., joint opinions 11 and 13.

14. Ibid., J. Blackmun, p. 22.

15. Ibid., joint opinion 25 and J. Blackmun, p. 3.

16. Daniel O. Conkle, "The Second Death of Substantive Due Process," *Indiana Law Journal* 62 (1987): 215–242.

17. *Planned Parenthood of Southeastern Pennsylvania v. Casey*, No. 91–744 (1992), joint opinion 9 and pp. 10 and 9.

18. Ibid., p. 14.

19. Rosenberg, *The Hollow Hope*, p. 5.

20. See Ronald Kahn, "The Supreme Court as a (Counter) Majoritarian Institution: Misperceptions of the Warren, Burger, and Rehnquist Courts," *Detroit College of Law Review* (Spring 1994), in press, for a detailed analysis of the *Casey* decision and other recent Rehnquist Court decisions that demonstrate that the Court's decision-making is constitutive, not instrumental like that of the Warren and Burger Courts, and will be more transformative in its jurisprudence than expected by most commentators.

21. 112 5. Ct. (1922), at 2655.

22. Ibid., at 2655, 2658, and 2671.

23. See Ronald Kahn, "God Save Us from the Coercion Test: Constitutive Decisionmaking, Polity Principles, and Religious Freedom," *Case-Western Reserve Law Review* 43 (1993): 983–1020, for an analysis of recent Rehnquist Court religion cases, including *Weisman*, and the view that the Rehnquist Court, like the Burger and Warren Courts before it, engages in constitutive decisionmaking.

24. *R.A.V. v. St. Paul*, no. 90–7675 (1992), p. 18.

25. See Edward A. Purcell, Jr., *The Crisis of Democratic Theory: Scientific Naturalism and the Problem of Value* (Lexington: University Press of Kentucky, 1973).

26. See Ronald Kahn, "Hermeneutics & Constitutional Faith, *Polity* 22 (Fall 1989): 165–179, and "Pluralism, Civic Republicanism, and Critical Theory," *Tulane Law Review* 63 (1989): 1475–1500, for a discussion of the conservative polity principles employed in the new civic republicanism, especially where authors, such as Perry, oppose the notion that foundational rights principles exist.

Bibliography

Abraham, Henry. *The Judicial Process.* 5th ed. New York: Oxford University Press, 1988.

Ackerman, Bruce. *Reconstructing American Law.* Cambridge, Mass.: Harvard University Press, 1984.

Adamany, David. "Legitimacy, Realigning Elections, and the Supreme Court." *Wisconsin Law Review* 1973: 790–845.

Baum, Lawrence. "Explaining the Burger Court's Support of Civil Liberties." *Political Science* 20 (1987): 21–28.

Bennett, Robert. "The Burger Court and the Poor." Pp. 46–61 in Vincent Blasi, ed., *The Burger Court: The Counter-Revolution That Wasn't.* New Haven, Conn.: Yale University Press, 1983.

Bickel, Alexander. *The Least Dangerous Branch.* Indianapolis: Bobbs-Merrill, 1962.

———. *The Morality of Consent.* New Haven, Conn.: Yale University Press, 1975.

———. "The Original Understanding of the Segregation Decision." *Harvard Law Review* 69 (1955): 1.

———. *Politics and the Warren Court.* New York: Harper and Row, 1965.

———. *The Supreme Court and the Idea of Progress.* New York: Harper and Row, [1970] 1978.

———. "The Supreme Court, 1960 Term—Forward: The Passive Virtues." *Harvard Law Review* 75 (1961): 40.

Blasi, Vincent. "The Rootless Activism of the Burger Court." Pp. 198–217 in Vincent Blasi, ed., *The Burger Court: The Counter-Revolution That Wasn't.* New Haven, Conn.: Yale University Press, 1983.

Brest, Paul. "Race Discrimination." Pp. 113–131 in Vincent Blasi, ed., *The Burger Court: The Counter-Revolution That Wasn't.* New Haven, Conn.: Yale University Press, 1983.

Breyer, Stephen G., and Stewart, Richard B. *The Administrative State and Regulatory Policy.* Boston: Little, Brown, 1985.

Brigham, John. *The Cult of the Court.* Philadelphia: Temple University Press, 1987.

Carter, Lief H. *Contemporary Constitutional Lawmaking: The Supreme Court and the Art of Politics.* New York: Pergamon, 1985.

———. "When Courts Should Make Policy: An Institutional Approach." Pp. 141–157 in John Gardiner, ed., *Public Law and Public Policy.* New York: Praeger, 1977.

Casper, Jonathan. "The Supreme Court and National Policy Making." *American Political Science Review* 70 (1976): 50–63.

Choper, Jesse. *Judicial Review and the National Political Process: A Functional Reconsideration of the Role of the Supreme Court.* Chicago: University of Chicago Press, 1980.

Conkle, Daniel O. "The Second Death of Substantive Due Process." *Indiana Law Journal* 62 (1987): 215.

Connolly, William, E., ed. *The Bias of Pluralism.* New York: Atherton, 1969.

Corwin, Edward S. *The Commerce Clause versus States Rights.* Princeton, N.J.: Princeton University Press, 1936.

296   _____. "The Passing of Dual Federalism." *Virginia Law Review* 36 (1950): 1–23.

Cox, Archibald. *The Role of the Supreme Court in American Government.* New York: Oxford University Press, 1976.

_____. *The Warren Court: Constitutional Decision as an Instrument of Reform.* Cambridge, Mass.: Harvard University Press, 1968.

Dahl, Robert. "Decision-Making in a Democracy: The Supreme Court as a National Policy-maker." *Journal of Public Law* 6 (1957): 279–295.

_____. *Democracy in the United States.* 4th ed. Boston: Houghton Mifflin, 1981.

_____. *A Preface to Democratic Theory.* Chicago: University of Chicago Press, 1956.

Davis, Rufus S. *The Federal Principle.* Berkeley: University of California Press, 1978.

Ely, John Hart. "The Constitutionality of Reverse Racial Discrimination." *University of Chicago Law Review* 41 (1974): 723.

_____. *Democracy and Distrust: A Theory of Judicial Review.* Cambridge, Mass.: Harvard University Press, 1980.

_____. "The Wages of Crying Wolf: A Comment on *Roe v. Wade.*" *Yale Law Journal* 82 (1973): 920–949.

Epstein, Lee, and Joseph F. Kobylka. *The Supreme Court and Legal Change: Abortion and the Death Penalty.* Chapel Hill: University of North Carolina Press, 1992.

Fiss, Owen. "Objectivity and Interpretation." *Stanford Law Review* 34 (1982): 739–773.

Freund, Paul. *The Supreme Court of the United States: Its Business, Purpose, and Performance.* Cleveland, Ohio: World Publishing, 1961.

Funston, Richard Y. *Constitutional Counter Revolution?: The Warren Court and the Burger Court: Judicial Policy Making in Modern America.* Cambridge, Mass.: Schenkman, 1977.

_____. "The Supreme Court and Critical Elections." *American Political Science Review* 69 (1975): 795–811.

Garvey, Gerald. *Constitutional Bricolage.* Princeton, N.J.: Princeton University Press, 1971.

Gillman, Howard. *The Constitution Besieged: The Rise and Demise of Lochner Era Police Powers Jurisdiction.* Durham, N.C.: Duke University Press, 1993.

Graber, Mark A. "The Non-Majoritarian Difficulty: Legislative Deference to the Judiciary." *Studies in American Political Development* 7 (1993): 35–73.

Greenstone, J. David, and Paul E. Peterson. *Race and Authority in Urban Politics.* New York: Russell Sage Foundation, 1973.

Harris, William F. *The Interpretable Constitution.* Baltimore: Johns Hopkins University Press, 1993.

Hart, Henry, and Albert Sacks. "The Legal Process: Basic Problems in the Making and Application of Law." Unpublished manuscript, 1958.

Hirsch, H. N. *A Theory of Liberty: The Constitution and Minorities.* New York: Routledge, 1992.

Kahn, Paul. "The Court, the Community and the Judicial Balance: The Jurisprudence of Justice Powell." *Yale Law Journal* 97 (1987): 1–60.

Kahn, Ronald. "The Burger Court, Boundary Setting, and Local and State Government Power." *Proteus* 4 (1987): 37–46.

_____. "The Burger Court, Equal Protection of the Law, and the Ascent of Pragmatism: A Critique." Paper presented to 1990 Annual Meeting, American Political Science Association, San Francisco, August 30–September 2, 1990.

_____. "God Save Us from the Coercion Test: Constitutive Decisionmaking, Polity

Principles, and Religious Freedom." *Case Western-Reserve Law Review* 43 (1993): 983–1020.

———. "Ideology, Religion, and the First Amendment." Pp. 409–441 in Michael McCann and Gerald Houseman, eds., *Judging the Constitution: Critical Essays on Judicial Lawmaking*. Boston: Scott Foresman, 1989.

———. "Pluralism, Civic Republicanism, and Critical Theory." *Tulane Law Review* 63 (1989): 1475–1500.

———. "Polity and Rights Values in Conflict: The Burger Court, Ideological Interests, and the Separation of Church and State." *Studies in American Political Development* 3 (1989): 279–293.

———. "Process and Rights Principles in Modern Constitutional Theory" (book review). *Stanford Law Review* 37 (1984): 501–517.

———. "Review Essay." *American Political Science Review* 80 (1986): 1315–1318.

———. "Review Essay: Hermeneutics and Constitutional Faith." *Polity* 22 (Fall 1989): 165–179.

———. "The Intersection of Polity and Rights Principles on the Burger Court." *Legal Studies Forum* 11 (1987): 5–28.

Kalman, Laura. *Legal Realism at Yale, 1927–1960*. Chapel Hill: University of North Carolina Press, 1986.

Kronman, Anthony. "Alexander Bickel's Philosophy of Prudence." *Yale Law Journal* 94 (June 1985): 1567.

Kurland, Philip. *Politics, the Constitution, and the Warren Court*. Chicago: University of Chicago Press, 1970.

Lamb, Charles, and Stephen C. Halpern, eds. *The Burger Court: Political and Judicial Profiles*. Urbana: University of Illinois Press, 1991.

Landynsky, Jacob W. "Justice Lewis Powell: Balance Wheel of the Court." Pp. 276–314 in Charles Lamb and Stephen C. Halpern, eds., *The Burger Court: Political and Judicial Profiles*. Chicago: University of Illinois Press, 1991.

Lee, Francis Graham. *Neither Conservative nor Liberal: The Burger Court on Civil Rights and Liberties*. Malabar, Fla.: Robert E. Krieger, 1983.

Levinson, Sanford. *Constitutional Faith*. Princeton, N.J.: Princeton University Press, 1988.

Levy, Leonard. *The Supreme Court under Earl Warren*. New York: Quadrangle Books, 1972.

Lewis, Anthony. "Earl Warren." Pp. 1–31 in Richard Sayler, Barry B. Boyer, and Richard E. Gooding, Jr., eds., *The Warren Court: A Critical Analysis*. New York: Chelsea House, 1969.

———. "Foreword." Pp. vii–ix in Vincent Blasi, ed., *The Burger Court: The Counter-Revolution That Wasn't*. New Haven, Conn.: Yale University Press, 1983.

———. "Historic Change in the Supreme Court." Pp. 73–81 in Leonard Levy, ed., *The Supreme Court under Earl Warren*. New York: Quadrangle Books, 1972.

Lowi, Theodore, *The End of Liberalism: The Second Republic of the United States*. 2d ed. New York: W. W. Norton, [1969] 1979.

Lytle, Clifford M. *The Warren Court and Its Critics*. Tucson: University of Arizona Press, 1968.

McCann, Michael W. *Taking Reform Seriously*. Ithaca, N.Y.: Cornell University Press, 1986.

McCloskey, Robert. *The American Supreme Court*. Chicago: University of Chicago Press, 1960.

298   McConnell, Grant. *Private Power and American Democracy*. New York: Alfred A. Knopf, 1966.
———. *The Modern Presidency*. New York: St. Martin's Press, 1976.
MacKinnon, Catharine. *Toward a Feminist Theory of the State*. Cambridge, Mass.: Harvard University Press, 1989.
Marx, Karl. "On the Jewish Question." Pp. 26–52 in Robert C. Tucker, ed., *The Marx-Engels Reader*. 2d ed. New York: W. W. Norton, 1978.
Maveety, Nancy. *Representation Rights and the Burger Years*. Ann Arbor: University of Michigan Press, 1991.
Michelman, Frank I. "Foreword: Traces of Self-Government." *Harvard Law Review* 100 (1986): 4–77.
———. "Political Markets and Community Self-Determination: Competing Judicial Models of Local Government Legitimacy." *Indiana Law Review* 53 (1977–1978): 145–206.
———. "States Rights and States Roles: Permutations of 'Sovereignty' in *National League of Cities v. Usery.*" *Yale Law Journal* 87 (1977): 1165–1195.
———. "Welfare Rights in a Constitutional Democracy." *Washington University Law Quarterly* 1979: 577–593.
Murphy, Walter F. *Elements of Judicial Strategy*. Chicago: University of Chicago Press, 1964.
———. "Constitutional Interpretation: The Art of the Historian, Magician, or Statesman?" Pp. 130–159 in M. Judd Harmon, ed., *Essays on the Constitution of the United States*. Port Washington, N.Y.: Kennikat Press, 1978.
Murphy, Walter F., and Joseph Tanenhaus. *The Study of Public Law*. New York: Random House, 1972.
Murphy, Walter F., James E. Fleming, and William F. Harris. *American Constitutional Interpretation*. Mineola, N.Y.: Foundation Press, 1986.
O'Brien, David M. *Storm Center: The Supreme Court in American Politics*. 1st, 2d, and 3d eds. New York: W. W. Norton, 1986, 1990, and 1993.
———. "The Supreme Court: From Warren to Burger to Rehnquist." *Political Science* 20 (1987): 12–20.
Parker, Richard Davies. "The Past in Constitutional Theory—and Its Future." *Ohio State Law Journal* 42 (1982): 223–261.
Perry, H. W. *Deciding to Decide: Agenda Setting in the United States Supreme Court*. Cambridge, Mass.: Harvard University Press, 1991.
Perry, Michael. *The Constitution, the Courts, and Human Rights*. New Haven, Conn.: Yale University Press, 1982.
———. *Morality, Politics, and Law*. New York: Oxford University Press, 1988.
Peterson, Paul. "Federalism, Economic Development, and Redistribution." Pp. 246–275 in J. David Greenstone, ed., *Public Values and Private Power in American Politics*. Chicago: University of Chicago Press, 1982.
Pritchett, C. Herman. *Civil Liberties and the Vinson Court*. Chicago: University of Chicago Press, 1954.
———. *The Roosevelt Court: A Study in Judicial Politics and Values, 1937–1947*. New York: Macmillan, 1948.
Provine, Doris. *Case Selection in the United States Supreme Court*. Chicago: University of Chicago Press, 1980.
Purcell, Edward A., Jr., "Alexander M. Bickel and the Post-Realist Constitution." *Harvard Civil Rights–Civil Liberties Law Review* 11 (1976): 521–564.

_____. *The Crisis of Democratic Theory: Scientific Naturalism and the Problem of Value.* Lexington: University Press of Kentucky, 1973.

Rosenberg, Gerald. *The Hollow Hope: Can Courts Bring about Social Change?* Chicago: University of Chicago Press, 1991.

Savage, David G. *Turning Right: The Making of the Rehnquist Court.* New York: John Wiley, 1992.

Saylor, Richard, Barry Boyer, and Richard E. Gooding, Jr., eds. *The Warren Court: A Critical Analysis.* New York: Chelsea House, 1969.

Schattschneider, E. E. *The Semi-Sovereign People.* New York: Holt, Rinehart & Winston, 1960.

Schwartz, Bernard. *The Ascent of Pragmatism: The Burger Court in Action.* New York: Addison-Wesley, 1990.

_____. *Super Chief: Earl Warren and His Supreme Court—A Judicial Biography.* New York: New York University Press, 1983.

Schwartz, Herman, ed. *The Burger Years: Rights and Wrongs in the Supreme Court, 1969–1986.* New York: Penguin Books, 1987.

Shapiro, Martin. "The Constitution and Economic Rights." in M. Judd Harmon, ed., *Essays on the Constitution of the United States.* Port Washington, N.Y.: Kennikat Press, 1978.

_____. "Fathers and Sons: The Court, the Commentators, and the Search for Values." Pp. 218–238 in Vincent Blasi, ed., *The Burger Court: The Counter-Revolution That Wasn't.* New Haven, Conn.: Yale University Press, 1983.

_____. *Law and Politics in the Supreme Court: New Approaches to Political Jurisprudence.* Glencoe: Free Press, 1964.

_____. "Political Jurisprudence, Public Law, and Post-Consequentialist Ethics: Comment on Professors Barber and Smith." *Studies in American Political Development* 3 (1989): 88–102.

_____. "The Supreme Court: From Warren to Burger." Pp. 179–211 in Anthony King, ed., *The New American Political System.* Washington, D.C.: American Enterprise Institute, 1978.

_____. "The Supreme Court: From Early Burger to Early Rehnquist." Pp. 47–85 in Anthony King, ed., *The New American Political System*, 2d version. Washington, D.C.: American Enterprise Institute, 1990.

_____. "The Supreme Court's 'Return' to Economic Regulation." *Studies in American Political Development* 1 (1986): 91–141.

_____. *Who Guards the Guardians?* Athens: University of Georgia Press, 1988.

Smith, Rogers M. *Liberalism and American Constitutional Law.* Cambridge, Mass.: Harvard University Pres, 1985.

Spaeth, Harold, and Stuart H. Teger. "Activism and Restraint: A Cloak for the Justices' Policy Preferences." Pp. 277–301 in Stephen C. Halpern and Charles M. Lamb, eds., *Supreme Court Activism and Restraint.* Lexington, Mass.: D. C. Heath and Company, 1982.

Sprague, John. *Voting Patterns of the United States Supreme Court: Cases in Federalism.* Indianapolis: Bobbs-Merrill, 1968.

Stewart, Richard B. "The Reformation of American Administrative Law." *Harvard Law Review* 88 (1975): 1669.

Storing, Herbert. *What the Anti-Federalists Were For: The Political Thought of the Opponents of the Constitution.* Chicago: University of Chicago Press, 1981.

Sunstein, Cass R. *The Partial Constitution.* Cambridge, Mass.: Harvard University Press, 1993.

300   "Symposium: Constitutional Adjudication and Democratic Theory." *New York University Law Review* 56 (1981): 259–582.

"Symposium, Judicial Review and the Constitution—The Text and Beyond." *University of Dayton Law Review* 8 (1983): 443–831.

"Symposium: Judicial Review versus Democracy." *Ohio State Law Review* 42 (1981): 1–434.

Thomas, William R. *The Burger Court and Civil Liberties*, rev. ed. Brunswick, Ohio: King's Court Communications, 1979.

Tribe, Laurence. *Abortion: The Clash of Absolutes*. New York: Norton, 1990.

_____. "The Abortion Funding Conundrum: Inalienable Rights, Affirmative Duties, and the Dilemma of Dependence." *Harvard Law Review* 99 (1985): 330–343.

_____. *American Constitutional Law*. 2d. ed. Mineola, N.Y.: Foundation Press, [1978] 1988.

_____. *Constitutional Choices*. Cambridge, Mass.: Harvard University Press, 1985.

_____. "The Emerging Reconstruction of Individual Rights and Institutional Design: Federalism, Bureaucracy, and Due Process of Law Making." *Creighton Law Review* 10 (1977): 422–439.

_____. *God Save This Honorable Court*. New York: Random House, 1985.

_____. "Perspectives on *Bakke*: Equal Protection, Procedural Fairness, or Structural Justice?" *Harvard Law Review* 92 (1979): 873–877.

_____. "The Puzzling Persistence of Process Based Constitutional Theories." *Yale Law Journal* 89 (1980): 1063–1080.

_____. "Seven Pluralist Fallacies: In Defense of the Adversary Process—A Reply to Justice Rehnquist." *University of Miami Law Review* 22 (1976): 43–57.

_____. "Structural Due Process." *Harvard Civil Rights–Civil Liberties Law Review* 10 (1975): 269–231.

_____. "The Supreme Court, 1972 Term, Forward: Towards a Model of Roles in the Due Process of Life and Law." *Harvard Law Review* 87 (1973): 1–53.

_____. "Unraveling National League of Cities: The New Federalism and Affirmative Rights to Essential Government Services." *Harvard Law Review* 90 (1977): 1065–1104.

Truman, David. *The Governmental Process: Political Interests and Public Opinion*. New York: Alfred A. Knopf, [1951] 1964.

Tushnet, Mark. *Red, White, and Blue: A Critical Analysis of Constitutional Law*. Cambridge, Mass.: Harvard University Press, 1988.

Unger, Roberto. *Law in Modern Society*. New York: Free Press, 1976.

Wechsler, Herbert. "The Political Safeguards of Federalism: The Role of the States in the Composition and Selection of the National Government." *Columbia Law Review* 54 (1954): 543–560.

_____. "Towards Neutral Principles of Constitutional Law." Pp. 3–48 in Herbert Wechsler, ed., *Principles, Politics, and Fundamental Law: Selected Essays*. Cambridge, Mass.: Harvard University Press, 1961.

White, G. Edward. *The American Judicial Tradition*, exp. ed. New York: Oxford University Press, [1976] 1988.

_____. "Earl Warren as Jurist." *Virginia Law Review* 67 (April 1981): 461–551.

_____. *Earl Warren: A Public Life*. New York: Oxford University Press, 1982.

Wood, Gordon. *The Creation of the American Republic, 1776–1787*. New York: W. W. Norton, 1969.

List of Cases

Pre–Warren Court

Colegrove v. Green, 328 U.S. 549 (1946).
Corfield v. Coryell, Fed. Cas. No. 3,230 (Cir. E.D. Pa 1823).
Edwards v. California, 314 U.S. 160 (1941).
Everson v. Board of Education, 330 U.S. 1 (1946).
Korematsu v. United States, 323 U.S. 214 (1944).
Lochner v. New York, 198 U.S. 45 (1905).
McLaurin v. Oklahoma State Regents, 339 U.S. 637 (1950).
Meyer v. Nebraska, 262 U.S. 390 (1923).
Missouri ex. rel Gaines v. Canada, 305 U.S. 337 (1938).
Nixon v. Herndon, 273 U.S. 536 (1927).
Pierce v. Society of Sisters, 268 U.S. 510 (1925).
Shelley v. Kraemer, 334 U.S. 1 (1948).
Skinner v. Oklahoma, 316 U.S. 535 (1942).
Strauder v. West Virginia, 100 U.S. 303 (1880).
Sweatt v. Painter, 339 U.S. 629 (1950).
United States v. Carolene Products, 304 U.S. 144 (1938).
Yick Wo v. Hopkins, 118 U.S. 356 (1886).

Warren Court—1953–1969

Aptheker v. Secretary of State, 378 U.S. 500 (1964).
Baker v. Carr, 369 U.S. 186 (1962).
Board of Education, Central School District v. Allen, 392 U.S. 236 (1968).
Brandenburg v. Ohio, 395 U.S. 444 (1969).
Brown v. Board of Education (Brown I), 347 U.S. 483 (1954).
Brown v. Board of Education (Brown II), 349 U.S. 294 (1955).
Brown v. Louisiana, 383 U.S. 131 (1966).
Carrington v. Rush, 380 U.S. 89 (1965).
Douglas v. California, 372 U.S. 353 (1963).
Epperson v. Arkansas, 393 U.S. 97 (1968).
Gomillion v. Lightfoot, 364 U.S. 348 (1960).
Griffin v. Illinois, 351 U.S. 12 (1956).
Griswold v. Connecticut, 381 U.S. 479 (1965).
Harper v. Virginia Board of Elections, 383 U.S. 663 (1966).
Kent v. Dulles, 357 U.S. 116 (1958).
Kramer v. Union Free School District No. 15, 395 U.S. 621 (1969).
Loving v. Virginia, 388 U.S. 1 (1967).
NAACP v. Button, 371 U.S. 415 (1963).
Reynolds v. Sims, 377 U.S. 533 (1964).
Roth v. United States, 354 U.S. 476 (1957).
Shapiro v. Thompson, 394 U.S. 618 (1969).
United States v. Guest, 383 U.S. 745 (1966).

Rehnquist Court (1986–   )

Index